CRITICAL THEORY AND SOCIAL TRANSFORMATION

Critical Theory and Social Transformation provides an exploration of the major themes in critical social theory of recent years. Delanty argues that a critical theory perspective can offer much-needed insights into the pressing socio-political challenges of our time. In this volume, he advances the need to reconnect social theory and social research and to return to the foundational concerns of critical social theory. Delanty engages with the key topics facing critical social theorists: capitalism, cosmopolitanism, modernity, the Anthropocene, and legacies of history. The connecting thread is that the topics are all contemporary challenges for critical theory and relate to major social transformations. The notions of critique, crisis, and social transformation are central to the book.

Critical Theory and Social Transformation will be of interest to the broad readership in social and political theory. It will appeal to those working in sociology, political sociology, politics, and international studies and to anyone with an interest in any of the chapter-specific topics, such as public space, memory, and neo-authoritarianism.

Gerard Delanty is Professor of Sociology and Social and Political Thought at the University of Sussex, Brighton, UK. He is the author of eleven books, including *Inventing Europe: Idea, Identity, Reality* (1995), *The Cosmopolitan Imagination* (2009), *Formations of European Modernity: A Historical and Political Sociology of Europe*, 2nd edition (2018). He has edited numerous volumes, including the *Routledge Handbook of Cosmopolitanism Studies*, 2nd edition (2018). His most recent book is *The European Heritage: A Critical Re-interpretation* (2018).

CRITICAL THEORY AND SOCIAL TRANSFORMATION

Crises of the Present and Future Possibilities

Gerard Delanty

LONDON AND NEW YORK

First published 2020
by Routledge
2 Park Square, Milton Park, Abingdon, Oxon, OX14 4RN

and by Routledge
52 Vanderbilt Avenue, New York, NY 10017

Routledge is an imprint of the Taylor & Francis Group, an informa business

© 2020 Gerard Delanty

The right of Gerard Delanty to be identified as author of this work
has been asserted by him in accordance with sections 77 and 78 of the
Copyright, Designs and Patents Act 1988.

All rights reserved. No part of this book may be reprinted or reproduced or
utilised in any form or by any electronic, mechanical, or other means, now
known or hereafter invented, including photocopying and recording, or in
any information storage or retrieval system, without permission in writing
from the publishers.

Trademark notice: Product or corporate names may be trademarks or
registered trademarks, and are used only for identification and explanation
without intent to infringe.

British Library Cataloguing-in-Publication Data
A catalogue record for this book is available from the British Library

Library of Congress Cataloging-in-Publication Data
Names: Delanty, Gerard, author.
Title: Critical theory and social transformation : crises of the present and
future possibilities / Gerard Delanty.
Description: Abingdon, Oxon ; New York, NY : Routledge, 2020. |
Includes bibliographical references and index.
Identifiers: LCCN 2019051291 (print) | LCCN 2019051292 (ebook) |
ISBN 9780367276409 (hardback) | ISBN 9780367276416 (paperback) |
ISBN 9780429297045 (ebook)
Subjects: LCSH: Critical theory. | Social sciences—Philosophy.
Classification: LCC HM480 .D453 2020 (print) | LCC HM480 (ebook) |
DDC 142—dc23
LC record available at https://lccn.loc.gov/2019051291
LC ebook record available at https://lccn.loc.gov/2019051292

ISBN: 978-0-367-27640-9 (hbk)
ISBN: 978-0-367-27641-6 (pbk)
ISBN: 978-0-429-29704-5 (ebk)

Typeset in Bembo
by Apex CoVantage, LLC

CONTENTS

Introduction   1

PART 1
Critical theory revisited   **5**

1 Spectres of critique: the legacy of the critical theory of the
   Frankfurt School   7

2 Critical engagements: varieties of critique in social science   38

3 Critical theory and social transformation: modernity,
   capitalism, and technology   62

PART 2
Capitalism, cosmopolitanism, the Anthropocene   **87**

4 Questioning *homo economicus*: have we all become neoliberals?   89

5 Imagining the future of capitalism: trends, scenarios, and
   prospects for the future   108

6 The prospects of cosmopolitanism and the possibility of
   global justice: new directions for critical social theory   124

7 Cosmopolitics and the challenge of the Anthropocene:
   the new politics of nature   144

vi Contents

PART 3
Space, memory and legacies of history 165

8 The future of public space: crisis and renewal 167

9 Modernity and memory: historical self–understanding and
the burden of the past 182

10 Looking back at the twentieth century: Europe's contested
legacies of history 198

11 The crisis of the present: authoritarianism and social
pathologies 213

12 Conclusion: on the future 234

Index *247*

INTRODUCTION

This book provides an exploration of the major themes in critical social theory of recent years. My aim is to show how a critical theory perspective offers new insights into our time. In doing so, I am also seeking to make a case for the revival of what was the original aim of the critical theory tradition, namely, the link between philosophy and social research.

One of the characteristic features of critical theory is the combination of sociological analysis within a philosophical framework. This is because the nature of social phenomena is such that they cannot be discerned only through empirical knowledge; critique requires knowledge of core constitutive forces, which are the grounds of the possibility of society. These elements were often referred to, following the philosophy of Kant and Hegel, as Reason. While critical theory has led to path-breaking results in social theory and in the philosophy of social science, the critical theory tradition has, on the whole, now become a largely philosophical project concerned with internal debates and divorced from sociological research. A consequence has been the waning of critique. My hope is that this book will show how a critical theory perspective offers valuable insights into many important topics which are in different ways connected to how the future can be conceived.

Aside from the link between social research and philosophy, an additional and related feature of critical theory is its concern with big questions, including ones that are not easily answered through empirical social theory, but which can be illumined through social theory by being placed in a broader context of sociological interpretation. Much of the critical theory legacy in any case has been taken up by social theory more generally as an interpretation of current times, which the older critical theory often referred to as a 'diagnosis of our times'.

Critical theory is not neutral, but, as a form of critique, it offers an assessment of current trends and crises in order to identify future possibilities. In this book, I place a strong emphasis on social transformation, but argue that this needs to

2 Introduction

be embedded in a theoretical framework that conceptualizes how possibilities for change could be normatively defended. Critical theory provides such a framework for understanding how a total transformation of society might be possible.

The term critical theory today has become somewhat blurred. It is traditionally associated with the so-called Frankfurt School group of thinkers, principally Adorno, Horkheimer, and Marcuse and the wider circle around Horkheimer after their re-location to Columbia University in the late 1930s. This generation of critical theorists also includes Walter Benjamin and extends into the so-called second generation around Jürgen Habermas and, more recently, Axel Honneth. Taken together, especially the seminal contributions of Adorno, Benjamin, and Habermas, this is the tradition of social thought that I am working with in this book. This tradition produced some of the most important and inspiring works of the twentieth century. I resist the temptation to refer to it with capital letters (i.e. Critical Theory) since critical theory has become more recently a wider and less-specific approach that also draws on other critical approaches, including ones from very different intellectual traditions, and more generally has become synonymous with radical thought. However, while this has undoubtedly opened up some new perspectives, as I discuss in Chapter 1, the result is that it is now somewhat unclear as to its scope and defining tenets. Hence, the need for conceptual clarification. But more than this, there is also a need for a re-integration of sociology and philosophy.

My concern is far from a reconstruction of the critical theory tradition or to suggest that there is a rigorous approach that needs to be rescued. My aim is rather to clarify what characterizes a critical theory approach in terms of its core philosophical ideas, its methodology, and its theory of society. The second objective (in Parts 2 and 3) is to look at a number of topics in light of the theoretical framework.

In Part 1 I attempt to outline the general framework of critical theory. Chapter 1 offers an explication of the core philosophical arguments deriving from the Left-Hegelian tradition. It also offers an appraisal of the philosophical framework more generally in light of criticisms and recent controversies. Chapter 2 shifts the focus to the methodology of critical theory. To this end, it offers an assessment of varieties of critique in social theory today with a view to identifying the distinctiveness of critical theory. But more than this, the chapter will discuss the main alternatives to critical theory with a view to identifying ways in which critical theory can learn from the encounter with these approaches. The third chapter is concerned with the mainstream social theory of critical theory and is specifically addressed to the literature within this tradition on modernity, capitalism, and technology. (There are, of course, others, but these are taken here in order to elucidate the main aspects, including the limitations, of the social theory of critical theory.)

The rest of the book is organized into two parts dealing with substantive topics. Part 2 is focussed on three major topics: capitalism, cosmopolitanism, and the Anthropocene. The latter topic, of great importance today, takes up the question of nature in critical theory but looks at it through a different lens and one informed by cosmopolitanism, which, I argue in the previous chapter, is directly relevant to a wider and more globally oriented critical theory.

Part 3 takes up a number of themes that have been central to the critical theory tradition, such as public space and the public sphere, memory and legacies of history, and the nature and dynamics of authoritarianism. By way of conclusion, I offer some thoughts on how the future might be conceived from a critical theory perspective.

The chapters in Parts 2 and 3 are not direct applications of critical theory but rather are informed by it. Each chapter topic can be read separately. Some chapters more than others contain more extensive consideration of the critical theory legacy, as for example the chapters on memory and totalitarianism. Chapter 10 is perhaps less directly concerned with the writings of the critical theorists but nonetheless reflects some of the major themes in critical theory on the decline of utopia and the overcoming of the experience of historical catastrophe in the twentieth century.

In writing this, book I have brought together some of my published and unpublished papers over the past six years. Chapters 2, 5, 6, and 7 are based on journal articles and have been revised for this book. Acknowledgements, where relevant, and references are to be found at the end of each chapter.

I am grateful to Estevão Bosco, Neal Harris, Filipe Maia, William Outhwaite, and Piet Strydom for reading through the manuscript and for their comments. I am also grateful to three readers who provided invaluable comments on the initial proposal. Gerhard Boomgaarden and Mihalea Ciobotea at Routledge provided helpful support for the book from beginning to completion.

My wife Aurea has been a constant source of inspiration in writing this book, which is dedicated to her and our son Dario.

PART 1

Critical theory revisited

1

SPECTRES OF CRITIQUE

The legacy of the critical theory of the Frankfurt School

This book seeks to demonstrate the relevance of a critical theory of society for the present day. In this chapter, I set out the core ideas that define the nature and scope of critical theory.[1] It is necessary to do so as, I argue in what follows, critical theory has lost direction due to both internal and external developments. On the one side, critical theory has inevitably undergone considerable transformation from the original project associated with the early Frankfurt School to the varieties of post-Habermasian theory that now exist, of which Honneth's recognition theory is perhaps the most influential. On the other side, since Foucault and postmodern theory, there has been a plethora of critical approaches in the human and social sciences that are very different from the Left-Hegelian tradition of the Frankfurt School. This spectrum would include Bourdieu's critical sociology, critical realism, and Boltanski's critical pragmatism, but it also includes what now also claims to be critical theory, namely, the French post-structuralist tradition, especially stemming from Foucault, postcolonial and de-colonial theory, and Lacanian feminism. Critical theory today has become a general term to refer to all of these traditions of radical thought which are reflected in a concern with the advancement of progressive politics. But beyond that they do not have much in common.

Such cross-fertilization of traditions – as in the confluence of Adorno and Foucault, once seen as incompatible – has undoubtedly been productive in interpretations of now classical authors (Allen 2016; Cook 2018). This has been acknowledged by thinkers associated with the postmodern turn such as Jameson and Lyotard.[2] However, in my view, such re-interpretations have a limited capacity to open up new avenues for critical theory as a programme of social research, which requires a macro-sociological re-direction. The limitations of the older approaches from Adorno and Horkheimer to Habermas are now all too clear, especially in light of the need to take into account a more global perspective and the necessity to address problems of Eurocentrism. A major limitation of the Frankfurt School tradition

8 Critical theory revisited

has been its preoccupation with European modernity and a lack of engagement with race and empire and the North–South relationship. The prominence of these concerns in social and political thought in recent times has led to a much wider and more diverse conception of critical theory. However, the result of such theoretical pluralization is that critical theory lacks both theoretical specificity and a theory of society.[3] It is also evident that the various traditions of critique have not come together in a way that provides clear methodological directions for social research to address major questions for our time. One reason for this is simply because, beyond a certain level of agreement on the need for critique and the need to address legacies of colonialism, many approaches are simply incompatible and have different views on the meaning of critique and political praxis. While the Left–Hegelian tradition has much to learn from critical philosophies inspired by, for instance, Foucault, there are clear differences in these different traditions of critical theory. Despite some conceptual similarity and the concern with the total transformation of society, Foucault's project was fundamentally different, as were his politics, given his ambivalent relation to neoliberalism.[4]

My position in this book is that the Left–Hegelian tradition of critical theory offers the most robust basis for critical theory as a framework of critical social research as opposed to a social or political philosophy. However, it will need to engage and learn from other conceptions of critique. I also argue for the need for a certain self-correction in the direction Left–Hegelianism has taken in recent years with recognition theory. While recognition theory has been one of the most fruitful developments in critical theory in re-connecting philosophy with social research, this has been at the cost of reducing the scope of critical theory to issues that can be framed in terms of a politics of recognition. I am not arguing for a return to an earlier kind of critical theory, such as Adorno's, but for a re-appraisal and clarification of the core concepts. This is with a view to applications in social science rather than within philosophy. Critical theory has today become a largely philosophical project conducted mostly by philosophers. The original project for the integration of philosophy and sociology has been lost, despite some attempts to revive it, as in the work of Rahel Jaeggi (2018) and Hartmut Rosa (2015, 2019). This is not because of the retreat into philosophy but because sociology in recent times has not been sufficiently receptive to critical theory. As I see it, what is lacking is a concern with macro-sociological questions. Indeed, the reception of recognition theory, as perhaps the last remnant of the critical theory tradition, has mostly been in micro-sociology.

A brief overview of critical theory is in place in order to identify the core concepts and principal aims, beginning with the legacy of Left–Hegelianism. Critical theory operates at a high level of philosophical abstraction, with its key texts based on concepts derived from German idealism. This presents a number of difficulties which are compounded by different interpretations of the philosophical systems of Kant and Hegel. Moreover, the critical theorists more or less never explicitly defined their core concepts, such as their master concept of Reason (see Jay 1996/1973: 63). Despite the problems this all presents, an understanding of

Spectres of critique **9**

these concepts is necessary since they provide a framework for understanding the processes and conditions that render society possible and which are not discernible from empirical data as such.

The legacy of Left-Hegelianism

The intellectual legacy established by Hegel for later critical theory was a conceptual system for the analysis of the world in terms of the realization of Reason. While Kant, in the *Critique of Pure Reason,* had confined the critique of Reason to the critique of metaphysical ideas that are transcendent and not derived from experience, Hegel posited Reason as unfolding historically in social reality. The critique of Reason thus became the critique of social reality, and Reason was historical rather than timeless.[5] Rather than being limited, as in Kant, it was a phenomenological process of self-formation. Critical theory, despite its Hegelian and Marxist lineage, retains a distinctive Kantian influence in that Hegel appropriated Kant's philosophy as, for example, in the notion of ideas of Reason. Later critical theorists, such as Habermas, re-affirmed the Kantian background as a corrective to Hegel's historical re-working of Kant's transcendental arguments. The Kantian tradition asserted the importance of what has to be presupposed in any account of the world (for example, a capacity for learning, for morality, for human judgement). Such presuppositions (which are 'transcendental' conditions) are not primarily empirical since they are more akin to principles and capacities integral to the make-up of human beings and society. Thus, for example, ideas of Reason such as peace, democracy, life, the person, humanity, and so on are not empirical as such in that nothing empirical corresponds to them. They are rather ideas of universal significance that make possible the formation of more specific empirical realities. They are the conditions of the possibility of social phenomena. Kant more than Hegel stressed this distinction, which illustrates how the social world is constituted and (though not Kant's preoccupation) how it can be transformed. Hegel's philosophy and Marx's later provided critical theory with a way to develop a theory of social transformation which required going beyond the limited horizon of Kant's concerns.

As developed in 1807 in *Phenomenology of Spirit* and in 1812–16 in the *Science of Logic* and applied from 1833 in the lectures on the philosophy of history,[6] the elusive notion of Reason refers to the ideas of the modern world that attempt to shape the world according to how we think it should be. Now, for Hegel that largely revolved around the idea of freedom and how it might be realized and flourish in social reality. It was Hegel's belief that freedom was the essential promise of modernity and that it was slowly emerging in the modern world with ever-greater possibilities for self-realization. As an emergent idea, it was more than an idea; it was part of the modern world and signaled the total transformation of society. However, it was also incomplete. It was this difference between the signs of its appearance and its incomplete existence that gave rise to the need for a critique of Reason. So, Reason is always present, but it is incomplete or unevenly developed. It is thus, in

10 Critical theory revisited

part, a condition of negativity in that it is not fully actualized, but it is also real in so far as it is manifest in reality.

While Hegel made much of the idea of freedom, which was the basis of emancipation, today this notion would need to be extended to include a wider spectrum of 'ideas of Reason', such as liberty, democracy, peace, truth, justice, equality, and autonomy. The legacy of Left-Hegelianism since the 1840s is to see these concepts as having normative relevance for the present and the basis of progressive politics. Left-Hegelianism was an interpretation of Hegel's thought that stressed less metaphysics – and the realization of spirit – than the social and historical manifestation of Reason and in ways that offer a means for the present to transcend itself. As summed up by Habermas, since the first generation after Hegel, philosophy became 'post-metaphysical' while retaining the notion or Reason (Habermas 1992: 29). The Left-Hegelian tradition also established a methodology for social interpretation rather than relying on a philosophy of history. While such concepts as freedom, Reason, and so on may take an ideological form in justifying the existing state of affairs, they also have a transformative capacity to make possible new realities. As Marcuse wrote in 1941 in *Reason and Revolution*, a key work in transmitting Hegel's more radical ideas to later critical theory: 'Hegel did not declare that reality is rational (or reasonable), but preserved this attribute for a definite form of reality, namely, actuality. And the reality that is actual is the one wherein the discrepancy between the possible and the real has been overcome. Its fruition occurs through a process of change, with the given reality advancing in accordance with the possibilities manifest in it' (Marcuse 1977: 153).

The idea of Reason, as expressed in Freedom, or these wider ideas of Reason, are concepts that are actualized to a degree in reality. They are not entirely abstractions in the sense of not having a concrete existence but refer to the accumulated cognitive potential that the world has built up in the course of history in shaping social reality. There is an immanent relationship between Reason and historical reality. The aim of philosophy is to reveal that relationship. To follow Marcuse again: 'As such the real is not yet "actual", but is at first only the possibility of an actual' (p. 150). So, Reason refers not only to ideas that transcend social reality; it is also manifest in social reality. In other words, it is immanent in reality. For Honneth, 'it amounts to the general thesis that each successful form of society is possible only through the maintenance of its most highly developed standard of rationality' (Honneth 2009: 23). We can therefore say that Reason forms the basis of the Hegelian ontology, a characteristic of which is the incompleteness of reality. In order to understand how Reason is actualized, two other key concepts are required: mediation and dialectics.

By mediation, Hegelianism posits processes that connect (i.e. mediate) the different parts and dimensions of social reality. Thus, the realization of freedom in one part of the world connects with other parts, and the realization of freedom in one aspect of society, for example, civil society, filters through to the domain of the state. Processes of mediation bind social reality together such that the ideas of Reason become inherent in the world and in time become manifest at the level of consciousness as self-consciousness whereby the self sees itself reflected in the world. The existence of something is dependent on its relation to something else. Mediation is thus a concept of interdependence. It is how a unity is forged out of diversity. Thus, through recognition, to refer to another famous Hegelian term and which could be seen as a process of mediation, the self is a self by being recognized by another. More generally, mediation refers to the ways in which subject and object are mutually constituted through ideas of Reason rather than, as in Kant, residing in a dualism or in differentiated spheres of Reason. According to Susan Buck-Morss (2009), Hegel took inspiration from the Haitian Revolution of 1791, which made possible emancipation from slavery and colonialism. It is possible that this interpretation inspired the famous discussion of master and slave in the *Phenomenology of Spirit*. If this is the case, it would suggest that this radical idea of freedom had a profound mediating influence in the modern world in stemming from Haiti as much as from Paris.

The mediation of Reason in the world is not a simple matter of the manifestation of ideas in social reality or a linear and harmonious process. It is achieved through dialectics, by which is meant relations of antagonism and contradiction through which new realities are created. The notion of dialectics captures the transformative process by which ideas of Reason become actualized or mediated in the world. It signifies a notion of reality as manifest in processes of transformation by which ideas work through reality to create new forms. While Hegel frequently fell into the trap of idealism, in seeing the relation of ideas to reality as one-sided, with reality simply reflecting ideas of Reason, his philosophy in fact informed a more radical interpretation that gave a stronger emphasis to the transformative moment in which reality undergoes a fundamental shift as a result of the development of its own ideas and latent possibilities.

This path of development, which makes possible developmental logics, is played out in terms of the interrelations of three worlds or levels of reality: the subjective world, the intersubjective world of social relations, and the objective world of nature. The combination of these levels is one of the critical factors in the shaping of reality. A critical theory approach requires taking all of these dimensions into account. It is this larger picture of the world that necessitates a macro-sociological approach and a theory of society that encompasses the learning capacities of society.[7]

The core of the intellectual legacy of Hegel's philosophy, as taken up by the left-wing tradition of Hegelianism – the so-called Young Hegelians such as, most famously, Ludwig Feuerbach, Bruno Bauer, Max Stirner and, of course, Karl Marx – was a conception of critique that was addressed to the contradictions, struggles, paradoxes, and crises of modernity across these dimensions. Since Marx, the dialectical conception of history gave a special place to social struggles as advancing the realization of Reason in the world. It became integral to a tradition of critical thought that strongly defended a normative view of society, that is, the belief that a better world is possible. Unlike utopian thought, with which it had much in common, the critical mind did not accept that a better world was impossible or

12 Critical theory revisited

not of this world. In other words, the normative position of critique was rooted in an ontological position that social reality contained within itself the capacity for transcendence. This ontological position had a strong degree of negation built into it, though it was until Adorno's *Negative Dialectics* [1966], with its key concept of non-identity, that this dimension of negativity was fully developed and given central prominence (because with Hegel it frequently appeared to be the case that Reason was actual). The possibility for transcendence is thus held to be latent or immanent within social reality.

The kind of critique it requires is therefore immanent critique, namely, a form of critique that is self-reflexive in seeking to show the discrepancy between idea and reality or the incomplete realization of an idea or its future possibilities. This began with Kant, who introduced the notion of 'an idea or concept of reason' in the *Critique of Pure Reason*, but only formally as an epistemology and not with respect to social reality. Hegel thus gave an ontological basis to critique as rooted in the actuality of ideas (de Boer 2011). It is therefore misleading to say that Hegel remained only on the level of ideas, for his entire endeavor was to see ideas as embedded in social reality. Yet, this was never adequately developed by Hegel, who famously saw the Prussian state as the embodiment of Reason, and, on the other extreme, he often saw ideas as self-manifestations rather than being created by revolutionaries (who Hegel disapproved of as the agents of Reason, which could only be discerned after its actualization and thus could not be wilfully brought about).

While for Kant, ideas of Reason had a transcendental function in that they allowed the immanent to be known, Hegel reduced Reason too much to the immanent level. The result was that it was never clear how Reason would become actualized. By historicizing the Kantian ideas, Hegel made a critical step in envisaging more specifically and potentially more concretely their relevance at the level of historical actuality. But, ultimately, he failed to come to grips properly with the process by which such ideas of Reason become actualized. This was the root of Marx's criticism that his idealism had the effect of curtailing the critical potential of his dialectics, that is, depriving it of the moment of praxis and the transformative action of social agents that would render it real.

Nonetheless, despite the absence of social agents, the intellectual basis was established for immanent critique. It should be noted that immanent critique is not a localized or an internal critique that simply sees Reason as manifest in social reality. This would be to domesticate it of its radical direction. Immanent critique receives its impetus from transcendence in that it is addressed specifically to those ideas of Reason that open social reality to future possibilities. As Fraser and Jaeggi (2018: 138–40) also argue, immanent critique is about deep potentials that have evolved in history. It is not then simply about a given social order not living up to its claims. It concerns latent possibilities that are the presuppositions of social transformation. In this way, the Hegelian notion of critique, as received in the Left-Hegelian tradition, avoids both an external and an internal conception of critique whereby the normative position is either external to social reality or resides within it. As summed up by Marcuse: 'Hegel's concept of reason . . . has a distinctively critical and polemic character. It is opposed to ready acceptance of the given state of affairs. It denies the hegemony of every prevailing form of existence by demonstrating the antagonisms that dissolve it into other forms' (p. 11).

The Hegelian notion of immanent critique was taken up by the Frankfurt School theorists, who made it the intellectual basis of a new critical theory of society. The distinctiveness of the philosophical approach of this tradition is that ideas of Reason are not merely abstract or general concepts that exist above social reality, but are rather real in that they are incorporated into social action. Thus, the idea of freedom or the notion of justice has a quasi-universal significance in that, despite taking a variety of culturally specific forms, they have the capacity to transform reality when they reach a higher level of reflexivity. This is in effect what mediation means: what is at first merely existing in a variety of forms and is often only expressed in the particular is given actual significance by being mediated in and through the medium of universal ideas or concepts possessing reality. To take an example, a sense of injustice exists in many different contexts, but it is only when these situations are connected (i.e. mediated) with a radicalized notion of justice that they have the capacity to bring about a fundamental transformation. In that sense, what is real becomes actualized through a re-working of latent ideas.

Critical theory – a brief overview of its conceptual framework

Since Horkheimer's 1937 signal essay, 'Traditional and Critical Theory', and Marcuse's 1941 *Reason and Revolution*, the Frankfurt School's programme of critical theory has been the most systematic attempt to re-establish the Hegelian heritage as received by Marxism on new foundations by linking the Hegelian-Marxist tradition with insights drawn from Freudian social psychology and classical sociology, in particular Weber (Horkheimer 1972a; Marcuse 1977).[8] Critical theory – as a new synthesis of Hegel, Marx, Weber, and Freud – began as a form of immanent critique[9] that was normative, diagnostic, and reconstructive. It was normative critique in that it was constructed on the basis of a vision of an alternative – even if it could not be precisely named – to the prevailing social and political order. As in Horkheimer's classic essay, it concerned social transformation and the elimination of social injustice, but above all it was concerned with the key problem of domination and social irrationality.[10]

Social injustice, the concern of classical Marxism, was seen as too limiting in view of the rise of new kinds of domination and unfreedom. The concern with domination arising from the spread of instrumental rationality to all spheres of life was one of the distinctive features of critical theory. The approach was normative in its concern with an alternative to the prevailing order but immanent in the recognition that existing social relations contain within them the means for their own overcoming. Critique is thus more than opposition to oppression or the pursuit of emancipation; it is about the identification of alternatives within the present in order to transform the present. Methodologically, critical theory proceeds

14 Critical theory revisited

reconstructively, that is, to say it seeks to reconstruct the immanent possibilities for transcendence, or, in other words, the possibilities contained in an actual situation for the overcoming and resolution of social problems. In Strydom's interpretation, critical theory seeks the reconstruction of ideas of Reason that point beyond or transcend every particular context as manifest in social reality (Strydom 2011). In order to accomplish this task, in line with Hegelian thought, it seeks to give form to a reality that already exists but disparately.

Critical theory requires a distinction between data and facts. The former require interpretation by reference to a theoretical system. Data are thus not then simply self-evident facts but must be made sense of. This requires both a philosophically based theory as well as a theory of society that would allow the critical theorists to place a given phenomenon in a large context. In this respect, critical theory draws heavily on the Marxist concept of totality (see Jay 1984a).

Reconstructive critique – the term that Habermas has generally preferred for immanent critique – entails a strong commitment to explanation through, for example, revealing the mechanisms of domination. As regards what kind of social problems or issues that are pertinent for critical social theory, the notion of reconstruction entails a relation to how society itself sees things. The theorist does not decide alone what is a problem but rather begins with what from the perspective of social actors are problems. In this way, critical theory incorporates into its self-understanding from the beginning a reflective relationship between social praxis and social scientific analysis. But the objectivity of social problems is always a necessary reference for the critical theorists, not simply the subjective views of the social actor. In other words, social actors might misunderstand the nature of social reality or the cause of social suffering, especially if they live under the conditions of what Horkheimer and Adorno referred to as mass deception or delusion. For this reason, critical theory regards domination as an objective condition that shapes consciousness and gives rise to suffering. However, the theoretical presumption that is the basis for the methodology of critical theory is that the experience of suffering gives rise to a desire to transcend the irrationalities of society. For this to occur the subjective experience of suffering must be illuminated by ideas – for instance the idea of justice – that bring about a transformation of the situation by challenging the source of the suffering. We shall set aside for now the problem as to whether in fact domination does necessarily always take such a total and singular form and necessarily gives rise to suffering. It is evident that today domination is more complicated and cannot be so easily seen in terms of a totalizing system that obliterates freedom and individual autonomy.

In line with the Hegelian-Marxist dialectical method, the Frankfurt School theorists held that social reality was contradictory and that the seeds of future possibility were contained within the struggles of the present. The normative ideas of modern society were not realized or only partly actualized. These ideas, following Hegel's ideas of Reason, represent both future potential and at the same time a false consciousness in that they do not appear to members of society as having a transformative potential, and consequently they take only an ideological form in

Spectres of critique **15**

that they end up affirming the status quo. Understood in these terms, normative critique was based on the central idea of immanent transcendence, namely, the notion that society can transcend or transform the given through a re-working and re-appropriation of its own self-understanding. Normative critique, understood in these terms, required a diagnostic approach to modern society in order to interpret the immanent signs of transcendence and the overcoming of pathologies. Normative diagnostic critique, as a form of transcendence, proceeds immanently, as opposed to being an external perspective or an attitude that sees political transformation as deriving from outside the horizons of a given society. Critical theory thus gave expression to a moral vision of the future possibilities of society as deriving from a process of social transformation driven forward by the internal dynamics of society. The Frankfurt School theorists stressed that this included the transformation of the individual's psyche as well as institutional change. Critique was the key to this, and a critical sociology was defined methodologically as one that sought to identify possibilities for critical thinking. These are always only latent and need to be reconstructed through social scientific investigation. It is for this reason that great importance was attached to empirical social research rather than purely philosophical analysis. There were nonetheless differences between Horkheimer and Adorno's conception of critique. While Horkheimer saw the task of critique to be about the uncovering of irrationalities, in the manner of ideology critique, Adorno argued for a stronger and more dialectical kind of critique that required a different form of negative thinking (Müller-Dohm 2005: 139).

Influenced by psychoanalysis, one of the early key critical theorists, Erich Fromm, developed in the 1930s and 1940s the idea that the subject suffers from pathological disorders as a result of living within irrational social structures (Burston 1991; Harris 2020). There is thus a lived, experienced harm to social irrationality that gives rise to a desire for transcendence. However, it was Marcuse's later interpretation in *Eros and Civilization* that established the most comprehensive synthesis of Freud into Marxist theory (Marcuse 1955). Although Marcuse, unlike Fromm, sought to retain Freud's key theories, the use of critical theory made by Freud was fundamentally different from Freud's concern with establishing psychoanalysis as a positivist medical science. The psychoanalytical model of transcendence provided critical theory with a way to deepen the Hegelian–Marxist conception of immanent transcendence; truth had to be dialectically demonstrated as a way of understanding social phenomena that were capable of expressing contradictions and thus contained unresolved tensions and possibilities (see also Chapter 11 on the Studies in Prejudice programme). Immanent transcendence signals a form of critique based on the internal transformation of society through processes of self-reflection. In this way, theory and practice are linked since critical theory is aimed at bringing about a better world through a 'diagnosis of the times'.

The kind of critical theory that the early Frankfurt School fostered was primarily 'ideology critique' – the de-masking of processes of domination – and did not always live up to the promises of its project of immanent critique. Much of it became simply cultural critique, as in the later writings of Adorno, who also

16 Critical theory revisited

contributed heavily to aesthetic theory and musicology. This was both a strength and a limitation of its scope. It was a crucial ingredient in the rise of cultural studies and post-representational theories of culture; it provided sociology with a normative foundation in the critical diagnostic analysis of ideology in order to demonstrate the workings of false consciousness and to identify possibilities for social transformation (see Benzer 2011). Yet, Adorno, despite his earlier attempt to link empirical social research with the Hegelian-Marxist philosophy, grew skeptical that empirical research and theoretical argument could easily go together. However, he did not abandon the aspiration to link sociology and philosophy, as is evident from his efforts at Frankfurt University since 1953 and earlier in California with the *Authoritarian Personality* [1950] project (see Chapter 11).[11]

The Frankfurt School is now best remembered as somewhat 'bourgeois Marxists' who wrote on modern mass culture, which they disdained, but their programme originally embraced empirical sociology grounded in a political and normative conception of society. Their endeavour represented the theoretically most sophisticated alternative to what Horkheimer termed 'traditional theory', namely, all forms of inquiry – whether hermeneutic or positivistic – that take the given as the only form of reality. Honneth has argued that the conception of critique at work here is that of a 'disclosing critique'. Critique proceeds by means of a disclosure – or a diagnosis – of the social world whereby new interpretations are possible and which endeavor to alter our way of seeing the world: 'A disclosing critique of society that attempts to change our value beliefs by evoking new ways of seeing cannot simply use a vocabulary of argumentative justification; rather, it can achieve its effects only if it employs its resources that, by condensing or shifting meanings, show facts hitherto unperceived in social reality' (Honneth 2009: 123; see also Bonacker 2006; Herf 2012).

As a result of the circumstances surrounding the Second World War and the Holocaust, the first generation of critical theorists tended to abandon immanent critique as well as empirical sociology as a result of their growing pessimism that the present society contained within itself the seeds of a better future. In 1947, in the *Eclipse of Reason*, Horkehimer wrote about the 'self-liquidation of reason' (see Jay 2016). The *Dialectic of Enlightenment* described human history as one of universal destruction whereby Enlightenment ideas such as freedom and happiness became in the end forms of mass deception that disguised the self-destructive ends of Reason. Despite being forerunners of cultural analysis, their critique of modern popular culture failed to understand the nature of cultural reproduction, which they tended to see as only oppressive. This was not confined to popular culture. Adorno was equally critical of many forms of so-called high culture, as in the music of Wagner (Adorno 1981 [1952]). The result was a methodological failure to link critique to a viable programme of social research. Social critique lost its way as cultural critique arose, which saw as its objective merely the documentation of domination in what Marcuse in *One-Dimensional Man* (1964) called, 'the totally administered society'. By this time, however, normative critique lost its connection with any notion of a political subject that could be a reference point for empirical sociology. The reason

Spectres of critique **17**

for this is perhaps because for the Frankfurt School the Holocaust became the overwhelming event of modernity. The attempt to understand the Holocaust and the wider context of totalitarianism consequently tended to give the earlier focus on capitalism a secondary significance, or to locate capitalism as part of a more deeply rooted anthropological instrumental rationality. For this reason, the *Dialectic of Enlightenment* became the real legacy of the Frankfurt School, despite the apparent message it contained of the end of immanent critique. Due to these developments, the theme of domination became central to critical theory.[12] One of its chief manifestations was in anti-Semitism. The pioneering research on anti-Semitism instigated by Horkheimer in the 1940s in the USA, leading to the Studies in Prejudice publications, saw anti-Semitism as a singular phenomenon that was more than simply a form of racism but an expression of totalitarianism (see Chapter 11).

While Adorno's greatest work has generally been held to be his *Aesthetic Theory* (2013 [1970]), his other late work, *Negative Dialectics* [1966], provided a philosophical basis for immanent critique. Neither of these works, perhaps due to their highly abstract nature, had much impact on critical theory in social science and were mostly taken up within specialist fields in philosophy. It is clear that Adorno's legacy is within philosophy, as is evident from the large volume of interpretative work (see O' Connor 2012; Bernstein 2001; Bowie 2013; Freyenhagen 2013). The famous enigmatic opening sentence of *Negative Dialectics* – 'Philosophy, which once seemed obsolete, lives because the moment to realise it was missed' – makes clear that it is philosophy that is Adorno's main concern.

Adorno's own preoccupations on returning permanently to Germany in 1953 were less in furthering the earlier project of a critical theory of society than in his new more public role as a critical intellectual in the Federal Republic. Despite his preoccupation with what he called in his 1951 work, *Minima Moralia*, 'damaged life', his later essays reflected a more positive view of possibilities for redemption and political renewal for a new generation of German people trying to come to terms with the legacy of the past. I return to this theme on memory and history in Chapter 10. In one of his final essays, 'Critique', in 1969, Adorno wrote: 'Critique is essential to all democracy. Not only does democracy require the freedom to criticize and need critical impulses. Democracy is nothing less than defined by critique' (Adorno 1998a: 281).

It is nonetheless worth returning to *Negative Dialectics* for a more systematic conception of critique that is still of relevance today. Despite the pivotal legacy of the *Dialectic of Enlightenment* [1944/1947] in the legacy of the Frankfurt School, it is arguably the case that *Negative Dialectics* is more in keeping with the critical theory tradition, even if it also moves beyond the notion of immanent critique. The central concept in the work is the notion of 'the non-identical', which takes up Hegel's emphasis on negation as part of the dialectical process by which reality is constituted. Adorno sought to develop a form of critique that would capture negation and absence as part of the ontological structure of reality and thus, as itself, real. Negative dialectics is opposed to all kinds of affirmative thinking that sees reality as defined exclusively by facticity or immediacy. In terms of immanence,

18 Critical theory revisited

the transcendental moment is contained within negativity as an open horizon. Adorno's negative dialectic thus can be seen as a corrective, on the one side, to the identification of critique with facticity or with an affirmative conception of dialectics, as in, for example, orthodox Marxism, which sees a direct relation between dialectics and socialism. On the other side, it is an alternative to the pessimistic or anti-modernist position that sees history devoid of any potentiality for a radical transformation of the present. Negative dialectics sees the future as open and not predetermined in any way by a goal. This suggests that for Adorno the critical analysis of the present must contain an orientation to the future. This is so even if the creations of human beings are so great that they overwhelm their capacity to bring about social transformation. It is also because of the centrality of the experience of suffering. In *Negative Dialectics* the objectivity of suffering: 'The need to lend a voice to suffering is a condition of all truth. For suffering is objectivity that weighs upon the subject; its most subjective experience, its expression, is objectively conveyed' (Adorno 1990: 17–18).

For this reason, it can also be said that Adorno's own conception of critique was not confined to immanent critique since he was aware that the present may not in fact offer a direction for the future. Immanent critique requires the unmasking of contradictions in the present rather than seeking an external point of reference, for example, a utopian alternative. However, immanent critique may have to accept that the present does not have anything to offer for the future other than hope and belief in the possibility of redemption. Thus, for example, democracy could be seen as having lost its capacity to make a better society possible because it has been fully absorbed into the administered society of late capitalism or perhaps because the nature of social life is such that democracy may be irrelevant (people might, for example, prefer to live a life of delusion). There is also a further problem with immanent critique, namely, how to judge which aspects of the present are desirable but unfulfilled. It may transpire that such ideas of Reason – peace, human rights, democracy, freedom, and so on – may be forms of tyranny or merely a continuation of a deeply flawed world. Immanent critique – as an expression of immanent transcendence – operates on the assumption that such ideas of Reason do have a means of transcending 'damaged life' without a clear sense of what the good life consists. That is why it is most probably the case that in the final analysis, Adorno's notion of critique was more strongly a negative critique. Martin Jay has pointed out that in *Minima Moralia,* Adorno believed immanent ideology critique was losing its capacity to provide a critical leverage in the world (Jay 1984b: 43). In this context, there is the more general problem of establishing clarity on exactly what domination is and whether or not it requires suffering. Many people are deluded about global warming and the nature of capitalism, but they are not necessarily suffering.

Negativism, as in negative dialectics, rests on the belief that it is possible to know that something is wrong without knowing what is right. This position, while not being incompatible with immanent critique, is nonetheless in tension with it. Kracauer, one of the early critical theorists, complained about *Minima Moralia* that the reader was left in the dark about the 'criteria by which the author had judged "mere existence"' (quoted in Müller-Doohm 2005: 343). According to Freyen-hagen (2013: 11), Adorno's position was that 'we can only know the bad (or part thereof), not the good, in our modern social world, and that this knowledge of the bad is sufficient to underpin his critical theory (including his ethics of resistance)'. The message of *Minima Moralia* was that the 'good life' is no longer possible, and hence philosophy can only show the damage 'to read the ruins of ethical life as a negative expression of what has been lost and/or what we intend to hope for' (Bernstein 2001: 40). This is captured in the famous statement 'Wrong life cannot be lived rightly' (Adorno 2005: 39). It is also intimated at the end of *Minima Moralia*: 'The only philosophy which can be responsibly practised in face of despair is the attempt to contemplate all things from the standpoint of redemption' (2005: 247). A theme implicit in much of Adorno's work is that culture, even where it is com-plicit with domination, always contains traces of refusal.[13] I agree that a normative position is possible in the absence of knowing what the good life is or what is right and just. It is often enough to recognize that something is bad to justify resistance. But that does not offer much guidance in dealing with other social challenges that are not primarily ones of suffering and domination. In any case, with the mature work of Adorno we have two models of critique: negative critique and immanent critique. They cannot be entirely separated, and it is unclear to what extent Adorno shifted position. However, it is evident that he saw theoretical reflection as the basis of both scientific and political practice. In one of his last essays, based on a radio broadcast, 'Resignation', he clarified his notion of critical thinking, which perhaps best exemplifies his mature thought:

> the uncompromisingly critical thinker, who neither signs over his conscious-ness nor lets himself be terrorized into action, is in truth the one who does not give in. Thinking is not the intellectual reproduction of what already exists anyway. As long as it doesn't break off thinking has a secure hold on possibility. Its insatiable aspect, its aversion to being quickly and easily satisfied, refuses the foolish wisdom of resignation. The utopian moment in thinking is stronger the less it – this too a form of relapse – objectifies itself into a utopia and hence sabotages its realization. Open thinking points beyond itself. . . . Whatever has once been thought can be repressed, forgotten, can vanish. But it cannot be denied that something of it survives. For thinking has the ele-ments of the universal.
>
> *(Adorno 1998b: 292–3)*

Habermas and the revival of critical theory

The programme of critical theory launched by Habermas sought to restore critical theory within sociological theory. As argued, critical theory with the earlier Frank-furt School had lost a direct connection with social research and did not seem rele-vant to the changed circumstances of the late twentieth century. This is not to say it had no relevance. The critical theory of Adorno and Horkheimer remained a major

20 Critical theory revisited

alternative to positivism or, to be more precise, to neo-positivism, as represented by Popper's critical rationalism and the dominant naturalistic understanding of social inquiry (Adorno et al 1976). On the other end of the epistemological spectrum, their conception of a critical social science was also an alternative to interpretative social science, including hermeneutics and phenomenology. However, the debate, as in the positivist dispute in German sociology, was largely confined to the philosophy of social science and did not lead to a new social theory beyond clarifying epistemological questions on method.

The creation of a new critical theory based on a theory of society was the task of Habermas, whose first major epistemological contribution sought to ground critical theory in a notion of emancipation tied to a theory of 'human interests'. The concern with emancipation from domination was always a major concern of Left-Hegelianism, but it never led to fruitful applications other than in a call for such domination to be transcended in the name of emancipation. While Habermas (1972 [1968]), in *Knowledge and Human Interests,* made a fruitful connection between Freud's psychoanalysis and Marxism, this contribution remained stuck at a very normative level with an unclear relationship between the epistemological position and social theory (other than a general embracing of anti-positivism within social science). This was to change both normatively and methodologically with the publication of the *Theory of Communicative Action* in 1981 and in publications of the preceding years, most notably *Communication and the Evolution of Society* in 1976 (Habermas 1984/1987, 1979). The new beginning also led him out of the philosophical and methodological impasse of his first work, *The Structural Transformation of the Public Sphere,* in 1962, which was effectively a story of the decline of Reason (Habermas 1989). The book had another problem for which he was much criticized: it was unreflectively Eurocentric in its argument that modernity in western Europe was the high point of the actualization of Reason, which subsequently went into decline.[14] The work was based on a historical model of the public sphere and more generally a historical model of European modernity that supposedly crystalized before the maturation of capitalism, which had a regressive impact on the public sphere whose history could only be one of decline.

With his mature work, critical social theory had the precise goal of locating transcendence within the immanent structures of communication and thus was not tied to a historical moment of emergence. The theory of communicative action shows that communicative rationality is as much a part of modernity as is instrumental rationality. The latter, the focus of Weber and Adorno and Horkheimer, is only one dimension of modernity. Equally central to modernity is communicative rationality, as reflected in the nature of social interaction, socialization, identities, and social institutions. Communicative rationality is not derivative of the former, nor is it merely an epiphenomenon or part of the superstructure of society. The key to social transformation resides in the relation between the forms of rationality. For Habermas, the basis of modernity is the accumulation of a normative potential within communicative rationality, as reflected in socialization processes, the design of social institutions, and the critique of power. In this way, immanent critique is no longer dependent on negative dialectics. While the critique of capitalism does not disappear, it is not the only focus of critical theory since domination can reside in other domains.

From his early work on the public sphere to his theory of communicative action and the later discourse theory of democracy (Habermas [1992] 1997), Habermas has brought about a major reorientation of critique based on a new theory of society. In line with the Hegelian-Marxist tradition, the defining feature of critical theory is the task of illustrating how the regulative ideas of Reason are articulated by social actors in situations of crisis and conflict where contrary political positions force deeper discursively achieved results. Normative critique thus becomes linked to a critical cognitive theory of developmental change in societal learning, which in turn is based on a theory of learning on the level of the individual as well as on the collective level (see Habermas 1979 [1976]). The *Theory of Communicative Action* concludes by giving a central prominence to social movements as the agents of progressive social change. This is one major departure from the older Frankfurt School, which did not have a theory of a collective actor capable of bringing about social change. (I return to this in more detail in Chapter 3.)

Influenced by Karl-Otto Apel, who advanced a critical philosophy of social science that drew on C. S. Peirce's philosophy of pragmatism as well as Hegelian-Marxism, Habermas recast the terms of dialectical mediation as a relationship between the 'ideal community' and the 'real community', whereby the former is already anticipated by the latter as a counter-factual alternative. Apel's work on what became discourse ethics opened a path for Habermas to rethink the normative foundations of critical theory in terms of the linguistic structures of communicative rationality. While in Apel's writings (1980 [1973]) it was often unclear where the ideal community resides, in Habermas's appropriation of his work, both as a philosophy of social science and as a social theory, it became clear that both the ideal and real community are to be found in the deeper domains of social reality. However, Apel did make it clear that the 'unlimited communication community is postulated in any argument, indeed in any human world' and 'in the historically given society the ideal communication community is always still to be realized' (Apel 1980: 140). The key point is that the nature of communicative rationality offers resources for people in concrete situations of social struggle to think critically and to find alternatives. Drawing from Apel's work, which introduced to critical theory the work of the American pragmatists, in particular C. S. Peirce, and gave a new significance for Kant, Habermas argued for a mediation of explanation and understanding in order to meet 'the challenge to all to transform causally explicable modes of behaviour into intelligible actions by a process of talking stock' (Apel 1980: 72). This was Apel's philosophical and more Kantian argument for a deeper and more hermeneutic 'critique of ideology', which he saw in terms of 'self-diagnosis and explanatory science'.

Critique is thus forward-looking and concerned with shifts in the self-understanding of societies and modernity more generally. It gives a clear direction for reconstructive critique as a methodology for a critical social science. Situations

22 Critical theory revisited

of major crisis – capitalist crisis or the wider conflict of system and life-world – give rise to social struggles in which social movements shape the future (to be discussed in Chapter 3). Habermas's critical theory directs empirical analysis to those sites of contestation where cognitive changes for a better world are likely to form. In essence, critique as a methodology for social science is addressed to a critical problem and seeks to explain the specific form normative or regulative ideas take as a result of competing positions and the identification of pathologies. Critique proceeds from a critical issue or crisis to an account of the normative ideas that are involved to an analysis of how social actors position themselves with respect to the problem. In this way, macro issues are translated into the micro level of analysis. The stress is thus on the objective problem that produces a crisis, which requires a subjective response leading in turn to social struggles.

Habermas's revision of critical theory, in drawing on Apel and Peirce, led to the insight that the objective condition of society is not a matter of total domination – in the sense of Adorno's concern with a totalizing domination that eliminates the capacity for transcendence – but at the same time it also brings into play something else, which at least implicitly invokes the illumining light of an idea of Reason pointing beyond the subjective situation of suffering and which challenges the sources of domination. This could be a sign or a symbol or a word or concept that transcends the given situation. It may be rooted in a memory or in an anticipation of an alternative world. This process of self-transformation can be understood in terms of the Hegelian notion of 'mediation' as the process by which consciousness arises in ways that link suffering or oppression with the objective condition of domination. The mediation of the subjective and the objective allows a sense of an opposite (e.g. a sense of not being violated, of not being subjected, of being free) to emerge. As Strydom has outlined in his reconstruction of the methodology of critical theory, the early critical theorists treated this dimension in a subdued manner, Adorno taking it in the negative sense of the 'non-identical' to avoid the reification entailed by 'identity thinking', while the later ones sought to bring it out in their own ways: 'formal pragmatic world concepts' plus 'communicative reason', in the case of Habermas, or with Honneth, the 'modern recognition order' (see Strydom 2011). Habermas's mature work, since the early 1980s also brought critical theory into the concrete sociological implications of postmetaphyical philosophy in that it now had to address the pluralization of modern forms of life (Habermas 1992, 1988).

While Habermas's use of the critical method in social research has been relatively limited, others have developed it in ways that connect more firmly macro-societal analysis with micro-analysis of specific communicative situations.[15] Furthermore, Habermas's earlier sociological approach, which was located within the Hegelian-Marxist tradition, has increasingly been overshadowed by a more explicitly developed Kantian normative political philosophy. Despite the turn from social theory to a normative political and legal philosophy in his work since the 1990s, it is clear that Habermas has not departed from the idea of a reconstructive critical theory in that transcendent ideas are embedded in social reality, as in, for example, the ways in which the norms and practices of democracy are institutionalized in most societies. The presumption then is that the normative order of modern society, in particular in the public sphere where political communication takes place, contains within itself the means to attain a better future. It may indeed be the case that the dialectical moment has lapsed, but this was always the case once the over-normative notion of emancipation confronting domination was displaced by the theory of communicative rationality and the recognition that transcendent possibilities are immanent in social reality.

Habermas's later work on law and democracy broadened the scope of critical theory to encompass areas that had been regarded as part of the sphere of instrumental reason, including in his own earlier work. This came at the price of a loss of the critical focus on what became a philosophy of deliberative democracy. The place and significance of the older concerns of critical theory with domination and capitalism receded. It also led to uncertainty on the role of explanation in social science.[16] While much of this can be attributed to Habermas's embracing of Rawls's normative model of deliberative democracy, it should not be forgotten that Habermas's project was different in that the category of deliberation had a transcendental rather than only a normative significance in that it referred to immanent structures in society and the validity claims embedded in human communication. Rawls's political philosophy was explicitly a normative critique and as such did not require addressing the immanent possibilities within the existing society to attain the demands of an ideal political community. For this reason, even though it reshaped political thought around an alternative political order, there is no basis in his work for a critical theory of society.

Post-Habermasian critical theory: Honneth and recognition theory

It is against this background of a loss in the explanatory power of critical theory as a theory of society that Honneth attempted to develop a deeper level of microanalysis in terms of struggles of recognition. Where Habermas posited a basic conflict between instrumental rationality and communicative rationality, or system and life-world, Honneth has put struggles of recognition at the centre of critical social theory. We return to the macro social theoretical shift in Chapter 3, as the focus here is on the epistemological and ontological framework of critical theory. While Habermas located communication as the core of social relations and the basis of the very possibility of society, Honneth posits recognition as the chief concern of critical theory. His central question is: 'how is it that the experience of disrespect is anchored in the affective life of human subjects in such a way that it can provide the motivational impetus for social resistance and conflict, indeed, for a struggle for recognition?' (1998 [1996]: 132). With this move, the relation between self and society undergoes major reconceptualization. The individual figures more centrally, and, as a consequence, the collective actor recedes in importance. Honneth's main concern is with the 'moral grammar of social life'. It cannot be denied that this is

24 Critical theory revisited

important, but it does take critical theory down a different path despite the continuity that certainly does exist with his project and that of the earlier Frankfurt School (see Basure 2011).

Recognition theory, as a critical theory of society, is still grounded in 'diagnostic critique' – which is Honneth's formulation of his particular approach to immanent critique – but one that seeks the identification of a pathology that has the effect of blocking recognition, which Honneth divides into three categories (emotional, legal, and social) which are linked, respectively, to rights, love, and esteem. In this approach, which links the early writings of Hegel to social psychology, critique moves from macro-level accounts of crisis in terms of societal structures to a micro-level analysis of how social pathologies arise as a result of individuals' failure to achieve recognition. Although this turn in critical theory is not incompatible with macro-sociological analysis, it has inevitably brought critical theory in the direction of micro-analysis.[17]

For Honneth, the early Hegel emphasized the essentially moral nature of social life and thus a view of social actors as moral as opposed to egoistic or rational. The basic structure of *Sittlichkeit* rather than Reason – or Kant's notion of *Moralität* – becomes more important in the social ontological and anthropological foundations of this new development in critical theory. The human being in recognition theory is basically vulnerable to harm and suffering. This is a universal anthropological fact of the human condition. Honneth's critical theory directs social struggles to problems of recognition rather than to a more general conception of domination that can be resisted by deliberative reasoning. Thus, the denial of recognition, which takes the form of disrespect in any of the three spheres of recognition, generates struggles for recognition. The task of critique is to demonstrate how these struggles arise and how they derive from more fundamental moral questions of recognition deriving from, for example, the experience of suffering, disrespect, the denial of rights, or exclusion. Honneth's argument opens up a more pluralist conception of social struggles than in Marxism and offers greater specificity than in Habermas's over-generalized conception of social movements resisting systemic forces, but the result is that social struggles are confined to recognition claims that can easily be contained within the *status quo*. Certainly, the structure of global society is not in question. Many such struggles pertain to the realm of personal self-realization (see Honneth 2004).

Honneth's revision of Habermas's critical theory solved a number of problems. Habermas's reliance on what was effectively an ontological theory of communication led to the neglect of dimensions of human experience that do not quite fit into the model of communication, for example, emotion, the pre-cognitive and pre-linguistic, and the experience of suffering. It offered an argumentative conception of social action that was best exemplified in the domain of democratic discourse. But not all social action or communication more generally accords with the deliberative model of language. As often noted, Habermas postulated a strong dualism of life-world and system with the result that the relation was destined to be antagonistic. Honneth's approach demonstrated that the domain of the system – for example, work – cannot be reduced to instrumental action and that the life-world is the realm of communicative action (Honneth 1982). Struggles for recognition pertain also to work, which cannot be reduced to the category of alienated labour. However, Honneth's theoretical framework in correcting a major problem in Habermas created further problems. In bringing to the fore of critical theory problems that cannot be conceived in terms of system and life-world, Honneth reduces social action to the fundamental problem of recognition. It is difficult to see how the category of recognition, however much differentiated, can be used as a framework for the many different issues facing social analysis.

As noted by several scholars (for example Heins 2008, 2010), it is very difficult to relate the category of recognition to global issues, for example, to the problem of global poverty or more generally to global politics. Honneth (2012), nonetheless, has attempted to apply recognition to demands for recognition between states. While this may cover some cases of struggle, for example, recognition of historical crimes, it hardly deals with global politics more generally. Nancy Fraser has criticized recognition theory for reducing other kinds of social struggles to demands for recognition. In her view, demands for social justice, especially those concerning the harsh social realities of market forces, are not primarily demands for recognition.[18] Throughout history, social struggles have not been primarily about recognition and have not been driven by suffering. The record of history is that social groups rebel when they perceive opportunities to improve their situation. More fundamentally, the problem is that recognition is primarily a category that pertains to the individual and their experience, especially of suffering. It does not account for the actions of people who do not suffer, such as social movements that act on behalf of marginalized people. It is also not clear why suffering would lead to struggles for recognition in view of the simple fact that it is the nature of much suffering that the subject is rendered unable to act to remedy their situation. In other words, it assumes that political action follows on from the experience of suffering.

While Honneth claims that recognition is a new normative standard for critique, it is not at all evident why this is the case. For instance, how would one distinguish between 'false' – or what Adorno would probably have called 'deluded' – claims to recognition, for example, where people might misunderstand their situation or the case of a claim to recognition by one group that, if realized, would have detrimental consequences for another. In view of these problems, recognition theory lacks a critical edge since the category of recognition does not provide a way to evaluate and make judgements on claims to recognition. In terms of immanent transcendence, Honneth has de-transcendentalized critique, which is reduced to operating within the structures of immanence. This has led to the accusation of a subjective turn in critical theory, which is reflected in Honneth's use of psychoanalysis in a somewhat apolitical manner, as in his turn to the work of Jessica Benjamin and Donald Winnicott's Object Relation approach. However, it is unclear whether this actually leads to an undue reliance on a moral psychologism, as critics often complain, since a subjective orientation is consistent with the broad aims of critical theory to place the historical subject as the primary agent of

26 Critical theory revisited

critique. It is nonetheless the case that despite his move away from Habermas's reliance on communication, he remains within the intersubjective framework that was also central to Habermas's endeavour and which is essential for a critical theory of society. Such a commitment to an intersubjective philosophy does not necessarily require extending recognition to all relations, such as the mother-child dyad as the infant has not attained the level of consciousness that the concept of recognition requires (McNay 2007: 134). The problem remains of the normative status of the category of recognition quite aside from its usefulness in dealing with the many facets of domination. As McNay argues in her critique of Honneth's recognition theory, it is a psychologically reductive social theory and gives a normative status to institutions such as the family as an imperfect realization of care, which leads to a reification of the domestic field and, moreover, fails to see that the family may itself be a source of domination (McNay 2007: 135–6). The problem, it seems, is that Honneth takes empirical trends and reads from them normative developments, such as the broad claim that modernity entails the spread of legal forms of recognition, without considering the regressive features of modernity. In a later work, *Freedom's Right*, Honneth (2014) argues for a model of gradual progress as the only way in which progress can work, and consequently critical theory does not need to concern itself with radical critique (Schaub 2015: 114–15).

In his incisive critique of recent critical theory, Michael J. Thompson argues that Honneth's recognition theory has lost sight of the central focus of domination stemming from capitalism. Instead, critical theory has become 'domesticated' by moving into the concerns of mainstream analytical political philosophy and thus abandoning the systemic imperatives of capitalism and the analysis of power and domination. 'The domestication of critical theory' means that 'it is rendered unable to critique the fundamental forms of social power that distort consciousness and therefore is unable to serve as a means of elucidating an emancipatory consciousness for social critique' (Thompson 2016: 18, see also Thompson 2019). In contrast, he sees the earlier Frankfurt School's project of seeking the analysis of the structures of consciousness that accompany advanced capitalism as now lost. In his view, Habermas and more recent contributions, for example Forst (2012), fall into a 'neo-idealist' trap in seeing the cognitive capacities of people to be independent of social pathologies and possessing an independent force that makes the power of social domination less important. Following Marcuse, Thompson sees the pathological effects of reified structures of thought present in language and communication, which cannot therefore be taken as an independent source of critical reason. Thompson may be going too far in his criticisms in that it is arguable that Habermas claims that communication exists in an undistorted form. Habermas, in fact, argues that communication entails validity claims that make it possible for power to be challenged. Moreover, Forst's argument that the right to justification does not derive from social conditions but from the universalist nature and logic of Reason is not in itself invalidated by the facts of history. Communicative action – including the moral status of human beings – is an ontological fact of the social world and does not reside in a separate domain of discourse. As such, it exists whether or not systems of power and domination distort it. A critical ontology of modernity cannot simply dismiss claims to justification and more generally critical reason as not integral to social reality. It is the whole point of Habermas's social theory to show that validity claims are immanent in social reality.

However, Thompson's critique is more pertinent to the limitations of recognition theory than to Habermas's theory of communicative action. Reification is not simply a matter of a failure of recognition that can therefore be solved by more authentic forms of recognition; rather it is a process that prevents the subject from having a critical grasp of society. While having critical elements, recognition is not itself a medium of critical thought. Thompson makes a key point in claiming that Honneth restricts recognition to a phenomenological operation, whereas Hegel saw it as the beginning of a higher form of reasoning. Thus, 'recognition is a crucial mechanism, but it can also be corrupted by defective social relations, institutions, and arrangements that are not detectable through recognition itself' (Thompson 2016: 77). In essence, recognition may produce pathologies and cannot on its own be a means out of a social world characterized by pathologies. Thompson does not deny the importance of recognition in itself nor its relevance to critical theory but persuasively argues that it cannot be the primary basis of a critical theory of society. Recognition claims are not fundamentally different from identity claims since recognition is a key dimension of identity. Constructing a critical social theory around identity presents major limitations to the scope and relevance of social theory in that whatever critical insights might follow will not be able to connect a micro-analysis with a macro-analysis of social structures. Such approaches also fail to address what has always been central to critical theory, namely, the focus on totality, that is, a view of society as a whole and the location of the particular in a wider context. As argued in the foregoing, this would have to include the inter-relationships between the subjective, the intersubjective, and objective worlds.

Recognition has been highly successful as a framework for social research. Its usefulness in addressing many social issues cannot be questioned, especially those concerning vulnerable groups. However, as argued in the foregoing it is limited when it comes to the analysis of major social transformation – the main concern of this book – but it also loses a critical impetus when it comes to the topics to which it has often applied. As Harris (2019) shows, the recognition framework considerably limits if not distorts the analysis of social pathology. While being a dimension of pathology, the problem of social pathology is not primarily one of recognition. I return to this in Chapter 3.

Critical theory after postcolonialism

A problem that runs through the entire critical theory tradition is that it has not been successful in responding to postcolonial critiques and above all to the problem of Eurocentrism. Honneth's conception of recognition assumes a largely western perspective and the historical condition of western modernity. Indeed, it has often been noted that his model of struggles of recognition pertains to the modern national state and its categories of legal recognition. But, in light of postcolonial and de-colonial critiques, how does this theory fare when it comes to claims of recognition that cannot be met within the societal or civilizational context of modernity? The presumption is that the modern national state provides the basic structures by which struggles for recognition can be realized. This is a major problem when it comes to colonial and racial relations and has led to new calls for the decolonizing of critical theory (Allen 2016; Baum 2015; Coulthard 2014; McCarthy 2009; Steinmetz 2006). It is also a problem that pervades the notion of immanent critique. In the context of conflicts that run very deep, it is very difficult to see how the relationship between the colonized and colonizer can be conceived in terms of recognition. The politics of de-colonization go far beyond the superficial level of recognition to question the formation of the subjects in question. Coulthard argues against the politics of recognition with the claim (which is not specifically directed at Honneth) that instead of making possible peaceful coexistence, the notion of reciprocity or mutual recognition in fact reproduces the very forms of colonial power that indigenous peoples have historically struggled against.

This postcolonial criticism is in particular a problem for recognition theory, which is very much a theory addressed to a particular problem in contemporary society, but it is more generally a problem for the entire Left–Hegelian tradition of critical theory. As Edward Said noted, it is remarkable that the critical scholarship fostered by the Frankfurt School never addressed the centrality of colonialism in the making of modernity (Said 1994: 278). The concerns of critical theory have always been heavily western. Much of this can be accounted for by the fact that the older critical theorists were Jewish and were responding to the Holocaust, which they saw as the central and defining moment of modernity. The focus on the Holocaust and the wider historical experience with totalitarianism – from Hitler and Mussolini to Stalin and the incipient forms analyzed in the *Authoritarian Personality* [1950] – tended to bring critical theory away from the study of capitalism (Adorno 2019). The impact and allure of the *Dialectic of Enlightenment* gave a further anti-political direction to critical theory as well as an obsession with Europe's inner demons. It is remarkable that no connection was made between the anti-Semitism that made possible the Holocaust and colonialism. However, the problems run deeper in that the earlier writings of the Frankfurt School before the rise of Hitler also did not address colonialism, despite the fact that at this time the major western societies were still colonial powers. Slavery and modern racism were never discussed as a significant dimension of modernity and constituted specific forms of domination. However, unlike Hannah Arendt, who was also highly Eurocentric, the Frankfurt School theorists did not subscribe to racist views.[19]

The silence about race and empire in the making of modernity is also apparent in Habermas's work, which praises Europe's culture of critique but fails to consider its relevance to the wider world and the historical experience with colonialism. It has been a central assumption of Habermas's theory of modernity that the structures of western modernity provide the essential resources to make possible emancipation. But if that very modernity is itself implicated in forms of domination that are themselves grounded in modernity's own self-understanding, might it limit, if not invalidate, the capacity for critique? It is evident that Habermas believed that the colonial legacy was less important to Germany, a matter that German historians are now questioning. However, in view of Britain and France as his major points of reference for modernity, it is nonetheless remarkable that race and empire do not enter into the narrative and critique of modernity. Western Europe was never entirely western and neither was it entirely European.[20]

There are two issues here as regards the alleged Eurocentrism of critical theory: one of scope and focus and one of conceptual reasoning. First, there is certainly a Eurocentrism in that the critical theory tradition has been primarily focussed on western societies. There were some minor exceptions but, even in these cases, critical theory as such had little impact (see Jay 1996/1973: 134–5). However, that narrow empirical focus in itself, while limiting its relevance, does not make it methodologically Eurocentric if by that term is meant a view of the superiority of the West over the non-western world. Adorno, Horkheimer, and Habermas clearly have a great admiration for modern European culture but hardly claim that it is morally superior to other cultures. Their uncompromising critique of fascism is surely evidence of critical theory's critique of the European legacy as engendering barbarism. *The Dialectic of Enlightenment* saw self-destruction as a universal logic in civilization and not just European. Habermas's writings stress the centrality of rupture within modernity and rejects the idea of a historical narrative of progress unfolding. Second, a more important question is whether its theoretical framework is Eurocentric in that the very concepts it uses are relevant to historical experiences beyond western modernity or to an understanding of de-colonization. This second question raises two issues. One is that its concepts might not be able to capture the experiences of other cultures, such as those for whom colonization was central to their experience with modernity (or even indigenous societies whose structures of consciousness cannot be comprehended through the categories of Left-Hegelianism). The Holocaust might be less central to the historical experience of the non-western world and thus not a central point of reference. If this were the case, it would mean that critical theory can only be a theory of western modernity. So long as it understands itself as such, there is no reason why this might be a problem (other than being somewhat limited). Indeed, much of postcolonial theory is confined to a critique of western scholarship. Nonetheless, I would suggest that it is not the case that critical theory sees itself as a theory only of the modern western world. Habermas clearly attributes a universal significance to his arguments on the learning and communicative features of all modern societies. The core insight in the transcendental thesis is that validity claims are implicit in language rather than in cultural traditions. It is the former that are universal, not the historical form in which they appear. The implication of this, which escapes most if not all postcolonial critiques, is that the basis of the theory of communicative action is in learning processes, not in a historical progress as such.

Second is the more serious charge that the concepts of Left-Hegelianism are somehow tainted if not fully implicated in colonialism and are therefore to be

30 Critical theory revisited

rejected if they are to address the challenges of de-colonization, which in demanding a de-colonization of the mind requires rejecting the core normative ideas of modernity. This latter position is more or less the claim made by Amy Allen in *The End of Progress* (Allen 2016, see also 2017). She argues that ideas of historical progress, social evolution, and sociocultural learning are western concepts – a claim that is stated rather than argued – and rooted in western modernity. Critical theory, in adhering to these views, presents an obstacle in engaging with postcolonial studies that do not accept the assumptions of Left-Hegelianism. Her argument, despite drawing attention to what is without doubt a failure in critical theory, is nonetheless problematical in that it rests on the presumption of a normative theory of progress as the basis of critical theory. It is also unclear why these concepts are western only. All societies have a capacity for learning. Moreover, her account does not demonstrate how critical theory can be advanced as a theory of society.

Problems of successful dialogue between different intellectual traditions are common place across the human and social sciences, but that does not mean that one tradition is at fault or that one tradition should engage with another one. The problem may equally well reside in the epistemology of postcolonial studies in not understanding Left-Hegelianism. However, I do not deny that critical theorists have been particularly slow to take on board postcolonial arguments. In my view, this is not the main problem. The problem with the charge of Eurocentrism, unless it remains on the level of scope, is that it makes the assumption that the concepts of Left-Hegelianism are in themselves limited, if not invalid, when it comes to the politics of de-colonization because they are of western lineage. For this claim to be cogent, it would need to be shown that the concepts are indeed of western origin and specific to the western historical experience. While critical theorists from Adorno to Habermas and Honneth undoubtedly saw their intellectual tradition as a western one, it is by no means self-evident that notions such as progress, emancipation, freedom, and so on are not of universal relevance. It is one thing to claim that western modernity has been deeply intertwined with colonialism; it is another thing to claim that all concepts associated with western modernity are products of the relationship with colonialism and that they are specific to the West. This is where one current within de-colonial theory departs from postcolonial critique, namely, Dussell's call for critical thought to be a dialogue of the critical legacies of all intellectual traditions (see Bartholomew 2018: 635). The fact that certain concepts have been more extensively theorized in the western tradition does not mean that they are western or of no relevance to non-western societies. Allen is justified in drawing attention to the neglect of colonialism and race in Left-Hegelianism and seeking to advance dialogue between postcolonialism and critical theory. However, it is not enough to invoke colonialism as the prism through which everything has to be viewed, not least as many concepts such as freedom preceded western dominance and drew from non-western traditions, such as the Arabic and earlier Indian thought. Regardless of how the dark side of history is to be viewed – whether the stress is on the history of colonialism, racism, the Holocaust, totalitarianism – the vast canvas of history includes many other legacies,

Spectres of critique **31**

including counter-movements. Allen's important book is focussed on the idea of progress, which is perhaps an easier target than other concepts in critical theory, central to which I have argued is the notion of an imminent form of transcendence. Such a perspective requires less the identification with the facticity of history than the transcendent forces immanent within an historical context. But progress is also more complicated, as Adorno recognized in one of his last essays, 'Progress', in which he recognized both its negative and its positive connotations: 'the concept of progress dissolves upon attempts to specify its exact meaning, for instance what progresses and what does not' (1998b: 141). He observes that the idea of progress articulates both the moment of society and at the same time contradicts it: 'Having arisen societally, the concept of progress requires critical confrontation with real society. The aspect of redemption, no matter how secularized, cannot be removed from the concept of progress [which] requires critical confrontation with real society. The fact that it cannot be reduced neither to facticity nor to the idea indicates its own contradiction' (1998b [1969]: 148). Benjamin also questioned the idea of progress, as in his remarks on the idea of progress in the *Arcades Project*: 'Overcoming the concept of "progress" and overcoming the concept of "period of decline" are two sides of the same things (1999: 460). He goes on to write that "the concept of progress must be grounded in the idea of catastrophe" (472). He rejects it as an 'uncritical hypostatization rather than a critical interrogation' and 'counter to the critical theory of history' (478).

In sum, my position is that the key concepts of critical theory are not reducible to the historical experience of western modernity and have a wider significance, including addressing the challenges posed by postcolonialism. The fact that the critical theory tradition did not critically reflect sufficiently on its own western presuppositions and consider the wider global and historical context should not detract from the relevance of its concepts for other traditions of thought. In short, I do not see the 'ideas of Reason' as reducible to western history – even if they first arose in Europe – nor to the specific use the critical theory tradition made of these concepts. The same applies to concepts whose origins lie in non-western contexts but can be relevant to western societies (the history of science and of Christianity offers many examples). In my view, despite Habermas's location of modernity within the context of the West, there is no reason to suppose that his theoretical framework necessarily presupposes western history, which in any case takes multiple forms. Allen's proposal to return to Adorno's more skeptical position of the idea of progress is an interesting way in which to connect Adorno to philosophies more critical of the idea of progress, such as Foucault. However, this argument does not solve the problem of the lineage of concepts since it can equally be argued that the notion of progress as social learning in Habermas can be read in non-historicist terms as pertaining to logics of development and learning processes in every social formation. This I see as a cosmopolitan challenge for critical theory (Delanty 2009).

There is also a wider question, which I will not engage with further in the present context, but it can be noted as it is relevant. It is by no means apparent that there is a basic divide between western and non-western societies today.

32 Critical theory revisited

All societies today are implicated in each other, and there are no pure forms of thought. Concepts and ideas of western origin have been transformed as a result of global diffusion and cross-fertilization so that they are effectively today no longer western concepts. Indeed, many concepts often associated with western thought are themselves products of centuries of inter-civilizational encounters and cannot be regarded as western. This in fact was recognized by Ernst Bloch in his account of the origins of emancipatory elements of modern thought in interpretations of Aristotle by medieval Islamic philosophers, such as Avicenna (Bloch 2019 [1963]).

There is, however, one consideration that does need to be taken into account as regards the alleged obsolescence of critical theory. The possible 'end of progress' is not in my view because the idea of progress and related ideas of Reason do not address the concerns of postcolonialism, but that these concepts might be undermined by societal trends that exist in all societies, as in, for example, the question as to whether we now have a post-public sphere and the transformation of the category of the individual. This will be discussed in Chapter 3 and with respect to the public sphere in Chapter 8).

My position is not that Left-Hegelianism is the most advanced or best theoretical framework, nor am I claiming that it does not need to engage with other schools of thought, including non-western ones. I am arguing that many of its basic ideas are still relevant for the present and that they need to address more directly the charges of postcolonial critiques, but they are not invalidated by those criticisms. Notwithstanding these defences of the critical theory tradition against some of the most serious criticisms, at this point I have conceded that post-Habermasian critical theory has lost the critical impetus. In order to recover it, dialogue with other conceptions of critique is essential. In this regard, postcolonial theory is important in correcting the limited scope of critical theory in relation to race and racism and North-South asymmetries. However, it does not offer an alternative, not only because in most cases it relies on other western thinkers, but because it does not have an alternative methodology for the social science. It hardly accounts for the full range of research topics for the social sciences. Kerner (2018) usefully shows some of the commonalities between critical theory and postcolonial theory and the need for fruitful dialogue, but does not appreciate that the core ideas of the former are different and rooted in a philosophy of social science. In any case, it is obvious that the concerns of postcolonial theory are not to advance a theory of society nor link philosophy with sociology.

Conclusion

In this appraisal of the core ideas of critical theory, I have stressed as the distinctive characteristic of critical theory, deriving from the Left-Hegelian tradition, the concern with social transformation. This relates to possibilities for the future that are latent in the present but need to be identified by a normatively grounded critique that seeks to advance progressive politics. The received tradition of critical theory from the early Frankfurt School to Habermas and Honneth is in need of revision

Spectres of critique **33**

due to its failure to address global and postcolonial challenges. However, I see this largely as a corrective rather than a new direction. Rather than abandon the path-breaking work of Adorno, Habermas, and Honneth, the future of critical theory needs to build upon their work. However, a return to the past as, for example, a turn to Adorno's philosophy will not in itself achieve much. The future of critical theory will inevitably involve the re-integration of philosophy and sociology. Critical theory, I have argued, entails a theory of society that encompasses the subjective, inter-subjective, and objective. Critical theory, unlike many other conceptions of critique, is based on the claim that there are certain assumptions that render society possible and which provide the basic possibilities for social transformation. These assumptions, which have been generally conceived within the realm of Reason, or the ideas of Reason, are not empirical realities as such but are nonetheless real in that they are present in the logic of societal formation. To develop this perspective fully, which is beyond the scope of this book, there will need to be a greater focus on macro-sociological analysis. The next chapter offers some reflections on the specificity of critical theory as a sociological approach.

Notes

1 My thanks to Neal Harris, Patrick O'Mahony, and Piet Strydom for comments on an earlier version of this chapter.
2 See Martin Jay's Preface to the 1996 issue of his classic history of the Frankfurt School (Jay 1996/1973).
3 Two recent volumes are indicative of current trends in critical theory, Deutscher and Lafont (2017) and Bohmann and Sörrensen (2019).
4 See Zamora and Beherent (2016).
5 A fuller account would have to acknowledge that Hegel did not see Reason unfolding only in social reality but also in nature. Reason was in turn a manifestation of a more metaphysical Spirit.
6 Posthumously published in 1833 as the *Philosophy of History*.
7 This relates to what Strydom terms the cognitive order of society (Strydom 2020b).
8 For a history of the Frankfurt School, see Abromeit (2013), Jay (1996/1973), Wheatland (2009) and Wiggershaus (1994). The literature on critical theory is wide. Some general interpretative works are Benhabib (1986), Bronner (1994), Calhoun (1995), Dubiel (1985), Geuss (1981), Held (1980), Hohendahl (1991), Kellner (1987), Outhwaite (2012), Schecter (2010, 2013), Strydom (2011). See also Jeffries's (2016) collective biographical history of the critical theorists.
9 The term immanent critique is generally held to be the broad philosophical form of critical theory (see Antonio 1981; Browne 2008; Finlayson 2014; Jaeggi 2018; Ng 2015; Strydom 2020a).
10 Horkheimer, in his early work, established the intellectual foundations of critical theory (Horkheimer 1972b, 1974a, 1974b). Adorno's work was undoubtedly of greater enduring significance for the future of critical theory.
11 See Müller-Dohm's biography of Adorno, Müller-Dohm (2005). It is also apparent from the posthumously published lectures at Frankfurt University that Adorno gave in 1964 that a theory of society required the mediation of sociology and philosophy (Adorno 2019).
12 According to Honneth, the concern with immanent critique always remained even in the *Dialectic Imagination* and in *Minima Moralia*.
13 See for example his reflection on culture and lies in *Minima Moralia* (Adorno 2005: 44).

34 Critical theory revisited

14 For some of the main critical perspectives see Calhoun (1992).
15 See for example O'Mahony (2013).
16 A later paper did return to some of the social scientific questions Habermas (2006).
17 Honneth's later work, *Freedom's Right*, suggests a revival of a macro-sociological approach to modernity (Honneth 2014).
18 See the debate about recognition or distribution, Honneth and Fraser (2001).
19 Arendt clearly held racist views on the superiority of white European over black people and upheld racial segregation. See Grosse (2006).
20 I have explored this in Delanty (2018).

References

Abromeit, J. 2013. *Max Horkheimer and the Foundations of the Frankfurt School*. New York: Columbia University Press.

Adorno, T. W. 1981 [1952]. *In Search of Wagner*. London: Verso.

Adorno, T. W. 1990 [1960]. *Negative Dialectics*. London: Routledge.

Adorno, T. W. 1998a [1969]. Critique. In: *Critical Models: Interventions and Catchwords*. New York: Columbia University Press.

Adorno, T. W. 1998b [1969]. On Resignation. In: *Critical Models: Interventions and Catchwords*. New York: Columbia University Press.

Adorno, T. W. 1998b [1969]. Progress. In: *Critical Models: Interventions and Catchwords*. New York: Columbia University Press.

Adorno, T. W. 2005 [1951]. *Minima Moralia: Reflections from Damaged Life*. London: Verso.

Adorno, T. W. 2013 [1970]. *Aesthetic Theory*. London: Bloomsbury Academic.

Adorno, T. W. 2019 [1950]. *The Authoritarian Personality*. London: Verso.

Adorno, T. W. 2019 [2008/1964]. *Philosophical Elements of a Theory of Society*. Cambridge: Polity Press.

Adorno, T. W. et al 1976. *The Positivist Dispute in German Sociology*. London: Heinemann.

Adorno, T. W. and Horkheimer, M. 1979 [1944]. *Dialectic of Enlightenment*. London: Verso.

Allen, A. 2016. *The End of Progress: Decolonizing the Normative Foundations of Critical Theory*. New York: Columbia University Press.

Allen, A. 2017. Adorno, Foucault, and the End of Progress: Critical Theory in Postcolonial Times. In: Deutscher, P. and Lafont, C. (eds.) *The End of Progress: Decolonizing the Normative Foundations of Critical Theory*. New York: Columbia University Press.

Antonio, R. 1981. Immanent Critique as the Core of Critical Theory: Its Origin and Development in Hegel, Marx, and Contemporary Thought. *British Journal of Sociology*, 32: 330–45.

Apel, K-O. 1980 [1973]. *Towards a Transformation of Philosophy*. London: Routledge & Kegan Paul.

Bartholomew, J. 2018. Decoloniality and Decolonizing Critical Theory. *Constellations*, 25: 629–40.

Basure, M. 2011. Continuity Through Rupture with the Frankfurt School: Axel Honneth's Theory of Recognition. In: Delanty, G. and Turner, S. P. (eds.) *Routledge International Handbook of Social and Political Theory*. London: Routledge.

Baum, B. 2015. Decolonizing Critical Theory. *Constellations*, 22 (3): 420–34.

Benhabib, S. 1986. *Critique, Norm, and Utopia: A Study of the Foundations of Critical Theory*. New York: Columbia University Press.

Benjamin, W. 1999. *The Arcades Project*. Cambridge, MA: Harvard University Press.

Benzer, M. 2011. *The Sociology of Theodor Adorno*. Cambridge: Cambridge University Press.

Bernstein, J. M. 2001. *Adorno: Disenchantment and Ethics*. Cambridge: Cambridge University Press.

Bloch, E. 2019 [1963]. *Avicenna and the Aristotelian Left*. New York: Columbia University Press.

Bohmann, U. and Sörrensen, P. (eds.) 2019. *Kritische Theorie der Politik*. Berlin: Suhrkamp.

Bonacker, T. 2006. Disclosing Critique: The Contingency of Understanding in Adorno's Interpretative Social Theory. *European Journal of Social Theory*, 9 (3): 363–83.

Bowie, A. 2013. *Adorno and the Ends of Philosophy*. Cambridge: Polity Press.

Bronner, S. E. 1994. *Of Critical Theory and Its Theorists*. Oxford: Blackwell.

Browne, C. 2008. The End of Immanent Critique? *European Journal of Social Theory*, 11 (1): 5–24.

Buck-Morss, S. 2009. *Hegel, Haiti, and Universal History*. Pittsburgh: University of Pittsburgh Press.

Burston, D. 1991. *The Legacy of Erich Fromm*. Cambridge, MA: Harvard University Press.

Calhoun, C. (ed.) 1992. *Habermas and the Public Sphere*. Cambridge, MA: MIT Press.

Calhoun, C. 1995. *Critical Social Theory: Culture, History and the Challenge of Difference*. Oxford: Blackwell.

Cook, D. 2018. *Adorno, Foucault and the Critique of the West*. London: Verso.

Coulthard, G. 2014. *Red Skin, White Masks: Rejecting the Colonial Politics of Recognition*. Minneapolis: Minnesota University Press.

de Boer, K. 2011. Hegel's Concept of Immanent Critique. In: de Boer, K. and Sonderegger, R. (eds.) *Conceptions of Critique in Modern and Contemporary Philosophy*. London: Palgrave.

Delanty, G. 2009. *The Cosmopolitan Imagination: The Renewal of Critical Theory*. Cambridge: Cambridge University Press.

Delanty, G. 2018. *The European Heritage: A Critical Re-Interpretation*. London: Routledge.

Deutscher, P. and Lafont, C. (eds.) 2017. *Critical Theory in Critical Times: Transforming the Global Political and Economic Order*. New York: Columbia University Press.

Dubiel, H. 1985. *Theory and Politics: Studies in the Development of Critical Theory*. Cambridge, MA: MIT Press.

Finlayson, G. 2014. Hegel, Adorno and the Origins of Immanent Criticism. *British Journal of the History of Philosophy*, 22 (6): 1142–66.

Forst, R. 2012. *The Right to Justification: Elements of a Constructivist Theory of Justice*. New York: Columbia University Press.

Fraser, N. and Jaeggi, J. 2018. *Capitalism: A Conversation*. Cambridge: Polity Press.

Freyenhagen, F. 2013. *Adorno's Practical Philosophy*. Cambridge: Cambridge University Press.

Geuss, R. 1981. *The Idea of Critical Theory*. Cambridge: Cambridge University Press.

Grosse, P. 2006. From Colonialism to National Socialism to Postcolonialism: Hannah Arendt's *Origins of Totalitarianism: Postcolonial Studies*, 9 (1): 35–52.

Habermas, J. 1972 [1968]. *Knowledge and Human Interests*. London: Heinemann.

Habermas, J. 1979 [1976]. *Communication and the Evolution of Society*. London: Heinemann.

Habermas, J. 1984/1987 [1981]. *The Theory of Communicative Action*. Vols. 1. London: Polity Press.

Habermas, J. 1989 [1962]. *The Structural Transformation of the Public Sphere*. Cambridge: Polity Press.

Habermas, J. 1992 [1988]. *Postmetaphysical Thinking*. Cambridge: Polity Press.

Habermas, J. 1997 [1992]. *Between Facts and Norms: Contributions to a Discourse Theory of Law and Democracy*. Cambridge: Polity Press.

Habermas, J. 1998 [1996]. *The Inclusion of the Other: Studies in Political Theory*. Cambridge, MA: MIT Press.

36 Critical theory revisited

Habermas, J. 2006. Political Communication in Media Society: Does Democracy Still Enjoy an Epistemic Dimension? The Impact of Normative Theory on Empirical Research. *Communication Theory*, 16: 411–26.

Harris, N. 2019. Recovering the Critical of Social Pathology Diagnosis. *European Journal of Social Theory*, 22 (1): 45–62.

Harris, N. 2020. Reconstructing Erich Fromm's 'Pathology of Normalcy': Transcending the Recognition-Cognitive Paradigm in the Diagnosis of Social Pathologies. *Social Science Information*, 58 (4): 714–33.

Held, D. 1980. *Introduction to Critical Theory*. Berkeley: University of California Press.

Heins, V. 2008. Realizing Honneth: Redistribution, Recognition, and Global Justice. *Journal of Global Ethics*, 4 (2): 141–53.

Heins, V. 2010. Of Persons and Peoples: Internationalizing the Critical Theory of Recognition. *Contemporary Political Theory*, 9 (2): 149–70.

Herf, J. 2012. The *Dialectic of Enlightenment* Reconsidered. *New German Critique*, 117 (Fall): 81–9.

Hohendahl, P. U. 1991. *Reappraisals, Shifting Alignments in Postwar Critical Theory*. Ithaca, NY: Cornell University Press.

Honneth, A. 1982. Work and Instrumental Action: On the Normative Basis of Critical Theory. *Thesis Eleven*, 5–6: 16–84.

Honneth, A. 1996 [1992]. *The Struggle for Recognition: The Moral Grammar of Social Conflicts*. Cambridge: Polity Press.

Honneth, A. 2004. Organized Self-Realization: Some Paradoxes of Individualization. *European Journal of Social Theory*, 8 (2): 171–91.

Honneth, A. 2009. *Pathologies of Recognition: On the Legacy of Critical Theory*. New York: Columbia University Press.

Honneth, A. 2012. *The I in We: Studies in the Theory of Recognition*. Cambridge: Polity Press.

Honneth, A. 2014. *Freedom's Right: The Social Foundations of Democratic Life*. Cambridge: Polity Press.

Honneth, A. and Fraser, N. 2001. *Recognition or Distribution: A Political-Philosophical Exchange*. London: Verso.

Horkheimer, M. 1972a [1937/1968]. Traditional and Critical Theory. In: *Critical Theory: Selected Essays*. New York: Herder and Herder.

Horkheimer, M. 1972b [1968]. *Critical Theory: Selected Essays*. New York: Herder and Herder.

Horkheimer, M. 1974a [1947]. *The Eclipse of Reason*. New York: Continuum.

Horkheimer, M. 1974b. *Critique of Instrumental Reason: Lectures and Essays Since the End of World War 11*. New York: Seabury Press.

Jaeggi, R. 2018. *Critique of Forms of Life*. Cambridge, MA: Harvard University Press.

Jay, M. 1984a. *Marxism and Totality: The Adventures of a Concept from Lukacs to Habermas*. Berkeley: University of California Press.

Jay, M. 1984b. *Adorno*. Cambridge, MA: Harvard University Press.

Jay, M. 1996/1973. *The Dialectical Imagination: A History of the Frankfurt School and the Institute of Social Research, 1923–1950*. London: Heinemann.

Jay, M. 2016. *Reason After Its Eclipse: On Late Critical Theory*. Madison: University of Wisconsin Press.

Jeffries, S. 2016. *The Lives of the Frankfurt School*. London: Verso.

Kellner, D. 1987. *Critical Theory, Marxism and Modernity*. Cambridge: Polity Press.

Kerner, I. 2018. Postcolonial Theories as Global Critical Theories. *Constellations*, 25: 614–28.

McCarthy, T. 2009. *Race, Empire and the Idea of Human Development*. Cambridge: Cambridge University Press.

McNay, L. 2007. *Against Recognition*. Cambridge: Polity Press.

Marcuse, H. 1955. *Eros and Civilization*. Boston: Beacon Press.

Marcuse, H. 1964. *One-Dimensional Man*. London: Routledge & Kegan Paul.

Marcuse, H. 1977 [1941]. *Reason and Revolution*. London: Routledge & Kegan Paul.

Müller-Dohm, D. 2005. *Adorno: A Biography*. Cambridge: Polity Press.

Ng, K. 2015. Ideology Critique from Hegel to Marx in Critical Theory. *Constellations*, 22 (3): 393–405.

O'Conner, B. 2012. *Adorno*. London: Routledge.

O'Mahony, P. 2013. *The Contemporary Theory of the Public Sphere*. Brussels: Peter Lang.

Outhwaite, W. 2012. *Critical Theory and Contemporary Society*. New York: Continuum.

Said, E. 1994. *Culture and Imperialism*. New York: Vintage.

Schaub, J. 2015. Misdevelopments, Pathologies, and Normative Revolutions: Normative Reconstruction as a Method for Critical Theory. *Critical Horizons*, 16 (2): 107–30.

Schecter, D. 2010. *The Critique of Instrumental Reason from Weber to Habermas*. New York: Continuum.

Schecter, D. 2013. *Critical Theory in the Twenty-First Century*. London: Bloomsbury.

Steinmetz, G. 2006. Decolonizing German Theory. *PostColonial Studies*, 9 (1): 3–13.

Strydom, P. 2011. *Contemporary Critical Theory and Methodology*. London: Routledge.

Strydom, P. 2020a. On the Origin of the Left-Hegelian Concept of Immanent Transcendence. *Journal of Classical Sociology*, 20.

Strydom, P. 2020b. The Modern Cognitive Order, Cosmopolitanism and Conflicting Models of World Openness. In: Delanty, G. (ed.) *Handbook of Cosmopolitanism Studies*. London: Routledge.

Rosa, H. 2015. *Social Acceleration: A New Theory of Modernity*. New York: Columbia University Press.

Rosa, H. 2019. *Resonance: A Social Theory of Our Relation to the World*. Cambridge: Polity Press.

Thompson, M. J. 2016. *The Domestication of Critical Theory*. New York: Rowman & Littlefield.

Thompson, M. J. 2019. Hierarchy, Social Psychology and the Failure of Recognition Theory. *European Journal of Social Theory*, 22(1): 10–26.

Wheatland, T. 2009. *The Frankfurt School in Exile*. Minneapolis: University of Minnesota Press.

Wiggershaus, R. 1994. *The Frankfurt School: Its History, Theories, and Political Significance*. Cambridge: Polity Press.

Zamora, D. and Beherent, M. (eds.) 2016. *Foucault and Neoliberalism*. Cambridge: Polity Press.

2
CRITICAL ENGAGEMENTS
Varieties of critique in social science

The previous chapter looked at the legacy of critique in left-Hegelanism with a view to identifying the core ideas, major points of reference, and some of the main critiques of the Frankfurt School's tradition of critical theory. This chapter seeks to position that tradition of critical theory in relation to other critical approaches in social science, especially in sociology. Critical theory has a particular relation with sociology, which it sought to link with philosophy. This was a major dimension of the early Frankfurt School, and, in the period of American exile when the Institute of Social Research was very active, it was much enhanced, as reflected in the empirical studies of anti-Semitism and the *Authoritarian Personality* study, and the relation with Paul Lazarsfeld in the 1940s. The re-opening of the Institute for Social Research in Frankfurt in the 1950s sought to revive the tradition of critical sociology and philosophy.

The tendency in recent times is that the sociological dimension has been lost with critical theory becoming a field in its own right and, as I argued in the previous chapter, that it is essentially located in philosophy, including political philosophy. As I argued, its relevance for social research has weakened as a result. In that sense, critical theory has become too much of a theory and less of a critical sociology. This is in part due to the influence of Adorno, whose concerns were ultimately in philosophy. The turn to philosophical abstraction may also be traced back to Adorno's clear preference for philosophical abstraction as a grounding for social research. Somewhat paradoxically, this occurred when the very term 'Frankfurt School' became widely used after Adorno and Horkheimer returned to Germany and pursued different goals, as did those who remained within the United States, such as Marcuse, Neumann, and Lowenthal (see Wheatland 2009: 343). However, there can be no doubt that the philosophical turn is also due to a significant degree in the work of Habermas since the early 1990s, when he brought about an augmented normative shift in critical theory which led to many of his followers focussing on the problem of normative justification. This turn, with its narrow proceduralist concerns, should not be seen as contrary to the aims of reconstructive or immanent critique, but it inevitably led to a shift from social theory to political theory in the general reception of Habermas's later work and thus a decline in critical sociology. It is, of course, the case that Honneth tried to reverse this turn to political philosophy by bringing critical theory in the direction of a social philosophy, but, as argued in the previous chapter, this shift produced a range of other problems, such as a loss in the critical edge of critical theory and its relative impotence in addressing global issues and other macro-level problems.

This book is a defence of the project of a critical sociology and against what critical theory has effectively become, namely, a critical philosophy based on readings of its major philosophical texts. It is clear, of course, that Left-Hegelianism gave to critical theory a rich legacy of writings. Much of this has been discussed in the previous chapter. However, the danger is that it has become too much self-absorbed into this copious body of thought and that the texts themselves have become the principal focus for critical theory. The project of de-colonization, although necessary to divest critical theory of its latent Eurocentrism, contributes to this (since it operates on the level of philosophical debates). I argue that critical theory should recover its sociological dimension in providing a critical interpretation of contemporary society and that it should offer a framework for social research. To be clear, I am not suggesting that the philosophical turn in critical theory is to be opposed. It has led to some important insights; for example, it has revealed some of the limits of critical theory on major questions of ontology and around Eurocentrism. The philosophical turn – the impact of the positivist dispute, the influence of Apel's introduction of Peirce and Rawl's theory of justice on Habermas – without doubt made crucial contributions to the elaboration of critical theory beyond the first generation concerning key issues on epistemology, ontology, and normative foundations. However, unless critical theory recovers its sociological relevance, it will remain trapped in its own discourse. As I argue in this chapter, it needs to engage with some of the other critical approaches in social science. A major challenge that these approaches offer is a clear methodological direction for their theoretical framework and a less abstract philosophical grounding in German idealism. So, in essence, this is an argument for the sociological re-appropriation of critical theory.[1]

The self-understanding of much of sociology, at least since the 1970s, included a significant critical dimension. In this respect, sociology undoubtedly differs from the other social sciences whose relation to critique is rather more distant. While mainstream sociology, whether in its neopositivistic or Weberian traditions, maintained a certain distance from the critical tradition, the pluralization of sociology over the past more than four decades or so has led to a much stronger presence of a critical temperament in both the theory and practice of sociology. There are a number of reasons for this, and they are connected with the inter-disciplinary nature of sociology. The origins of sociology are various, but at its source lies the Enlightenment tradition of social theory. In the vast range of works in European social thought during the pre-disciplinary period, roughly from the early eighteenth to

40 Critical theory revisited

late nineteenth century, sociology emerged as a theoretically grounded reflection on modern society (Strydom 2000; Wagner 1994). This was far from sociology as it later emerged as a discipline from the end of the nineteenth century, but the basic orientation of the discipline was shaped in this pre-disciplinary formative period. A major part of this early history was the presence of the critical mind and the influence of the German philosophical tradition with its concern with critique. However, critique, it should be noted, was more characteristically French, as in the writings of Pierre Bayle, who wrote a *Historical and Critical Dictionary* in 1697. Along with the political and philosophical ideas nurtured by the French Revolution, it had a major impact on German thought since Kant, who announced his time to be the age of critique. As this historical self-understanding shifted from an epistemic condition (Kantian) through (with Hegel) a philosophy of history to (with Marx) a critique of political economy related to the formation of a political subject, critical sociology received its main inspiration. In this tradition of thought, which was augmented with the incorporation of Freud's psychoanalysis into sociology by the Frankfurt School and related thinkers such as Erich Fromm, critique involved something more than mere criticism: it entailed the reflective transformation of the subject as it confronts an external problem.

I begin the chapter with a discussion of the conceptions of critique stemming from the Enlightenment. This will be followed by a summative statement of what can be said to be defining concepts of the Left-Hegelian tradition of critical theory. The remainder of the chapter will discuss the main alternatives to critical theory with a view to identifying ways in which critical theory can learn from the encounter with these approaches.

Modernity and critique

Four major concepts of critique originated within Enlightenment thought and led to different understandings of critique, all of which had implications for critical sociology. The first is the inter-linkage of crisis and critique described by Reinhart Koselleck (1988) in a classic work, *Crisis and Critique*, which claimed that alternative conceptions of political authority emerged as a challenge to the prevailing order at times of crisis. Modernity, as described by Koselleck, in its formative period in the early modern and Enlightenment period, was marked by a divergence of state and society, leading to the emergence of autonomous intellectuals who are the source of new models of political authority. But, for Koselleck, critique is largely subversive of the modern state – for example, the Enlightenment critique led to the ideas of 1789 – and ultimately does not offer a solution to the problems of the modern polity. For these reasons, in the 1830s, Auguste Comte, as the founder of sociology, had termed sociology a 'positive' science of society as opposed to the 'negative' or critical knowledge of the Enlightenment intellectuals. In any case, the first notion of critique approaches the model of political criticism and is closely associated with the Enlightenment critique of intellectuals and the formation of political modernity.

As a contrast to this sense of political critique, a second understanding of critique is the one associated with Kant's critical philosophy. Kant's philosophy established a concept of critique as a method of demarcating empirical, factual, or scientific knowledge from speculative or metaphysical knowledge. For Kant, critical knowledge is autonomous and not subservient to dogmatic authority. The Kantian notion of critique has been reflected in positions as starkly divergent as Karl Popper's critical rationalism and Theodor Adorno's critical theory of society. It provided a strong transcendental foundation for modern thought, which (not to be confused with transcendence) concerned the need to discern the universal elements of reality.

While Kant's critical philosophy laid the foundations for a modern philosophy of science as well as the philosophy of the modern idea of the university, a more radical version emerged with Hegel's rendering of critique as the capacity to see within the given facts of consciousness a reflexive process of continuous transformation by which the new emerges out of the old. Marx's recasting of the Hegelian dialectic into a theory of modern capitalism opened up the possibility of a critical theory of society that had divested itself of much of the abstract theorizing of the Enlightenment thinkers. This third understanding of critique, as formulated in the Hegelian-Marxist tradition, has been the most influential tradition of critique in modern sociology.

The fourth tradition is the humanistic one of *Bildung*. Although less evident in the sociological tradition, the German romantic notion of *Bildung* – literally education as a formative process for personality – referred to a notion of critique that has many resonances in later sociology, namely, the emancipatory moment that occurs when the individual is confronted with knowledge. The Enlightenment idea of a university education bringing about a critical transformation in personality signals a tradition of critique that continued to be relevant to the role of sociology as an established subject in higher education.

The influence of Freud and Foucault, arguably the two most significant thinkers of the twentieth century, subsequently gave the critical tradition an additional impetus beyond the earlier Enlightenment concerns in demonstrating the dark forces that lie within the self and the sense that emancipation may be only another guise of domination. But it was in the Enlightenment period that the tone was set for critique, as Foucault acknowledged in a much-discussed essay (Foucault 1984a). If the subsequent institutionalization of sociology as a discipline entailed a certain renunciation or domestication of critical knowledge, it was never entirely silenced. The critical tradition was most notably preserved in social theory, which partly diverged from sociology. But even in mainstream sociological theory, the diagnostic and interpretative concerns of classical social theory were evident. The presence of the critical tradition in sociology is undoubtedly related to its uncertain status as a discipline in its own right, with its own subject matter and methodology, and its transdisciplinary self-understanding as a science of society which builds upon the fruits of the other social and human sciences. In this respect, sociology is a critical endeavor in that it is a diagnostic theory of society with a normative orientation. Even Parsonian sociological theory, which had no specific foundation in the critical

42 Critical theory revisited

tradition, certainly has at the core of its self-understanding nothing less than a diagnosis of the age that was grounded in certain normative values. But in the tradition of critical sociology, which, for example, was represented by the anti-Parsonians, C. Wright Mills (1970) and Alvin Gouldner's (1970) critique had a more forcible purpose in aligning itself with emancipation. Sociology as a critical science of society can be seen as a major philosophical and methodological alternative to the dominant (neo-)positivist and interpretative traditions. The critical, the interpretative, and the positivistic traditions in twentieth-century philosophy of social science have provided not just sociology but much of the social sciences with their basic epistemological and methodological foundations. This has been much documented (see Delanty and Strydom 2003), but the situation today warrants a new assessment of the nature and status of critique in sociology which will have to go beyond the critique of positivism and hermeneutics.

First, arising out of the linguistic and cultural turn in the philosophy of social science, there has been a plethora of approaches and positions that are not easily located within the dominant traditions. The Foucauldian concept of critique, more a product of modern anti-science than revolutionary praxis, does not fit very comfortably with the Hegelian-Marxist tradition with its concern with the constitution of political subjectivity.

Second, the critical tradition itself has seen an internal pluralization of positions, none of which appear to share much with the others. Habermas, Bhaskar, and Bourdieu do not share a common epistemology, despite their somewhat loose Marxist (at least in the former two) backgrounds and commitment to critical sociology. Many developments that can be broadly located within a critical frame of reference take as their point of orientation both the critical and the interpretative tradition. In fact, it can be argued, that there has been a certain migration of critical sociology towards the interpretative tradition, leading to a diffusion of critique into opaque positions (as in the work of Boltanski and Thévenot).

Third, critical sociology, in its traditional self-understanding as a normatively grounded diagnosis of the age, has now largely retreated into social theory, having abandoned sociology (Turner 2008). Even within social theory, there is some evidence that the critical tradition is losing its ground against challenges from other approaches. In this chapter, I argue that the cultural turn in opening up sociology to new possibilities for critique has, in doing so, led it in the direction of a self-understanding that has transformed critique into a concern with 'practices'. In this move, which is reflected in several approaches, critique becomes absorbed into micro-analysis leading to a loss of focus for macro-analysis. This, I argue, represents a loss for a critical sociology. However, my main purpose in this chapter is to attempt a schematic analysis of the diversity of understandings of critique in sociological theory today with a view to discerning the shape of a new critical theory of society which must learn from these currently competing approaches.

I argue that there are five main varieties of critique in critical social science. Although critique can be related to many approaches, and scientific knowledge is, as Popper argued, by its very nature critical, and as Burawoy (2005) has claimed, an essential part of sociological practice, I confine this discussion to those positions that explicitly invoke a notion of critique as linked to the formation of the political subject as their epistemological and methodological approaches.[2] For this reason I do not discuss the hermeneutic tradition of critique of the 'masters of suspicion', to use Ricoeur's (1977) term, to refer to the common purpose of Marx and Freud, or the critique that is implicit in every act of interpretation, as in the work of Gadamer, Taylor, and Walzer. The present discussion is also confined to those conceptions of critique that have influenced sociology and sociological theory and which have distinct methodological implications for social research (see Strydom 2011; Bohman 1991). The five examples are: normative-diagnostic critique as in the Frankfurt School tradition, critical realism, Bourdieu's critical sociology, Foucault's genealogical critique, and the variety of positions that have emerged around the notion of critical practice. By way of conclusion, I shall offer an assessment of the positions under discussion with a view to clarifying exactly what is at stake in invoking critique as a methodological approach in sociology.

Critical theory

As discussed in the previous chapter, the outcome of Honneth's recognition theory was a recovery of the link between social research and critical theory. Now, while this has led to much fruitful research and at first appeared to be an advance beyond Habermas's project, it is limited in scope to issues of recognition.[3] Other more sociologically based approaches that adopt a critical theory perspective can be found in the work of sociologists such as Klaus Eder and Max Miller, who also draw on other traditions of inquiry, such as discourse analysis and collective identity theory[4]. A tendency in their work and that of others who can be broadly related to the critical theory tradition is the methodological shifting of critique to the analysis of public discourses around critical events. The work of Benhabib, although not specifically sociological, on identity and difference could also be included here (Benhabib 1986). Other key theorists in the critical theory tradition would include Fraser and Jaeggi, who have given a new significance to theorizing on capitalism and alienation (see Fraser and Jaeggi 2018; Jaeggi 2014). The distinguishing feature of critical theory is the identification of new discourses that have transformative potential. The centrality of crisis, disputes over legitimation in the public sphere, and cognitive shifts loom large in the work of these authors as well as others and represents the most promising direction for critical sociology (see O'Mahony 2013). The following is a brief summary of the key concepts as discussed in the previous chapter that constitute the theoretical framework of critical theory.

Immanent transcendence: This is the notion that there is something immanent in social reality that forces, motivates, or guides social actors to transcend the given society through a re-working and re-appropriation of its own self-understanding and its understanding of its social, economic, cultural, and possibly also natural conditions. The sources of immanent transcendence are generally unrecognized latent forces below the surface that from time to time give rise to something new,

44 Critical theory revisited

such as a sign, action, movement, or intervention. Such latent forces are drawn out by means of the mediating influence of ideas, concepts or principles (e.g. freedom, justice) or their embodiment in some cultural artefact or model (international law, democracy). The concept draws attention to the construction and transformation of society, including the generative forces as well as the structuring conditions of transformation, as the focus for social analysis and research.[5]

Ideas of Reason: Deriving from Hegel's revision of Kant, ideas of Reason refer to the normative ideals of modernity that represent future possibilities. They include notions such as freedom, equality, solidarity, peace, democracy, and self-determination. Ideas of Reason are the conceptual and cognitive conditions representing the transcendent dimension immanent in social reality. As such, they are an integral part of the cognitive and normative order of society. These ideas are of an abstract nature while taking a concrete form in normative applications or interpretations (e.g. liberal democracy is a normative model that is based on the more abstract idea of democracy, but it is only one such normative model of democracy).

Dialectics: This relates to relations of antagonism and contradiction through which new social realities are created. It concerns the transformative process by which ideas of Reason lead to a re-interpretation of the self-understanding of a society or a radicalization of one or more ideas of Reason and corresponding forms of transformative action. It signifies an ontological notion of reality as manifest in processes of transformation.

Critique: The critical theory tradition invokes a wide range of notions of critique, all of which are varieties of the more general notion of 'immanent critique', the term preferred by Adorno and the one most in keeping with left Hegelianism. This term refers to the immanent possibilities for transcendence, or, in other words, the possibilities contained in an actual situation for the overcoming and resolution of social problems. Critique proceeds by means of a disclosure of the social world whereby new interpretations are possible and which endeavor to alter our way of seeing the world. It is sometimes referred to by Honneth as a 'disclosing critique'. The older Frankfurt School tradition used the term 'ideology critique' to refer to the more specific negatively oriented critique of ideologies as a form of de-masking of contradictions. Habermas has tended to use the related term 'reconstructive critique', which methodologically seeks the reconstruction of ideas of Reason as manifest in social reality. It draws attention to social transformation and the positive potentials inherent in social reality as the empirical focus for critical social analysis.

Critical realism

Principally associated with the work of Roy Bhaskar (1975, 1979), critical realism has become increasingly influential in social science. Originally termed variously critical naturalism and transcendental realism, it has now been taken up under the heading of critical realism. Within sociology, Margaret Archer (1995) and Andrew Sayer (2000) developed important applications that make it relevant to the analysis of cultural phenomena, though they are generally skeptical of the adequacy of much of contemporary cultural theory. Critical realism is opposed to traditional positivistic conceptions of science as well as to hermeneutic or interpretative approaches. A product of post-empiricist philosophy of science, it shares with much of late-twentieth-century philosophy a view of reality that stresses its contingent and non-observable nature. While critical realists are hostile to the critical theory tradition, which they see as an extension of the interpretative tradition, they share a common concern with the latter in that their aim is a critique of power and what Bhaskar has termed a 'transformational model of human activity' (see also Vandenberghe 2014).

Critical realism, which cannot be equated with naive realism or a positivistic conception of reality, seeks to promote a transformational as opposed to an affirmative account of the social world. In the view of critical realists, the critical theory tradition of the Frankfurt School lacks explanatory power, which is why they argue it has not much more to offer than interpretation. The aim of social science, as science, is to provide convincing explanations of the social world. I shall not consider in detail whether or not this is a correct assessment of critical theory since my aim is rather to outline in what sense critical realism offers a viable model of critique for sociological inquiry. However, it can be briefly remarked that this is undoubtedly a misunderstanding of the Frankfurt School tradition which sought to advance a methodology that was both explanatory and interpretative. Yet, despite this failure to understand critical theory, critical realism has been on the whole more successful than critical theory has been in devising a robust methodological framework for social research. A central contention of critical realism is the underlying or objective reality of the world, which exists independently of our knowledge of it. Unlike other critical approaches, it places less emphasis on action than on the structures that shape or condition action. Margaret Archer has pursued this line of argument in a direction that has led to a strong criticism of the position held by Giddens, which can be characterized as a hermeneutical one that conflates agency and structure. Critical realists are characteristically concerned with the primacy of ontological arguments over epistemological ones since, in their view, it is the structure of social reality that needs to be understood.

One of the core ideas in critical realism is that while reality can be known, it is not observable. Observations on what is manifest or experienced by people do not tell us much about the nature of reality. For this reason, critical realism is critical in that it requires a problematization of the ways in which reality is perceived by social actors. Perceptions and ordinary knowledge are a poor guide to reality in the view of critical realists, who are equally critical of empiricism or empirical realism as they are of any position that could be called constructivist. A critical methodology as opposed to a constructivist one is called for simply because reality is separate from our consciousness of it. The notion that reality can be reduced to its discursive construction limits the scope of social science too much to cultural phenomena. This skepticism towards broadly culturally oriented approaches, too, marks critical realism off from postmodernism, which is not sufficiently critical with regard to coming to grips with the objective reality of the world. But reality

46 Critical theory revisited

is not just an objective force that can be reduced to primary causes. Critical realists stress the emergent nature of reality as manifest in the fact that certain things have consequences. To understand these consequences is the task of critique in the most straightforward sense.

Many applications of critical realism in social science are simply demonstrations of the complex nature of connections between things and references to mechanisms that have the power of determining consequences. However, the ontological framework has a more developed conception of the emergent nature of reality. Three levels of reality can be specified: the empirical, the actual, and the real. Critical realists aim to draw attention to the fact that reality is more than the empirical and the actual, with which it is frequently conflated. In this framework, the empirical level is the level of perceptions, how the world is experienced by people. It corresponds to everyday knowledge and consciousness. The actual refers to things that occur and have direct consequences, the world of events. The real refers to the underlying structures or 'generative mechanisms' that have determining or causal powers, many of which are indirect. The mechanisms involved can be structures, as in institutional arrangements, or the result of the influences of individual social actors. The objective of social science as a form of critique is to demonstrate that beyond the empirical and the actual is the objective reality of the real. Both the actual and the empirical are a poor guide to reality because our perceptions could be wrong and not everything is actualized and that which exists cannot be explained without recourse to mechanisms. These mechanisms are to be understood as the means through which effects operate and thus have powers and properties.

This theoretical framework is undoubtedly coherent and an attractive methodological proposal for social scientists seeking to place empirical social research on a philosophically grounded footing. It is possible to find many applications of how these ontological levels map on to familiar phenomena. Thus, for example, from a critical realist perspective social conflicts can be looked at in terms of the powers wielded by particular actors, their actual manifestations in terms of, for instance, control over legislation or the distribution of wealth, and the level of perceptions. As with many Marxist-inspired approaches, including critical theory, critical realists are not content to remain on the level of the actual (the status quo) or the empirical level (consciousness) but want to penetrate deeper into the depth structures of the real that define and shape the other levels. With its concern with reality and the underlying distinction between the real and our knowledge of it, critical realism differs from the critical theory of the Frankfurt School tradition in being less concerned with a normative or moral theory of society. It shares with critical theory the attempt to go beyond consciousness but has a much stronger concern with ontology. This inevitably leads less in the direction of a normative critique than an explanation-driven kind of critique. The claims of critical realism to be a form of critique ultimately consist in its capacity to demonstrate the mechanisms that make consequences possible. The logic of argument is thus something like this: reality is layered, or morphological in nature, in that different things have consequences by virtue of the mechanisms that connect one thing to another. The purpose of a critical realist science is to uncover these mechanisms.

The critical realist methodology is without doubt more robust than the Frankfurt School's ideology critique and has the added value in its capacity to demonstrate the web of relations that make up social reality in all its complexity. The threefold model of reality is the key to its methodology. As a post-empiricist philosophy of science, it operates with a strong sense of the need for anti-reductionism and the recognition of multi-causality. The success of critical realism as a critical social scientific research approach undoubtedly consists of its ability to offer social scientists a robust methodology. It lacks the vagueness of constructivist approaches, which operate with an undifferentiated conception of reality, and unlike critical theory it lends itself to applied social research. The aims of critical realist methodology direct the critical sociologist to identifying mechanisms and inter-linkages between the three levels of the social world and thus to correcting false understandings of the world that derive from uncritically accepting the empirical. As with Foucauldian methodology, to be looked at next, it is also centrally about power. But unlike Foucault, power is not everything, a generalized all-pervasive entity, but something that exists in the form of specific generative mechanisms. The strengths of critical realism are also its main weaknesses.

The limits of critical realism as a critical approach lie in its inability to articulate possibilities within the real world for social change. Although Bhaskar speaks of a 'transformational model of social activity', the approach does not offer much by way of an interpretation of how social change happens. Critical realism is rather dismissive of the empirical and is primarily concerned with gaining access to the real. In this respect, the critical theory of the Frankfurt School offers a wider scope for critique. An approach that is ultimately confined to illustrating the consequences of generative mechanisms deriving from the real, it does not address the full range of challenges facing social science; in particular, the challenge of articulating alternative conceptions of the world, such as those that might be at stake in various forms of resistance. While Sayer (2000) attempts to develop critical realism as a normative critique, in the view of many critics the approach is limited by a concern with the elaboration of an ontological framework that is prior to social research (Kemp 2005). A more fruitful debate is possibly to follow the proposal of William Outhwaite (1987), who has argued for the overall compatibility of critical theory and critical realism. His thesis is that a realist epistemology underpins not only Bhaskar and Habermas, but it is also an assumption underpinning Habermas and Bourdieu and which he associates with reflexivity.

Bourdieu's critical sociology

One of the classical approaches to critique in social science is Pierre Bourdieu's critical sociology. Over several decades Bourdieu developed a distinctive sociological critical approach that still remains influential not only within sociology but across the social sciences. While Bourdieu shares with critical realism and critical theory a common concern with a critical methodology and a broad background in western Marxism, the similarities end there. Bourdieu has been vehemently opposed to a social scientific method that is in any way derivative of philosophy.

48 Critical theory revisited

His work has reflected a disdain for philosophical elaboration and a strong belief in sociology's own methodological autonomy from philosophy. Moreover, his critical method is less driven by ontology, as is the case with critical realism, than by epistemology in that he is primarily concerned with the creation of a framework that separates a social scientific perspective from the perspective of common sense. While this does in fact lead him in a similar methodological direction to that of critical realism, the conclusions are different. His approach is also remarkably different from the normative diagnostic approach of critical theory in that his model of critique is non-normative in the sense that it is not designed to articulate alternative visions of political possibility and does not proceed by ideology critique or by the analysis of what Habermas has termed distorted communication in order to reveal alternative kinds of communication.[6]

Less burdened by philosophical systems, Bourdieu's model of critique is more sociological than that of critical realism, which has been concerned with the development of a much broader philosophical approach for all of science. Bourdieu has developed an approach that primarily aims to show the connections, or homologies, that exist between habitus and fields leading to the reproduction of social structures. However, the international reception of his work, especially in the Anglo–American world, has been in the context of the cultural turn in the social sciences, and his work has contributed to new ways of pursuing research on culturally constituted phenomena. His methodological approach has proven to be a highly flexible framework for research that demonstrates the material origins of cultural phenomena in terms of an analysis based on the habitus, capital, and fields of power. Despite accusations of determinism and structuralist inclinations, Bourdieu succeeded in providing a firm foundation in methodology for a range of culturally oriented interests and made a decisive contribution to a view of socially governed 'practices'.

His framework can be summed up as follows. Social actors are positioned in the social world in the structural context of a particular field by their habitus, which provides each actor with a set of dispositions that more or less shape their view of the world and determine their scope for action. The possibilities afforded by the habitus are not adequate to a fully critical understanding of the social world since these reside on the level of common sense, a term that is perhaps roughly the equivalent of ideology in critical theory. Critique or critical reflection is possible, but it is always partial and lacks a capacity for transcendence.

While Bourdieu claims to offer a theory of the habitus that avoids a dualism of structure and agency, his approach has often been seen as one that prioritizes structure over agency. Yet, the idea of practice was intended to move away from the objectivity of structure as a way to conceptualizes the ways in which social actors are socially contextualized. It has undoubtedly been an unfair complaint that Bourdieu's contextualist approach was deterministic since he is methodologically primarily focussed on the social actor's mode of being in the world. The problem of structure and agency has overshadowed a bigger problem, namely, an inadequate account of the nature of culture or cultural models. Alexander has drawn attention to this problem which, in his view, is a failure to address the objectivity of culture. This is not the place to enter into a debate on Alexander's (1995) critique of Bourdieu's concept of culture. In the terms of the approach adopted here, the problem with culture in Bourdieu's approach is less its objectivity than the existence within the cultural constitution of society of what can be termed regulative ideas of Reason. The domain of culture cannot be reduced to practices and related strategies of accumulation and exchange, as is the case for Bourdieu. Social actors in Bourdieu's sociology are primarily motivated by the pursuit of capital, which takes different forms (cultural, economic, social, political) and is accumulated and exchanged by strategic moves. So, the first methodological step for Bourdieu is to show how social actors are located within the milieu of the habitus; the next methodological step is to show how and why they pursue different kinds of capital in the context of the field or fields in which they engage in practices; and in a further step it is demonstrated how these forms of capital are exchanged and in the process of exchange undergo symbolic violence in which social structures are reproduced. Social actors, in Bourdieu's portrayal of the social world, cannot do much more than accumulate and exchange forms of capital. An account of these strategies – or practices – will allow a wider and more macro-level of analysis on the structural homologies that exist between power and the class structure of society, in particular around the fundamental fact of inequality. The assumptions on which this is based are that people live in a world of inequalities in terms of capital, and people seek to gain recognition through its accumulation.

For Bourdieu, it would appear that social action is never capable of the high degree of critical rationality that Habermas believes is possible under certain circumstances. Thus, while the Habermasian critical approach seeks to reconstruct the critical capacities of social actors, Bourdieu sees this as an activity that is essentially different and requires an alternative kind of reflexivity. This does not mean that he accepts the neo-positivist belief in scientism, science as a context-transcending activity that requires no self-problematization. Bourdieu's conception of critique is double-edged. On the one side, it is a critique of power and inequality and, on the other, it is a critique of the received wisdom and institution of science, which he terms 'doxa'. Critique is thus both aimed at the viewpoint of the habitus and scholarly 'doxa'. Against the latter he aims to show that social scientific knowledge is caught up in the paradox of being an account of the social world while itself being a creation of a specific institution of the social world, for science is an institution. Indeed, many of Bourdieu's studies have been designed to apply the self-critique of social science to itself, showing how particular fields of power and the habitus lie behind academic activity.

In later work, Bourdieu termed his critical sociology a reflexive sociology (see Bourdieu and Wacquant 1992; Bourdieu 2004). Critique operates reflexively in problematizing itself by seeking to understand its conditions of existence. This is true both of common-sense forms of reflexivity as well as scholarly forms of reflexivity. But what he has termed practical reflexivity, as expressed in everyday life and common sense, does not have the same powers of critique that are found in the critical reflexivity of a social science that can gain critical distance from

50 Critical theory revisited

doxa. Doxa within science, it would appear, is less constraining than the habitus. The notion of critique in Bourdieu shares with critical realism a concern with explanation. Where critical realism was concerned with the limits of the empirical, Bourdieu aims to unmask the limits of common sense. But there are problems of extending Bourdieu's critical reflexive sociology beyond its usual application in constructing homologies between societal structures based on the habitus and group identities out of which society reproduces its structures. The primary methodological force of the critique it affords is ultimately one that can show only strategies of accumulation and exchange and structural processes of reproduction. While this has generated valuable sociological research, the notion of critique at stake lacks both normative and transformational force. From the vantage point of the methodology of critical theory, Bourdieuian critical sociology offers an inadequate account of culture as a domain of interpretation in which is contained normative structures and ideas which can have a transformational impact depending on how they are invoked. The demonstration of homologies and the context specificity of the habitus does not provide a sufficiently adequate foundation for a critical theory of society.

Genealogical critique

While the previously discussed conceptions of critique, despite their differences, share a common background in the Enlightenment conception of critique and the possibility of radical politics in which sociological critique can play a role in clarifying the mechanisms of domination, the Foucauldian approach to critique is entirely different. Critique is no longer based on the priority of truth over power, which Habermas, Bhaskar, and Bourdieu take for granted. Instead, critique must oppose the very notion that truth is separate from power. With Foucault, critique becomes deconstructive and loses its concern with normativity since it rejects the possibility of a transcendental stance. Indeed, most features of the modernist conception of critique are rejected, such as the notion of a political subject and the possibility of a different kind of society. The contrast with Bourdieu is striking, for the two critical thinkers operate with radically different conceptions of method. In the debate with Habermas, too, stark differences become apparent in both the interpretation of modernity and in the self-understanding of social science. It is debatable whether or not what Foucault offers is a notion of critique, given his rejection of the traditional assumptions on which critique depends, such as the possibility of correct versus false knowledge and the advancement of progressive politics. However, there can be little doubt that Foucault's methodology offers a basis for critique and that he understood his project to be a critical undertaking. The intellectual roots of this thought lie in a mix of Freud, Marx, and Nietzsche (Foucault 1984b, 2007; see also Dean 1994; Flyvberg 2001). Nietzsche is without doubt the key figure in the genealogical method he developed, though one cannot neglect the impact of Claude Levi-Strauss in laying the foundations for the removal of subjectivity that was a feature of almost every other philosophy from Marxism to phenomenology and existentialism. The post-humanist moment had in fact already occurred in structuralism, not in post-structuralism, which in many ways was a continuation of what Lévi-Strauss had set out to achieve. In the simplest possible sense, the form of critique that Foucault practiced was deconstructive or genealogical, as he termed it.

Genealogy can be described as a mode of critique that aims to show the process by which something is constructed as opposed to being natural or taken for granted. As such, it is primarily a de-naturalizing mode of critique (Bevir 2010). In his early work, whilst still under the influence of Levi-Strauss's structuralism, he termed it 'archaeological' in so far as it was an attempt to reveal the structures by which modern systems of knowledge were created. Under the heading of genealogy, this became more explicitly focussed on the analysis of power. Foucault specifically aimed to show how with modernity the self was constructed in discourses in which power relations were established around the formation of subjectivity by the application of particular modes of knowledge. Hence, the critical method is genealogical in that it aims to show how the modern self was constituted in relations of power; it is deconstructive in that it seeks to reveal that knowledge is not emancipatory but heavily implicated in the shaping of social institutions in modern society.

The reception of Foucault's work has been extensive and often has been taken up, especially in the Anglo-American context, in ways very different from Foucault's original concern with a historical analysis of institutions such as a hospital, prison, or asylum and the formation of modern sexuality. Indeed, it is only with some difficulty that his pioneering studies can be applied to the social world of the present day. The idea that everything is constructed, which was his main purpose, has lost the critical edge that it once had. However, Foucault was arguably the single most important figure in shaping the historical and cultural turn in the social and human sciences and opened the social sciences to new perspectives in which the critical tradition of Hegelian-Marxism and the various interpretative traditions underwent a process of reorientation and alignment. In the present context, what can be commented on is the nature of critique that can be associated with Foucault's genealogical approach. Foucault is much invoked in social science in terms of theory and in terms of methodology, but closer inspection will reveal that there are different points of emphasis, especially when it comes to methodology. In particular from a critical and a methodological point of view, Foucauldian genealogy can mean at least three possible strategies.

As a critical approach to social research, Foucault first directs the social researcher to the analysis of the self in terms of positionality. This notion, which Foucault did not explicitly use, draws attention to the ways in which the individual or self is shaped as a result of being positioned in a particular location. The viewpoint that one has is always a perspective from a particular position. The study of positioning makes possible a critical analysis of the self-understandings of social actors, including identity, which from a Foucauldian perspective is the product of a position rather than underpinned by an autonomous subject. This emphasis on positionality is not unique to Foucault but is also a characteristic of Bourdieu (May 2000; see also Davies and Harré 1990). But what is distinctive about Foucault in this respect

52 Critical theory revisited

is the emphasis on subject positions as productive of power, not as in Bourdieu as a strategy to achieve a goal but as the very condition of the possibility of the self. In this sense, then, the Foucauldian approach entailed a post-humanist notion of the construction of the subject.

A second dimension of this understanding of critique points to the key notion of discourse as constitutive of the self. The notion of discourse in Foucault, as opposed to other approaches, such as critical discourse analysis, involves language that is more centrally about the application of knowledge to the organization of the social world. Foucauldian discourse also gives greater recognition to institutional arrangements and is not merely a matter of the use of language. Discourses for Foucault are also not primarily sites of debate, as in Habermas, but sets of rules as opposed to words and meaningful communication, and they have more of an epistemic than a communicative function. Knowledge, as a way of knowing the world, is a feature of modernity for Foucault and has the specific function of providing a means of categorization. Thus, genealogical critique is the analysis of modes of categorization by which individuals are positioned and classified by epistemic regimes. The notion of discourse can be related to the preference for practices as opposed to action or notions of identity or consciousness that might imply an autonomous subject. Genealogical critique is often identified as governmentality and with a particular application to the study of biopower in terms of the discursive constitution of the self around practices of knowledge, such as medicalization.

Under the heading of governmentality, as famously put forward in his signal essay on the topic, Foucault (1991) intended the critical analysis of modes of constructing the self. Governmentality concerns the expression of forms of power that derive less from the central organs of the state than from modern institutions such as the medical profession and the regulation of sexuality, where the object of control is the body. In these forms of power, which are discursive formations, the modern subject is shaped in disciplinary regimes in which knowledge is exercised through various technologies of surveillance. Governmentality draws attention to those forms of power exercised by 'technologies of the self' and which cannot be reduced to economic or overtly political forms of power emanating from the state. In this view, power is not just force, coercion, or domination in which one agent acts on another; rather it is a discourse into which the actor enters and in which the actor is shaped. In Foucault's terms, power is productive as opposed to being repressive in that it makes possible action and in doing so determines its shape.

The previously discussed three dimensions of Foucault's critical method can be viewed as different approaches to his central concern with power and the discursive constitution of the self as a subject. The tremendous international reception of his work over the past three decades has drawn attention to an additional dimension of his approach that has an important implication for the methodological application of critique. This concerns less power than resistance. While Foucault always recognized that where there is power there is also resistance, it was not until his later work that this became more pronounced. One of the major political implications of Foucault's work has been the shift he brought about in drawing attention to the perspective of the 'subjugated' and, more generally, the view from the margins. His history of the hospital, for instance, drew attention to the perspective of the patient as opposed to the perspective of the doctor. This shift in perspective has been significant in bringing critique in the direction of the study of marginality. Yet, the influence of Foucault in the social sciences ultimately resides in his theorizing of power. His theoretical concepts, despite their lack of precision, have been a huge inspiration for innovative social research and in opening up new avenues of inquiry (see, for example, Chapter 3 in relation to technology and Chapter 4 with regard to neoliberalism). Of all the poststructuralist thinkers, he has been the one who has made the most fruitful contribution to social science. Nevertheless, there are some significant shortcomings in Foucauldian methodology when it comes to many areas of social life. The underlying assumptions about society run into much the same problems that the Frankfurt School's social theory encountered, namely, an inability to come to terms with expressions of subjectivity that cannot be explained in terms of a notion of disciplinary power.

Critical practice

As noted in the previous section, the notion of critique in critical theory, critical realism, and the critical sociology of Bourdieu was considerably displaced by Foucault, with whom a decisive shift occurred in the very idea of a critical social science. Critique loses both normativity and a relation to a political subject, as well as its world-disclosing function. The various classical conceptions of critique underwent internal transformation as well as bearing the influence of Foucault and the wider cultural turn in the social sciences. Most varieties of critique that have emerged in recent years are characterized by a concern with practice, reflexivity, and with discourse. In different ways, these terms mark a turn to the location of critique in a specific context. Foucault has been associated with a movement away from modernity and the project of the Enlightenment. While it is evident that he did not see his work as postmodernist in the sense often attributed to him, his legacy has been to redefine critique as the analysis of the micro-order of power without any concern with the identification of alternative visions. The reorientation of critique referred to here is evident in a number of developments. Critical theory, it has been widely noted, has undergone a pragmatic turn (Bohman 1998; Ray 2004). The two traditions share a common concern with a possible re-conceptualization or a new way of searching for problem solving alternatives based on self-transformative capacities. For this reason, James Bohman has argued for a merging of critical theory and pragmatism. Seila Benhabib (1986) has brought critical theory forward via a consideration of questions of difference that have been opened up by the cultural turn. Rainer Forst (2002), for instance, has stressed the necessity of locating normativity in specific contexts of justice. A particularly important development for critique within sociology and which has significant methodological implications is the shift that has taken place in French critical sociology with the work of Boltanski and Thévenot, which is the focus of the present discussion.

54 Critical theory revisited

In their view, both Foucault and Bourdieu were too preoccupied with a vision of the social world as essentially about power and thus an 'unlivable world' (Wagner 1999: 349). As discussed above, Bourdieu excluded from critique the perspective of social actors whose 'practical sense' was rather the object of analysis for critical sociology. Luc Boltanski and Laurent Thévenot, in a major reorientation of critical sociology, outlined a new approach in which critique was considerably pluralized. Their sociology of critical pragmatism – or simply pragmatic cultural sociology – as originally outlined in French in 1991 in *On Justification* – put at the forefront the notion of justification as a contextual basis for critical capacity (Boltanski and Thévenot 2006, see also 1999). In this approach, critique is based on the capacity of people in quite ordinary contexts for evaluating claims and engaging in criticism. The normative basis of critique is a set of rules or normative principles that emerge from a particular context (work, politics, family, consumption, and so on). What they term 'repertoires of justification' are the discursive means by which social actors seek to justify the views, beliefs, and attitudes they have about specific issues with reference to some notion of a common good or a principle of a shared interest. These can be understood as elementary grammars or schemas that are available to social actors who in using them transform them. As Lamont and Thévenot (2000) demonstrate, there are also national cultural variants. As in critical theory, a crisis disrupts the normal course of events, and the social actors bound up in it engage in conflict. Boltanski and Thévenot emphasize arguments and conflicts into which common norms are appealed. However, these norms are usually specific to the context in which the debate arises but can be used in different contexts leading to a plurality of modes of justification. Unlike Habermas's notion of justification, which appeals to the possibility for discursive consensus based on common presuppositions, Boltanski and Thévenot see a plurality of orders or repertoires of justification, each invoking different notions of justification. However, they do not exclude the possibility of translation between these orders because people often use modes of evaluation drawn from different repertoires.

The concrete implication for critique in this approach is that disagreements, arguments, and conflicts should be analyzed in terms of modes of justification.[7] A mode of justification is the key to the approach and should be seen as a way of normative evaluation that has a specific format or mode of application. Boltanski and Thévenot speak of 'repertoires of justification' or broad 'orders of worth' to which correspond specific modes of evaluation. These modes of evaluation are the discursive formats or regimes of truth in which social actors evaluate critical issues that arise with respect to situations governed by the repertoires of justification. *On Justification* outlined, somewhat arbitrarily, six repertoires of justification which they related to major political philosophies. However, more important than these orders for their methodology is the mode of evaluation that is invoked in a specific case. Critical action is simply the mobilization of a repertoire of justification around various modes of evaluation in a given situation. The methodology that follows from this approach would be one that first tries to clarify the repertoires of justification in question in a particular critical situation. The next step is to identify the modes of evaluation that are invoked. It would then seek to establish whether and how different criteria from different repertoires compete with each other.

The critical edge of this approach emerges in the analysis of the actual criteria of evaluation that social actors use in a particular critical case. Where Bourdieu's critical sociology prioritizes the structural limits of what social actors could do, pragmatic sociology emphasizes people's capacities to act in different ways. For this reason, Boltanski and Thévenot have been criticized for not addressing structural inequalities and placing too much emphasis on social actors' critical capacities. Moreover, there is little consideration given to collective struggles or the formation of a political subject. Critique is always pluralized into competing discourses and actualized in everyday contexts. Where Habermasian critical theory overstates normativity, Boltanski and Thévenot relativize it to context specific discourses where discursively achieved consensus is not possible. Across the various repertoires of justification, there can be only compromises but no consensus. In sum, in the move beyond Bourdieu's critical method, critique now becomes a matter of practice around moral issues of judgement. But in this displacement of critique, they end up with a characterization of the social world as one of unending disputes over different orders of justification. It can nonetheless be concluded, despite these problems, that pragmatic sociology has been one of the most promising developments in recent conceptions of critique. In addition to its methodological applicability, it has given a more grounded approach to critique that is lacking in the critical theory tradition. The important point is that pragmatic sociology has developed a productive kind of interpretivism. Although it offers a limited capacity to explain macro-processes and long-term trends, it offers a useful approach to understanding social conflicts.

Conclusion

The five varieties of critique discussed in this chapter draw attention to different dimensions of critique. I argue that a new critical theory needs to incorporate elements from all traditions. Bourdieu and critical realists in their different ways provide the strongest kind of critique as a methodologically useful tool for social research and one that offers a sound basis for social explanation. The disadvantage is a relatively narrow conception of the purpose of critique. As we have seen in the case of Bourdieu, critique is largely an exercise to demonstrate the limits of everyday forms of knowledge, while critical realism is primarily concerned with the discovery beneath the empirical and the actual of the structuring forces of the real. Critical theory on the other hand, while also operating with a general notion of ideology critique, has a broader normative concern with the formation of political subjectivity and the identification of forms of self-transformation. The resulting notion of a world-disclosing critique lacks methodological specificity, and lately critical theory has become increasingly embroiled with other approaches but in ways that are methodologically unclear when it comes to designing a programme of research.

56 Critical theory revisited

Foucault's work marks the critical juncture of an entirely new turn in the notion of a critical social science. The emphasis on discourse and the related notions of positionality and formation of subjectivity has opened up critique to important new insights. Already evident in Foucault, recent developments have highlighted the turn to practice. However, the turn to practice, which has brought critique closer to interpretative approaches, has been at the cost of a certain neutralization of critique in a multiplicity of critical projects. It has also more or less jettisoned explanation and macro-sociological analysis. One of the many implications that arise from recent developments around the tie between discourse and critique is the uncertain relation of critique for macro-analysis. The discursive turn has mostly been taken up in micro-analysis. The concern with major societal transformation that was a feature of the older approaches, in particular that of the Frankfurt School tradition, seems to have been somewhat diluted in a view of critique that has become increasingly focussed on the constitution of the self. The outcome of the Foucauldian turn to discourse and practice has been a certain neutralization of critique in a constructivist mode of analysis.

The analysis on varieties of critique in this chapter suggests that the most promising framework is still the normative-diagnostic model of the critical theory of the Frankfurt School. However, this has now to be reconceived, and dialogue with other approaches is essential. Critical theory's concept of immanent transcendence is relevant to a transformative conception of the social that is also at work in other approaches. This concept suggests a notion of self-transformation, including subject transformation and wider societal transformation. It has long been recognized in the Hegelian-Marxist tradition that society, due to its internal dynamics which are related to class struggle, is self-transformative. It has been variously theorized as, in the terms of Alain Touraine (1977), 'the self-production of society', or the notion of creativity that, according to Castoriadis (1987), is integral to the radical imaginary of the social, and it is also implicit in Habermas's theory of the self-constitution of society through collective learning processes. A transformative conception of the social can be broken down into subject transformation and societal transformation. By subject transformation is meant the shaping of consciousness and identity on the level of individuals and on the level of collective actors. Self-transformation also pertains to the wider shaping of society in terms of processes of institution and norm-building. To identify such forms of self-transformation is the key methodological challenge for critical theory. Concretely, this will be related to the identification of various forms of autonomous agency as, for instance, in expressions of individuation and forms of democratic self-organization. I conclude by summing up what might be considered the main characteristics of critique in social science and which might serve as a methodological guide for social inquiry. Critique as a methodologically grounded approach entails four – or, if necessary, five – dimensions, which can be derived from the general epistemological framework of immanent transcendence in so far as this concerns the identification of society's immanent possibilities for transcendence.[8]

Critical engagements **57**

The four core features of critique concern: diagnostic analysis of a problem or crisis situation, reconstructive critique of social actors' communication and action, explanatory critique of the objective structures or mechanisms, and disclosing critique of practically realizable normative possibilities. These roughly correspond to the moments of description, interpretative reconstruction, explanation, and normatively connecting with practice. The fifth feature, namely, genealogical critique, enters in conjunction with the second phase, if necessary, to test the status of the normative principles interpretatively reconstructed from communication and action.

First, critique takes as its starting point a sense of a problem or crisis in the objective order of society. This is where the critical theory tradition is particularly relevant to the grounding of critique in the analysis of domination. The need for critique arises because social actors experience a problem that has normative roots, for instance, social injustice or a social pathology. It may be addressed to a tension, discrepancy, or contradiction between normative ideas and social reality. The perception of the problem could be the result of a sudden change, the emergence of a new social actor, a discursive shift, or a breakdown in solidarity. The experience of suffering due to, for instance, unjust treatment, discrimination, exploitation, or reification could serve as an instance of problem disclosure. The centrality of violence in modern societies has been one of the most significant contexts for engagement with the world for many people. This level of critique is largely descriptive and diagnostic and operates principally yet imaginatively on the empirical level.

The second level of critique has a stronger interpretative dimension to it but may be termed reconstructive critique in that its aim is to reconstruct the immanent possibilities in a given situation as well as the guiding situation-transcendent normative principles or cultural models with reference to the social actors' positions, identities, communication, and action. The context of interpretative reconstruction is the objective problem situation with which social actors are confronted. This need not be restricted to an immediate or urgent issue in everyday life, although this is the most likely context, but can be a deep-seated issue which has not yet found the necessary vocabulary for it to be publicly articulated. This level of critique is concerned with the definitions of the actual situation with which social actors operate and their actions and relations. As such it operates on the micro- and meso-level, but it can only proceed on the basis of the reconstructed transcendent normative guidelines. On this level, the critical capacities of ordinary social actors, resistance, and discursive formation are key features of the situation taken into account by the critical method. The insights offered variously by pragmatic sociology and Foucauldian theory are particularly relevant in giving to the critical method a direction beyond ideology critique. This is also the dimension where Foucault's type of genealogical critique becomes relevant and even necessary. Its purpose is to make sure that the reconstructed normative principles which make reconstructive critique possible have not become hollowed out, suffered reversal into their very opposites, or completely lost their meaning.

58 Critical theory revisited

The third level is the deeper and more explanatory level whereby the critical theorist seeks to explain the nature of the problematic or crisis situation in such a way that its cause or causes are critically exposed. It is at this level that reality as such comes more firmly into focus. This kind of critical explanation or explanatory critique requires going beyond not only descriptive, interpretative, and discourse-based approaches, but even also the normative reconstructive approach which is defining of critical theory's second methodological level. The logic of critical explanation or explanatory critique necessary to address the objective and typically macro-structures of society requires going beyond these different approaches for various reasons. Explanation in critical theory does not take the form of the search for laws nor for intentionality models. Nor does it exhaust itself by accounting for rational connections between actions and reasons, as is characteristically done at the second level. Its defining concern is rather accounting for non-intentional, institutional, and structural forces in the shaping of society and for the presence of power in social relations associated with such forces. In order to explain the consequences of structural forces, such as power relations, critical theory must make reference to causal mechanisms, and beyond this it must also be able to demonstrate how these arose. For this reason, an explanatory account must have a macro-reference and be able to postulate generative mechanisms whereby social structures are not only reproduced but also are deformed or distorted. In a certain respect, the concern with explaining underlying structures or mechanisms characteristic of Bourdieu's critical sociology and of critical realism has some relevance to the kind of critique that the critical method aims at here. However, while critical theory can draw from some of these methodological conceptions, the characteristic feature of explanation in critical theory – that is, providing an explanation which not only delivers a critical insight but connects it to practice – distinguishes it from both critical sociology and critical realism. This leads to the final level.

The fourth level has a world-disclosing role in so far as it aims to provide society with the means to solve major problems and/or to reconstitute the social world. We can term it, following Adorno, Habermas, and Honneth, as a disclosing critique in that it brings to light possible interpretations and solutions to social problems and opens social reality up to as yet unrealized or even alternative possibilities. As a disclosing critique, it ties critique to a social praxis by addressing the enlightening insight made available by the critical explanation to critical theory's addressees or, more generally, the audience. Here belongs critical theory's defining concern with subject formation, from individual self-transformation to the formation of a political subject, and the stimulation of processes of mobilization. This link between critique and social praxis has been a key feature of much of the critical tradition in that social science is supposed to have a practical role in resolving social problems and in transforming the social world. While normative reconstruction at the second level is situation transcendent, disclosing critique's role is more explicitly transcendent at the level of practice than any of the other ones, for it is through this role that social science connects with public discourse and social praxis. Theory and practice, science and politics, have ultimately complementary functions in that science provides

Critical engagements **59**

democracy with self-reflection and critique based on research, while democracy opens up social science to public interests.[9]

These proposals might open the way for the recovery of critique in social science. The model proposed here has, in addition, the advantage of making critique relevant to macro-analysis as well as to social praxis and corrects the tendency towards a constructivist view of social reality as constituted in practices or discourses needing only interpretation. The position advanced here ties practice to a stronger normative purpose built on the foundations of empirical and theoretical analyses of social reality.

Notes

1 This chapter is partly based on 'Varieties of Critique in Sociological Theory and Their Methodological Implications for Social Research'. *Irish Journal of Sociology*, 2011, 19 (1): 68–92. It has been revised for this chapter. An earlier version was a given as a semi-plenary lecture for the European Sociological Association conference in Lisbon in September 2009.
2 By formation of a political subject, I mean broadly a political conception of critique that sees as its task political enlightenment. I do not consider conceptions of criticism that do not generally define their methodological purpose as one of critique (e.g. Allen 1998; Walzer 1987, 1988).
3 See Honneth's reflections on this (Honneth 2002).
4 Their work is discussed in Chapter 8 of Strydom (2011).
5 My thanks to Piet Strydom for advice on clarifying the term.
6 Despite this qualification, Bourdieu clearly saw his critical sociology as having a political role. However, it was only in his later writings that he took up a political position.
7 For interpretations, see Benatouïl (1999), Wagner (1999), Silber (2003) and Celikates (2006).
8 I am grateful to Piet Strydom for suggestions on this point and on much of the following.
9 For this reason, pragmatism and critical theory are closely related (see Bohman 2011; Strydom 2011)

References

Alexander, J. C. 1995. The Reality of Reduction: The Failed Synthesis of Pierre Bourdieu. In: Alexander, J. C. (ed.) *Fin de Siècle Social Theory*. London: Verso, pp. 182–217.
Allen, J. 1998. The Situated Critic or the Loyal Critic? Rorty and Walzer on Social Criticism. *Philosophy and Social Criticism*, 24 (6): 25–46.
Archer, M. 1995. *Realist Social Theory: The Morphogenetic Approach*. Cambridge: Cambridge University Press.
Benatouïl, T. 1999. A Tale of Two Sociologies: The Critical and Pragmatic Stances. *European Journal of Social Theory*, 2 (3): 379–91.
Benhabib, S. 1986. *Critique, Norm, Utopia*. New York: Columbia University Press.
Bevir, M. 2010. Rethinking Governmentality: Towards Genealogies of Governance. *European Journal of Social Theory*, 13 (4): 423–4.
Bhaskar, R. 1975. *A Realist Theory of Science*. Leeds: Leeds Books.
Bhaskar, R. 1979. *The Possibility of Naturalism*. London: Routledge & Kegan Paul.
Bohman, J. 1991. *New Philosophies of Social Science: Problems of Indeterminacy*. Cambridge, MA: MIT Press.
Bohman, J. 1998. Theories, Practices, and Pluralism: A Pragmatic Interpretation of Critical Social Science. *Philosophy of the Social Sciences*, 29 (4): 459–80.

60 Critical theory revisited

Bohman, J. 2011. Methodological and Political Pluralism: Democracy, Pragmatism and Critical Theory. In: Delanty, G. and Turner, S. (eds.) *Handbook of Contemporary Social and Political Theory*. London: Routledge.

Boltanski, L. and Thévenot, L. 1999. The Sociology of Critical Capacity. *European Journal of Social Theory*, 2 (3): 359–77.

Boltanski, L. and Thévenot, L. 2006. *On Justification: Economies of Worth*. Princeton, NJ: Princeton University Press.

Bourdieu, P. 2004. *Science of Science and Reflexivity*. Chicago, IL: Chicago University Press.

Bourdieu, P. and Wacquant, L. 1992. *An Invitation to Reflexive Sociology*. Chicago, IL: Chicago University Press.

Burawoy, M. 2005. For Public Sociology. *British Journal of Sociology*, 56 (2): 259–94.

Castoriadis, C. 1987. *The Imaginary Institution of Society*. Cambridge: Polity Press.

Celikates, R. 2006. From Critical Social Theory to a Social Theory of Critique: On the Critique of Ideology After the Pragmatic Turn. *Constellations*, 13 (1): 21–40.

Davies, B. and Harre, R. 1990. Positioning: The Discursive Production of Selves. *Journal for the Theory of Social Behaviour*, 20 (1): 43–63.

Dean, M. 1994. *Critical and Effective Histories: Foucault's Methods and Historical Sociology*. London: Routledge.

Delanty, G. and Strydom, P. (eds.) 2003. *Philosophies of Social Science: The Classic and Contemporary Readings*. Buckingham: Open University Press.

Flyvberg, B. 2001. *Making Social Science Matter*. Cambridge: Cambridge University Press.

Forst, R. 2002. *Contexts of Justice: Political Philosophy Beyond Liberalism and Communitarianism*. Berkeley: University of California Press.

Foucault, M. 1984a. What Is Enlightenment? In: Rabinow, P. (ed.) *The Foucault Reader*. New York: Pantheon.

Foucault, M. 1984b. Nietzsche, Genealogy, History. In: Rabinow, P. (ed.) *The Foucault Reader*. New York: Pantheon.

Foucault, M. 1991. Governmentality. In: Burchell, G., Gordon, C. and Miller, P. (eds.) *The Foucault Effect: Studies in Governmentality*. London: Harvester Wheatsheaf.

Foucault, M. 2007. What Is Critique? In: Lotringer, S. (ed.) *The Politics of Truth*. New York: Semiotext(e).

Fraser, N. and Jaeggi, R. 2018. *Capitalism: A Conversation*. Cambridge: Polity Press.

Gouldner, A. 1970. *The Coming Crisis of Western Sociology*. London: Heinemann.

Honneth, A. 2002. An interview with Axel Honneth: The Role of Sociology in the Theory of Recognition. *European Journal of Social Theory*, 5 (2): 265–77.

Jaeggi, R. 2014. *Alienation*. New York: Columbia University Press.

Kemp, S. 2005. Critical Realism and the Limits of Philosophy. *European Journal of Social Theory*, 8 (2): 171–91.

Koselleck, R. 1988. *Critique and Crisis: Enlightenment and the Pathogenesis of Modern Society*. Cambridge, MA: MIT Press.

Lamont, M. and Thévenot, L. 2000. *Rethinking Comparative Cultural Sociology: Repertoires in France and the United States*. Cambridge: Cambridge University Press.

May, T. 2000. A Future for Critique? Positioning, Belonging and Reflexivity. *European Journal of Social Theory*, 3 (2): 157–73.

Mills, C. W. 1970. *The Sociological Imagination*. London: Penguin.

O'Mahony, P. 2013. *The Contemporary Theory of the Public Sphere*. Brussels: Peter Lang.

Outhwaite, W. 1987. *New Philosophies of Social Science: Realism, Hermeneutics and Critical Theory*. London: Palgrave Macmillan.

Ray, L. 2004. Pragmatism and Critical Theory. *European Journal of Social Theory*, 7 (3): 307–21.

Ricoeur, P. 1977. *Freud and Philosophy: An Essay in Interpretation*. London: Routledge.

Sayer, A. 2000. *Realism and Social Science*. London: Sage.

Silber, I. F. 2003. Pragmatic Sociology as Cultural Sociology: Beyond Repertoire Theory. *European Journal of Social Theory*, 6 (4): 427–49.

Strydom, P. 2000. *Discourse and Knowledge: The Making of Enlightenment Sociology*. Liverpool: Liverpool University Press.

Strydom, P. 2011. *Contemporary Critical Theory and Methodology*. London: Routledge.

Touraine, A. 1977. *The Self-Production of Society*. Chicago, IL: University of Chicago Press.

Turner, S. 2008. The Future of Social Theory. In: Turner, B. S. (ed.) *The New Blackwell Companion to Social Theory*. Oxford: Blackwell.

Vandenberghe, F. 2014. *What Critical About Critical Realism?* London: Routledge.

Wagner, P. 1994. *A Sociology of Modernity: Liberty and Discipline*. London: Routledge.

Wagner, P. 1999. After Justification: Repertoires of Evaluation and the Sociology of Modernity. *European Journal of Social Theory*, 2 (3): 341–57.

Walzer, M. 1987. *Interpretation and Social Criticism*. Cambridge, MA: Harvard University Press.

Walzer, M. 1988. *The Company of Critics: Social Criticism and Political Commitment in Twentieth Century*. New York: Basic Books.

Wheatland, T. 2009. *The Frankfurt School in Exile*. Minneapolis: University of Minnesota Press.

3

CRITICAL THEORY AND SOCIAL TRANSFORMATION

Modernity, capitalism, and technology

While the previous chapters dealt with the core philosophical and methodological ideas underpinning critical theory, the focus of this chapter shifts to the social theory of the Frankfurt School and is specifically concerned with the theme of social transformations in modernity. The central question that I am addressing can be formulated as follows: what are the major social transformations of modernity from a critical theory perspective? A distinctive feature of critical theory has been its attempt to locate the present in the context of a historical account of modernity. This concern with history is not for the sake of understanding the past but for interpreting the present and future possibilities contained within the present. This is perhaps what distinguishes critical theory from Foucault's genealogical approach with which it has some similarities in being also 'a history of the present'. However, unlike for Foucault, the task for critical theory is always to identify openings to the future, hence the key theme of social transformation in the formation of modernity.

The chapter begins with an account of modernity as understood by critical theory. This leads to a discussion on capitalism in relation to modernity and the problem of whether capitalism is to be understood as the defining characteristic of contemporary society. The chapter then moves on to look at the problem of technology, which was one of the main expressions of the Frankfurt School's critique of modernity. In the current context of the digital age and so-called surveillance capitalism, the critical theory of technology has become once again highly salient.

Critical theory and modernity

Since the early Frankfurt School to post-Habermasian social theory, the concept of modernity has been central to critical theory. Despite the significant shifts in critical theory from Adorno through Habermas to Honneth, there is general agreement that modernity is defined by its future possibilities, which needed to be redeemed from the present. As discussed in the previous chapters, a critique of modernity is about the disclosing of such possibilities through an analysis of the nature and mechanisms of domination, including social pathologies and regression. To use the apt words of Johann Arnason, the concept of modernity in critical theory must be seen as a 'field of tensions' (Arnason 1991). On the most general level, this can be understood in terms of the dialectical conception of history whereby the present is defined by immanent relations of contradiction, process, and becoming. The critical theory of modernity thus concerns the identification of social struggles, major moments of crisis, transformational shifts in the self-understanding of modern society, and the formation of a critical consciousness.

Since Marx, a central theme in the critical theory tradition is that the immanent forces, at least potentially, transcend the limits of society. In Marx and Lukács, such forces resided in labour; with Marcuse they were generated by human drives; Adorno related them to mimetic behaviour; Habermas and Honneth shifted such immanent forces to the domain of communication and recognition.

Perhaps one central theme that runs through the entire social theory of modernity is the tension between domination, consciousness, and the normative order of society. The normative order of society – as in the Kantian and Hegelian ideas of Reason – is embedded in consciousness, and both are entangled in systems of domination. Freedom and unfreedom, progress and regression, enlightenment and pathologies, emancipation and domination are mutually implicated. But domination is never total, and the normative order of society can be a source of resistance if and when the appropriate forms of consciousness develop. In that sense, the idea of critique is linked to a project of 'consciousness-raising'. Where critical theorists have differed is in their accounts of the relations between these elements and in the generative processes by which a critical consciousness is formed.

Three main paradigms can be identified in critical theory: instrumental reason, communicative reason, and recognition. The conception of modernity in the writing of Adorno and Horkheimer was strongly influenced by Lukács's Marxist appropriation of Weber's theory of rationalization in his 1923 essay, 'Reification and the Consciousness of the Proletariat', which is one of the main chapters of *History and Class Consciousness* (Lukács 1972). This seminal text with its famous notion of reification gave the basic orientation to the Frankfurt School's critical theory of modernity (see Feenberg 2011; Honneth 2008). It made capitalism and domination a key concern of critical theory. The phenomenon of reification, according to Lukács, is that 'a relation between people takes on the character of a thing and thus requires a "phantom objectivity", an autonomy that seems so strictly rational and all-embracing as to conceal every trace of its fundamental nature: the relation between people'. Lukács goes on to argue, following Marx, that commodity fetishism is 'the specific problem of our age, the age of modern capitalism'. It becomes the 'universal category of society'. Closely related to it, alienation is made possible by the fundamental condition of reification whereby the commodity form becomes the generalized condition of modern society. The principle at work, he argues, is 'the principle of rationalization based on what is and what can

64 Critical theory revisited

be calculated'. Following Weber, rationalization is defined as the ability to predict with ever greater precision all the results to be achieved and is achieved through the exact breakdown of every complex into its elements. This process is one of pure calculation and leads to the fragmentation of both the object and the subject. Lukács emphasized atomization and fragmentation as consequences of rationalization in industrial capitalism. It embraces every aspect of life. He goes on to describe bureaucracy in terms of the formal standardization of social life that reduces all social functions to their elements and organized into segregated partial systems.

In sum, Lukács's account of what he refers to as 'an inhuman, standardized division of labour' is in essence a Marxist reading of Weber's famous motif of the 'iron cage' of modern capitalism. Unlike for the politically conservative Max Weber, what is needed for Lukács is a radical transformation to overcome reification. 'But a radical change in outlook is not feasible on the soil of bourgeois society'. Lukács's essay shaped the direction of critical theory in giving central place to the core problem of domination as a form of reification that eats into consciousness and gives rise to the problem that radical change requires a new consciousness, but this is held in check by the very forms of reification that it seeks to overcome.

The first generation of critical theorists was never clear on from where this new consciousness comes. As Marcuse wrote in *One Dimensional Man*: 'Confronted with the total character of the achievements of advanced industrial capitalism, critical theory is left without the rationale for transcending this society' (Marcuse 1964: xiv). The result was a conception of modernity that stressed in a decidedly one-sided manner instrumental rationality and more generally capitalism. This was compounded by the rise of anti-Semitism, which was theorized by the Frankfurt School in the 1940s as an expression of the related rise of totalitarianism. Anti-Semitism and the broader phenomenon that it represented was a danger to liberal democracy, as much in the United States as in Europe. As such, a possible opposition would be the preservation of democratic values. This at least accounts for some of the support that the Studies in Prejudice research gained in the USA in the 1940s (see Wheatland 2009: 227ff). However, the problem of the wider trend towards reification in modern society will not necessarily be reversed. The argument of the *Dialectic of Enlightenment* remained the over-arching legacy of the Frankfurt School rather than what might be seen as the liberal presuppositions of the Studies in Prejudice that were designed to appeal to American academia.

The problem of a counter-consciousness nonetheless remains and cannot be separated from the related question of the normative structure of society, which was also under-theorized in the critical theory tradition of Adorno, Horkheimer, and Marcuse. Habermas attempted to rectify this problem with a conception of modernity that counter-posed communicative rationality to instrumental rationality. In this account, which we can term the communicative paradigm, modernity is shaped by the conflict between the instrumental forces of capitalism and on the other side by communicative forms of reason, which include public critiques of power, social movements, and democracy. This dual model of modernity is related to the system versus life-world distinction, namely, a conception of society in terms of systemic forms of integration (the state, law, economy, bureaucracy, and so on) and social integration (through social institutions, socialization, cultural traditions, and the like). In this reconceptualization of modernity, domination is resisted by forms of consciousness emanating from the life-world and which are anchored in the normative order of society (as in modern political ideas, such as rights, justice, democracy, and so on). As discussed in Chapter 1, contrary to criticisms of Habermas, communicative reason does not exist on a level above and beyond social reality but is itself as much a part of the social reality as are structures of domination. This immanent perspective on modernity opened up a more dialectical vision of social change as well as offered a perspective on social agency that sees social movements as the major agents of social transformation. On the one side, there is a dialectical relationship between consciousness and the normative order of society, whereby shifts occur in consciousness through the expansion and radicalization of normative ideas and the cognitive horizons of society. On the other hand, the resulting transformation in consciousness leads to wider societal change when forms of domination are challenged.

Habermas's theory of modernity thus stressed modernity in terms of the expansion of communicative forms of rationality, for instance, the expansion in democracy, constitutional solutions to conflict, rights, and so on (Habermas 1979 [1976], 1984/1987 [1981]). At a time when postmodernism – in general French poststructuralist philosophy – was becoming influential in offering a different account of modernity, Habermas defended the basic orientation of modernity as containing unfulfilled yet necessary normative potential for the future and for progressive politics. The postmodernist approach, much opposed by Habermas, as in the *Philosophical Discourse of Modernity*, tended to reject the very notion of modernity as entailing an emancipatory project (Habermas 1987 [1985]). Against this trend, Habermas's whole conception of modernity aimed to provide a normative horizon by which consciousness could be assessed in terms of opposition to domination. The most basic insight is that power can always be challenged by critical subjects so long as they possess the means of communication. If the communicative foundations of social action are destroyed, the result will be pathologies. This comes about through the 'colonization of the life-world' by systemic forces. In effect, Habermas's theory of modernity sees domination occurring as a result of the excessive impact of the system on the life-world. Emancipation occurs when the life-world resists such systemic forces. Habermas thus resolved the problem inherited from Lukács of how to explain resistance to domination. The source of such forms of resistance is in the communicative order of the life-world rather than, as for Lukács, in a political project, or as in Horkheimer's famous 'message in a bottle'[1]. This is supposed to explain some of the major transformations in modernity by which the old forms of domination were discarded and new societal structures created, for example, how the modern constitutional state arose as a way by which peaceful solutions could be found for political differences between elites and between states. The exercise of power is always entangled in claims to legitimacy, which Habermas sees as being further entrenched in the validity claims inherent in communication and which

66 Critical theory revisited

therefore, in terms of Kantian philosophy, take the form of transcendental presuppositions that must necessarily be taken into account in any analysis of modernity. The consequence of this, as outlined in *Legitimation Crisis* 1975 [1973], is that modern political order cannot rest only on the fact of legality – compliance with the procedural rule of law – but also involves legitimation claims. In essence, there are always problems of legitimacy in the exercise of power which makes possible the always-in-principle possibility for domination to be resisted. As Habermas argued in that work, late capitalism did not solve the problem of legitimation and created new societal problems which raise the spectre of new challenges.

Habermas's mature work on law and democracy, as in *Between Facts and Norms* ([1992] 1996) and *The Inclusion of the Other* ([1996] 1998), tended to move away from the system versus life-world conflict in order to account for a more complex view of modern law and its connection with democracy and the public sphere. While the new departure, based on the later developed theory of discourse ethics, led to some important insights concerning the normative order of society, it did not cast much light on understanding the nature of domination and moved the focus away from capitalism, which consequently receded from the lens of critical theory.

Honneth in part sought to bring problems of domination and issues of social justice in his revision of the direction critical theory had taken with Habermas's discourse ethics. However, as discussed in Chapter 1, his theoretical approach required seeing all such problems as problems of recognition. The recognition paradigm, despite the many advantages it offered, reduced modernity and social struggles to a narrow spectrum of issues (see McNay 2007). While recognition pervades many aspects of the social, not everything can be reduced to a struggle over recognition. Thus, for example, social pathologies are seen as pathologies of recognition rather than problems residing in the objective order of society. As mentioned earlier, the reception of recognition theory has mostly been in micro-sociology and consequently has not been integrated into a macro-sociological theory of society.

While Honneth corrected Habermas's view of work as instrumental action and thus devoid of normative significance, his solution reduced the normative critique to the problem of recognition in that all kinds of work require esteem. It is far from clear that the recognition approach can be fruitfully applied to new kinds of work that constitute the relatively new phenomenon of the precariat.[2] The actual nature of work itself cannot be ignored by critical theory, as Honneth does in an argument that reduces the problem of work to recognition through remuneration and status. As pointed out by critics such as Jean-Philippe Deranty, Christophe Dejours, and others, this does not take into account forms of work that are by definition alienating. In this sense, then, a critique of work cannot easily proceed immanently with a just society emerging simply from changes to recognition when people continue to have to perform the same kind of work.

The current situation, then, is that critical theory does not have a clearly articulated theory of modernity. Nonetheless, as indicated, there has been a general acceptance that modernity must be seen in terms of the formation of critical consciousness, the development of the normative order of society, and resistance to domination. It entails a view of modernity that is neither reduced to societal structures – for example, processes of instrumental rationalization, systemic structures – nor to its cultural forms. Modernity entails the development of transcendent structures in its normative and cognitive order as well as immanent forces that could at any time emerge and bring about a transformation of the present. However, modernity is thus not simply to be found in the normative order of society but in the immanent level of latent forces. The characteristic feature of the critical theory approach to modernity is the dialectical vision of a 'field of tensions' where the various elements act on each other, bringing about their mutual transformation.

Capitalism is central to modernity, but it is not its only dimension. Capitalism interacts with a wider spectrum of forces that constitute the field of modernity. In what follows, I explore the question of capitalism and discuss its relation to modernity.

Capitalism and modernity: a reconstruction of a contested concept

The term capitalism is extremely difficult to pin down, not least since the term was not used until the end of the nineteenth century.[3] The *Communist Manifesto* in 1848 used the term the 'bourgeois mode of production' and 'modern bourgeois society' rather than capitalism. Marx in later writings spoke of the 'capitalist era' and the capitalist 'mode of production' to refer to the emerging shape of the modern economy and of societal transformation more generally. When the term capitalism came into common currency in the twentieth century, its use revealed a political perspective on the desirability and permanence of capitalism as opposed to socialism. It therefore was connected with a critical-normative standpoint. Marxist-influenced approaches saw capitalism as a pervasive social and economic condition that would come to an end one day, while the defenders of capitalism preferred to see the modern economy in terms of free enterprise or the free market as part of a wider condition of liberty. In many sociological accounts, as in the writings of Raymond Aron (1967) and Ralf Dahrendorf (1957), the notion of industrial society was the preferred term to capitalism. As we have seen, for critical theory capitalism was a *bête noire* that was never fully defined but was regarded as the source of all problems and the main cause of domination. However, the Frankfurt School had a somewhat general view of capitalism, which seems to include Soviet industrialism. It was in many senses another term for instrumental reason. Perhaps this is why Habermas veered away from the preoccupation with capitalism, which was subsumed into his broader category of systemic integration. One major innovation in his theory of society was the retention of the centrality of capitalism but within the context of a wider conception of interacting societal forces. Only in this way could immanent possibilities of transformation be fully conceptualized. However, this was at the price of losing a perspective on the nature and logic of capitalism.

A critical theory of capitalism will need to establish clarity on what capitalism means. This is not just about a narrow preoccupation with definitions but of

68 Critical theory revisited

agreement on some of the defining features of capitalism and, I argue, critically, whether capitalism refers to the modern economy per se or to society. The general tendency in modern sociological theory is to see the economy as a subsystem of modern society, which, while not reducible to the economy, is very much shaped by it. This is most evident in Parsons and functionalist traditions where the emphasis is placed on the economy understood as the market. For Weber, in contrast, capitalism is an expression of more general trends in rationalization, which culminate in the societal condition of an 'iron cage' of universal rationalism. Nonetheless, despite their differences, for these classical theories, capitalism is a modern society and based on the centrality of markets. This is also the case with Karl Polanyi in his classic account of the 'Great Transformation' that saw markets becoming disembedded from traditional social institutions (Polanyi [1944] 2001). The result is the neutralization of the political nature of capitalism. In contrast, in Marxist theory, the economy is more than a market; it is primarily a system of production that has a determining effect over the rest of society and, as a mode of production, it became the dominant one since the sixteenth century, making possible the modern capitalist era. In the Marxist analysis, the status of the wider category of society is unclear and confusingly, as Williams (1976: 50–2) noted, is sometimes the 'bourgeois society' but also incorporates the capitalist mode of production. In all of these classical accounts, including the seminal contributions of Simmel, Sombart, and Schumpeter, the term capitalism is highly ambiguous. Either it is a term to refer to modern western society as a whole or a term to refer to the modern economy or a part of it.

There is some value in returning to Marx to see what can be salvaged from the many confused uses of the term. It is evident that the Marxist legacy is to see modern society increasingly shaped by the capitalist economy which transforms social relations through the progressive extension of exchange values into all social spheres. It is evident, too, that the notion of the 'bourgeois society' is of limited use and that Marx did not have a theory of society as such. The problem of reductionism that arose from the Marxist account has been the focus of considerable controversy, possibly to the neglect of the many important facets of Marx's analysis of the workings of capitalism. However, the relation between economy and society remains important in that the notion of the capitalist economy is not necessarily the equivalent of capitalist society. The solution, in my view, is not to jettison the term capitalism for simply the free market or a more general notion of the modern economy, for this would be to lose some of the most insightful analyses of modern capitalism.

The core of the Marxist account sees capitalism as an economic system, a mode of production, based on the unrelenting pursuit of profit, which is privately appropriated. However, it is also more than simply the economy conceived of as an autonomous domain in society. The strength of the Marxist approach is that capitalism is seen as a dynamic and destructive system that has created self-perpetuating forces that seek the maximization of profit and the conversion of everything into exchange values. Capitalism is an insatiable system of production and valorization that makes everything transferable into commodified forms that serve the

Critical theory and social transformation **69**

accumulation of capital. The notion of capital is thus the primary condition of capitalism and can be seen as a condition or force that is neither entirely economic nor social. 'Capital is not a thing but a process in which money is perpetually spent in search of more money' (Harvey 2010: 40). Capitalism is a commodified society. Its defining essence is the accumulation of capital. Kocka (2016: 21) offers a compelling definition: 'decentralization, commodification, and accumulation as basic characteristics'. In this respect, the core insight of Marx remains relevant, namely, that capitalism is based on capital. We can add to this that while not necessarily a necessary feature of capitalism, it has been a destructive force in the world in both the positive (removing the vestiges of feudalism) and negative senses of the term. The violent history of capitalism over nature and social life has dominated. The destructive force of capitalism is the cumulative effects of its constant search for sources of energy, sites of production, markets, and disposal zones.

While the analytical basis of this account in Marx resides in the Labour Theory of Value, which holds that the potential for production is greater than what the worker gets as a wage, the history of capitalism reveals a more complicated story than one that is essentially based on an account of the exploitative buying of labour for the production of commodities. As Schumpeter and the Frankfurt School theorists argued, the result of the buying and selling of labour does not lead inexorably to the immiseration of the proletariat. Indeed, the opposite has often been the case (at least in modern western societies) and which accounts for the relative success of capitalism in warding off political challenges that come from deprivation and exploitation. The history of the modern class system and social inequalities, in any case, can no longer be seen only in terms of nationally delineated societies where production and consumption coincide. Today, these are part of a global system that began with imperialism, as Wallerstein has argued. This is not something that can be discussed here (see Wallerstein 2011). A possible solution to the problem of what is the defining feature of capitalism is to take the core Marxist insight that capitalism is a dynamic system that converts everything into exchange values in order to generate profit. Here, the key point is the destructive logic of transformation and commodification leading to private appropriation and the accumulation of capital. For Marx, capital – the logic of accumulation and appropriation – is more important than capitalism as an economic system based on wage labour and the class system. Thus, for example, one major development in capitalism in recent times is the growth of the intangible economy which does not depend on wage labour and the related phenomenon of financialization (Haskel and Westlake 1997; Deutschmann 2011). Yet, it is an aspect of capitalism. So, too, is the persistence and return of what Marx called 'primitive accumulation', namely, the incorporation into capitalism of precapitalistic modes of production, which has today become significant with the worldwide exploitation of nature that has come with global agrarian capitalism and extractivism, such as mining.

Conceiving of capitalism in terms of the destructive logic of capital goes some way to answering the problem of what is capitalism and whether it is an economic system or another term for modern society. The upshot is that capitalism is a system

70 Critical theory revisited

of social relations that has commodifying effects, or, in the terms of Lukács, reification. These social relations are not confined to the relation between workers and capitalists or relations confined to the economic system. Conceiving of capitalism only as an economic system has the unsatisfactory outcome in that it does not account for its enormous impact on the rest of society; viewing capitalism as the equivalent of modern society, as in the outdated term 'bourgeois society', runs into problems of economic reductionism. In a similar way, the notion of democracy is not confined to the political system but pervades society more generally. But this does not mean that modern society is democratic.

In a similar vein, Fraser and Jaeggi have drawn attention to the important but neglected question of the relation of capitalism to social reproduction. The latter is necessary to the forms of work based directly on capitalism, (i.e. wage labour) and more generally services the requirements of capitalism (Fraser and Jaeggi 2018: 31–5). This perspective locates capitalism as part of a wider conception of social reproduction which includes the social conditions of capitalism that enable it. In this view, capitalism is not exclusively an economic system but is part of an 'institutionalized social order' or, in Jaeggi's terms, 'a form of life' (Jaeggi 2018).

Is capitalism the defining feature of our time?

In the foregoing, I argued that capitalism cannot be seen as residing in a specific sphere such as the economy and is therefore not reducible to the modern economy or market. It also has a wider cultural significance, which, for Arnason (2015), has a civilizational dimension to it. Since Weber, Simmel, and Schumpeter through the Frankfurt School to Jameson, capitalism has been theorized as having a cultural logic that brings it out of the economic domain. For Weber, capitalism 'is the most fateful force in our modern life' (Weber [1920] 1978: 17). It is driven by a 'spirit' that has come to shape the modern world in ways that go beyond the economic foundations of capitalism as an economic system. Marcuse (1964) argued capitalism had become the ideology of a one-dimensional society that could no longer conceive of an alternative. As Boltanski and Chiapello (2006) have shown, the spirit of capitalism is itself not immutable but changes over time and capitalism will always find a spirit to provide it with justifications and motivations (see also Konings 2015). What conclusion can we draw from this? Is contemporary society defined by some kind of spirit of capitalism that goes beyond the realm of economic activity to encompass the fabric of society? Has the global diffusion of capitalism over the past century to become more or less the only economic system in the world led to its final triumph over history?

This is what Marcuse claimed in *One Dimensional Man*. But if this is the case and capitalism is indeed the only game in town, it is very difficult to conceive of the end of capitalism or of alternatives to it. However, if capitalism is seen as part of modernity, rather than the primary condition of modernity, a different perspective is opened up. For this to be a viable position, the distinction between society and economy must be upheld. Capitalism may be the primary form of the modern economy – a mode of production, a market system, and forms of consumption – but the social is not only defined by economic forces, however dominant they are. We must not lose sight of the fact, recognized by Marx, Weber, and Schumpeter, that capitalism seeks to satisfy human needs and, in doing so, as Marcuse argued, it creates new needs which are met by the culture industry. In so far as it is part of, what Hegel called the 'system of needs', it is inextricably tied to forces that go beyond its institutional forms. In almost every account of the rise of capitalism, there is a general recognition that capitalism as an economic form cannot be separated from wider societal processes. Marx recognized that capitalism was parasitic on precapitalistic social institutions, such as religion, family, and gendered relations.

Polanyi's account, while flawed in many ways, shows how the formation of capitalism occurred through the disembedding of markets from established social and cultural institutions which consisted of largely segmented markets (Polanyi [1944] 2001). The self-regulating market that gained victory in the nineteenth century around the competitive labour market, the gold standard, and international free trade was unable to sustain itself. Aside from requiring an interventionist state to enable it to gain dominance, it provoked a counter-movement by the end of the century. For Polanyi, capitalist societies entail a 'double movement' around disembedding and embedding. Thus, socialism and its various offshoots, including the Chartist movements, trade unionism, social democracy, and so on, seek to subordinate the economy to democracy. This dialectical view of modern society was also the basis of Marx's theory of class conflict as an integral part of capitalism. While Marx saw conflict in terms of capital versus labour, Polanyi had a broader vision that can also be cast in terms of capitalism versus democracy, whereby social and political forces hold the destructive logic of capitalism at bay.

Theories of modernity vary greatly depending on the weight given to its economic, political, or cultural currents.[4] In the present context, the key question is the significance of capitalism, as the main form of economic modernity, in relation to other currents of which democracy is of particular importance. While it cannot be said to be the final word on modernity, one of its major expressions has been in the conflict between capitalism and democracy. It is possible, following Castoriadis (1987), to see both of these as expressions of imaginary significations that, as argued by Arnason (1991, 2003), produce civilizational configurations. Theorists of modernity have drawn attention to many features of the condition of modernity, and there is little consensus on what it entails other than that it takes a variety of forms. There is, however, agreement that modernity is not reducible to capitalism and wider processes of instrumental rationality, as in the writings of Weber and the Frankfurt School, and that it also takes other political and cultural forms. Of these, democracy is possibly the most important as the concrete and long-lasting legacy of modernity. This is not to neglect the fact that there have been major experiments with modernity that were not primarily products of democracy or even of capitalism, as the twentieth-century history of Soviet communism attests (Arnason 1993) and not forgetting the shorter-lived fascist experiments. While the history of modern societies bears testimony to many different trajectories of modernity, there can be no

72 Critical theory revisited

doubt that in the present day the two most fateful forces are those of capitalism and democracy. It is possible to view these forces in more general terms, as in the social theory of Habermas, for whom modernity is essentially a struggle between instrumental rationality (as part of a broader functional rationality) and communicative rationality or a conflict between system and life-world (Habermas 1984, 1987). Touraine (1995) offered a similar if vaguer framework in terms of a conflict at the heart of modernity between Reason and the subject (see also Touraine 2014). In this way, as the destructive forces of capitalism colonize the social world, they meet with resistance drawn from other currents in modernity. As Wagner (2012: 81–106) has argued, democracy sits in a relation of tension with capitalism, but in many of its forms – as, for example, 'democratic capitalism' in the post 1945 period in western societies – it has also accommodated capitalism by reducing its potential challenges around equality and inclusion. However, in line with this argument and Marx's own vision of the future, capitalism does not remove opposing forces but in fact increases the scale of counter-currents. Therein resides the sources of its demise. The normative, and more generally the cognitive, order of society offers resources for various forms of resistance to domination. Democracy is only one, but an important one.

While a definitive answer to the question about whether capitalism is the defining feature of our time is probably impossible, the argument given in this chapter is that whatever the answer, consideration must be given to the field of tensions in which capitalism operates. It was argued in the foregoing that capitalism cannot be seen as entirely encased within the economic sphere of society and, as the legacy of Marx shows, is embedded in social relations and produces systemic crises that have the effect of constantly transforming the social fabric of societies. Capitalism meets with resistance and thus is inextricably bound up with political modernity, of which, as argued, democracy is one of the most significant forms. Even if democracy is much absorbed into the systemic structures of modern society, it nonetheless retains a normative surplus that always makes it possible for power to be contested. This perspective is in line with the immanent conception of critique in critical theory, that is, an approach that sees the counter-currents to capitalism impregnated within capitalism.

Since the early 1980s when neoliberalism entered mainstream politics, it gained ideological supremacy in many parts of the world and could be said to be the dominant ideology of contemporary societies. The celebration of *homo economicus* – as embraced by post-communist regimes, right-wing governments in Latin America in the 1980s, and the PRC – can indeed be viewed as the final victory of capitalism. However, the theoretical perspective of critical theory would see capitalist ideology, such as the neoliberal doctrine of the free market, as entangled in countervailing forces (see the next chapter for a more extensive discussion of neoliberalism). Democracy – in the wide sense of popular movements for social justice – remains a powerful force in the world, often resisting capitalism, but also supporting capitalism and in many cases being co-opted by capitalism, as Nancy Fraser has argued. Democracy and capitalism have existed in various degrees of tension, ranging from coexistence – as in democratic capitalism or liberal democracy – to outright antagonism, as in anti-capitalism protest movements (Bowles and Gintis 1986). More or less every democracy has been capitalist. The confluence of both can be accounted for by the fact that democracies require wealth creation and capitalism has been able to deliver enough for many democracies to thrive and settle with capitalism. While capitalist societies – China and Chile under Pinochet – do not have to be democracies, they cannot entirely eliminate the quest for democracy. This does not necessarily imply the 'end of history' scenario in the sense of the worldwide victory of liberal democracy as argued by Fukuyama, since democracy develops in a variety of forms and can also herald authoritarianism.

A tentative answer to the question, then, as to whether capitalism is the defining feature of our time, must take into account the fact that capitalism exists in a state of perpetual crisis. As David Harvey (2010), following Marx, has shown, capitalism is not a static system but produces ongoing crises. The history of capitalism is a story of one crisis leading to the next. This is because of its tendency towards violent destruction, beginning with the destruction of nature. Such a perspective is in line with the main argument of the *Dialectic of Enlightenment*, which asserts that the domination of human beings was the consequence of the domination of nature. The domination of nature has today become a major focus for contemporary politics in late modernity (see Chapter 7).

By placing capitalist crisis at the centre of the analysis, it can be shown that in a longer historical perspective there were four major moments of crisis in modern society when capitalism and democracy collided, leading to new societal configurations and paradoxical outcomes for democracy. These moments, briefly characterized, are: the crisis of the 1870s, which saw the first crisis of economic liberalism leading to the rise of the protectionist state; the crisis of 1929 and the Great Depression which finally saw the emergence of Keynesianism since 1945; the crisis of 1973 which saw the crisis of the preceding era of 'democratic capitalism' and the rise of neoliberalism; the crisis of 2008 in which the neoliberal order imploded but with uncertain outcomes. Since the crisis of 2007-8, a fundamental shift in perspective is needed since it is now apparent that there are major contradictions and paradoxes in the relationship between capitalism and democracy. The shock of Brexit and Trump has deepened this sense of crisis, which cannot be seen either as the victory of capitalism or democracy.

From a critical theory perspective, the present time is characterized by a deep uncertainty as to the future. This mood of uncertainty is probably more a defining condition of our time than the ideology of *homo economicus* or the simple belief in capitalism as a one-dimensional reality. Yet, the quest for social justice and for meaningful forms of democratic empowerment are not silenced and are as much a part of social reality as is capitalism. While democracy is constantly thwarted by big business and the apparent penetration of capitalism into human subjectivity invalidates some of the presumptions of humanist Marxism, the moral and political horizons of societies can never be entirely closed.

74 Critical theory revisited

The question of technology

The critical theory of the early Frankfurt School had a particular concern with technology. In view of the enormous implications of technology today in shaping not only the cultural realm of society but also the social fabric of societies and, since 2016 Brexit and Trump, politics, the contribution of critical theory is of considerable relevance. While in many ways the critique of technology from Benjamin through Adorno and Horkheimer to Marcuse and Habermas does not seem relevant to the new digital technologies of the present, a closer inspection of their work does in fact indicate considerable significance despite the limitations of their view of technology as a form of instrumental rationality. Their conception of technology differed from the modernist view of technology as an unquestioned instrument of progress, but they did not accept the anti-modernist nostalgia to a return to a pre-technological age. The first generation of critical theorists were in some respects influenced by the anti-technological trust of much of early to mid-twentieth-century thought, as in, for example, most famously, Martin Heidegger in the *Question Concerning Technology* ([1954] 1977), but also Lewis Mumford (1934) and Jacques Ellul ([1954]1964). However, they were not anti-modern and saw the potential value of technology, although this is mostly applicable to Benjamin, because it is evident that despite their critical assessment of technology, Adorno, Marcuse, and Habermas had very little understanding of technology, which on the whole was seen as contrary to the logic of social relations.

Since Lukács in *History and Class Consciousness* in 1923, the Marxist theory of capitalism addressed technology in less-generalizing terms as ingrained in the very form of capitalism (but went beyond Marx's emphasis on technology as machinery). Weber's theory of rationalization, as in the famous motif of the 'iron cage', gave a further sociological foundation for critical perspectives on technology as a form of instrumental rationality, though Weber himself did not take up this direction. As argued earlier, Lukács was a major figure in shaping the sociological direction of critical theory, including his account of technology as embroiled in modern industrial capitalism, which by its very nature was technologically driven. The Marxist approach was developed later by Braverman (1974) in a classic work on scientific management as a tool by which monopoly power is established over knowledge in the control of the labour process.

The question of technology in critical theory is somewhat more complicated than in the straightforward Marxist account, as in Lukács or Braverman. Walter Benjamin was a significant influence on Adorno and Horkheimer for whom he offered a more nuanced view of technology. His seminal 1935–6 essay, 'The Work of Art in the Age of Mechanical Production', with the famous thesis of 'that which withers in the age of mechanical reproduction is the aura of the work of art', is one of the most important statements of the critique of technology (Benjamin 1973: 223). Modern culture, he argued, is no longer based on an original that has a presence in time and space. Culture, especially through the medium of photography, is reproduced mechanically today and therefore loses its aura and hence its authenticity. The essay introduced a material perspective on technology as integral to modern aesthetics such that it is now no longer possible to see culture as a realm separate from technology, which according to Benjamin 'detaches the reproduced object from the domain of tradition'. Modern culture is post-auratic, which leads to the 'shattering of tradition' that comes with a change in perspective.

Unlike the classic Marxist critique of technology, which looks back to a pre-technological time when human beings supposedly had an authentic relationship with nature, Benjamin – for whom modern technology was epitomized by the invention of the camera – had a different insight into the tremendous transformation that modern technology introduced: 'for the first time in world history, mechanical reproduction emancipates the work of art from its parasitical dependence on ritual' (p. 226). With modernity, art is now designed for its reproductability and thus no longer exists for its own sake, as with the doctrine *l'art pour l'art* or earlier when art was attached to ritual and tradition. 'Instead of being based on ritual, it begins to be based on another practice – politics'. With cinema and photography, and mechanical reproduction, the potential exists for a radical transformation of culture, which requires the loss of the autonomy of art and the end of the bourgeois institution of art, which confined art to be the representation of something outside itself. The invention of the camera fundamentally changed this very idea of an image. Modern culture is produced for the public rather than for a private audience. This process of de-aestheticization is all made possible by technology, but it is double-edged in that it can facilitate both regressive as well as critical responses. Benjamin notes how capitalism appropriates the cinema but also how it creates critical spaces which can be appropriated by regressive as well as progressive politics. Fascism, for instance, made use of technology to create an aestheticized politics. Although Benjamin's analysis of the transformation of modern culture by technology was Marxist in terms of seeing culture shifting as a response to changes in the material and technological forms of society, he nonetheless saw possibilities for progressive politics in the era of post-auratic art. In this respect, he was clearly influenced by Brecht, with whom he was closely associated, and was criticized by Adorno in that his analysis did not sufficiently take into account the capacity of capitalism to create a culture industry that would thrive on new possibilities for entertainment and even make possible a pseudo-authenticity.

Benjamin's essay brought new perspectives to bear on technology and culture that greatly influenced critical theory as it embraced ideology critique, which now encompasses the critique of popular culture. His essay revealed an ambivalence at the heart of modern technology between its redemptive and its regressive character. In contrast, Adorno and Horkheimer in the *Dialectic of Enlightenment* clearly tended towards a critical view of technology as an instrument of domination and a major source of reification. Although there is some evidence that Adorno saw potentially progressive applications in the use of radio as opposed to television, which was regarded by its regressive nature, his overall position was clearly to see technology as an expression of an instrumental rationality that has penetrated from work to politics and culture and has entered all spheres of life. In this respect, Marcuse's position was more nuanced.

76 Critical theory revisited

In an essay published in 1941, 'Some Implications of Modern Technology', Marcuse (1982) discusses the double face of technology. He notes how technology can promote authoritarianism in that the 'Third Reich is indeed a form of "technocracy"' and the basis of the war economy. More generally, according to Marcuse social relationships are now 'mediated by the machine process'. 'The machine that is adored is no longer dead matter but has become something like a human being'. In line with Lukács's thinking, technology is given social content: 'Expediency in terms of technological reason is at the same time, expediency in terms of profitable efficiency, and rationalization is, at the same, monopolistic standardization and concentration' (p. 144). Marcuse's somewhat functionalist argument that technology strips people of their individuality would have to be corrected today in light of a more complicated situation that has come about whereby technology also facilitates possibilities for individuation and even resistance. The general position is that modern technological rationality, as reflected in industrial capitalism, is based on convenience, expediency, efficiency, and standardization; it leads to adjustment and compliance, the concentration of power, atomization, and the loss of personal autonomy. Technological rationality erodes critical rationality. 'The standardization of thought under the sway of technological rationality also affects critical truth values' (p. 147). Nonetheless, Marcuse believed that a critical rationality can prevail but only if it resists technological rationality and creates a radically different society. He does concede that technology can be in the service of critical rationality and he opposes anti-technological politics, such as an 'anti-industrial revolution'. 'The philosophy of the simple life, the struggle against big cities and their culture frequently serves to teach men [sic] distrust of the potential instruments that would liberate them' (p. 160). That technology can be humanized and democratized seems to be his conclusion. Indeed, 'mechanization and standardization may one day help to shift the gravity from the necessities of material production to the area of free human realization' (p. 160).

Both Benjamin and even more so Marcuse believed in the utopian possibility of a science and technology that would deliver a better future. The solution was not a nostalgic rejection of technology for a premodern age but the political necessity to create a new society. Setting aside the question of what kind of politics would be required to bring such a society into being, the problem remained as to whether a new kind of technology is what is required and if this is at all possible. Marcuse's concept of technology was confined to examples that fall into the general category of industrial standardization, such as the Fordist assembly line. On the one side, such instrumental kinds of industrial technology could be used for human liberation, but they are also the very core of industrial capitalism and difficult to disentangle from capitalism. However, in a post-capitalist society, even such forms of technology could be employed to service human needs. It is indeed possible too that entirely new kinds of technology could be created.

In *One-Dimensional Man*, the critique of technology became part of a more general critique of ideology: 'Our society distinguishes itself by conquering the centrifugal social forces with Technology rather than Terror, on the dual basis of an overwhelming efficiency and an increasing standard of living' (1964: x). Technology is both a means of social control and an ideology in itself. It is an ideology in the sense that the pervasive spread of technological rationality makes impossible the conception of an alternative society or way of thinking. Marcuse insists that technology is not neutral: 'Technology as such cannot be isolated from the use to which it is put; the technological society is a system of domination which operates already in the concept and construction of techniques'. 'Technological rationality has become a political rationality' (*xvi*). A machine can be neutral in the sense that it can be used for different purposes, but it is always located in a social context and its uses are determined by that context (see also Marcuse [1958–9] 1989). While making material progress possible, including an improved quality of life, it produces from a new unfreedom because it prevents the individual from becoming autonomous. The result is what he famously termed in an inversion of Freud's concept of sublimation a 'repressive desublimation', whereby repression is achieved not through the suppression of the pleasure principle (i.e. its sublimation), but by making pleasure itself compatible with reality: 'The Pleasure Principle is Absorbed by the Reality Principle' (p. 72).

Chapter 1 begins with the statement: 'A comfortable, smooth, reasonable, democratic unfreedom prevails in advanced industrial civilization, a token of technical progress' (p. 1). This is possible because people come to recognize themselves only in their commodities, and social control is anchored in the new needs which capitalism produces. Marcuse's account of technology does not mention specific technologies – other than passing references to consumer goods such as the TV and the car – and it is difficult to see what might be an alternative since a world without technology or less technology would not necessarily be better. Cars may be objects of desire that are not really necessary and thus part of capitalist ideology, but washing machines reduce tedious manual work (mostly done by women) and are thus emancipatory, even if they do not lead directly to critical reason. It is also not evident that technology per se prevents the individual from becoming autonomous: some do, while others do not, but it more or less depends on the use made of them. Marcuse's target is perhaps not in the end technology but what he calls 'technological rationality', namely, the instrumental use of technology for domination. This includes the more general worship of technology as a religion or as the ultimate expressions of modernity (see also Noble 1999; Nye 1994). Reverence of technology cultivates an affirmative view of society and thus conceals an ideology of uncritical acceptance.

The general direction of critical theory on the question of technology has been either to evade it (as in recognition theory, which fails to see that recognition is mediated by technology) or to see it as embedded in instrumental rationality and part of what Marcuse called the general 'transformation of the natural world into a technical world'. Thus, in the critical social theory of Habermas with its concern with a counter-instrumental rationality, it was inevitable that technology would also be seen as an expression of instrumental rationality. As a consequence of the elision of technology, the insights of Benjamin were side-lined as politically naive.

78 Critical theory revisited

Unlike Benjamin, Habermas has been decidedly negative about technology. His first and major statement on technology is the 1968 essay, 'Technology and Science as "Ideology", which was dedicated to Marcuse on his 70th birthday (Habermas 1970). He disagrees with what he takes to be Marcuse's belief that a New Science would be possible and that it would make possible a New Technology. This is a utopian position that he finds in Marcuse, despite the latter's critical view of technology. In any case, whether or not Marcuse believed that a different kind of technology would be possible, a point on which he was very vague, it is evident that Habermas does not see such a possibility and that technology belongs to the domain of purposive-rational action. For Habermas, from a normative perspective technology is a matter of the technical control of nature and thus to a degree it is neutral so long as it is confined to that domain. He contrasts it to communicative forms of action, which in contrast are not primarily instrumental but social. Since the end of the nineteenth century, he argues, there has been a tendency towards the 'scientization of technology' whereby science and technology have become a leading productive force and an integral part of capitalism. Habermas does not see technology or science as able to deliver emancipation because they have become a substitute for politics in that increasingly in the planned economy politics is only a technocratic matter of finding technical solutions to societal problems. In this specific sense, technology is ideological in that political solutions are seen as technical ones. Moreover, technological rationality invades the social world, distorting communicative rationality. This position fails to see that technology might be a medium that enables communicative action.

An intimation of his later critique of biogenetics is the claim: 'Technocratic consciousness reflects not the sundering of an ethical situation but the repression of "ethics" as such as a category of life' (1970: 112). Habermas reached a contradictory position early in his writings that saw technology as outside the domain of communication, and as such it is non-social, but at the same time it is a possible source of domination when it becomes a substitute for politics. As Feenberg (1996) has shown, Habermas is committed to a view of technology as essentially neutral in that it is bound up with what Habermas called a cognitive interest in technical control, a theory developed in *Knowledge and Human Interests* in 1968 (Habermas 1992).[5] The thesis of the colonization of the life-world does not discuss specifically technology as a medium of colonization. However, there is also the view that science and technology have become ideologies of late capitalism, which would suggest that it is therefore inseparable from capitalism and thus a form of instrumentalization. The basic assumption that pervades his work is that technology is non-social is deeply problematical as is the contrary view that technology is necessarily a form of domination. The claim made in *Knowledge and Human Interests* that knowledge of nature is based on prediction is also deeply problematical in its assumption that predictive-based knowledge is value free if not applied to the social world. Habermas's objection was against the application of the methods of the natural sciences to the human and social sciences. While this generated important insights in the shaping of post-positivistic social science, it did not question the rationality of the

Critical theory and social transformation **79**

natural sciences. The problem, in essence, is that Habermas, as with Lukács, Adorno, and Horkheimer, and, albeit to a lesser extent, Marcuse, sees technology in terms of the model of machinery or a non-social instrument.

In *The Future of Human Nature*, his view persists that new forms of technology such as genetic engineering are at odds with the very category of the human being in that any attempt to alter the genetic constitution of the human being ultimately undermines personal autonomy (Habermas 2003 [2001]). Genetic engineering, as preventive clinical action, may enable in some areas the enhancement of personal autonomy, but as a form of 'technical fabrication', it can lead to more general problems that cannot easily be anticipated. His main argument, which appears to be directed at 'liberal eugenics' and the sinister spectre of 'human breeding', is that the selection of an embryo by means of genetic assessment and testing, as well as its genetic modification of the human genome, entails a new kind of instrumental domination over human beings that denies their autonomy since it violates human nature. New reproductive technologies can increase individual autonomy, but they also play into the hands of a neoliberal biotechnology (in which case they cannot be neutral). This reasoning and its questionable assumptions about human nature, which we cannot assess here, is in line with the general trend in critical theory towards a view of technology as a form of reification and inherently instrumentalizing. While the question remains as to whether technology is social or neutral, Habermas clearly sees it is as an instrument of domination that should be confined to the realm of technical mastery. He does concede that the problem is not genetic engineering 'but the mode and scope of its use' (2003: 43). Notwithstanding this concession, it is evident that he sees such kinds of technology as overall negative due to their tendency towards 'an instrumentalization of human nature'. While it is difficult to disagree with his call for the regulation of genetic engineering and the need for a new human 'ethical understanding', his analysis leaves open the question of whether the very fabric of social life is in fact now technologized in ways that are not reducible to the notion of an all-pervasive technical rationality. It is difficult to see why, for example, gene therapy is predominantly an instrument of domination or why human nature cannot be changed for the better. In sum, it seems unsustainable to see technology as neutral or residing within a non-social realm. This is above all the case when it comes to digital technology. The basic insight was in any case contained in Benjamin's work, which already in the 1930s recognized the mediatized nature of human experience in modernity. Technology today must be seen as wider than something that can be understood in terms of the model of the machine, an instrument to achieve a purpose. In many ways, technology is everywhere and is not something other than social relations.

The critical theory of the Frankfurt School nonetheless offers important insights into technology. Whatever problems might be raised by their work on the state of technology when they wrote are present to an even greater degree when it comes to new kinds of technology today. Habermas's intervention on genetic engineering is without doubt one of the more sophisticated discussions of technology on critical theory, but it, too, as discussed, ultimately fails to understand the nature

80 Critical theory revisited

of technology. The general view of technology in critical theory is that it is an instrument of domination, and an all-pervasive technical rationality has pervaded modern society which impedes or blocks critical reason through the mechanism of reification. The kind of technology that the critical theorists were addressing were the products of industrial capitalism. Now, while it was once at least theoretically possible to see industrialization developing in terms of a model of society in which social relations are primarily determined by social interaction or where there was a limited degree of technological mediation, this is clearly not possible today. Technology today has become part of the fabric of social life such that it cannot be seen as residing in a separate domain or as an instrument employed by autonomous social or political actors. Technology, in short, is everywhere. The new technologies of the digital age – various forms of screens and software – are not hard, static, and given but are soft, fluid, mobile, and personalized. They are interwoven into the structures of the social world in ways that cannot be seen in terms of a colonization of the life-world by external systemic forces. Neither can they be so easily subsumed under the category of standardization and nor are they necessarily designed for consumption. Digital uses of Facebook, for example, are not only consumers – even in the case of paid-for platforms as in dating sites – but are also part of the productive system. Digital technology, while being in itself a reality, is also manifest as discourses about reality. The notion of discourse, rather than ideology, highlights the productive role of technology in the construction of reality in the sense of being a body of knowledge within social reality, everyday life, social institutions, and so on (see Fischer 2010: 235). In short, the model of instrumental rationality inherited from Weber and Lukács is not adequate to account for technology. The underlying problem in the critical theory tradition was the tendency to reduce technology to *technik*, or 'technique', as it has been generally rendered. This led to a predominately instrumental conception of technology.[6]

Berry (2014) discusses the shift from the culture industry to the computational industries with a view to applying critical theory to the digital age in order to be able to understand its democratizing and totalizing powers. On one level, digital technologies can be seen as calculative rationalities, but it is clear that they have gone beyond purely instrumental uses for production and the storage of information. Digital technologies can be empowering but they are also instruments of reification and the basis of new kinds of neoliberal governmentality. This is not unlike the tremendous transformation brought about by the invention of printing and the arrival of print capitalism, which today is undergoing yet another transformation into what Seymour sees as the dystopian world of platform capitalism (Seymour 2019).

When confronted with the relatively new phenomenon of algorithmic governmentality, the need for a critical perspective is all important, but it will need to draw on insights beyond the Frankfurt School's general recourse to technical rationality. Incorporating a Foucauldian perspective, it can be said that the age of big data makes possible modes of governmentality that are not so much based on the individual as on relations; according to Rouvroy and Berns (2013), what has now come about is a 'governance of relations'. Algorithmic governance is a shift beyond traditional statistical governance (which was based on averages). It involves the collection and automated storage of unfiltered mass data, which is then 'mined' or processed to identify correlations between them with a view to creating probabilistic statistical knowledge by means of profiles to anticipate individual behaviour. However, algorithmic governmentality does not produce something like a subject; it is not aimed at identifying a person: 'it circumvents and avoids reflexive human subjects, feeding on infra-individual data which are meaningless on their own, to build supra-individual models of behaviours or profiles without ever involving the individual and without ever asking them to themselves describe what they are or what they could become' (Rouvroy and Berns 2013: 10). Thus, domination is not aimed at the individual and their sense of needs, as in Marcuse's notion of the 'totally administered society'; domination occurs through multiple profiles that have been created by digital traces in everyday activity. Needs and desires are created rather than simply met. Algorithmic governance does not signal the end of the individual but also does not create new kinds of autonomous individuation. It can be seen as an accentuated technical rationality but one that requires hyper-subjectification in that while often passing over the heads of individuals in terms of intentionality, subjects the individual to a plethora of modes of options. It may also portend the end of the very category of the future, reduced to an algorithmic projection. James Bridle (2018) thus sees contemporary society lost in the vast amount of information available. What he calls 'computational thinking' – which can be compared to Adorno's notion of identity thinking – is the belief that any problem can be solved by the application of computation. This amounts to a new standardizing ideology that reduces critical thinking to the search for an app (see also, Seymour 2019).

The growth of the digital economy, social media, and electronic communication of all kinds can be seen as a process of total commodification but one that can be reversed (Lanier 2013). From a critical theory perspective, the transformation of society by technology is not to be accounted for by technological determinism. We must not forget that the digital age is predominately a product of capitalism. While the origins of the internet are not specifically in capitalism, it developed within the structures of capitalism. Domination and capitalism coalesce in the phenomenon of surveillance capitalism. Facebook is now more powerful than many nation states, and even the most powerful ones cannot control it. According to Shoshana Zuboff, the digital economy has brought into being an ominous new kind of capitalism based on surveillance: 'Surveillance capitalism unilaterally claims human experience as free raw material for translation into behavioural data'. The accumulation of big data produces, what she calls, a 'behavioral surplus' which is used not only to predict human behaviour but also to modify it (Zuboff 2019: 8). The product is not the user, as is often said, but rather the user provides the input in the form of behavioural data which is then used to predict the behaviour of the user. Her argument takes up one of the main themes in the critical theory of the Frankfurt School. Surveillance capitalism gives rise to a new kind of power, which she terms 'instrumentarianism'. It works its way through a complex system of 'smart'

82 Critical theory revisited

networked devices. This was all spear-headed by Google which perfected surveillance capitalism in much the same way as General Motors invented and perfected managerial capitalism. This model spread to Facebook and later to Microsoft and more recently to Amazon. Surveillance capitalism accumulated huge quantities of data about us but in ways that can be known to us. By doing so they have created behavioural future markets. Zuboff's work on this new kind of capitalism, which she says is unpreceded, is that while employing many technologies, such as algorithms, it is not simply a case of technological determinism; it is, in short, a capitalistic enterprise and thus driven by the imperative for capitalism accumulation. As Zuboff points out, during the early period of Google, created in 1998, behavioural data was largely in the service of the user and led to improved services in terms of speed, accuracy, and relevance of data that was freely at the disposal of the user (p. 69). This was all quickly to change within a few years when Google discovered behavioural surplus, which meant that it ceased to mine data to improve services but instead sought to predict behaviour by matching ads to the profiles of users that were constructed from traces of online behaviour. This move, which was driven by the simple reality that advertising feeds on data, marks a turning point in the history of capitalism in that surveillance becomes the path to profit. Instead of serving the needs of people, as an older capitalism did, it sells predictions of people's behaviour.

A recent work by James Bridle on how technology is shaping a new post-truth age recalls the chilling argument of the *Dialectic of Enlightenment*. Despite increased information, there is more darkness than enlightenment in our digital age, which has produced post-truth, alternative facts, and fake news. Untruth travels faster than truth. In the *New Dark Age,* Bridle reveals the political nature of technology. 'A close reading of computer history reveals an ever-increasing opacity allied to a concentration of power, and the retreat of that power into ever more narrow domains of experience' (Bridle 2018: 34). Finance capitalism changes in response to new technologies, for example, in the creation of cables that can process information faster. New technologies impact negatively on the lives of Amazon workers and Uber drivers in the creation of ever-more alienating environments (pp. 113–115). Technological complexity, especially those reliant on algorithms, presents risks and increases the propensity for crises with flash crashes (p. 122). Despite ever-increasing data (and FOI Acts) there is less and less accountability and transparency. 'Technology extends power and understanding; but when applied unevenly it also concentrates power and understanding' (p. 120). In an argument that is very similar to the Frankfurt School's critique of technology, Bridle discusses the impact of computational logics on consciousness and cognition as a form of reification. Increasingly people think in Boolean, adopt the language and logics of computers, and defer to technology over their own analysis ('automation bias') (p. 40). More worryingly still, because technology is forever an incomplete representation of the present, the more we adopt computational ways of thinking (target driven, quantitative, Boolean, or modelled) we lose parts of our capacity to comprehend reality. As Bridle writes, 'reality itself takes on the appearance of a computer; and our modes of thought follow suit' (p. 43). Facebook initially only allowed users to identify as 'liberal' or 'conservative' in their dropdown choice of 'political affiliation' and so on. Other examples would include predictive policing and the use of historical data for training. The result is that calculations of behaviour take on the force of natural law.

In view of these developments – whether termed algorithmic governmentality or surveillance capitalism – it is evident that some of the perspectives in critical theory on technology are still relevant. A distinctive feature of the critical theory approach to technology is to oppose the dominant view of technology as neutral and as deterministic. Instead, it must be seen as shaped by society and specifically by capitalism (while admitting of the possibility that it can be shaped by other modes of social and economic organization). While the nature of digital technologies today is vastly different to anything the critical theorists had in mind when they referred to technology, the new technologies can be seen as part of the wider edifice of capitalism. Technology is not neutral and neither is it a self-determining power but is engrained in capitalism. All the major organizations of digital social media are capitalistic businesses whose driving force is the profit imperative. As Marcuse argued of a different era of capitalism, technology embodies ideology in that the technological products bear the imprint of social arrangements and service the system that produces them. Despite the apparent power they wield in our lives, they are not total systems of control and can be controlled and resisted. Moreover, technological systems, while not neutral in that they are products created under certain conditions, are often not in themselves inherently good or bad. It is the use that is made of them that is good or bad. Clearly, surveillance capitalism is capable of considerable manipulation of user behaviour. This is not only covert and often illegal practices but extends to voter behaviour as in the practice of governments and political parties buying Facebook ads.[7] However, it must also be recognized that despite the propensity for domination and the reification of everyday life, digital technology has diverse applications and can also facilitate a critical rationality as much as enable an all-pervasive technical rationality.

The challenge of surveillance capitalism is that it is not easily brought under sway of the normative order of society, which evolved to deal with quite different forms of social and economic organizations. Much of the debate today is about bringing mega-digital giants such as Facebook under the legal and democratic control of the constitutional state through, for example, legislation of privacy, criminality, and political use of data. In view of the fact that the current situation is not much more than a decade old, it is difficult to foresee the future other than to suggest that it is likely to be linked to the wider fate of capitalism (which will be discussed in the next chapter).

Notes

1 In a letter written on 29.6.1940 Horkheimer wrote: 'In view of everything that is engulfing Europe and perhaps the whole world our present work is of course essentially destined to being passed on through the night that is approaching: a kind of message in a bottle' (cited in Wheatland 2009: 347).

84 Critical theory revisited

2 For critical perspectives on work, see Deranty (2008), Dejours et al (2018), Doogan (2009), Sennett (1999, 2006), Standing (2011).
3 This section and the next draw from my article, 'The Future of Capitalism: Trends, Scenarios and Prospects for the Future' *Journal of Classical Sociology* 2019, 19 (1): 10–26.
4 For an account of theories of modernity, see Wagner (2012).
5 See other work by Feenberg on technology, critical theory, and modernity Feenberg (1991, 1995).
6 See Schatzberg (2018) for a critical reconstruction of technology.
7 See Chun (2006), Fuchs (2014, 2018), Frischmann and Selinger (2018).

References

Arnason, J. 1991. Modernity as a Project and a Field of Tension. In: Honneth, J. and Joas, H. (eds.) *Communicative Action*. Cambridge: Polity Press.
Arnason, J. 1993. *The Future that Failed: Origins and Destinies of the Soviet Model*. London: Routledge.
Arnason, J. 2003. *Civilizations in Dispute Historical Questions and Theoretical Traditions*. Leiden: Brill.
Arnason, J. 2015. Theorizing Capitalism: Classical Foundations and Contemporary Foundations. *European Journal of Social Theory*, 18 (4): 351–67.
Aron, R. 1967 [1963]. *Eighteen Lectures on Industrial Society*. London: Weidenfeld and Nicholson.
Benjamin, W. 1973. The Work of Art in the Age of Mechanical Reproduction. In: *Illuminations*. London: Fontana.
Berry, D. 2014. *Critical Theory and the Digital*. London: Bloomsbury.
Boltanski, L. and Chiapello, E. 2006 [1999]. *The New Spirit of Capitalism*. London: Verso.
Bowles, S. and Gintis, H. 1986. *Democracy and Capitalism: Property, Community, and the Contradictions of Modern Social Thought*. London: Routledge & Kegan Paul.
Braverman, H. 1974. *Labour and Monopoly Capital*. New York: Monthly Review.
Bridle, J. 2018. *The New Dark Age: Technology and the End of the Future*. London: Verso.
Castoriadis, C. 1987 [1975]. *The Imaginary Institution of Society*. Cambridge: Polity Press.
Chun, W. 2006. *Control & Freedom: Power & Paranoia in the Age of Fiber Optics*. London: MIT Press.
Dahrendorf, R. 1957. *Class and Conflict in Industrial Society*. Stanford: Stanford University Press.
Dejours, C., Deranty, J-P., Renault, E. and Smith, N. 2018. *The Return of Work in Critical Theory*. New York: Columbia University Press.
Deranty, J-P. 2008. Work and the Precarisation of Existence. *European Journal of Social Theory*, 11 (4): 443–63.
Deutschmann, C. 2011. Limits to Financialization: Sociological Analyses of the Financial Crisis. *European Journal of Sociology*, 52 (3): 347–98.
Doogan, K. 2009. *New Capitalism? The Transformation of Work*. Cambridge: Polity Press.
Ellul, J. 1964 [1954]. *The Technological Society*. New York: Vintage Books.
Feenberg, A. 1991. *Critical Theory of Technology*. Oxford: Oxford University Press.
Feenberg, A. 1995. *Alternative Modernity: The Technical Turn in Philosophy and Social Theory*. Berkeley: University of California Press.
Feenberg, A. 1996. Marcuse or Habermas? Two Critiques of Technology. *Inquiry*, 39 (1): 45–70.
Feenberg, A. 2011. Rethinking Reification. In: Bews, T. and Hall, T. (eds.) *Georg Lukacs: The Fundamental Dissonance of Existence*. New York: Continuum.

Fischer, E. 2010. Contemporary Technology Discourse and the Legitimation of Capitalism. *European Journal of Social Theory*, 13 (2): 229–52.

Fraser, N. and Jaeggi, J. 2018. *Capitalism: A Conversation*. Cambridge: Polity Press.

Frischmann, B. and Selinger, E. 2018. *Re-Engineering Humanity*. Cambridge: Cambridge University Press.

Fuchs, C. 2014. *Digital Capital and Karl Marx*. London: Routledge.

Fuchs, C. 2018. *Digital Demagogue: Authoritarian Capitalism in the Age of Trump & Twitter*. London: Pluto Press.

Habermas, J. 1970 [1968]. Science and Technology as 'Ideology'. In: *Towards a Rational Society*. London: Heinemann.

Habermas, J. 1992 [1968]. *Knowledge and Human Interests*. London: Heinemann.

Habermas, J. 1975 [1973]. *Legitimation Crisis*. Boston: Beacon Press.

Habermas, J. 1979 [1976]. *Communication and the Evolution of Society*. London: Heinemann.

Habermas, J. 1984/1987 [1981]. *The Theory of Communicative Action*. Vols. 1. London: Polity Press.

Habermas, J. 1987 [1985]. *The Philosophical Discourse of Modernity*. Cambridge: Polity Press.

Habermas, J. 1996 [1992]. *Between Facts and Norms: Contributions to a Discourse Theory of Law and Democracy*. Cambridge: Polity Press.

Habermas, J. 1998 [1996]. *The Inclusion of the Other: Studies in Political Theory*. Cambridge, MA: MIT Press.

Habermas, J. 2003. *The Future of Human Nature*. Cambridge: Polity Press.

Harvey, D. 2010. *The Enigma of Capital and the Crises of Capitalism*. Oxford: Oxford University Press.

Haskel, J. and Westlake, S. 1997. *Capital Without Capitalism: The Rise of the Intangible Economy*. Princeton: Princeton University Press.

Heidegger, M. 1977 [1954]. *The Question Concerning Technology*. New York: Harper & Row.

Honneth, A. 2008. *Reification: A New Look at an Old Idea*. Oxford: Oxford University Press.

Horn, E. 2016. *The Future as Catastrophe: Imagining Disaster in the Modern Age*. New York: Columbia University Press.

Jaeggi, R. 2018. *Critique of Forms of Life*. Cambridge, MA: Harvard University Press.

Kocha, J. 2016. *Capitalism: A Short History*. Princeton, NJ: Princeton University Press.

Konings, M. 2015. *The Emotional Logic of Capitalism*. Stanford: Stanford University Press.

Lanier, J. 2013. *Who Owns the Future?* London: Allen Lane.

Lukács, G. 1972 [1923]. *History and Class Consciousness*. Cambridge, MA: MIT Press.

McNay, L. 2007. *Against Recognition*. Cambridge: Polity Press.

Marcuse, H. 1964. *One Dimensional Man*. London: Routledge & Kegan Paul.

Marcuse, H. 1982 [1941]. Some Implications of Modern Technology. In: Arato, A. and Gebhardt, E. (eds.) *The Essential Frankfurt School Reader*. New York: Continuum.

Marcuse, H. 1989. From Ontology to Technology: Fundamental Tendencies of Industrial Society. In: Bronner, S. E. and Kellner, D. (eds.) *Critical Theory and Society*. London: Routledge.

Mumford, L. 1934. *Technics and Civilization*. New York: Harcourt, Brace & Company.

Noble, D. 1999. *The Religion of Humanity: The Divinity of Man the Spirit of Invention*. London: Penguin Books.

Nye, D. 1994. *American Technological Sublime*. Cambridge, MA: MIT Press.

Polanyi, K. 2001 [1944]. *The Great Transformation*. Boston: Beacon Press.

Rouvroy, A. and Berns, T. 2013. Algorithmic Governmentality and Prospects of Emancipation: Disparateness as a Precondition for Individuation Through Relationships? *Reseaux*, 177: 163–96.

Schatzberg, E. 2018. *Technology: Critical History of a Concept*. Chicago: Chicago University Press.

86 Critical theory revisited

Seymour, R. 2019. *The Twittering Machine*. London: Indigo Press.

Sennett, R. 1999. *The Corrosion of Character: The Personal Consequences of Work*. New York: Norton.

Sennett, R. 2006. *The Culture of the New Capitalism*. London: Routledge.

Standing, G. 2011. *The Precariat: The New Dangerous Class*. London: Bloomsbury.

Touraine, A. 1995. *Critique of Modernity*. Cambridge: Polity Press.

Touraine, A. 2014. *Beyond NeoLiberalism*. Cambridge: Polity Press.

Wagner, P. 2012. *Modernity: Understanding the Present*. Cambridge: Polity Press.

Wallerstein, I. 2011. *Historical Capitalism*. London: Verso.

Weber, M. 1978 [1920]. *The Protestant Ethic and the Spirit of Capitalism*. London: Allen & Unwin.

Wheatland, T. 2009. *The Frankfurt School in Exile*. Minneapolis: Minnesota University Press.

Williams, R. 1976. Capitalism. In: *Keywords: A Vocabulary of Culture and Society*. London: Fontana.

Zuboff, S. 2019. *The Age of Surveillance Capitalism*. London: Profile Books.

PART 2

Capitalism, cosmopolitanism, the Anthropocene

4

QUESTIONING *HOMO ECONOMICUS*

Have we all become neoliberals?

It has become an axiom of contemporary social and political science that we live in neoliberal times and that the state and capitalism itself have become neoliberal. We have all become neoliberal subjects, if not Hayekian at least Foucauldian, it would seem. But is this correct? Have disembedded markets usurped society and the state? Has greed become the new God?[1]

Neoliberalism has undoubtedly been one of the most consequential of ideologies in the past four decades or so. It has fundamentally changed the relationship between state and economy. However, there is widespread confusion as to what it actually is today and how extensive its influence has been. There is a pronounced tendency to see neoliberalism as an account of the wider condition of society and of the individual in an era of globalization. In many ways, our neoliberal world bears testimony to the early Frankfurt School's characterization of the victory of capitalism over society and the self. However, neoliberalism is not a topic that figures into the critical theory accounts of capitalism and is also strangely absent from Habermas's social theory. In the classic works of the critical theorists, the model of capitalism presupposed western industrial capitalism in the era of monopoly capitalism and big government. The current situation is different with the predominance of finance capitalism, global markets, and several decades of neoliberalism.

In the writings of many theorists, especially those adopting a critical approach, neoliberalism is very much the defining spirit of the age (see, for instance, Brown 2019; Greenhouse 2010; Saad-Filho and Johnson 2005). In the work of Nancy Fraser (2013) and Jodi Dean (2009) neoliberalism is another word to describe contemporary capitalism. Crouch (2011), in an assessment of the fate of neoliberalism, sees it as the dominance of the corporation rather than any longer a state policy. It has been characterized as the basis of a 'new social order' (Duménil and Lévy 2005) and feeding off a permanent 'state of exception' (Ong 2006). For Fraser the goals of feminism have contributed to the neoliberal project of the rule of the market. David

90 Capitalism, cosmopolitanism, Anthropocene

Harvey (1991) in an influential work described postmodern thought as much the same as neoliberalism, and more recently (2005) he characterizes neoliberalism as the condition of global capitalist accumulation in which the figure of the 'disposal worker' emerges as its prototype. Others, for instance Wolfgang Streeck (2014), see the European Union as entering a new neoliberal phase in which the social model has been overshadowed by the Lisbon agenda of the competitive economy undermining the European social model. In a polemical piece, Pierre Bourdieu (1998) spoke of the 'essence of neoliberalism' as a methodical destruction of collectives', a project that aims 'to create the conditions under which the "theory" can be realised'. The theory in question was the utopia of a pure and perfect market, which requires severing the economy from society and the state.

Contemporary left scholarship often presents the social world as one of totalized neoliberalism. In this chapter, I wish to dispute some of these claims that equate neoliberalism with contemporary capitalism in general or with the current societal condition and to offer a more differentiated analysis of neoliberalism, which I do not think should be generalized to an extent that it loses any specificity. My aim is not simply to define neoliberalism, though I think agreement on the main elements is needed, but to identify counter-trends to capitalism and to provide critical sociology with more than a critique of neoliberalism that leaves very little scope for conceiving of alternatives to an all-dominant system. Defining neoliberalism as the rule of the market is as helpful as defining democracy as the rule of the people.

While I do not deny the obviously pervasive and reifying influence of neoliberalism, I wish to show that it is a false characterization of many dimensions of the social world to see only the hand of neoliberalization at work. It is also to accept neoliberalism's own account of the world. My argument is that too much is included within the concept of neoliberalism for it to be a useful concept.[2] However, as with the term capitalism, I am not suggesting the term should be jettisoned, as it offers a critical perspective on contemporary capitalism. What is needed is a clearer account of some of the defining elements of neoliberalism and its various phases and forms in order to assess what aspects of state and society are today neoliberal and which are more accurately seen as the result of other influences.

In this chapter, I identify five different conceptions of neoliberalism and suggest that while there is neither a common trajectory nor a common intellectual nor ideological source to all five, there is nonetheless one common thread. If neoliberalism is less extensive than it is held to be in critical social science, it raises the question of how capitalism and the market should be understood today. My argument is that much of what can be seen in terms of neoliberalization can also be seen as the result of other trends, some of which have morphed into new variants of neoliberalism. It is also a question of what theoretical perspective is taken. Many accounts of neoliberalism are influenced by a Marxist analysis that sees neoliberalism as the final victory of capital over labour. With the ascendancy of finance capitalism, this argument is more difficult to sustain in the classic Marxist formulation but has been adapted in interesting ways to the circumstances created by the 'financialization of society' by, *inter alia*, Lazzarato (2012, 2015, 2017; Vogl 2017).

From an institutionalist perspective, neoliberalization can be seen as less pervasive with diverse institutional responses to the market (see for example Campbell and Pedersen 2001). Much of recent theorizing, as reflected in the writing of Jodi Dean (2009) and Wendy Brown (2015, 2019), for example, has been influenced by Foucault's work on subject formation in order to account for the formation of a neoliberal subjectivity that encompasses a wider spectrum than market forces.

From a critical theory perspective, as developed in the previous chapters, a key issue in contrast is the identification of transformational capacities, critical junctures, and moments of crisis in which signs of alternatives become visible. However, there can be no doubt that when it comes to neoliberalism, the analytical lens of critical theory must be widened in light of Foucault's path-breaking writings on neoliberalism in the 1978–9 lectures (Foucault 2008). Nicholas Gane (2012) persuasively shows how for Foucault neoliberalism has its own governmental logic and should not be identified exclusively with the free market as such. Foucault's key insight was that neoliberalism is not simply about de-regulation, privatization or governing through 'freedom', but surveillance and the extension of the market into all aspects of social and cultural life as well as the sphere of the state. According to Gane, this aspect of neoliberalism has often been missed by commentators more concerned with the disempowerment of politics and the dismantling of the welfare state. The implication of a Foucauldian perspective is indeed that neoliberalism has become the condition of our time, a condition that has been enhanced by the growing importance of finance capitalism and the financialization of the economy.[3] If this is the case, then it would seem we have all become neoliberals. However, I argue form a late critical theory perspective that society – and hence the political subject – is never entirely colonized by capitalism. My questions, then, are the following: what exactly is neoliberalism? To what extent is contemporary society neoliberal in terms of the relationship between market, society, and state? How extensive is *homo economicus*?

What is neoliberalism? Five conceptions

It is often said that neoliberalism, like liberalism itself, is not one thing but many things. This is true of most ideologies, such as republicanism, socialism, nationalism, and Marxism, which are notoriously difficult to pin down. This, however, does not mean that they cannot be defined. One solution is to define the concept as it is actually used. This approach works for many concepts but can be limiting when the concept is used pejoratively as an attribution and thus suggests a critical attitude. This indeed was how Mannheim in *Ideology and Utopia* defined the notion of ideology, as the ideas of one's opponents and thus somehow the wrong ideas (Mannheim 1960 [1936]). In many ways, neoliberalism has become such a negative term, as in the slogan, Thatcherism or Reaganomics. Few today would style themselves neoliberals, but this does not mean that neoliberalism is dead (see Davies 2017). Since the 2008–10 banking crisis, there has been a massive onslaught on unregulated markets in finance and widespread recognition that unregulated markets are destructive

92 Capitalism, cosmopolitanism, Anthropocene

of markets themselves. It is, of course, the case that while there have been moves against unregulated markets, neoliberalism lives on and possibly has been saved by such measures (see Mirowski 2013). If this is the case, then it must have changed in the course of such renditions. However, I argue it has not undergone such radical transformation that it has no core or defining rationale.

A related problem is that other terms may be used with much the same meaning, such as in the US the term neo-conservatism carries much the same meaning as the more widely used term neoliberal. However, neo-conservatism is different in that it is a wider right-wing ideology that encompasses a conservative morality. Moreover, neither term is entirely pejorative, though positive meanings are probably less common today than they were in the 1990s when the ideological appeal of neoliberalism waned, even if in practice it continued, as Crouch (2011) has argued in new forms. The problem of measuring the impact of neoliberalism is that many of its core tenets underwent a transmutation into other forms, such as 'the Third Way' and lost their specificity. Yet, it has substantial and demonstrable elements which have had clear influences in spheres of life that lie outside the primary concerns of neoliberal doctrine. However, these influences may be more limited than often thought, and a stronger argument can be made that some of the most prevalent influences today are counter-neoliberal. Campbell and Pedersen (2001) have argued that there is no convergence towards a common neoliberal paradigm and that neoliberalism has not undermined the state's capacity to regulate markets. Indeed, as Foucault showed, neoliberalism required the state to implement its project (see also Brown 2019). More generally, the implications of institutionalist analysis, for instance, the varieties of the capitalism approach (Hall and Soskice 2001) or the neo-institutionalism of Powell and DiMaggio (1991), imply greater diversity in state, market, and society relations than suggested by Marxist prognoses of a universal trend towards the victory of the market over state and society (see the next chapter).

In the following, I outline five ways of defining neoliberalism and argue that the latter three are only superficially neoliberal since they entail entanglements with other societal processes. Yet, underpinning all varieties of neoliberalism is the restructuring of state and society to serve the interests of capitalism. Consequently, the classic understanding of neoliberalism as the retreat of the state must now be revised to account for the transformation of the state to serve the interests of capitalist accumulation. The state does not back off but becomes more and more involved in capitalism. My argument is that to the extent to which neoliberalism since the mid-1990s morphed into other social and political forms, it also becomes entangled in political subjectivities of resistance as well as in social practices that are contrary to the fundamental logic of neoliberalism.

Hayekian neoliberalism as a political philosophy

The economic and political philosophy of Friedrich von Hayek provides the basic philosophical ideas of the doctrine that became known as neoliberalism. His work and others, most notably Ludwig von Mies, established the view that economic liberty underpins political liberty and that neither can be achieved by central planning. Hayek's arguments were put forward as a critique of the centrally planned economy in an era that witnessed the decline of lassez-faire capitalism and the rise of monopoly capitalism along with totalitarianism. While in many ways he was an adherent of classical liberalism, he departed from classical liberalism and classical economic theory in one important respect: the market works in ways that make it impossible to be planned. This is because our knowledge of the market is always incomplete. Classical liberalism in contrast held to a view that the state is important in achieving liberty. Hayek, who did not deny the importance of the state, indeed Maynard Keynes agreed much with him, saw the market not as a perfect system but as a highly complex system that is not amenable to planning since the price system can make the necessary adjustments to produce an optimal equilibrium between supply and demand. He set up a basic opposition between competition and planning, which in effect was a conflict between economics and politics. Neoliberalism seeks to break the subservience of the former from the latter.

The Road to Serfdom was published in 1944 in an era that had embraced the spirit of planning, as in the New Deal in the US, the expansion of the welfare state in the UK and in most European countries, the rise of European integration, and so on. Hayekian liberalism was against the current of the age until the 1970s (Hayek 1944). By this time, it had consolidated as a powerful intellectual movement. The crisis of capitalism of the 1970s opened up an opportunity for it to enter the mainstream of economic and political thinking within the neoconservative right. The Hayekian notion of neoliberalism, a term that goes back to the first meeting of the Mont Pèlerin Society in 1938, can be summed up as the view that the competitive spirit and freedom are linked and a contrast to monopolies and to the centrally planned economy, which is anathema to freedom.

The notion that the planned economy would necessarily require dictatorial rule is undoubtedly a problematical claim and one that is not entirely explained by the context of the day. However, it should be noted that when Hayek defended competitive individualism rather than collectivism as the basis of society, he was not arguing for the extension of the market – or some notion of market fundamentalism – to everything, but rather the reverse, namely, that non-market forces should not intrude into the domain of the market (see Shearmur 1996). In this sense, his neoliberalism reflected the liberal conception of negative as opposed to positive freedom. This, after all, was an era when the market was on the defensive. To defend the market in 1944 was different from doing so in the present day, when the market has asserted itself in ways unimaginable in that era. However, by the time of his death in 1992, he did not fundamentally disagree with the aggressive neoliberalism of that era. In any case, neoliberalism as a political project promotes a stronger and essentially a different position than negative liberty in that it opposes the reliance of economic goals on moral and political foundations. Hayek's political philosophy led the way to a technocratic conception of politics as devoid of normative concerns.

94 Capitalism, cosmopolitanism, Anthropocene

Thatcherism and neoliberalism as economic policy

The second conception of neoliberalism can be characterized in a number of ways and which are not all directly attributable to the political philosophy of F. A. Hayek. Hayek was not very clear on the policy implications of his thought, which remained at a high level of theoretical abstraction. This was left to others to develop, and there was no shortage of willing politicians and academics. The transmission of his work to a new generation of right-wing politicians – most prominently Pinochet in Chile (who is often conveniently forgotten as the pioneer of neoliberalism), Reagan and Thatcher – in the 1970s by Chicago based economists such as Milton Friedman, marks the rise of neoliberalism as the Washington Consensus as a more assertive positive conception of market freedom (and in which political freedom is more or less jettisoned). I will not elaborate on the well-known story of the diffusion of neoliberal political philosophy into economic theory and into policy making in the 1970s and 1980s. Accounts of this vary from Harvey's (2005) critical analysis to Naomi Klein's chilling *Shock Doctrine* (Klein 2008) to recent histories of the neoliberal movement by Seidman Jones (2012), Peck (2010) and Mirowski and Plehwe (2009).[4]

The most important and defining elements of neoliberalism, once it gained ascendancy, can be summed up as involving ways of implementing market liberalization through: (1) the de-regulation of the economy; (2) the privatization of those parts of the economy that had been owned and managed by the state; 3) the liberalization of trade through global markets; 4) policies aimed at lower general taxation; 5) the emphasis on monetarism as opposed to fiscal policy in order to combat inflation; and 6) anti-labour politics in an era when western societies were still predominantly industrial. These policies, of which the first three are the bedrock of neoliberalism, were put into practice systematically by Margaret Thatcher and Ronald Reagan during the 1980s and in Latin American countries. This was an era when there was systemic restructuring of the state and the declared end of the so-called postWW2 consensus around the pursuit of full employment as a goal of state policy, the rejection of the 'Great Society' vision of Lyndon Johnson in the 1960s, as well as the abandonment of national wage bargaining and the Keynesian welfare state. In this sense, then, neoliberalism is an economic policy rather than a condition or type of capitalism. As mentioned, it was initially largely negatively defined in terms of the removal of market barriers as opposed to positive measures. However, this was to change when it embraced more assertive positive measures in creating a new kind of society subservient to the interests of capitalism. There is much to show that when the state implemented radical market reforms, the measures went far beyond anything that can be described in terms of negative action: the example of Chile under Pinochet, and the Iraq war – when it became entangled with the neo-conservative security agenda – are two pertinent examples of where neoliberalism was imposed through military intervention by the state in its drive to open up new markets, thus contradicting the basic presuppositions of neoliberal theory. The contradiction here is not simply that the state is useful for markets, which cannot create their own conditions of existence, but the contradiction of means and ends, which Hayek claimed was the problem with socialism in that the means was detrimental to its ends (rather than the ends in themselves as a problem); but when it came to the neoliberalism ends, it did not appear to matter too much that the means might be destructive of the desired ends.

Although the term neoliberal capitalism is often used, it is properly speaking an approach towards the management of the economy, in particular to those parts under aegis of the state, rather than a condition of capitalism. Yet, it is true that neoliberalism had a transformative effect on capitalism, freeing large parts of it from state control and opening up new opportunities for it on a transnational level. Setting aside the decreasing importance of organized labour, which was on decline in the western world since de-industrialization, it was the large corporations that ultimately benefited, as Crouch (2011) has argued. This, of course, raises the interesting question of whether the organizations that benefited from three decades of neoliberal policies are also the causal agents.

While de-regulation, the liberalization of trade, and privatization of state assets are the foundations of neoliberalism, there is also the further dimension, which follows from privatization, of a retrenchment of the welfare state. This latter element is not uncontroversial since it has been argued that, at least in the UK in this period, there was not a decline in spending on welfare, while others have argued that cuts to welfare began with the previous Labour government. Paul Pierson has argued in extensive studies of welfare that the welfare state is resilient and Thatcher did not succeed overall in cutting the welfare state despite her intentions (see Pierson 1994, 2001). European experiences differ hugely, as is strikingly illustrated by Spain where the welfare state expanded, albeit under socialist governments. Yet, it cannot be disputed that Thatcherism has been consequential as well as divisive and contradictory. For instance, while the British Conservative Party initially supported UK membership of the then EEC in 1973, which it saw as furthering the aims of market liberalism, by the 1980s it shifted when it became apparent that European integration did after all require a degree of planning that was not permitted by the neoliberal mindset and, of course, one that appeared to challenge notions of state sovereignty. The contradictions were huge; as is now well known, the neoliberal state required the building up of the state edifice not its retraction. It was far from a minimal state, as the period saw the building of the world's most powerful military state and more generally the massive expansion in the state military complex. Why is this if neoliberalism seeks to promote market freedom and is opposed to the strong hand of the state? The answer is that it needs the state to further its aims. The planned state that Hayek was opposed to was a state that sought the protection of labour; the neoliberal strong state seeks to advance the interests of capital, and for this reason it is re-designed to serve market needs. Only in this way is it possible to understand the worldwide trend towards the co-option of the state for big business. An important example of this trend is in the massive expansion of the military economy, which depends on the state.

96 Capitalism, cosmopolitanism, Anthropocene

It should be noted that neoliberalism was adopted only by some western governments following the crisis of capitalism in the 1970s, not before, and often as in France, only piecemeal. Although it did not ultimately solve the fiscal crisis of the state, nor did it succeed stemming the rising inflation and unemployment facing those governments, it was not itself to blame for the problems that led to its emergence. Undoubtedly, the long period of ideological maturation helped it to present itself as a remedy. However, despite the proclamations of neoliberals, it was certainly not part of the solution, even though some elements of neoliberalism can be defended on grounds other than market fundamentalism, for instance, de-regulating the airways and telecommunications were undoubtedly necessary measures, while in the case of the banking sector it was a case of the remedy being worse than the illness. There is presumably a difference between mobile phones and banks. Not all de-regulation is detrimental to the common good. In the area of health and education an overall assessment is difficult to make due to the diversity of national trajectories, changed demographic conditions, and the previously mentioned issue of welfare state spending apparently increasing rather than decreasing. The emergence of public-private partnerships, a later development, cannot entirely be understood in neoliberal terms, since the state continues to fund and manage large parts of the public sector. Indeed, it can be argued that the role of the state has increased as has the extent of re-regulation, as is also evidenced by the Obama health care reforms.

Did neoliberalism come to an end? It has almost certainly never come to an end as such and has continued in a piecemeal fashion by later governments, which took on board some of the premises and dropped others, as in the case of Third Way-style politics. The French, German, and, more recently, Swedish governments have variously adopted neoliberal policies. It is most vividly and with devastating consequences survived in the form of the de-regulation of the banking sector. Major world organizations such as the IMF, the World Trade Organization and the World Bank are based on neoliberal policies and represent the continuation of neoliberalism after it ceased to be a dominant national policy.

Managerialism and organizational change

The growth of managerialism and bureaucratization in organizations is often seen as an expression of neoliberalism and evidence of its widespread impact on areas of life other than the economy. Examples of neoliberalism within organizations would include the adoption of strategies such as outsourcing costs, flexible employment, the pursuit of growth, and competitiveness. In the case of organizations within the ambit of the state, partnerships with private businesses are often taken to be instances of the pervasiveness of neoliberalism whereby market forces enter into domains that were previously outside the market. A relevant example of market-based reforms is the National Health Service in the UK since 1996. While these examples certainly bear the imprint and influence of neoliberal doctrines, the differences between neoliberal de-regulation and the move towards the 'social investment' model is less marked than would appear from some of the debates to which it has given rise. Taylor-Gooby (2008) describes this as a shift in European social policy towards a third phase from one of social provision to one of social investment. This third phase can only with difficulty be termed neoliberal. The adoption of what can also be described as greater rationalization within organizations is not simply due to the impact of the market. The post-Fordist economy is not a product of neoliberalism, even if there are some similarities and co-emergence, but a development of capitalism. Another and complicating perspective is that there has been as much re-regulation today as de-regulation (see Campbell and Pedersen 2001).

The embracing of the market is not always attributable to neoliberalism: markets can be liberating. The German system of apprenticeships, for instance, with its closely knit relation between education, vocational training, and work preceded neoliberalism and illustrates a more socially embedded model of capitalism. The post-1945 'ordo-liberalism' in Germany was clearly very different from the Washington Consensus. The increased power of managers in organizations is not directly linked to free-market economics and has had different sources. Managerialism preceded neoliberalism, as James Burnham demonstrated in the *Managerial Revolution* in 1941 and cannot therefore be seen as a product of neoliberalism, which ideologically is opposed to the managerial tendency towards planning. From a neo-institutionalist perspective, including the world polity approach of John Meyer, the global spread of formal organization and its penetration into most spheres of society cannot be understood in terms of a model of instrumental rationalization or standardizing power. Meyer and Bromley (2014) emphasize the causal role of cultural change in the spread of formal organization, which cannot be attributed to neoliberalism. Despite what may appear to be co-emergence, the cultural change preceded neoliberalism. Macro-level cultural change in science, rights, and education tends to lead towards the expansion of organizational complexity, including accounting and management, which is not easily explained by market forces.

While it can be conceded that elements of neoliberal discourse have crept into domains of social life that lie outside the market, much of what has been attributed to neoliberalism can be explained simply by capitalist development and the simple fact that all organizations, including non-profit ones, have to operate in conditions that are dictated by markets even if they are not capitalistic, such as educational institutions. A significant development in this respect is the rise and diffusion of New Public Management – sometimes referred to as New Public Governance – the process by which strategies and techniques of neoliberal management are adopted by non-capitalistic public organizations, such as universities and hospitals (Osborne 2010). Thus, one of the pervasive legacies of neoliberalism has been the widespread adoption of business-like practices such as outsourcing, micro-managing, target setting and performance management, the client as customer, value for money, efficiency, and so on. In this sense, as the public service imitates business, neoliberalism has come to have a wide impact on social institutions beyond the capitalist economy.

However, for every instance of the extension of the market another can be found to illustrate counter-market tendencies. This is where Hayek meets Polanyi.

98 Capitalism, cosmopolitanism, Anthropocene

As Polanyi (2001) demonstrated in *The Great Transformation*, which was published in 1944, the same year as *The Road to Serfdom*, the extension of the market generates counter tendencies towards social protection, thus setting limits to its reach. Boltanski and Chiapello (2006) have shown a similar logic at work in *The New Spirit of Capitalism* with the argument that the very nature of capitalism has been transformed by critiques of capitalism. Capitalism, including neoliberal policy making, needs to anchor itself in justifications and cannot be entirely detached from the normative order of society. The discourses of New Public Management seek legitimacy by appealing to efficiency and can be challenged when they fail to deliver. The pervasive impact of neoliberal practices does not mean the unchallenged rule of unbridled markets.

The individualization of risk and responsibility

A widespread view today — and which is especially prevalent in sociology — is that states are being transformed around a new political project aimed at the individualization of risk and responsibility. The Keynesian state was based on a benevolent approach to the individual — essentially the (male) industrial worker — as the recipient of benefits. Since the rise of neoliberalism there has been less a retrenchment of the welfare state than what can be described as a transformation of some of its key functions. This is most evident in the relation between the individual and the state. The old social liberalism of the post WW2 period was based on collective assumptions about citizenship, while current policies are marked by a strong concern with the individual as responsible for their own lives. The individual is no longer to be a passive recipient but an active agent, who must work and be responsible for their health and well-being and so on. Rose (1999), from a critical Foucauldian perspective on neoliberalization, has referred to this as 'neoliberal governmentality' (see also Miller and Rose 2008). As noted, for Foucault neoliberalism is not just an economic policy but has become part of the state apparatus which applies the basic principles of neoliberalism to itself and to society more generally. It thus does not simply rest on the market alone, which, if left to its own devices, does not, as Hayek incorrectly believed, generate freedom.

There has undoubtedly been a significant shift in the social welfare policies since the 1990s towards the 'individual as a consumer' and the adoption of the previously discussed practices of New Public Management. Gone is the old commitment to national cohesion and solidarity to be achieved through distributive means and full employment. The new policies, generally described as repressive, punitive, or disciplinary, rest on the individualization of responsibility and a new spirit of individual achievement. The citizen has become a Foucauldian agent internalizing the demands of external pressures and transforming them into life projects. The shift in social policy is paralleled by changes in the nature of work. The new capitalism is often characterized by precariousness (Sennett 2006; Standing 2016; Young 2007). Nonetheless, how much of this is to be attributed to neoliberalism is unclear. There are two different issues here: changes in welfare policies — 'from welfare to workfare' – and changes in the nature of capitalism. One does not follow from the other. The thesis of the increasing precariousness of work (Deranty 2008) is one side of a situation in which, in this period, women were incorporated into the work force, which, in the western world, has also undergone a huge demographic transformation. It is rather difficult to explain all of this by reference to neoliberal policies, which are perhaps more evident in the transformation of public services.

As far as the welfare state is concerned, the changes can only be partly described as neoliberal. The language of the citizen as consumer has become pervasive, but is this only due to the impact of neoliberalism? We can certainly find ample evidence in education of managerialism with target setting, monitoring, performance setting, the client as customer, and so on. A new conception of the individual is behind notions of life-long learning, transferrable skills, learning as opposed to teaching, the empowered individual, and so on. However, the discourse of individualization cannot be simply wholly attributed to neoliberalism, which is only one strand in a more complicated story. The field of education is a good example of individualism as what is often referred to as individuation, namely, the capacity for personal autonomy (see Beck and Beck-Gernsheim 2001). Individuation cannot be reduced to the so-called neoliberal subject, who is reconfigured to respond to the exigencies of the market.

As argued by Yasemin Soysal in an insightful article, the notion of individualism has been very much bound up with the idea of the rights-bearing individual since the 1970s in European education when progressive pedagogies of self-centred learning, critical thinking, creativity, and problem-solving were promoted (Soysal 2012: 13–14). She stresses how an empowered notion of the individual became attached to a strongly rights-conscious movement within and beyond education. Personal autonomy and education are inextricably linked, as in the notion of *Bildung* with its normative, cognitive, and aesthetic notion of the individual as developmental. These ideas not only historically precede neoliberalism but have origins different from the liberal conception of the individual itself. Today the notion of personal autonomy has an additional cosmopolitan dimension in that the language of rights, including human rights, has shaped the individual as participative or active as opposed to a passive agent. As Meyer and Bromley (2014: 370) have argued, there is now a worldwide expansion of education that has empowered individuals. In combination with a new culture of rights and the expansion of the knowledge-based society, the expansion of education has huge implications for the shape of the contemporary organization. This condition arose from circumstances that have had an independent origin from neoliberalism. It may be argued, as Nancy Fraser (2013) has said of feminism, that education has become embroiled in the neoliberal project. The opposite can equally be argued, namely, that neoliberalism has been subverted by alternative conceptions of the individual. To mistake these for neoliberalism is to fundamentally misunderstand the logic of personhood and the nature of societal learning. As Weber noted of the entwinement of capitalism and Protestantism, it is inevitable that different processes can become mutually implicated due to processes of intersection and imbrication, but they can still retain their own logics of development.

100 Capitalism, cosmopolitanism, Anthropocene

To take another example: European integration in the new era of so-called austerity. It has been increasingly commented that the neoliberal agenda has become prevalent, especially since the Lisbon Treaty and more so with austerity politics in the wake of the 2007–9 financial crisis (Schafer and Streeck 2013). Is austerity an example of neoliberalism? In some ways it is in that governments and the EU have adopted policies of nationalizing sovereign debt to save private banks.[5] However, this is by no means quite so straightforward in that it was the acknowledged failure of neoliberal de-regulated markets that led to the problem in the first instance for which austerity was the proposed solution. The fact that the remedy does not work or is hard to digest does not make it neoliberal. In any case, perhaps with the exception of Greece, austerity policies are imposed by neoliberal-inclined national governments, not by the EU. The Republic of Ireland was one of the most neoliberal countries at the time of the financial crisis, but it was national governmental policy that implemented austerity reforms. The wider thesis is of course that the EU has become neoliberal with the goal of market competitiveness becoming firmly established with the Lisbon agenda. However, this raises at least three problems. First, market competitiveness was central to European integration from the beginning in an era when European integration was part of the 'big state'. Market competitiveness was the primary rationale for the free movement of capital, goods, labour, and services. Second, this economic rationale, which preceded neoliberalism, was complemented by other goals which were not purely economic and which arguably became more important. In this context, Favell (2014) argues that the fourth freedom of human mobility cannot be reduced to neoliberal policy. It is difficult to explain some of the central policies as neoliberal, for instance the Common Agricultural Policy. Third, there is no reason why market competitiveness is not compatible with non-neoliberal goals, such as those of egalitarianism and democracy, which presumably require wealth creation, or the idea of a European social model. Obviously, the EU is a complicated mosaic of many currents, which include neoliberal orientations as well as other currents.

Economic globalization and global markets

Neoliberalism is often equated with the increasing importance of global markets, which have supposedly undermined the capacity of the national state for social protection and cohesion. Markets are thus supposed to be becoming disembedded, and states are increasingly powerless, leading them to shift from being provider states to other functions, such as regulation (which contradicts the neoliberal temptation towards de-regulation). This is largely true, especially in relation to global finance markers, but it is an incomplete and misleading account. Neoliberalism is the legislation for privatization, de-regulation, and the liberalization of markets. This was first implemented within some national contexts but ultimately had repercussions beyond the national context in opening global markets, which came to rest on foundations other than nation states, such as those of global organizations, the WTO, World Bank, and IMF. In that wider sense, neoliberalism is a global project.

Questioning *homo economicus* **101**

It is thus the case that neoliberalism is about opening up as much of the world as possible to markets. However, it should be noted that this is not specifically a neoliberal strategy and has been inherent in capitalism since the seventeenth century. It is also difficult to apply neoliberalism to the national economic policies of some of the most important economies in the world today, such as China, India, Russia, and South Africa. For reasons of space, I cannot comment in detail on this complex issue, but all of these examples, which are hugely significant in terms of globalization, are not neoliberal regimes but reflect very different state-organized forms of capitalism. Along with other Latin American countries – notably Mexico, Chile, and Argentina – Brazil adopted neoliberalism from 1994 to 2000 during the Cardoso presidency, but during the Lula presidency there was a major societal re-orientation from neoliberalism, which has been much discredited there following the economic disasters it produced, such as the bankruptcy of Argentina in 2001. This, of course, changed since 2018 with the election of Bolsonora.

A qualification must be made in the case of Russia, where following the demise of communism, neoliberal style politics were quickly adopted by the new elites (who were in fact not quite so new, but the old communist guard in new clothes). This was also the case in much of central and eastern Europe. While Harvey (2005) includes China since 1978 with the reforms led by Den Xiaoping as part of the global spread of neoliberalism, in my view this makes very little sense unless the notion of neoliberalism is generalized to include all forms of capitalism. A modified version of neoliberalism was adopted in India, but this was relatively moderate in a country where the national state remains central to the economy.

Finally, the thesis of a generalized condition of neoliberalism sits uncomfortably with the theory of varieties of capitalism (Hall and Soskice 2001; see also Amable 2003). According to this approach, to be discussed in the next chapter, there is not one type of capitalism but two generic types – coordinated economies and liberal market economies – with many countries falling in between these poles, which can also be seen as ideal types. For reasons of space, I cannot go into the implications of this further but will comment that the notion of a variety of national and regional models of capitalism seriously questions assumptions of the universality of neoliberalism as the defining condition of our time.

Despite these controversial issues around what is neoliberalism and what it is not, there are good grounds for re-contextualizing neoliberalism with the emergence of the 'financial subject'. Inspired by the Foucauldian theory of the formation of subjects through power relations, fruitful applications have been made to make sense of developments relating to the financialization of the economy and – one of the main results of neoliberalism – the de-regulation of global finance markets. The phenomenon of financialization and the shift it has brought from economies of savings to economies of investment has brought about new relationships of subservience between private households and global finance markets. This has led to a fundamentally different kind of capitalism than one based on labour in that it is now the private individual who is the focus of capitalism and connected by many links in the forms of loans, credit cards, and various kinds of borrowings

102 Capitalism, cosmopolitanism, Anthropocene

(Payne 2012). This extends into domains beyond mortgages to include private pensions and student loans. The volatility of finance markets creates condition of uncertainty, risk, and precariousness for large segments of the population who are at the same time forced to be responsible for their finances. The interaction of people and personal finance with global finance has made possible the ascendancy of finance capitalism and has led to the creation of a 'financial subject' (see Mulcahy 2016; Langley 2008). This refers not to personal identities but 'to the creation of individuals as subjects of finance through institutional discourse and practices, so that individuals recognize themselves and their goals in relation to financial economic and political policies' (Mulcahy 2016: 217). Financialization has penetrated deep down into everyday life and has brought about new and more extensive relations of borrowers and investors. The resulting financial subject has become a key figure in contemporary capitalism and more generally in twenty-first-century culture. If credit was the economic form of the boom time, debt is the economic form of crisis. As McClanahan shows in a study on the cultural forms of debt, debt is a figure for unpaid or defaulted credit (McClanahan 2017: 15). Credit is no longer a means for spending on nonessential goods but has become a necessary means for survival for many people.

It is evident that neoliberalism does not take simply one generic form. The above account distinguishes between the philosophical project, as in the writings of Hayek, its political implementation in the 1980s, later incarnations when neoliberalism was adopted more widely by transnational organizations, and by 'Third Way' style politics. It took more diffuse forms with the ascendancy of finance capitalism, and aspects of neoliberalism are adopted outside the sphere of the state in a variety of institutional settings. If anything underlies all these forms, it is the transformation of the state and society by market forces. Thus, neoliberalism is not the divorce of the economy from state and society, but as Foucault has shown, it is the radical restructuring of state and society to serve the interests of capitalism.

Conclusion: how extensive is *homo economicus*?

Since Marx, Weber, and Polanyi, we are now more attuned to the massive expansion of the market in social life. Above all, capitalism, once an aspect of the social world, has become the dominant force in the modern world. It is difficult to disagree with the persuasive argument of Wendy Brown that neoliberalism seeks to limit and control the scope of the political and that four decades of neoliberalism have led to a profoundly anti-democratic culture that made possible the rise of neo-authoritarian politics (Brown 2019: 88). Neoliberalism attacks and fragments the social, which is the foundation of the possibility of progressive politics. But does this mean that neoliberalism has become all dominant to the extent that markets entirely rule over our lives and that the political has been entirely eroded? Have the counter-vailing currents been absorbed into the neoliberal economy? I do not think so.

Capitalism has become the dominant, if not the exclusive, form of the economy. With the end of the USSR and the centrally planned socialist economy, there are no alternatives to capitalism. However, the global spread of capitalism does not mean that capitalism has become the only societal model. We may live in a capitalist economy but not in a capitalist society. Society is shaped by forces other than capitalism, and it follows that neoliberalism does not rule unchallenged or that it has succeeded in co-opting everything to its needs. Democracy, for instance, is equally pervasive and often a counter-force to capitalism. De-regulation in one area often leads to more regulation in another or simply to re-regulation, as in the banking sector, as anyone who has sought a mortgage since 2009 has found out. Moreover, capitalism does not simply take one form but many. Economies today, which are predominantly capitalist to be sure, also contain large swathes of non-capitalist activities. It is certainly the case that much of non-capitalist activity is often co-opted by capitalism – as in family functions serving the needs of capitalism – but this does not mean that neoliberalism is an all-dominant ideology.

Markets, it should also be considered, are not necessarily capitalist. Crouch (2011: 79–82) distinguishes between marketization and privatization, noting that the former does not necessarily lead to the latter, which involves the selling of a previously owned state asset to a private firm. There is today a plethora of new kinds of markets, which are not primarily capitalistic, by which I understand an operation that is exclusively aimed at the making of a profit for private appropriation. This is not to deny the rise of entirely new kinds of markets and capitalistic activities that are largely unregulated, as John Urry (2014) has documented.

In arguing that the condition of neoliberalism has been inaccurately attributed to areas of contemporary life, my intention is not to absolve neoliberalism, which has been a pernicious ideology in many ways, of polluting politics or to underestimate its impact; nor is it my intention to declare its premature demise. Thatcherism has been hugely divisive and many neoliberal reforms counterproductive, as is best illustrated by the de-regulation of the banking sector and the rise of fat-cat elites. The drive for Brexit since 2016 has been led by neoliberal politicians who see Brexit as a way to de-regulate markets from EU regulatory regimes.

Undoubtedly, de-regulation was necessary in many areas of the economy, as in telecommunications and the airlines, and privatization in some areas has led to beneficial outcomes, but where these policies were taken too far the outcome has been detrimental to the prospects of a fairer and more egalitarian society. My argument is that a differentiated analysis of capitalism today will show that it is embroiled with democracy with multiple points of resistance. This leads to different normative conclusions than an argument that sees neoliberalism as a one-dimensional reality. As argued in the previous chapter, modernity entails a field of tensions whereby capitalism is entangled with the normative and cognitive order of society. Out of this mix of opposing forces various points of resistance are generated. In line with the basic animus of critical theory, in particular Habermas's social theory, neoliberal governance is not exempt from the need to provide justifications. It is possible that today the legitimation claims of neoliberalism are becoming openly questioned in ways that they were not previously.

104 Capitalism, cosmopolitanism, Anthropocene

I would like to put forward the claim that contrary to the spectre of a new age of neoliberal capitalism and a supine state that administers austerity remedies on docile and disciplined populations, the opposite tendency is also in evidence. Democratization, the language of rights, and a politics of personal autonomy are powerful currents in the world today. Far from being entirely subsumed into a neoliberal project, they are equally likely to subvert and transform it. The vast and complicated field of European integration, seen by some as part of the neoliberal project, can equally well be seen as creating the conditions of the possibility for societal diversification and transformation.

Businesses are increasingly being forced to adopt the logic of non-capitalist organizations, as illustrated by the examples of corporate social responsibility, and what Stehr and Adolf (2010) have referred to as the 'moralisation of the market' leading to a blurring of the distinction between citizens and consumers. In this conception of the consumer, moral considerations enter into the picture, challenging the notion of a neoliberal subject. There is some evidence to demonstrate the existence of forms of economic value that lie outside commodification (see Arvidsson 2011). While one should be skeptical of corporate social responsibility, which, like many things, can be co-opted by capitalism and made to serve its interests, it is never entirely a discourse that is controlled by capitalism. It can be hypothesized that there are no pure markets: markets are always regulated – it is only a matter of degree – as are certain non-markets elements, such as norms and values that derive from other areas of social life. It can also be hypothesized, following institutionalist analysis, that the capitalist firm should not only be seen in terms of the market but has to organize around a new regime of rights, environment issues, transparency, and so on.

Neoliberalism provided the right with a powerful ideology for some three decades. It galvanized the right in a way that the left had nothing comparable at a time when its historical social basis, the western industrial working class, vanished or at least became much diminished in size and political influence. The Keynesianism and social democracy that it replaced lacked a comparable ideological appeal. A fateful development was that new kinds of progressive politics, such as feminism and more generally cultural politics, were not in themselves resistant to neoliberalism, which in its more progressive forms was compatible with progressive cultural politics. Today neither right nor left have an ideological alternative. The left needs more than a critique of neoliberalism if it is to really offer an alternative conception of how market, state, and society should be organized.

Notes

1 This chapter is based on a keynote lecture for the International Symposium on 'Children – Childhood – State – Education' University of Wuppertal, Germany, 10–11 July 2014. I am grateful to Professor Heinz Sünker for the invitation and for comments. The paper has subsequently been extensively re-written. I am also grateful to Neal Harris for helpful comments on an earlier version.

2 See also (Boas and Gans-Morse 2009) for whom the term neoliberalism, due to its terminological shifts, is one of the social sciences' essentially contested concepts and nowadays generally used as a slogan that lacks analytical usefulness.
3 There is an irony here in that Foucault himself was drawn towards certain aspects of neoliberalism, and his later work on biopower and economic liberalism suggests a modification to his earlier work. On Foucault and his ambivalent relation with neoliberalism, see Zamora and Behrent 2016).
4 See also Duménil and Lévy (2004), Peck (2012), Steger and Roy (2010), Turner (2008).
5 See Blyth (2013) for an incisive analysis of the history of the idea of austerity and its application to save banks.

References

Amable, B. 2003. *The Diversity of Modern Capitalism*. Oxford: Oxford University Press.
Arvidsson, A. 2011. New Forms of Value Production. In: Delanty, G. and Turner, S. (eds.) *International Handbook of Contemporary Social and Political Theory*. London: Routledge.
Beck, U. and Beck-Gernsheim, E. 2001. *Individualization*. London: Sage.
Boas, T. and Gans-Morse, J. 2009. Neoliberalism: From New Liberal Philosophy to Anti-Liberal Slogan. *Studies in Comparative International Development*, 44 (2): 137–61.
Boltanski, L. and Chiapello, E. 2006 [1999]. *The New Spirit of Capitalism*. London: Verso.
Bourdieu, P. 1998. The Essence of Neoliberalism. *Le Monde diplomatique*. http://mondediplo.com/1998/12/08bourdieu.
Blyth, M. 2013. *Austerity: The History of a Dangerous Idea*. Oxford: Oxford University Press.
Brown, W. 2015. *Undoing the Demos, Neoliberalism's Stealth and Revolution*. New York: Zone Books.
Brown, W. 2019. *In the Ruins of Neoliberalism: The Rise of Antidemocratic Politics in the West*. New York: Columbia University Press.
Campbell, J. L. and Pedersen, O. K. (eds.) 2001. *The Rise of Neoliberalism and Institutional Analysis*. Princeton, NJ: Princeton University Press.
Crouch, C. 2011. *The Strange non-Death of Neo-Liberalism*. Cambridge: Polity Press.
Davies, W. 2017. *The Limits of Neoliberalism: Authority, Sovereignty and the Logic of Capitalism*. London: Sage.
Dean, J. 2009. *Democracy and other Neoliberal Fantasies*. Durham, NC: Duke University Press.
Deranty, P. 2008. Work and the Precarisation of Existence. *European Journal of Social Theory*, 11 (4): 443–63.
Duménil, G. and Lévy, D. 2004. *Capital Resurgent: Roots of the Neoliberal Revolution*. Cambridge, MA: Harvard University Press.
Duménil, G. and Lévy, D. 2005. The Neoliberal (Counter-)Revolution. In: Saad-Filho, A. and Johnson, D. (eds.) *Neoliberalism: A Critical Reader*. London: Pluto Press.
Favell, A. 2014. The Fourth Freedom: Theories of Migration and Mobilities in 'Neo-Liberal' Europe. *European Journal of Social Theory on Europe in Crisis*, 17 (3): 275–89.
Foucault, M. 2008. *The Birth of Biopolitics: Lectures at the Collège de France, 1978–79*. London: Palgrave Macmillan.
Fraser, N. 2013. *Fortunes of Feminism: From State Managed Capitalism to Neo-Liberal Crisis*. London: Verso.
Gane, N. 2012. The Governmentalities of Neoliberalism: Panopticism, Post-Panopticism and Beyond. *The Sociological Review*, 60 (4): 611–34.
Greenhouse, G. (ed.) 2010. *Ethnographies of Neoliberalism*. Philadelphia: University of Pennsylvania University Press.

106 Capitalism, cosmopolitanism, Anthropocene

Hall, P. and Soskice, D. 2001. *Varieties of Capitalism: The Institutional Foundations of Comparative Advantage*. Oxford: Oxford University Press.

Harvey, D. 1991. *The Condition of Postmodernism*. Oxford: Blackwell.

Harvey, D. 2005. *A Brief History of Neoliberalism*. Oxford: Oxford University Press.

Hayek, F. 1944. *The Road to Serfdom*. Chicago, IL: Chicago University Press.

Klein, M. 2008. *The Shock Doctrine: The Rise of Disaster Capitalism*. London: Penguin Books.

Langley, P. 2008. *The Everyday Life of Global Finance: Saving and Borrowing in Anglo-America*. Oxford: Oxford University Press.

Lazzarato, M. 2012. *The Making of the Indebted Man: An Essay on the Neoliberal Condition*. Los Angeles: Semitext(e).

Lazzarato, M. 2015. *Governing by Debt*. Los Angeles: Semiotext(e).

Lazzarato, M. 2017. *Experimental Politics: Work, Welfare, and Creativity in the Neoliberal Age*. Cambridge, MA: MIT Press.

Mannheim, K. 1960 [1936]. *Ideology and Utopia*. London: Routledge & Kegan Paul.

McClanahan, A. 2017. *Dead Pledges: Debt, Crisis and Twenty-First-Century Culture*. Stanford: Stanford University Press.

Meyer, J. and Bromley, P. 2014. The Worldwide Expansion of 'Organization'. *Sociological Theory*, 31 (4): 366–81.

Miller, P. and Rose, N. 2008. *Governing the Present: Administering Economic, Social and Personal Life*. Cambridge: Polity Press.

Mirowski, P. 2013. *Never Let a Serious Crisis Go to Waste: How Neoliberalism Survived the Financial Meltdown*. London: Verso.

Mirowski, P. and Plehwe, D. (eds.) 2009. *The Road from Mont Pelerine: The Making of the Neoliberal Thought Collective*. Cambridge, MA: Harvard University Press.

Mulcahy, N. 2016. Entrepreneurial Subjectivity and the Political Economy of Daily Life in the Time of Finance. *European Journal of Social Theory*, 20 (2): 216–35.

Ong, A. 2006. *Neoliberalism as Exception*. Durham, NJ: Duke University Press.

Osborne, S. (ed.) 2010. *The New Public Governance: Emerging Perspectives on the Theory and Practice of Public Governance*. London: Routledge.

Payne, C. 2012. *The Consumer, Credit, Neoliberalsim: Governing the Modern Economy*. London: Routledge.

Peck, J. 2010. *Constructions of Neoliberal Reason*. Oxford: Oxford University Press.

Pierson, P. 1994. *Dismantling the Welfare State? Reagan, Thatcher and the Politics of Retrenchment*. Cambridge: Cambridge University Press.

Pierson, P. (ed.) 2001. *The New Politics of the Welfare State*. Oxford: Oxford University Press.

Polanyi, K. 2001 [1944]. *The Great Transformation*. Boston: Beacon Press.

Powell, W. and DiMaggio, P. (eds.) 1991. *The New Institutional Analysis in Organization Analysis*. Chicago, IL: University of Chicago Press.

Rose, N. 1999. *Powers of Freedom*. Cambridge: Cambridge University Press.

Saad-Filho, A. and Johnson, D. (eds.) 2005. *Neoliberalism: A Critical Reader*. London: Pluto Press.

Schafer, A. and Streeck, W. (eds.) 2013. *Politics in the Age of Austerity*. Polity Press.

Seidman Jones, D. 2012. *Masters of the Universe: Hayek, Friedman and the Birth of NewLiberal Politics*. Princeton, NJ: Princeton University Press.

Sennett, R. 2006. *The Culture of the New Capitalism*. London: Routledge.

Shearmur, J. 1996. *Hayek and After: Hayekian Liberalism as a Research Programme*. London: Routledge.

Soysal, Y. N. 2012. Citizenship, Immigration, and the European Social Project: Rights and Obligations of Individuals. *British Journal of Sociology*, 63 (1): 1–21.

Standing, G. 2016. *The Precariat: The New Dangerous Class*. London: Bloomsbury.

Steger, M. and Roy, R. 2010. *Neoliberalism: A Very Short Introduction*. Oxford: Oxford University Press.

Stehr, N. and Adolf, M. 2010. Consumption Between Markets and Morals: A Socio-Cultural Consideration if Moralised Markets. *European Journal of Social Theory*, 13 (2): 213–28.

Streeck, W. 2014. *Buying Time: The Delayed Democratic Crisis of Capitalism*. Cambridge: Polity Press.

Taylor-Gooby, P. 2008. The New Welfare State Settlement in Europe. *European Societies*, 10 (1): 3–24.

Turner, R. S. 2008. *Neo-Liberal Ideology: History, Concepts, Politics*. Edinburgh: Edinburgh University Press.

Urry, J. 2014. *Offshoring*. Cambridge: Polity Press.

Vogl, J. 2017. *The Ascendancy of Finance*. Cambridge: Polity Press.

Young, J. 2007. *The Vertigo of Late Modernity*. London: Sage.

Zamora, D. and Behrent, M. (eds.) 2016. *Foucault and Neoliberalism*. Cambridge: Polity Press.

5

IMAGINING THE FUTURE OF CAPITALISM

Trends, scenarios, and prospects for the future

The previous chapter offered an assessment of the state of neoliberalism and argued that while neoliberalism continues to be a major feature of current times, its dominance in many spheres of life does not foreclose the possibility of resistance or the emergence of alternatives. Capitalism may have survived its crises, but the dream of capitalism that neoliberalism sold to the world has gone. This raises the question of how critical theory should approach the future and in particular the future of capitalism.[1] A key consideration in this context is whether an immanent analysis – that is, one that proceeds from the current form that capitalism takes – is still relevant or whether the future should be viewed only in more dystopic terms as catastrophe without the possibility of redemption. This chapter is confined to a consideration of the future of capitalism. While Chapter 7 will look at the related but wider context of the Anthropocene for imagining the future of human societies in terms of a different relation to nature, Chapter 12 will explore other visions of the future.

What is the future of capitalism? Does it have a future? Indeed, we might ask does the future have a future? Are there alternatives to capitalism, and do they have a future or will capitalism also devour them? It is clearly not possible to answer the question of the future of capitalism with the certainty that might have been possible until the middle of the twentieth century when alternative scenarios of modernity were possible and when one of these prevailed for almost a century. The twentieth century inherited the legacy of the previous century for future-oriented thinking, but especially in the Marxist heritage there was greater emphasis given to transformations within the present as containing the conditions of possibility of the future. For much of the critical theory tradition these were, as in Ernst Bloch's 1935 book, *Heritage of Our Times*, the hidden possibilities of the age (Bloch 2009). Walter Benjamin wrote at the end of the *Arcades Project* of the demise of capitalism: 'The experience of our generation: that capitalism will die no natural death' (Benjamin 1999: 917).

The aim of the chapter is to provide a framework for critical thinking about how the question of the future of capitalism might be answered. A major consideration, as argued in Chapter 3, is that capitalism is not a purely economic condition but is entangled in other social spheres. Capitalism to varying degrees is more or less intermeshed with the legal and political structure of the state, and consequently it is unable to separate itself from democracy. Notwithstanding, new challenges to democracy, and capitalism and democracy together, constitute the defining features of the present day. The tensions that result from this dialectic will provide momentum for the main circuits of potential change.

Perhaps one major consideration is that today the question of the future of capitalism has to grapple with the fact that unlike until relatively recently, there is a much stronger sense of the uncertainty of the future (see Beckert 2016; Beckert and Bronk 2018). While arguably the future has always been uncertain, the modernist spirit since the Enlightenment believed strongly in the predictability of the future, even when reality indicated otherwise. Today that belief has gone and with it the illusion of a known future.

It is also now clearer than ever that there is no single trajectory for capitalism. Economies do not progress along linear paths. Although Marx in earlier writings referred to a succession of modes of production, his mature thought, as reflected in, for example, the Marx-Zasulich correspondence, revealed a more nuanced view of non-European trajectories of capitalism. While the received Marxist view that capitalism will come to an end simply because all modes of production come to an end can be criticized from such a perspective, it should be noted that Marx himself saw a post-capitalist society as arriving quite far into the future, which is presumably why he distinguished between socialism and – more distant in the future – the utopia of communism. To take a different example, it is now widely accepted that slavery did not end with the demise of the ancient modes of production but was perpetuated by modernity and by capitalism and today takes new and incipient forms. Capitalism existed prior to the modern capitalist economy and is unlikely simply to vanish in the near future. As the Marxist notion of 'primitive accumulation' suggests, capitalism is entangled in other forms of accumulation, which it transforms and renders subservient to its needs (see Costa and Goncalves 2020). There is also no reason to suppose that a post-capitalist society will be more desirable or democratic. From both a normative and immanent perspective, a critique of capitalism today must address those aspects of contemporary society that provide a foundation for a post-capitalist world, which cannot therefore be a total rupture from the present. The future is likely to consist of a variety of societal forms and trajectories. However, in such a variegated world it is possible that the dominant forms of capitalism that until now have prevailed will be much diminished. Not only are such forms diminished, but they do not offer a model for the future. For example, the post-1945 period of relative prosperity that also saw a certain harmonization of capitalism and democracy is no longer a model for the future, let alone a likely scenario. The presuppositions on which it was based no longer exist – the worldwide dominance of the US economy, the cold war, industrialized national

110 Capitalism, cosmopolitanism, Anthropocene

economies – and entirely new challenges, such as climate change, resource scarcity, and population growth in the non-western world, require different solutions.

Another general point can also be stated: just as economic orders will not evolve linearly, so too will political orders likely take a variety of shapes and forms. Today the most obvious example is China, where capitalism coexists with the one-party state which nominally subscribes to communism. While such multi-polarity offers a clear refutation of the end of history thesis, the worldwide diffusion of democracy does not necessarily lead to the triumph of liberal democracy. Democracy, too, exists in a variety of forms (Blokker 2012). A striking recent development is the consolidation of authoritarian democracy in many parts of the world. However, there are also important expressions of progressive collective action that offer alternative visions of political community (Mota and Wagner 2019).

Which current is likely to gain the upper-hand? In this chapter, I discuss five scenarios for looking at the future of capitalism: varieties of capitalism, systemic crisis of capitalism, catastrophic collapse, low-growth capitalism, and postcapitalism. In conclusion, I claim that there are various possibilities that can be understood in terms of transitions, breakdown, or transformation, but a likely future trend, what Robert Reich has called super-capitalism, will be curtailed, and there will be limits to the accumulation of capital.

Varieties of capitalism

The notion of capitalism in critical theory has generally been predicated on the transformation of nineteenth-century capitalism into monopoly capitalism. The debate about the future of capitalism and its possible collapse has been predicated on the presumption that capitalism takes one major form and that there is one direction of travel leading to its final collapse. This reasoning takes almost no account of one of the most influential sociological approaches to the study of contemporary capitalism, namely, the 'varieties of capitalism' approach (VoC). While Marx provided a robust theory of capitalism, the Marxist approach has not given sufficient attention to the fact that capitalism is highly variable as an institutional form. Indeed, the huge differences in the national and organizational forms of capitalism have led to many theorists rejecting the label capitalism.

According to Hall and Soskice (2001), in the most well-known account of the VoC argument, capitalist regimes vary greatly. The critical factor for them is the ways in which capitalist firms coordinate actions and the degree of institutional advantage they secure from state policies. They distinguish between two major types of capitalism, liberal market economies and coordinated market economies, with the latter more dependent on non-market relationships of production than the former, which depend more on competitive markets. The implication of the VoC approach is that capitalism differs greatly in national contexts due to the institutional advantages that national states offer to businesses. The theory suggests that globalization as a monolithic one-directional trajectory of universal de-regulation is less pervasive in that firms will not automatically move offshore when it may be cheaper to do so. Nations can prosper not by adopting neoliberal policies but by building on institutional advantages. This perspective offers a view on the significant differences between Scandinavian and German experiences, on the one side, and the more liberal models in the English-speaking world on the other. Other contributions to this debate include Albert's (1993) contrast of Anglo-Saxon and German, or 'Rhenish' capitalism.

While the main contrast in the VoC literature is the difference between neoliberal-oriented economies and the European model of what has been referred to as social capitalism (see Offe 2003), a wider conception of varieties of capitalism would need to take into account the quite significant differences in neoliberalism, which, as discussed in the previous chapter, is not a single monolithic force. The UK and the USA are often taken to be the major examples, but here the differences are very great as are the differences between Anglo-Saxon models and those that have emerged in the developing world, where neoliberalism has been arguably more pervasive and where democratization is weaker (Connell and Dados 2014).

While the VoC debate has mostly been confined to the OECD countries and micro-level analyses of the relationship between firms and state structures, it leaves open the wider global context. Amable (2004), for instance, identified five global forms of capitalism. The future of capitalism cannot be separated from the question of its forms and the diverse ways in which it interacts with states. Some forms may perish, while other types may prosper. It may indeed be the case that the collapse of states will lead to the collapse of the kinds of capitalism that they foster and not due to the inherent problems of capitalism. There is almost no significant instance of a capitalist economy that is not tied to the state to support it. Without such a support, capitalism is vulnerable. This perspective questions the assumption that neoliberalism brings about a transformation in the relation of economy to the state, where the state is restructured to serve the interests of economic forces. While this may be one course, it is not the only one.

One major trend worldwide is export-led industrialization, especially in Asian countries which have been transformed by the retail revolution in Europe and North America. Hamilton and Shin (2015) question the model of capitalism that Marx provided for East Asian countries. This was an analysis that was based on factory production and on the relations between owners and workers that was centred in European national economies. The resulting bias towards production and nationally delineated economies does not accommodate demand-responsive economies in most developing countries. While they do not speak of an Asian variety of capitalism, they stress the need to see capitalism in a variety of world contexts, but where there is a significant global interconnection that establishes links between centres of production and the main sites of consumption. This is clearly an essential aspect of capitalism today in that western consumption rests on major sites of production in Asia. It is possibly a reversal of nineteenth-century British capitalism, which depended on production in Britain but on markets in the overseas colonies that also provided the raw materials.

112 Capitalism, cosmopolitanism, Anthropocene

Looking at capitalism as variegated, it may be objected, does not provide an answer to the question of what its basic form takes. Obviously, if something exists in a variety of forms, there must be a common denominator that has undergone variation. The VoC approach does not clarify exactly what is capitalism. If the variation is very great, there is some justification in claiming that there is a variety of forms of capitalism. But if the varieties are not fundamentally different, the problem remains of what constitutes capitalism. The VoC literature has not provided a satisfactory account of this problem. Moreover, as previously suggested, the different forms of capitalism are connected through global processes (see the discussion of Wallerstein next). Thus, while the varieties of capitalism may be very different, they are all interdependent (as is illustrated in the trade war between the US and China). From a Marxist perspective, the varieties of capitalism are expressions of the uneven development of capitalism within a common historical era. So, it is not a question of a numerical order of different types that exist on their own. Demand for goods in Europe and North America drives industrial production in Asia. As Weber ([1927] 2003) wrote in his *General Economic History*, the history of capitalism itself reveals a variety of forms (see also Kocka 2016).

Despite these shortcomings, the VoC approach is an essential corrective of simplistic models of a unitary model of capitalism progressing towards a bright future or those that see it heading for the precipice. A very likely trend is that capitalism will morph into a variety of shapes and forms and that some will survive. It may indeed be the case that Asian models will continue to undergo transformation, especially as democratization in those countries deepens. So, this is in effect a scenario that sees a future for capitalism, though not necessarily a long-term one, since the varieties that survive will probably do so as long as the capitalist world system is in existence and that capitalism itself is not in question or threatened by external forces or political opposition. This bring us to the next scenario that addresses this problem.

Systemic crises of capitalism

Another scenario of the future of capitalism is that it does not have a future. It will simply come to an end and not simply morph into a variety of forms. In line with Marx's prognoses of the future of capitalism due to its inherent self-destructiveness, several theorists have offered new interpretations of the end of capitalism. It is the internal contradictions of capitalism that will bring about its end and not an external force or the appeal of an alternative economic system. For Marx, it was the falling rate of profit leading to a reduced capacity for growth. Other contradictions included improved technology leading to the over-production of goods that are worth less; the over-supply of credit, which, in combination with technology replaces human labour, leads to goods being produced that do not have enough people who can afford to buy them.

Schumpeter, in 1943, in *Capitalism, Democracy and Socialism*, offered a different prognosis of the end of capitalism arising from systemic crises (Schumpeter 2010).

While he disagreed with much of Marx's analysis, he shared his view that capitalism would not in the final analysis survive crises. Capitalism generates problems that have the capacity to destroy capitalism; indeed, he thought that the nascent neoliberal belief produces destructive outcomes. However, it was less a systemic crisis in the Marxist sense that was the problem but that the success of capitalism would lead it to destroy its own foundations. Capitalism, in generating wealth and prosperity, creates a new critical intellectual class that cultivates values hostile to capitalism. He also saw the process of innovation, central to capitalism, but leading to creativity (in this Schumpeter was almost certainly wrong). One of his main views was the decline of the figure of the entrepreneur and the rise of the decadent bourgeois and the technocrat. Schumpeter held that the driving force of capitalism was the heroic entrepreneur, but the twentieth century had ushered in a different kind of capitalism that was also faced with the challenge of socialism.

The global financial crisis of 2008–9 marked a new moment of crisis in the history of capitalism and gave a renewed significance to both Schumpeter's and Marx's theory of capitalism over others, such as Weber's or the neoliberal narrative of the triumph of the market. The Weberian legacy – despite in many ways complementing Marx's analysis of capitalism – ultimately had a different story to tell, namely, that due to the rationalizing logic of modernity, capitalism will always find ways to solve its problems. Through calculation, planning, and rational mastery, capitalism contains within itself solutions to the problems it brings to the modern world. Systemic crises that might engender the demise of capitalism had no place in this approach. The prospect of a systemic crisis of capitalism is also foreign to neoliberal theory and its canonical doctrine that markets operate through self-correcting pricing mechanisms. Contrary to the Weberian and Marxist positions, according to F. A. Hayek, any attempt to plan the economy would more likely lead to a breakdown, since prices – the basis of markets – operate in a context of risk and contingency. Both Marx and Schumpeter offered different accounts of the systemic crisis of capitalism. Obviously, they were writing about different eras and different crises, both economic and political. In Marx's time, socialism was only a possibility; in Schumpeter's day, a variant of socialism was an existing and very real alternative to capitalism.

A major work co-authored by Wallerstein and other prominent sociologists has accessed the prospects of capitalism coming to an end in the not-too-distant future (Wallerstein et al 2013). Wallerstein and Randall Collins, in their respective and different accounts, portray capitalism entering into turmoil followed by decline. Collins's argument is more specific and is best summed up first: the process of technological displacement of labour, in particular middle-class labour, will in the long run generate the terminal crisis of capitalism. The various solutions or escapes that capitalism had until now are becoming rapidly closed off. For example, the computerization of jobs led to new jobs, but now these are also disappearing and not being compensated by the creation of a sufficient number of new ones. This account stresses changes in the nature of work as a result of new technologies in bringing about the end of capitalism.

114 Capitalism, cosmopolitanism, Anthropocene

Wallerstein, in a far-reaching analysis of the demise of capitalism, claims that the capitalist world-system that consolidated over the past five centuries or so will come to an end as do all economic and political systems. His main argument, which is based on the so-called Kondratieff cycles, is that capitalism goes through roughly 50-year periods of booms and slumps and that the slumps are getting worse. This is a reversal of the neoliberal narrative that the booms bring about greater prosperity than the slumps. It also questions the neo-Keynesian claim that states can borrow their way out of the current crisis and thus advert austerity policies on the grounds that the prospect of a new boom is likely not to materialize. Capitalism is entering a new systemic crisis in which profits are plummeting.

His argument also runs against the varieties of capitalism perspective in that for him capitalism is organized on a world level and is not locked into national or even into regional variants. If capitalism were in fact regionally or nationally delineated, it is conceivably possible for systemic crises to be contained in the way, for example, that the EU has tried to contain the problem of Greek debt. However, there are also hegemonic crises, which are longer than the 50-year Kondratieff cycles, and occur in the transition from one hegemonic order to the next. The decline of the United States as the main hegemonic order brings with it a new crisis. In this account, capitalism requires a world hegemon – in the sixteenth century it was Spain, Britain in the nineteenth century, the USA in the twentieth century – but today there is no unchallenged hegemon, and consequently capitalism enters into an era of crisis.

Capitalism is driven by the relentless accumulation of capital. The maximization of capital requires a hegemonic order that imposes order on the world so that it is not hindered. States outside the hegemonic order benefit from the existence of a hegemonic power to the extent that they benefit from capitalism. In his analysis, the basic costs of production are rising, and the capitalist system as a whole cannot be brought back to equilibrium in that the mechanisms it relied on until now are not available. For these reasons, the possibilities for an endless accumulation of capital are declining. The demise of capitalism is accompanied by a situation in which large numbers of people no longer believe that they are benefiting from capitalism. 'We are consequently living in a structural crisis in which there is a struggle about the successor system' (Wallerstein in Wallerstein et al 2013: 35).

Wallerstein's prognosis of a deep structural crisis rests on a theory of capitalism that sees the core characteristic of capitalism to be the accumulation of capital. In effect, it is a theory of the systemic crisis of capital accumulation. It does not rule out the survival of capitalism on a more reduced scale and thus of the fourth and fifth scenarios discussed next. However, his notion of a historical systemic crisis describes the ending of one societal system and the transition to another. It is not clear what might come after the present crisis, which may continue for perpetuity. From a more critical perspective, there is a question to be asked as to whether current developments are indicative of a systemic crisis that portends the end of capitalism. The so-called crisis of capitalism in 2008-9 turned out in many ways to be a crisis of the state. The rise of austerity policies have not endangered capitalism, which recovered remarkably from the financial crisis. Streeck (2011, 2014a) is undoubtedly correct in describing the current crisis as one of the relationships between capitalism and democracy. However, the crisis of democratic capitalism, or in the terms of Habermas (1976), a legitimation crisis, does not necessarily signal a terminal crisis of capitalism. It is essentially a political crisis and may take the form of a crisis of governability. The notion of a systemic crisis, on the other hand, is an economic crisis that unfolds in the long-term. Such a prognosis might then be seen as compatible with other views that focus on the short-term (including the VoC approach). However, the problem with purely systemic accounts of crisis is that they do not adequately address other dimensions of crisis, such as the uncoupling of democracy from capitalism, new expressions of populism, or mass mobilization against the super-rich. Nonetheless, systemic approaches provide a wider picture of structural transformation on a global level. Perhaps such accounts are best seen less as a picture of the future of capitalism than a long-term account of historical transformation in the relation of society and economy in which quite fundamental shifts may occur in capitalism.

Catastrophic collapse

The notion of a systemic crisis of capitalism is based on a view of the internal dynamics of the capitalist economy leading in time to the end of capitalism. An alternative scenario can be considered, namely, the possibility of global catastrophe or a major regional catastrophe that would have global ramifications. Throughout history, as Jared Diamond has shown, there have been many examples of whole societies or civilizations collapsing as result of a catastrophe (Diamond 2011). Modernity has not eliminated the spectre of catastrophe but in fact has nurtured it. Since Byron's poem 'Darkness' in 1816, according to Eva Horn, the modern mind has been fascinated by the possibility of the end of the world and the figure of 'the last man' standing at the end of history. 'The future is not just the space for utopian promises and humanity's progress; it also opens up a catastrophic imaginary – the expectation of an abrupt change, a sudden disruption of all existing things' (Horn 2018: 23). Today such vistas concern an increase in temperature, but in the nineteenth century the fear was of a cooling of the earth. In more prosaic terms, Malthus's *Essay on the Principle of Population* in 1798 is perhaps the first prognosis of a counter-Enlightenment dystopian future arising from population growth outstripping the capacity of modern society to provide food for all. Another historical example and one rooted in reality as opposed to the romantic temperament or faulty science was the Lisbon earthquake of 1755, which had a major impact on Europe in that it illustrated the vulnerability of human societies to natural forces. It led to the destruction of Lisbon, which was mostly burnt and destroyed following a tidal wave that followed in the aftermath of the earthquake and heralded the collapse of its empire.

While the second half of the twentieth century was animated by the spectre of nuclear catastrophe, today in the post-Cold War era the most obvious possibility of global catastrophe is an ecological crisis resulting from severe climatic change.

116 Capitalism, cosmopolitanism, Anthropocene

Such an occurrence would not be entirely an external cause, since capitalism has been one of the major causes of climate change and, as Marx recognized, economic activity is embedded in nature.[2] However, ecological catastrophe is not in itself a systemic crisis, as normally understood, but a crisis in the relation of human societies with the planet (in Chapter 7 thus will be discussed more specifically in the context of the Anthropocene). Such crisis could directly have adverse consequences for turbo-capitalism in curtailing the supply of energy. Without access to energy, no economic system can function. This is particularly a danger for capitalism, which depends on access to large supplies of energy in order to drive growth.

Other possible catastrophic crises that might lead to the collapse of capitalism are biological, for example the global spread of a deadly virus or nuclear war. It should be recalled that the world's single greatest catastrophe was the Spanish Flu that killed between 50 to 100 million people in 1918-19. While this did not endanger capitalism as such, it had huge economic and more importantly political consequences; for example, between 13 to 18 million people died in India as a result of the flu. It paved the way to independence of India and to the worldwide creation of health care systems (see Spinney 2018). While these developments can also be seen as functional to the long-term requirements of capitalism, they nonetheless had the potential to be catastrophic for all societal systems. The twentieth century was fundamentally changed as a result of the epidemic, and it is therefore possible to imagine how a future epidemic, made possible by an even more interconnected world, would have similar catastrophic consequences.

Now, while none of these catastrophes, including the deployment of nuclear weapons, can be excluded in principle, it is difficult to see how worst-case scenarios of climate change – for example, a global increase in temperature of 2 to 4 degrees – will lead to the collapse of capitalism. Such events would be catastrophic for many parts of the world, leading to major displacement of populations, and rises in sea levels would affect most parts of the world and possibly lead to the collapse of some states. However, it is not evident that capitalism would collapse unless a much longer term of 50 to 100 years were taken when an ecological crisis may reach a level that endangers human societies. Until then, an ecological catastrophe is likely to contribute to the long-term systemic crisis of capitalism rather than be in itself the transformative force. As Frederic Jameson remarked in a much cited phrase, 'it is easier to imagine the end of the world than to imagine the end of capitalism' (Jameson 2003: 76).

Low-growth capitalism

Another scenario that is possibly a more realistic prognosis, at least for the short- to medium-term of the next 20 to 30 years, is a long period of low-growth capitalism bolstered either by an enhanced regulatory order or constrained neoliberal regimes. Predictions of the collapse of capitalism tend to be either premature or long-term. As noted, Marx himself saw it as an event in the distant future. The foreseeable future, based on current trends, is more likely to be one of the continued transformations of neoliberalism, but within the limits of low growth, if not stagnation. Predictions of the end of capitalism neglect the fact that capitalism is highly resilient. It is capable of considerable flexibility, and the fact that it is crisis-prone does not mean that a crisis portends its demise. Rather than one big crisis that will bring about the end of capitalism, there is a series of crises, and the resolution of one generates another. Crises can in fact be a necessary part of capitalism.

As Harvey and others have argued, the need for capitalism to find new sources of capital led to the extension of easy credit to the working class until it led to the crisis of private debt, which imploded in 2008 with the subprime mortgage crisis in the USA after reaching unsustainable levels. Thus, in Harvey's words, 'crisis tendencies are not resolved but moved around'. Crises also function as 'irrational rationalisers' of a system that is inherently contradictory. 'Crises are, in short, as necessary to the evolution of capitalism as money, labour, power and capital itself' (Harvey 2010: 117). David Kotz (2017) argues that if neoliberal accumulation continues, it will lead to a future of stagnation and instability. This situation is vividly apparent with the election of Trump and Brexit. Both events in 2016 can be seen as the expression of stagnant economies that saw a fall in the real value of wages and declining opportunities and quality of life for many low-income people. The political outcomes with the Trump presidency and Brexit led in turn to political instability. But neoliberal capitalism, despite some modifications, is basically in place. Pro-Brexit politicians in the UK thus seek to free the UK from the regulatory structure of European integration in order to make the UK a global free-trading nation, even if in the short-term there will be economic havoc and social mayhem since, from their perspective, an unfettered capitalism will triumph in the long-run.

As argued in the previous chapter, the reality of neoliberal capitalism is that it can readily adapt to changing circumstances. While neoliberalism has lost much of its ideological zeal, its policy consequences are with us (Crouch 2011). Many governments rely on neoliberal policies in some form or another. Low- or zero-growth economies will lead to increased unemployment that will be eased only by the rise of low-paid, temporary, and insecure forms of employment (Doogan 2009; Sennett 2006). Meanwhile the super-rich will retain their privileges, and global inequality will not decline significantly.

The reality of capitalism today, according to Thomas Piketty (2014: 571), is a great contradiction created by the fact that wealth accumulated in the past grows more rapidly than wages and output. It has led the entrepreneur to become a rentier. His analysis shows that the accumulation of wealth has led to divergence in equality, but 'divergence is not perpetual and it is only one of several possible future directions for the distribution of wealth' (p. 27). This conclusion is less apocalyptic than Marx's, who predicted zero growth in the long-run. Capitalism can flip the other way, leading to greater, not less, regulatory control, as reflected in the example of European integration as a stabilizing mechanism to restrain the worse effects of capitalism but without endangering capitalism. In this sense, the balance of democracy and capitalism may be re-set such that democratic demands may set limits to capitalism.

118 Capitalism, cosmopolitanism, Anthropocene

So, a possible future is the continuation of neoliberalism but with increased political instability arising from the on-set of low growth since low-growth economies will not generate sufficient recourses to meet the fiscal requirements of the state. Such trends will, of course, vary greatly throughout the world. The western world is clearly witnessing low growth, but this is not necessarily the case worldwide. While Brazil is in the throes of economic stagnation, this is not the case for India and East Asia. Yet, as these countries become richer, it is likely, according to Mann (2013: 97), that global economic growth will slow down due to a wider distribution of wealth. The resulting higher costs of labour everywhere will lead to lower profits. Mann disagrees with the notion of a systemic crisis simply on the grounds that societies are not systems but multiple overlapping networks of ideological, economic, military, and political networks of interaction. The lines of interaction are not systemic, and internal dynamics are not self-contained within a domain such as the economy. This leads him to being more sceptical of a terminal crisis of capitalism. His prognosis is instead for a lower-growth capitalism that reduces global inequality and consequently reduces the prospect of social revolution. The major world revolutionary movements in recent times that have brought about change are religious ones and do not have specific implications for capitalism.

The problem with low-growth capitalism as a long-term scenario for a domesticated form of capitalism is that it is fundamentally incompatible with the logic of capitalism, which requires unrelenting growth. The nature of capitalism is that it does not settle for low growth, even when forced to abide by limitations imposed upon it unless such limitations can be rendered functional to the interests of capitalism. Low-growth capitalism, furthermore, does not appear to be compatible with the long-term ecological survival of human societies. The notion of an ecologically sustainable kind of capitalism is now no longer a realistic option in that the parameters of sustainability cannot be met even by low growth.

It is precisely for this reason that a Polanyi-style counter-movement – the assertion of social protectionism against excessive market forces – while a likely development, will ultimately not solve the major problems that capitalism has produced (Polanyi 2001 [1944]). Polanyi's thesis was based on the presupposition of an era of capitalism that was already an inadequate account of his time, but today, with societies everywhere beholden to global forces and potentially catastrophic climate change, the future that beckons will be shaped by a more radical transformation of modernity than one that simply seeks to establish a relation of equilibrium between market forces and social protection.

Postcapitalism

It is possible to envisage a future in which capitalism – weakened as a result of systemic crises – coexists with non-capitalist forms of economic organization. We can call this order 'postcapitalism' to capture the sense of continuity, but also with some significant points of rupture and counter-trends. I refer to postcapitalism as more than simply low-growth capitalism. However, postcapitalism does not necessarily designate a condition that is non-capitalist, but only partly capitalist. To a degree, it may correspond to some form of socialist democracy.

For the immediate future, for reasons given above, it is difficult to envisage a whole-scale transition to a socialist society or some kind of non-capitalist society as a practical reality. The political forces that might create it are absent, even if latent. It is certainly possible to imagine a non-capitalist future, and there are many compelling manifestos and future scenarios of, for example, real utopian socialism or participatory economics.[3] The problem is how to create them. On the basis of current trends, the future of capitalism is more likely to lead in the direction of a post-capitalist world in which capitalism wanes but does not disappear. Capitalist accumulation may reach its limits for reasons of systemic contradictions but does not undergo a systemic collapse. This vision was set out by Drucker (1994), for whom the future that beckoned was essentially a post-capitalist one in so far as the new economy is knowledge based and thus supplants the proletarian-based capitalism of industrial capitalism. However, his claims of a technologically driven post-capitalist order do not stand up to much scrutiny since the reality of the knowledge economy is that it exists within the capitalist mode of production (Fuchs 2013). Nonetheless, as Mason argues, technological change could possibly lead the way to a post-capitalist society if it were accompanied by a major political transformation that made possible the eradication of many of the problems produced by capitalism (Mason 2016).

What if Schumpeter were right? According to Schumpeter, 'creative destruction' does not mean the end of capitalism but its transformation. While Marx saw the destructiveness of capitalism mostly in negative terms and as the expression of the demise of capitalism, Schumpeter saw destructiveness as potentially creative. Indeed, the history of capitalism bears Schumpeter out to a considerable degree in that major technological innovations have led to the renewal of capitalism. As Beckert argues, 'capitalism is an economic system oriented towards the future' (2016: 269). It will not therefore be easily defeated by the future. According to Beckert, capitalism has an inherent disposition to create novelty, without which it cannot survive. It is an economic system oriented to the future. Innovation does not therefore lead to a post-capitalist future since the demonic forces of capitalism have the capacity to fashion the future.

A postcapitalist world is still a realistic possibility because of the major changes brought about by technology that cannot be controlled by capitalism. Technology has reduced the need for work, releasing a surplus population that will not be easily subdued. Automation has the potential to improve the quality of life for all (Bastani 2019; Srnicek and Williams 2016). There is a remarkable rise of the shared economy; that is, goods and services that do not depend on the rule of the market and managerialism (see Elder-Vas 2018). This position is at odds with Collins's argument discussed previously. However, technology alone does not determine the future. And the sharing economy is not quite so shared as the example of Airbnb shows. It is also a question of how such changes interact with other developments. As argued, capitalism is embedded in social institutions, cultural practices, and normative orders, which may generate counter-currents to capitalism. However, capitalism also has a tremendous capacity to co-opt alternatives as well as its critiques. The transformative moment probably does not reside in technology as such but in political creativity and the capacity to imagine the future in ways that challenge the logic of capitalism.

In the context of, on the one side, the systemic weakening of capitalism and the resulting decline in capitalist accumulation, and, on the other, the reassertion of the democratic constitutional state and other forms of collective action, the field of tensions that has always defined modernity is once again reconfiguring (see Mota and Wagner 2019). Calls for neo-Keynesianism, while not amounting to a critique of capitalism as such, as in the writing of Joseph Stigliz and Paul Krugman, have led to considerable rethinking of the merits of neoliberalism, which no longer enjoys hegemonic status (see also Davies 2015). It is possible to envisage a world in which other and more democratic kinds of economic organization develop – for example, a universal basic income – and coexist alongside capitalism, thus setting limits to its capacity to shape the world (Standing 2017). Such a prospect, again, is more likely if the future is envisaged in terms of multiple paths rather than one direction of travel. This is Calhoun's position against Wallerstein's argument of a systemic crisis of capitalism. 'Capitalism could decline without collapsing, simply organizing less of economic activity as alternative systems organize more' (Calhoun 2013: 159). In this view, capitalism persists but is less dominant, and in time a new economic system might develop. It is possible to see a variation of this argument along the lines of Robert Reich's claim that capitalism needs to save itself from the most destructive forms of neoliberal super capitalism (Reich 2015, see also 2008).

The political impact of climate change in the next decade or so may lead to major changes in consumption, which is currently based on the myth of sustainability. It is evident that if current consumption continues, the ecological impact will be catastrophic and reduced consumption may be the only viable option to turbo-charged growth and super-capitalism. If this were to happen, it would lead to reduced capital accumulation and possibly alternative forms of social life. It is very likely that in the age of the Anthropocene, ecological challenges to capitalism will be critical in stemming its destructive tendencies (see Chapter 7). The likelihood of such a development raises once again the question of a new relationship between capitalism and democracy since it is unlikely that capitalism on its own will lead the way.

Conclusion

Theorizing about capitalism and its future has re-animated social and political thought in recent years. The legacy of classical social theory on long-term analyses of capitalism and other related major social and historical transformations needs to be revived to address the current situation. The analysis given in this chapter is that any consideration of the future of capitalism will need to clarify a number of points concerning its core elements since it is not possible to speak of capitalism as a single monolithic entity that has a single future. Neither is it a totalizing power that has eradicated alternatives, since, as argued in this chapter and in the previous two chapters, capitalism is not only an economic system that is separated from other social and political processes. In accord, with the social theory of Habermas, capitalism cannot dispense with the need for legitimation and is embroiled with latent forces that point to an alternative. However, unlike Habermas, I do not think the economy can simply be conceptualized as part of a functionally operative system that only requires fulfilling demands for legitimation. Economies, and, more general, the social system, are also much more irrational and chaotic than Habermas assumed and cannot be so easily tamed by legitimation or even by political rationality deriving from within the state.

The origins of capitalism in the transition from feudalism have been much discussed, and we have a general picture of the course of capitalism over the past five centuries and of its diffusion over the world. A challenge for today is to think through the present situation of capitalism. Some of Marx's most important ideas are still relevant, especially concerning the centrality of capitalist accumulation. However, the world that took shape in the second half of the previous century cannot be understood form the historical experience of the nineteenth. It is also arguably the case that the early twenty-first century is a fundamentally a different place than the world that existed until the end of the previous century in that capitalism has ceased to be contained within the parameters of a model of modernity that took shape in the nineteenth century. Since the end of the Soviet Union and the rise of Chinese economic dominance, capitalism has become a global system. However, it is far from having created a one-dimensional society in that there are now many signs within the present of alternative futures. Although the means to realize all but catastrophic visions is opaque, the political imagination has been awakened.

Building on recent work by Wallerstein et al., Streeck, Beckert, and others, I have proposed five possible scenarios that sum up current debates on the future of capitalism. These can be roughly divided into perspectives that emphasize transitions to a future non-capitalist world, to breakdown, and to transformations of the present. Arguments that emphasize the latter are more convincing in that there is not one end but several ends in sight for capitalism. One likely future will be what Robert Reich (2008) has called super-capitalism will be curtailed and there will be ecological limits to the accumulation of capital. The end of capitalism is a story about the degree to which its destructiveness can be controlled by political forces. The analysis offered in this chapter highlights the links between capitalism and other social and political processes, such as democracy, as the points of tension from which crises spring. From a critical theory perspective, any perspective on the future must be rooted in current trends and possibilities latent in the present. This is not simply as question of realizing the normative claims of modern society or a return to a previous condition. The notion of immanent critique entails a stronger demand for societal transformation and consideration of latent forces that contain the seeds of a different future.

122 Capitalism, cosmopolitanism, Anthropocene

Notes

1 My thanks to Aurea Mota, Neal Harris, William Outhwaite, Piet Strydom, and Frederic Vandenberghe for comments on an earlier version. The chapter is based on a revised version of the main section of an article, 'The Future of Capitalism: Trends, Scenarios and Prospects for the Future' in the *Journal of Classical Sociology*, 19 (1): 10–26 in 2019, which was part of a special issue on the bicentenary of the birth of Karl Marx. I am grateful to the editors of the special issue, Iain Wilkinson and Larry Ray, for comments on an earlier version. Other versions of the paper were given at a symposium at the University of Kent, Canterbury, UK on 5 June 2018 and as a lecture at the University of Brasilia on 15 September 2018. I am grateful to the participants at both events for comments.
2 On climate change and capitalism, see Harrison and Minkler (2014), Klein (2014), Moore (2016), Newell and Paterson (2010).
3 For example, see Ackerman et al (2005), Callinicos (2003), Hannel and Wright (2016).

References

Ackerman, B., Alstott, A. and Van Parijs, P. 2005. *Redesigning Distribution: Basic Income and Stakeholder Grants as Cornerstones for an Egalitarian Capitalism*. London: Verso.

Albert, M. 1993. *Capitalism Against Capitalism*. London: Whurr.

Amable, B. 2004. *The Diversity of Modern Capitalism*. Oxford: Oxford University Press.

Arnason, J. 1993. *The Future that Failed: Origins and Destinies of the Soviet Model*. London: Routledge.

Arnason, J. 2015. Theorizing Capitalism: Classical Foundations and Contemporary Innovations. *European Journal of Social Theory*, 18 (4): 351–67.

Bastani, A. 2019. *Fully Automated Luxury Communism*. London: Verso.

Beckert, J. 2016. *Imagined Futures: Fictional Expectations and Capitalist Dynamics*. Cambridge, MA: Harvard University Press.

Beckert, J. and Bronk, R. (eds.) 2018. *Uncertain Futures: Imaginaries, Narratives, and Calculation in the Economy*. Oxford: Oxford University Press.

Benjamin, W. 1999. *The Arcades Project*. Cambridge, MA: Harvard University Press.

Bloch, E. 2009 [1935]. *Heritage of Our Times*. Cambridge: Polity Press.

Blokker, P. 2012. *Multiple Democracies in Europe*. London: Routledge.

Calhoun, C. 2013. What Threatens Capitalism Now? In: Wallerstein, I., et al (eds.) *Does Capitalism Have a Future?* Oxford: Oxford University Press.

Callinicos, A. 2003. *An Anti-Capitalist Manifesto*. Cambridge: Polity Press.

Connell, R. and Dados, N. 2014. Where in the World Does Neoliberalism Come from? The Market Agenda in Southern Perspective. *Theory and Society*, 43: 117–38.

Costa, S. and Goncalves, G. 2020. From Primitive, Accumulation to Entangled Accumulation: Decentring Marxist Theory of Capitalist Expansion. *European Journal of Social Theory*, 20 (2).

Crouch, C. 2011. *The Strange non-Death of Neo-Liberalism*. Cambridge: Polity Press.

Davies, W. 20015. The Return of Social Government: From 'Socialist Calculation' to 'Social Analytics'. *European Journal of Social Theory*, 18 (4): 431–50.

Diamond, J. 2011. *Collapse: How Societies Choose to Fail or Succeed*. 2nd edition. London: Penguin Books.

Doogan, K. 2009. *New Capitalism? The Transformation of Work*. Cambridge: Polity Press.

Drucker, P. 1994. *Post-Capitalist Society*. New York: HarperBusiness.

Elder-Vas, D. 2018. Moral Economies of the Digital. *European Journal of Social Theory*, 21 (2): 141–7.

Fuchs, C. 2013. Capitalism or Information Society? The Fundamental Question of the Present Structure of Society. *European Journal of Social Theory*, 16 (4): 413–34.

Habermas, J. 1976. *Legitimation Crisis*. London: Heinemann.

Hahnel, R. and Wright, E. O. 2016. *Alternatives to Capitalism: Proposals for a Democratic Economy*. London: Verso.

Hall, P. and Soskice, D. 2001. *Varieties of Capitalism: The Institutional Foundations of Comparative Advantage*. Oxford: Oxford University Press.

Hamilton, G. and Shin, S. I. 2015. Demand-Responsive Industrialization in East Asia: A New Critique of Political Economy. *European Journal of Social Theory*, 18 (4): 390–412.

Harrison, N. and Minkler, N. 2014. *Liberal Capitalism and Climate Change*. London: Palgrave Macmillan.

Harvey, D. 2010. *The Enigma of Capital and the Crises of Capitalism*. Oxford: Oxford University Press.

Harvey, D. 2014. *Seventeen Contradictions and the End of Capitalism*. London: Profile Books.

Horn, E. 2018. *The Future as Catastrophe: Imagining Disaster in the Modern Age*. Cambridge: Cambridge University Press.

Jameson, F. 2003. Future City. *New Left Review*, 21 (May–June): 65–79.

Klein, N. 2014. *This Changes Everything: Capitalism and Climate Change*. London: Allen Lane.

Kocka, J. 2016. *Capitalism: A Short History*. Princeton, NJ: Princeton University Press.

Kotz, D. 2017. *The Rise and Fall of Neoliberal Capitalism*. Cambridge, MA: Harvard University Press.

Mann, M. 2013. The End may be Nigh, but for Whom? In: Wallerstein, I., et al (eds.) *Does Capitalism Have a Future?* Oxford: Oxford University Press.

Mason, P. 2016. *PostCapitalism: A Guide to Our Future*. London: Penguin Books.

Moore, J. 2016. *Anthropocene or Capitalism: Nature, History and the Crisis of Capitalism*. Oakland, CA: PM Press.

Mota, A. and Wagner, P. 2019. *Collective Action and Political Transformation: The Entangled Experiences in Brazil, South Africa and Europe*. Edinburgh: Edinburgh University Press.

Newell, P. and Paterson, M. 2010. *Climate Capitalism*. Cambridge: Cambridge University Press.

Offe, C. 2003. Can the European Model of 'Social Capitalism' Survive European Integration? *The Journal of Political Philosophy*, 11 (4): 437–69.

Piketty, T. 2014. *Capital in the Twenty-First Century*. Cambridge, MA: Harvard University Press.

Polanyi, K. 2001 [1944]. *The Great Transformation*. Boston: Beacon Press.

Reich, R. 2008. *Supercapitalism: The Transformation of Business, Democracy and Everyday Life*. Melbourne: Scribe Publications.

Reich, R. 2015. *Saving Capitalism: For the Many, Not the Few*. London: Icon.

Schumpeter, J. 2010 [1942]. *Capitalism, Socialism and Democracy*. London: Routledge.

Sennett, R. 2006. *The Culture of the New Capitalism*. London: Routledge.

Spinney, L. 2018. *The Spanish Flue of 1918 and How It Changed the World*. London: Vintage.

Srnicek, N. and Williams, A. 2016. *Inventing the Future: Postcapitalism and a World Without Work*. London: Verso.

Standing, G. 2017. *Basic Income: And How We Can Make It Happen*. London: Pelican.

Streeck, W. 2011. The Crisis of Democratic Capitalism. *New Left Review*, 71 (September–October): 5–25.

Streeck, W. 2014a. *Buying Time: The Delayed Crisis of Democratic Capitalism*. London: Verso.

Streeck, W. 2014b. How Will Capitalism End? *New Left Review*, 87 (May–June).

Wallerstein, I., Collins, R., Mann, M., Derluguian, G. and Calhoun, C. 2013. *Does Capitalism Have a Future?* Oxford: Oxford University Press.

Weber, M. 2003 [1927]. *General Economic History*. New York: Dover Publications.

6

THE PROSPECTS OF COSMOPOLITANISM AND THE POSSIBILITY OF GLOBAL JUSTICE

New directions for critical social theory

It has been widely recognized that a limitation of the critical social theory tradition has been its relative neglect of global challenges. As discussed in Chapter 1, it was also constrained by a tacit Eurocentrism. In this respect, it was probably no different from the mainstream currents in twentieth-century social and political thought. As argued in Chapter 1, postcolonial critiques and new perspectives in global history require a reconsideration of the entire critical theory tradition. As we have seen, the communicative and recognition turn brought about by Habermas and Honneth did nothing to address global challenges and remained trapped within a European understanding of modernity. In this chapter, I argue that critical theory needs a cosmopolitan turn, which I see as more far-reaching than a corrective of Eurocentrism in that it is not merely a re-setting of the cultural horizons of critique but of addressing pressing new concerns. I am principally concerned with global justice, which has become more a key topic for current critical theory than it was in the first generation of critical theory, which was more concerned with issues relating to domination and instrumental rationalization. The next chapter addresses the new politics of nature in the context of the Anthropocene.

In this chapter, I argue that cosmopolitanism and critical theory have much in common and that the former is best termed critical cosmopolitanism. The idea of a critical cosmopolitanism is relevant to the renewal of critical social theory in its traditional concern with the critique of social reality and the search for immanent forms of transcendence. It also offers a route out of the critique of domination and a general notion of emancipation that has so far constrained critical theory. It provides a promising approach to connect normative critique with empirically based analysis focussed on exploring new ways of seeing the world. Such forms of world disclosure have become an unavoidable part of social reality today in terms of people's experiences, identities, solidarities, and values. These dimensions represent the foundations for a new conception of critical theory's immanent transcendence. The notion of immanent transcendence constitutes the core of the cosmopolitan imagination in so far as this is a way of viewing the social world in terms of its immanent possibilities for self-transformation and which can be realized only by taking the cosmopolitan perspective of the Other as well as global principles of justice.

The idea of critical cosmopolitanism

The term critical cosmopolitanism signals the critical and transformative nature of cosmopolitanism.[1] This is what distinguishes it from other uses of the term, which are often unclarified. The term was probably first used by Rabinow (1986) and has been invoked by Mignolo (2000) and also Rumford (2008). For Mignolo critical cosmopolitanism is a de-colonial critique of the Eurocentric presuppositions of cosmopolitan thought. In the sense I am using the term it draws attention to the transformative potential within the present. Cosmopolitanism as a normative critique refers to phenomena that are generally in tension with their social context, which they seek to transform. This is what makes it particularly difficult to specify since it is a discourse or phenomenon that is expressed in its effects on social contexts and in its response to social problems that are experienced by people in different contexts.

Cosmopolitanism is thus both a normative theory (which makes cognitive claims) and also a particular kind of social phenomenon. Like many concepts in social and political science, it is both an empirical and a normative concept, that is, as is increasingly recognized now in the expanding literature, it is both an experience or reality – in the sense of a lived experience and a measurable empirical condition – and an interpretation of the experience of the encounter. In so far as it is an interpretation, normative aspects enter into it as common reference points. It can additionally be characterized as having a cognitive dimension. In this latter sense, cosmopolitanism can be held to be a critical attitude and, from the perspective of social science, a particular kind of analysis. This is an analysis that is essentially critical in that it is an approach to social reality that views social reality not only as an empirical phenomenon but also as given form by counter-factuals. It is the nature of these counter-factuals that they involve normative ideas. Cosmopolitanism can thus be said to concern empirical phenomena or reality, interpretations (which are also empirical but normatively guided), and evaluations (which are on a higher order and require explanations, and which is where critical sociology has a role).

One of the features of cosmopolitanism as a process of self-transformation is its communicative dimension. As a dialogic condition, cosmopolitanism can be understood in terms of critical dialogue or deliberation. A deliberative conception of culture and politics captures the cosmopolitan spirit of engaging with the perspective of the Other as opposed to rejecting it. This is where the tie between cosmopolitanism and critical theory is strong. Habermas's reorientation of critical theory towards communication and deliberative democracy still remains one of the more important resources for a theory of critical cosmopolitanism, though this has not received much attention. In this chapter, I am emphasizing the critical logic of cosmopolitanism in opening up new horizons. This is a condition in which cultures undergo transformation in light of the encounter with the Other. It can take different forms, ranging from the soft forms of multiculturalism to major re-orientations in self-understanding in light of global principles or re-evaluations of cultural heritage and identity as a result of inter-cultural encounters. What is noteworthy is the interactive dimension to the fusion of horizons, which is not a condition of external agency or a self-transcending subjectivity but an orientation that develops out of the interplay of Self, Other, and World relations.

This is essentially a dialogical relation. The cosmopolitan condition emerges out of the logic of the encounter, exchange, and dialogue and the emergence of universalistic rules rather than by the assertion of a higher order of truths. It has been recognized in classical sociological theory in the interactionist tradition (G. H. Mead) and in genetic psychology (Piaget) that processes of universalization, such as generalization and abstraction, emerge from the inter-relation of different points of view and in turn to the formation of second-order reflexive or cognitive meta-rules (see Aboulafa 2006; Strydom 2019a, 2011, 2020b). It is in this sense, then, it is of a relativization of universalism that the epistemological framework of cosmopolitanism is a post-universalism since it stands for a universalism that does not demand universal assent or that everyone identifies with a single interpretation. Depending on the social context or historical situation, social actors will interpret universal rules differently and put them to different uses.

It is this interpretative feature of cosmopolitanism that distinguishes it from older conceptions of universalism in the sense of a universal order of values. Cosmopolitanism, properly understood, is rather characterized by a 'post-universalistic' conception of truth. By this is simply meant that statements of truth and justice and so on are not absolute, immutable, or derivable from an objective order of universal values, but nonetheless it is still possible to make judgements and evaluations. Universalist claims on science are stronger than claims in the domain of culture and morality (see Chernilo 2019). For cosmopolitanism, then, universalism is best understood as differentiated. This understanding of universalism has been variously recognized by philosophers as different as Hilary Putnam, Richard Rorty, Jürgen Habermas, and Martha Nussbaum and virtually all of the analytical tradition. In other words, cosmopolitanism entails a weak universalism that is compatible with relativism, understood as, in Sahlins's formulation, 'the provisional suspension of one['s] own judgments in order to situate the practices at issue in the historical and cultural order that made them possible' (Sahlins 2000: 21). It accords with the Kantian notion of a transcendental presupposition, namely the position that something must be necessarily presupposed and to what extent it is universal.

As discussed in Chapter 2, a methodological feature of critical theory is its concern with the objectivity of a problem: critique is driven by the fact that the social world produces problems to which social actors and social science respond in their different ways. Social science seeks to offer explanations which have the critical function of assisting social actors and the wider society in finding solutions and in understanding the nature of the problem. This concern with societal problems is also what animates the cosmopolitan imagination and gives to cosmopolitanism a critical edge. For cosmopolitan thought, social problems are the primary challenge and are the context in which the broadening of moral and political horizons occurs. While the kinds of problems that critical theory has been traditionally concerned with are those associated with the 'critique of domination', the cosmopolitan reconstitution of critical theory would rather focus on those societal problems that are global in scope.

Both the history of cosmopolitanism and critical theory share a concern with war and violence. The background to much of the critical theory tradition before Habermas was the centrality of the Holocaust as the culmination of modernity. Cosmopolitanism, too, has been a response to the experience of war and violence in the twentieth century. The emergence of cosmopolitanism with its central concern with global justice after 1945 – as reflected in developments such as crimes against humanity, the UN Declaration of Human Rights, and the general movements towards worldwide democratization, the project of European integration – was in many ways shaped by the widely felt need to find global solutions based on dialogue rather than on violence.

Global justice and cosmopolitanism

The notion that global justice is both a challenge and a possibility is a relatively new idea. As noted, it has become more central to contemporary critical theory, as reflected in the work of theorists as different as Rainer Forst and Nancy Fraser. Notions of justice have traditionally been confined to territorially limited political communities, generally nation-states, and global justice a secondary or derivative matter. It was not very long ago when all questions of justice were thought to pertain to nationally defined political communities. This was certainly the assumption that Rawls made in *A Theory of Justice* in 1971 and which set the terms of debate for more than four decades. In the past two decades, there has been a steady increase in what may be called discourses of global justice, including theoretical conceptualizations and political practices that reflect notions of global justice. It would appear that global justice has become part of the *Zeitgeist* or the political imaginary of critical publics in contemporary societies as they address a range of global challenges.

To create new or possible worlds it is first of all necessary to be able to imagine them. The fact that we are unsure of what exactly global justice constitutes but nonetheless speak of it suggests that it is a reality of a certain kind. One might say it is a reality creating idea. The reality of global justice can now be declared to be a constitutive feature of political community. It is a way of judging the world and a way of thinking about the world, as well as a way of examining the world that challenges the exclusivity of national borders as determining the boundaries of justice. Global justice has a normative, a cognitive, and an epistemological dimension: it offers principles against which injustice can be measured; it offers a language to speak about human interconnectedness; and it is a topic on which knowledge can be acquired through social research. The concern with global justice is central to

128 Capitalism, cosmopolitanism, Anthropocene

the idea of cosmopolitanism, though not the only aspect of cosmopolitanism. In this chapter, I am largely concerned with the political dimension of cosmopolitanism, which I see as the context in which to discuss global justice. The aim of the chapter is to explore the considerations that are at stake in assessing the prospects of cosmopolitanism today as a political project. I argue that there is scope for fruitful dialogue between sociology and political philosophy around this question, which asks how a normative idea that is already ingrained in the social world can be studied empirically. Expressed more directly in the terms of critical theory, it is a question about how latent forces in social reality develop to a point that they bring about a transformation of social reality. In the next section, I discuss the notion of global justice before outlining a theoretical approach to the analysis of cosmopolitanism. The subsequent section moves on to look at the conditions of the possibility of cosmopolitanism before finally considering the prospects of cosmopolitanism.

Most academic discussions of global justice have concentrated on its normative significance. Political theorists, who have dominated the discussion on global justice, have mostly considered it in terms of a normative political project to be realized in the world. I would like to comment briefly on this before I move to discuss the other and more sociological dimensions, in particular the cognitive dimension, and more specifically the process by which global justice emerges. A striking feature of normative conceptions of global justice is that political theorists are in disagreement with the aims of global justice, which we can add to the lexicon of essentially contested terms. Much of this disagreement arises when it comes to the tricky problem of how to create policies to realize normative aims, assuming that these can be agreed on. There is perhaps wider agreement on the presuppositions of global justice as regards, for instance, the responsibilities of citizenship. Assuming that the aims of global justice derive from the responsibilities of citizenship, which entails not just rights but also obligations, a good place to begin is with the condition of citizenship.

There is general agreement that citizens have an obligation to others beyond those who are members of their community, generally taken to be a state, but disagreement on how far it should extend – to humanity at large, for instance, as Peter Singer (2004) has argued – and, moreover, there is disagreement on what the obligation entails and how far into the future such obligations should extend (for instance, to future generations). In the case of the debt crisis in Europe since 2009, especially in the context of the Greek debt crisis, there is the issue as to whether obligations extend to member states to assist those states in financial trouble on the grounds that the EU as a whole will benefit. In this case, it is evident that obligations are related to interdependence and thus to self-interest. However, if we have an obligation to people with whom we are not directly affected and have no direct material benefit from helping – to make that assumption – the question arises as to what kind of deeds should follow (donations, changes in consumption such as fair-trade, boycotting the products of exploitative companies, increased taxation to fund aid, and so on). This is often seen as a question of solidarity, whether it is a 'thin' or a 'thick' solidarity. There is a second debate as to whether responsibility falls on individuals or on states; for some it is enough that states fulfil the obligation, for instance, through humanitarian aid financed through general taxation, but for others, individuals as active citizens also have an additional obligation of a pro-active nature. Additionally, there are a range of pragmatic issues concerning efficiency, (i.e. who is best placed to achieve the desired results – states, inter-governmental organizations or global institutions) – and what kinds of action are required (e.g. military intervention, high interest loans or aid, changes to migration policies, reduced carbon emissions, and so on). There is an additional layer of complexity, too, if we add responsibility. To have an obligation to others is all the more stronger if one has a responsibility to them, but not all obligations are based on responsibility; they can be inspired by solidarity, which in turn rests on sources such as identity and is generally relational (in the sense of bonds that derive from having a direct relation to others). Indeed, I would argue that cosmopolitan solidarity does not necessarily derive from the obligation (or duties) of citizenship, which is largely determined by rights secured by a state. But this is a question that is essentially one of process or emergence rather than one of the projects of global justice; that is, it is a development that is determined by changing social realities and the outcome of how publics respond to problems in the social world.

As a political project, there are essentially four positions, ranging from fairly weak to strong views, depending on where one stands on the question of the limits of obligation and whether or not the norms that apply within a given state also should apply beyond the jurisdiction of the state. One position is that the aim of global justice is to alleviate poverty so that basic needs can be fulfilled. This is a fairly weak objective in that it is achieved once the problem of absolute poverty has been solved and very basic problems of health solved. This generally corresponds to humanitarianism and development aid and is inspired by a basic desire to provide assistance to vulnerable persons or societies that have experienced a major catastrophe. However, the obligation to provide assistance to those in need does not challenge the obligations of citizenship and does not necessarily lead to cosmopolitan consequences. A second position is to see the problem of global justice in terms of the pursuit of human rights. In this case, the objective is more focussed on individuals rather than on societies as a whole and is concerned with securing basic liberty. These are two weak demands since the aim is to bring societies up to a certain level or to eliminate specific obstacles or to make possible certain basic capabilities, as Martha Nussbaum (2002, 2006) argues, such as needs and freedoms. A third position is to see the aim of global justice to be the pursuit of equality, this being a stronger position, as Gillian Brock (2019, 2009) has convincingly argued, in that to achieve equality in many parts of the world it is necessary to change power relations in those countries and put in place new social structures. This is more than the satisfaction of basic needs but extends into the domain of the politics of recognition. Neither of these three positions – assuming effective means can be established on how to achieve them, which for positions one and two is rather less complicated than in the third – have any significant qualitative implications for the developed world or for planetary sustainability. They are compatible with liberal and statist as opposed to globalist arguments.

130 Capitalism, cosmopolitanism, Anthropocene

Finally, there is the stronger position that the aim of global justice is to achieve equality between states, as opposed to taking for granted the existing relations and achieving certain goals within states, such as the removal of absolute poverty, the enforcement of human rights, and greater equality. In this stronger position, which we can term globalist, the question of global justice is inescapably one of redistributive justice and strong demands of what obligation to others entails. In the case of migration, for instance, it may be necessary to create significant changes to membership of the polity. Strong conceptions of global justice also arise on re-distribution, challenging liberal humanitarianism. Once the satisfaction of basic needs and freedoms has overcome absolute inequality, the challenge of overcoming relative inequality remains. This puts egalitarianism to the test since, if the entire world were to achieve the standard of life in the developed world, the ecological sustainability of the planet would self-destruct. This, then, is where global justice and global environmentalism are inter-linked and where the objective of planetary sustainability may be the ultimate aim of global politics. Strong conceptions of global justice are also related to the idea of global democratization and call into question the statist and liberal assumptions of the other positions with the argument that global institutions need to be created rather than rely on existing states or the actions of individual citizens.

The first two positions have the merit of being achievable, while the second two, in particular the fourth, are less clear in terms of a way forward. The pursuit of the normative objectives of global justice cannot be separated from the means to achieve them, and we have to entertain the possibility that to ignore such problems the enforcement of global justice can be counter-productive, if not destructive. The mis-use of human rights, for instance, has brought the very notion of human rights into disrepute, though I strongly disagree with the view of critics such as Costa Douzinas (2000) that this has altogether discredited human rights (see for a different view Moyn (2012)). It does mean that global justice is a contested domain and historically variable. We only have to think of the atrocities committed in the name of regime change and liberal democracy. However, I reject the strong critique of global justice that argues that, while desirable, any attempt to create it is either impossible or oppressive due to the measures it would require. I think these positions are as wrong as the conservative realist position (espoused by David Miller and Michael Walzer, for instance) that only cohesive national communities are real, and we have no obligations beyond the borders of nation-states. To pursue this further it is, in my view, best to place the idea of global justice in the context of the broader framework of cosmopolitanism since this has generally provided the terms of analysis for the transformation of political community in the context of global challenges because, as I shall argue, global justice is part of a wider socio-cultural shift and thus tied to other processes of change. To understand the prospects of cosmopolitanism is especially important in the context of a great number of global challenges, ranging from ethnic-national conflicts, racism and the exclusion and discrimination of minorities, ecological destruction, human trafficking, the exploitation of vulnerable workers, and so on.

Cosmopolitanism and social change: a theoretical framework

Political philosophers will continue to debate the normative project of global justice. I am more interested in global justice as a discourse in contemporary societies that tells us something about the nature of social change and changing assumptions about what I refer to as the objectives of global justice, such as the bonds that constitute a political community or the perception of what responsibility requires. Rather than focus only on the normative project, we also need to consider the process by which cosmopolitanism and the related forms of knowledge on which it rests emerge. Beck (2006) has referred to this as 'cosmopolitanization', meaning the empirical manifestation of cosmopolitanism. The objectives of global justice will ultimately be determined by public argumentation and reflect the outcome of social processes in which normative ideals are contested and de-contested. It is possible to speculate that the outcome will be highly pluralist, with different objectives invoked for various problems. It is very unlikely, probably undesirable and certainly problematic, for the norms that apply in domestic national contexts to be simply transposed to the global context, as globalists would have us believe. In my view, a cosmopolitan position involves the recognition of differential levels of obligation and membership. For this reason, I have some sympathy for the enigmatic argument that Rawls proposed in his last work, *A Law of Peoples*, in 1999, that the norms that should be applied to the global context are (mostly) different from those that apply to domestic politics. However, in his concern with 'peoples' rather than persons, he confined the demands of distributive justice too much and effectively narrowed the range of global justice to exclude much of the cosmopolitan imaginary, which has made visible the cracks in the walls of the nation-state in ways that have implications for solidarity and how membership of the polity is perceived. This is because his main concern was with 'peoples' and with issues such as the promotion of autonomy, the prevention of persecution, and so on. Nevertheless his 'well ordered' 'peoples' end up looking very much like nation-states. It is not surprising then that cosmopolitan political theorists have been unhappy with Rawls, who did not take up the radical project in *A Theory of Justice* in a cosmopolitan direction, remaining instead within a narrow liberal position. I would like to make the argument that the liberal heritage, which to varying degrees may survive within the national state, is deeply problematical when it comes to global justice. While many cosmopolitan goals are compatible with liberalism, the challenge of global justice is not easily achieved within a liberal framework, which assumes a sovereign state.

The politico-normative appeal of cosmopolitanism is also due to the alternative it suggests to both nationalism and to globalization: it offers an alternative to the homogenizing aspects of globalization and related visions, such as, on the one side, the end of history scenario and, on the other, it challenges highly particularistic ways of life associated with nationalism and predictions of a worldwide clash of cultures. Broadly speaking, cosmopolitanism concerns ways in which diversity (different conceptions of the common good) and unity (belief in the possibility of a common good and the equality of all persons) can be reconciled both within given societies or cultures and in the wider global context through taking into account the perspective of others. For this reason, cosmopolitanism has an unavoidable cognitive dimension in that it is also about the degree to which societies can develop ways of thinking and feeling about justice; it is not simply a matter of the application of normative principles, such as the pursuit of freedom or specific human rights, since those principles themselves – which are best seen as metanorms – need to be interpreted and realized in different forms. The central issue, following Habermas, I would argue is learning: cosmopolitanism is centrally about learning; it is about how the moral and political horizons of individuals, groups, the public in general, and societies are broadened though the capacity for connectivity. The short answer to the question of realizing global justice is that it requires a major cognitive transformation, that it can only come following from shifts in the self-understanding of contemporary societies in the way they imagine the world. Just like nations have imaginaries, so, too, does cosmopolitanism have an imaginary dimension to it.

Against the commonly stated objection that cosmopolitanism is weak or non-existent due to the dominance of the national imaginary, I would reply by saying that, first, the cosmopolitan imaginary is already part of the nation today. There are few national identities that can exclude cosmopolitan challenges, be it the integration of minorities, human rights, or the need for global dialogue. Everywhere the nation has become the site of contested claims. It is possible to argue, as Scheffler (2001) has, that there are two competing claims within political community around local and global claims. Second, one could make the stronger claim that the cosmopolitan is in fact prior to the national imaginary in that the idea of the nation is always a particularization of the universal. This was how the modern idea of the nation first arose in the eighteenth century, as a particularization of the universal, and while there have been many attempts to deprive the nation of its universalistic legitimation, the connection is still preserved in the constitutions of most countries. Further examples of the priority of the universal over the particular would include the anti-slavery movement in the nineteenth century and the civil rights movement in the mid-twentieth century. In my view, it is important for the cosmopolitan project to locate itself within the category of the nation, rather than transcending it, for the nation is capable of redefinition in light of universalizing claims. For this reason, there is no fundamental antagonism between the national and the cosmopolitan: the latter can be seen as a counter-factual embedded within modern political community.

Before developing this further and suggesting how the prospects of cosmopolitanism might be assessed, I would like to outline the main intellectual sources of cosmopolitanism with a view to arriving at the core of the cosmopolitan imagination. While having Greek origins, it is essentially a product of modern societies as they address global problems. The origins of the term, of course, lie in stoic thought, at least in its most important philosophical legacy, and the early Christian thinkers, St Paul and St Augustine, made an important contribution in developing the ideas.

There were, of course, also non-western traditions that can be associated with cosmopolitanism, which should not be equated entirely with its European heritage.[2] However, despite its origins in antiquity and the civilizations of what Karl Jaspers has termed the Axial Age (see Bellah and Joas 2012), cosmopolitanism is an essentially modern movement in its concerns with global justice and the vision of the essential unity of the world but without presupposing a transcendental or sacred order. Cosmopolitan ideas are not just simply ideas projected on the world, as was the case in ancient thought, but are part of the modern world. The defining tenets of modern cosmopolitanism can be seen in the work of three key thinkers: Immanuel Kant, Alexander von Humboldt, and Karl Marx, who each gave to modern cosmopolitanism a key contribution.

In *Perpetual Peace* in 1795 Kant (1991) established the principle of hospitality as the defining tenet of cosmopolitanism, which he contrasted to internationalism, which for Kant was based on treaties between states. Cosmopolitanism in contrast is based on the centrality of the individual and the need for the rights of the individual to be recognized even where the individual is a foreigner. It is this idea of cosmopolitan law, rather than the vision of global government, which Kant believed was desirable but not realistic, and which has been the real legacy of modern cosmopolitanism. The writings of Alexander von Humbolt brought an additional contribution to the modern idea of cosmopolitanism. This consists of what he called 'world consciousness', a term that he coined and which has entered into language of cosmopolitan thought to refer to the inter-connectedness of the world. For von Humboldt the world was the primary reality of being and guaranteed the unity of humanity and nature. While Kant's world was the European order of republican nations, von Humboldt had a genuinely more cosmopolitan temperament and vision of the unity of the world, as reflected in his famous *Political Essay on the Island of Cuba* in 1856 (von Humboldt 2011) and his criticism of slavery, and in his major four-volume work *Cosmos* (see Walls 2009). Finally, Karl Marx articulated a cosmopolitan vision of political community with the claim that 'the workers of the world have no country' and the foundation of the First International. Neither Kant nor von Humbolt gave much thought to how the cosmopolitanism that they believed in would be possible. Marx in contrast had a very clear vision of a cosmopolitical project and one that would realize global social justice. For Marx, justice had to be social and had to be globally realized. Taking these three conceptions of cosmopolitanism, with their respective roots in European republicanism, romanticism, and socialism, we can arrive at a broad view of cosmopolitanism as based on the following dimensions.

It is in the first instance a condition of openness to the world in the sense of the broadening of the moral and political horizons of societies. It entails a view of societies as connected rather than separated.

Cosmopolitanism is made possible by the fact that individuals, groups, publics, and societies have a capacity for learning in dealing with problems and in particular learning from each other. In this sense, then, cosmopolitanism is not a matter of diversity or mobility but a process of learning.

134 Capitalism, cosmopolitanism, Anthropocene

Dialogue is a key feature of cosmopolitanism since dialogue opens up the possibility of incorporating the perspective of others into one's own view of the world. It can thus be associated with a communicative view of modernity.

Rather than being an affirmative condition, it is transformative and is produced by social struggles rather than being primarily elite-driven or entirely institutional. In this sense, cosmopolitanism can be related to popular and vernacular traditions rather than exclusively to the projects of elites (see Holton 2009).

From an epistemological perspective, cosmopolitan involves the production of essentially critical knowledge, such as the identification of transformative potentials within the present.

Finally, cosmopolitanism is related to subject formation: it is constitutive of the self as much as it is of social and political processes. This is reflected in the von Humboltian – in this case Wilhelm von Humboldt's – understanding of cosmopolitanism as a particular kind of consciousness that is best exemplified in education. In the acquisition of knowledge, the self undergoes a transformation, for *Bildung* is a form of self-formation and occurs through the encounter of the individual with the world. *Bildung* is a means of encountering the universal, as reflected in the category of the world, and is the aim of education.

These features of cosmopolitanism challenge the received view of normative ideas, such as global justice as transcending political community or as simply utopian. The conception of cosmopolitanism I am putting forward is that it is constitutive of modernity and part of the make-up of the political community. This is why cosmopolitanism is not a zero-sum condition, either present or absent, as its critics often argue and its defenders mistakenly argue in its support. It is present to varying degrees in contemporary societies.

In order to assess the prospects of cosmopolitanism it is therefore necessary to determine the extent to which cosmopolitan phenomena are present in the cultural model of societies and in their modes of social organization and institutions. By the cultural model, I mean the social imaginary of societies, the dominant forms of collective identity or self-understanding, and the ideas of Reason embedded within them. The cultural model of all modern societies involves the amplification and metamorphosis of transcultural ideas such as liberty, justice, freedom, autonomy, and rights, which, of course, are variously interpreted and are not always fully institutionalized. But the existence of such ideas (essentially meta-norms) means that societies have the cognitive means of reaching beyond themselves. For this reason, there is generally a tension in modern societies between the cultural model and institutions. Related to these levels of analysis is the dimension of subject formation, the cosmopolitan self. It is possible that any one time in the history of a society there is a tension between subject formation, the cultural model of society, and social institutions. It is for this reason that cosmopolitanism can be seen as a critical theory of society (see Delanty 2009): it shares with the critical heritage the concern with possibilities within the present or the immanent transcendence of society.

I am emphasizing, then, the formative dimensions of cosmopolitanism, which in other words is structure forming both the self and society. It entails a subject (the cosmopolitan subject), a discourse in which ideas, knowledge, and modes of cognition are produced, and social practices. Viewed in such terms, cosmopolitanism is a process as opposed to a fixed condition. It is marked by conflict, contradictions, negotiation. The implications of this view are that evidence of cosmopolitanism must be found not in an end state – a cosmopolitan society or state as opposed to a non-cosmopolitan one – but in the process by which it emerges. This is the sociological task to determine.

The conditions of the possibility of cosmopolitanism

What would be such evidence, and how can it be assessed? My proposal is for a three-fold level of analysis. First, four levels of cosmopolitanism can be specified. Second, three main processes can be identified by which norms or normative systems emerge. Third, a number of key areas can be identified for empirical evidence. The first two will be outlined in this section, with the third the focus of the final section of the chapter.

Cosmopolitanism can be understood in terms of four levels of relationships, as I have argued in *The Cosmopolitan Imagination* (Delanty 2009). These range from low to high levels of intensity and can also be seen as constitutive of subject formation and thus elements in the making of a cosmopolitan subject.

The first level of cosmopolitanism can be described as a cultural cosmopolitanism and typically concerns curiosity about other cultural values. One of its most pervasive forms is in consumption, but it can also be seen in educational programmes aimed at understanding other cultures. In these instances, cosmopolitanism entails a relation to the Other that does not involve extensive self-scrutiny or reflexivity and is fully compatible with most expressions of liberal tolerance. It may also exhibit a general tolerance of diversity, recognition of interconnectedness, and a disposition of openness to others. In sum, it is a soft kind of cosmopolitanism and akin to the condition of 'cultural omnivorousness'.

A second form of cosmopolitanism concerns a stronger and more positive recognition of the Other. Here cosmopolitanism can be related to political rather than purely cultural relations of alterity. In this case the question of the inclusion of the 'Other' is paramount, not just awareness or curiosity about differences. Such expressions of cosmopolitanism can be related to what Honneth and Taylor refer to as recognition, in particular recognition based on rights. The enlargement of the boundaries of political community in both the national and international context can be seen in terms of the cosmopolitan ethnic of what Habermas has referred to as a 'solidarity among strangers'. Expressions of solidarity as opposed to tolerance illustrate this deeper level of the engagement with the other. While such forms of cosmopolitanism can be found on the global level, it is more characteristic of local contexts.

While the second type of cosmopolitanism demands of the political subject a change in its relation to alterity, it does not require much more than the inclusion of the other. A third expression of cosmopolitanism is to be found in a stronger

136 Capitalism, cosmopolitanism, Anthropocene

reflexive and critical attitude whereby both self and other undergo transformation. This concerns the mutual evaluation of cultures or identities, both one's own and that of the other. To achieve it, a degree of cultural distance is required in order to create a space for critique and scepticism. This more critical kind of cosmopolitanism makes possible for people to mediate between cultures. Such forms of cosmopolitanism will be expressed in dialogic encounters and in deliberative style communication. This is also what allows for the critique of cultures and cross-cultural communication.

The fourth type of cosmopolitanism builds on the previous one in its orientation towards a shared normative culture. The characteristic expression of such forms of cosmopolitanism is not simply mutual critique but the formation of new social relations and institutions. This is where the consequences of the other levels become evident. In this case it is possible to speak of cosmopolitanism as a societal condition as opposed to being an aspect of political community or characteristic of people. Unlike the previous types it is also possible to relate this form of cosmopolitanism to an engagement with global problems or consciousness of the urgency for global justice and the need to find solutions that may require giving primacy to the non-national interest and the perspective of others. Thus, when cosmopolitan forms of consciousness penetrate beyond the level of individuals to reach the societal level creating not only new institutions but also wider social transformation beyond the national societies, we can speak of a global cosmopolitanism.

These four levels of cosmopolitanism are not necessarily consecutive and can be co-extensive. However, it makes sense to see them as analytically separate and embodying degrees of strength, from 'soft' to 'hard' forms. This approach offers a rejoinder to the common critiques of cosmopolitanism that tend to see it as a global condition unconnected with local contexts or a view of cosmopolitanism as necessarily 'thin' in contrast to 'thicker' local identities and solidarities. The differentiated conception of cosmopolitanism put forward here would, on the contrary, see it as engrained in all social contexts.

From a sociological perspective, the task is also to explain the emergence of cosmopolitanism, for instance, to account for how the different levels emerge and interact with each other. This can be seen in terms of three processes: generative, transformative, and institutionalizing.

Generative processes involve the creation of new ideas, new perceptions of problems, new interpretations of meta-norms (liberty, freedom, autonomy, equality, and so on), leading to new kinds and cycles of claim-making which challenge the given order. Such processes, which lead to an increase in variation, are associated with social movements, which are generally the initiators of social change. This is the first step in the emergence of norms. This may also involve the combination of different meta-norms, for instance equality and autonomy.

Transformative processes follow from the selection of the variety generated and occur typically when a dominant social movement brings about major societal change through the mobilization of large segments of the population and the transformation of the political system during a period of contestation. This is where the question of solidarity and identity is relevant: changes in consciousness occur following from new ways of framing problems.

Institutionalizing processes occur when a social movement succeeds in institutionalizing its project in a new societal framework, for example, in the establishment of a new state or in new legislation, and brings about the re-organization of state and society.

Cosmopolitanism is produced in all three processes; it is not then simply one level, such as an institutionalized policy, but the outcome of diverse movements and actions. In answering the question about whether or not cosmopolitanism is real, one needs to consider the process by which it emerges. Norms are produced in such processes and not simply given. It follows that there will be different interpretations of such norms in different contexts (including in different civilizational contexts). This approach would thus give centrality to agency in the shaping of cosmopolitanism, which ultimately derives from the capacity of social actors in specific places and at specific times to reinterpret their situation in light of new ideas or new interpretations of ideas, as in, for instance, the reinterpretation of the meaning of solidarity or rights. It is also a matter of how social actors interpret their situation in light of public interpretations of social issues.

This might be one way in which there could be useful cross-fertilization between political philosophy and sociology, for an under-researched area is exactly this, namely, how norms emerge and undergo change in light of new interpretations. Political philosophers simply postulate norms and debate their feasibility and desirability, while social scientists are interested in their empirical existence as something that can be measured. However, before something can be measured, it must first exist and, as I have argued, there are degrees of emergence.

At work in such processes is a mechanism which can be described as akin to the logic of translation. The key aspect is the transformation in meaning that occurs when a concept or idea is taken from one context and placed in another because a translation always involves a change in meaning. In a similar way the language of rights, for instance, undergoes a certain metamorphosis when the rights that apply normally in one context are applied to another or when one group uses the rights claimed by another. The history of democracy has been characterized by the constant contestation and negotiation of its terms and very meaning. The language of rights, obligations, democracy, and citizenship is never settled in its meanings but is perpetually open to new interpretations. This cognitive condition is ultimately what makes possible the generation of new norms; it makes possible the emergence of new politics and claims and enables the shaping of new institutions.

Viewed in such terms cosmopolitanism is not to be defined only with respect to normative change but also involves socio-cognitive shifts, namely, shifts in ways of seeing the world (see Strydom 2011, 2019a, 2019b). It is such changes in cognitive capacities that often make possible the articulation of new normative principles or their application in domains in which they previously did not apply. In this sense, then, cosmopolitanism entails learning capacities: individuals, collective actors, and societies find solutions to problems that require the critical reflexive capacity to

138 Capitalism, cosmopolitanism, Anthropocene

take the point of view of the other into account. The cognitive dimension of cosmopolitanism should be distinguished from its epistemic level, that is, the form of knowledge that it may engender. Many accounts and discussions of cosmopolitanism have been confined to its normative and symbolic levels of expression, that is, the level of norms and principles and the level of meanings and values. The concern with the normative has been more a feature of the political philosophy of cosmopolitanism while interest in the symbolic has been a feature of the culturally orientated social science, such as anthropology and cultural studies. This has been to the neglect of its cognitive dimension, which can be seen as a more basic level and one that provides the condition of the possibility of the normative and symbolic forms as well as knowledge. However, a fuller picture will involve looking at the interaction of all four forms. Specific examples of the cognitive order include reflexivity, self-problematization, critique, and connectivity. Of these an important one with regard to cosmopolitanism is the latter: shifts in cognition occur when individuals see new connections between things that were previously seen as separate. The capacity to see connections between phenomena is the basis of the possibility of global justice.

The prospects of cosmopolitanism

Finally, some reflections on the prospects of cosmopolitanism in view of the preceding considerations and the argument I have presented for a differentiated conception of cosmopolitanism with the emphasis on identifying the processes by which its various components and forms emerge. This entails giving attention to the cognitive, normative, symbolic, and epistemic levels. While cosmopolitanism may be less evidenced in terms of the fulfilment of a specific project, there is considerable evidence of the emergence of cosmopolitanism, at least of significant preconditions. For reasons of space, this can be only a brief sketch of some substantive topics to indicate the broad lines of empirical inquiry for critical theory guided by critical cosmopolitanism. Overall, the evidence suggests that there has been considerable progress in the past five decades or so in terms of cognitive shifts that reflect cosmopolitanism and some evidence of normative progress.

The rise of normative internationalism

Since 1945, arguably since 1941 with the Atlantic Charter, there has been a significant expansion in cosmopolitanism as reflected in global political institutions. The aftermath of WW2 led to the foundation of the UN and UNESCO, which was funded with an explicitly cosmopolitan mission, and later the various embodiments of what was to become the EU, which in turn provided a model for the worldwide spread of normative transnationalism, for example, NAFTA (and to a lesser extent MERCOSUR) in the Americas, the Organization of American States, ASEAN in Asia, and the Organization of African Unity. The statist underpinnings of these developments should not detract from the fact that in these decades a new breakthrough was made in international politics by which the national interest had to accommodate other claims, which were not always those of other states. The expansion in international legal and regulatory regimes was also due to the need to manage the problems that have their source within national society.

Developments in international law, the category of crimes against humanity, and the recognition of human rights – and in many cases its incorporation into national law through legislative changes and in judicial interpretations (Sassen 2011: 383) – have led to an entirely different situation than the pre-1945 world when international problems were more likely to be through war. As in technological innovation, once something is invented it has the tendency to remain and often to develop into new forms, as the example of the historical European integration reveals. Other examples can be found in the sphere of global dialogue, from the notion of a dialogue of civilizations to religious ecumenism. While new norms have emerged, the true significance of these developments rather lies in opening up the space of the political and creating the elements of a global as opposed to a national public sphere. In recent years, the imperative of a global response to climate change despite numerous setbacks, is now a significant dimension of global politics and has the potential to become a transformative force as the objectivity of the scale of global warming becomes apparent.

The spread of global civil society

The global spread of transnational activism is one of the most striking aspects of the relevance of cosmopolitanism, which is more present in social struggles than in institutional forms. It is particularly relevant to digital activism. As several theorists of global transnationalism have observed, for example Benhabib (2004), Castells (2012), the state now operates in a very complex field of contested norms. Organized social actors operating through global networks have challenged the capacity of states to exercise a monopoly. While not all such activism is necessarily cosmopolitan – as the 'Arab Spring' suggests – it can have the effect of producing the necessary preconditions, for instance, democratization and the opening of public spaces for cosmopolitanism to emerge. Global social movements are not always in direct opposition to states.

One of the most important developments in recent years has been a move in the direction of co-governance, whereby state-centred institutions collaborate with global social movements, as argued by Della Porta and Marchetti and others (see Della Porta and Marchetti 2011). Indeed, the very shift from government to governance is an example of a wider discursive shift in the way we now think of the political as due in no small part to the tremendous impact of global civil society movements. Sassen (2011) comments on the 'de-nationalization' of the state in the face of transnational opposition by which the powerless mobilize and win concessions from the state. Many of these come from the South and are locally based and challenge the hegemony of the North and the forms of globalization that emanate from the West. In general, such insurgent movements reflect a different

140 Capitalism, cosmopolitanism, Anthropocene

understanding of cosmopolitanism to notions of world government or global citizenship as well as to globalization more generally (see also Mota and Wagner 2019). In this context, the potential complementarity among diverse local mobilizations/interpretations of global cognitive models (democracy, human rights, and so on) should be noted. Boaventura de Souza Santos's diatopic hermeneutics of human rights provides a relevant theorization of this (Santos 1999).

The diffusion of cosmopolitanism in domestic politics

Undoubtedly the most extensive evidence of cosmopolitanism can be found within national societies. While it is not entirely possible to separate internal processes of change from those that are externally induced, it can be said with some confidence that social change over the past few decades has resulted in greater cultural and political pluralization within national societies. The impact of globalization has not undermined cultural diversity producing more homogenization, as has been demonstrated in the World Values Surveys (Norris and Inglehart 2009). The general trend has in fact been towards a greater emphasis on significant value change in the direction of what can be broadly termed cosmopolitan values. Homogenous national identities have increasingly come under scrutiny in societies that are more conscious of their multi-ethnicity. There is considerable empirical evidence in many societies of increased multiple identities, especially among young people. Viewing cosmopolitanism as a process of cultural opening and self-problematization, the nation is one of the main sites of cultural contestation. Examples of this can be found in debates around memory and commemoration, heritage, representations of the nation, the curriculum and educational policy and media, and popular culture. The recent surge of neo-authoritarian trends, especially since 2016 with Brexit and the Trump presidency, does not negate these trends. In fact, as is clearly illustrated with Brexit, the UK has witnessed a counter-trend in Europhilia precisely in reaction to Brexit (see Chapter 11).

Conclusion

In conclusion, the obvious rise of anti-cosmopolitan trends – xenophobic and recalcitrant nationalism, religious fundamentalism, new technologies of surveillance and population control – should not detract from the potential of cosmopolitanism to bring about alternatives. However, what is not present today is a significant cosmo-political project that would deliver greater global justice. The challenges for cosmopolitan social science are very great, but if the proposals made in this chapter are accepted, it follows that the focus of attention should be on the capacities and learning potential in contemporary societies for social change in the direction of cosmopolitanism. While a global cosmopolitan social actor as such does not exist, there is a plurality of such actors in the world and thus some indication of the making of a cosmopolitan subject. Moreover, the existence of cosmopolitan orientations in critical publics worldwide offers some hope for the prospects of

Cosmopolitanism to have a greater impact. This is where the real hope for global justice ultimately resides.

Global justice is not simply a set of normative principles of justice that are applied in given situations but a process that regulates and structures much of the political and is constitutive of social spaces. The normative order of justice with which cosmopolitan notions such as global justice is often associated is not permanent but open to contestation and to new interpretations, self-understanding, and narratives. So, what is occurring today is a cognitive expansion in the nature of justice. In this sense, then, global justice has a generative impact in opening up new ways of seeing the political community and in responding to injustice. In terms of the three mechanisms discussed in the foregoing, while cosmopolitanism is reflected in all three, it is more strongly evidenced as a generative process that provokes new challenges to the political community through enhanced consciousness of the interconnectivity of the world.

Evidence of major change can never be easily found in the short-term. Criticisms of cosmopolitanism that invoke the obvious presence of counter-cosmopolitan trends – which presumably presuppose cosmopolitan currents – are too short-sighted in focusing on a short time span or on reactive events. The Axial Age breakthrough itself took several centuries – 800 to 200 BC – to produce the first universalistic visions which laid the foundations for the emergence of cosmopolitanism, and the tumultuous history of democracy is itself is a reminder of the need to take a longer view on major social and political transformations. Thus, the fact that there is much evidence of global injustice or anti-democratic politics today does not mean that global justice is absent from the self-understanding of contemporary critical publics or that it has no consequences. The thesis of this chapter is that the most compelling evidence resides less in manifest institutional change, despite considerable gains, as discussed in the preceding section, than in socio-cognitive shifts in learning competences. Thus, the structuring impact that global justice has had on the political imagination in recent times is essentially more of a cognitive than a normative development in re-defining the self-understanding of the political community.

Notes

1 The idea of critical cosmopolitanism and its link with critical theory is developed in more detail in Delanty (2009). This section draws on Delanty (2012). The remainder of the chapter is based on 'The Prospects of Cosmopolitanism and the Possibility of Global Justice' *Journal of Sociology* 50 (2): 213–28. Earlier versions were presented as keynote lectures at the conference, 'Realizing Global Justice: Theory and Practice', 19 June 2013 at University of Tromsø' and the Annual Conference of the Global Studies Association, Roehampton University, London, 10 July 2013. I am grateful to Piet Strydom for comments on some of the ideas behind this paper and for inspiring the emphasis on the cognitive dimensions of cosmopolitanism. My thanks, too, to Estevao Bosco for comments on an earlier version.

2 For reasons of space, a consideration of the sources of non-western cosmopolitanism is not possible. On Asian cosmopolitanism see Pollock (2006). See also Holton (2009) and Delanty (2014).

References

Aboulafa, M. 2006. *The Cosmopolitan Self: George Herbert Mead and the Continental Philosophy.* Champaign: University of Illinois Press.

Beck, U. 2006. *The Cosmopolitan Outlook.* Cambridge: Polity Press.

Bellah, R. and Joas, H. (eds.) 2012. *The Axial Age and Its Consequences.* Cambridge, MA: Harvard University Press.

Benhabib, S. 2004. *The Rights of Others.* Cambridge: Cambridge University Press.

Brock, G. 2009. *Global Justice: A Cosmopolitan Account.* Oxford: Oxford University Press.

Brock, G. 2019. Equality, Sufficiency, and Global Justice. In: Delanty, G. (ed.) *The Routledge International Handbook of Cosmopolitanism Studies.* London: Routledge.

Castells, M. 2012. *Networks of Outrage and Hope: Social Movements in the Internet Age.* Cambridge: Polity Press.

Chernilo, D. 2019. There Is No Cosmopolitanism Without Universalism. In: Delanty, G. (ed.) *Routledge International Handbook of Cosmopolitanism Studies.* London: Routledge.

Della Porta, D. and Marchetti, R. 2011. Transnational Activitism. In: Delanty, G. and Turner, S. (eds.) *International Handbook of Contemporary Social and Political Theory.* London: Routledge.

Delanty, G. 2009. *The Cosmopolitan Imagination: The Renewal of Critical Social Theory.* Cambridge: Cambridge University Press.

Delanty, G. 2012. The Idea of Critical Cosmopolitanism. In: Delanty, G. (ed.) *Routledge Handbook of Cosmopolitanism Studies.* London: Routledge.

Delanty, G. 2014. Not All Is Lost in Translation: World Varieties of Cosmopolitanism. *Cultural Sociology,* 8 (4): 374–91.

Douzinas, C. 2000. *The End of Human Rights.* Oxford: Hart Publishing.

Holton, R. 2009. *Cosmopolitanisms: New Thinking and New Directions.* London: Palgrave Macmillan.

Kant, I. 1991. *Perpetual Peace: Political Writing.* Cambridge: Cambridge University Press.

Mignolo, W. 2000. *Local Histories/Global Designs: Coloniality, Subaltern Knowledge, and Border Thinking.* Princeton, NJ: Princeton University Press.

Mota, A. and Wagner, P. 2019. *Collective Action and Political Transformation: The Entangled Experiences in Brazil, South Africa and Europe.* Edinburgh: Edinburgh University Press.

Moyn, S. 2012. *The Last Utopia: Human Rights in History.* Cambridge, MA: Harvard University Press.

Norris, P. and Inglehart, R. 2009. *Cosmopolitan Communications: Cultural Diversity in a Globalized World.* Cambridge: Cambridge University Press.

Nussbaum, M. 2002. Capabilities and Human Rights. In: De Grief, P. and Cronin, C. (eds.) *Global Justice and Transnational Politics.* Princeton, NJ: Princeton University Press.

Nussbaum, M. 2006. *Frontiers of Justice: Disability, Nationality, Species Membership.* Cambridge, MA: Belknap Press.

Pollock, S. 2006. *The Language of the Gods in the World of Men: Sanskrit, Culture, and Power in Premodern India.* Berkeley: University of California Press.

Rabinow, P. 1986. Representations are Social Facts: Modernity and Postmodernity in Anthropology. In: Clifford, J. and Marcus, G. E. (eds.) *Writing Cultures: The Poetics and Politics of Ethnology.* Berkeley: University of California Press.

Rawls, J. 1971. *A Theory of Justice.* Cambridge, MA: Harvard University Press.

Rawls, J. 1999. *The Law of Peoples.* Cambridge, MA: Harvard University Press.

Rumford, C. 2008. *Cosmopolitan Spaces: Europe, Globalization Theory.* London: Routledge.

Sahlins, M. 2000. *Culture in Practice: Selected Essays.* New York: Zone Books.

Santos, B. 1999. Towards a Multicultural Conception of Human Rights. In: Featherstone, M. and Lash, S. (eds.) *Spaces of the Culture: City, Nation, World.* London: Sage.

Sassen, S. 2011. Limits of Power and Complexity of Powerless. In: Delanty, G. and Stephen, P. Turner (eds.) *Handbook of Contemporary Social and Political Theory*. London: Routledge.

Scheffler, C. 2001. *Boundaries and Allegiances*. Oxford: Oxford University Press.

Singer, P. 2004. *One World: The Ethics of Globalization*. New Haven: Yale University Press.

Strydom, P. 2011. The Cognitive and Meta Cognitive Dimensions of Contemporary Social and Political Theory. In: Delanty, G. and Turner, S. (eds.) *International Handbook of Contemporary Social and Political Theory*. London: Routledge.

Strydom, P. 2019a. The Modern Cognitive Order, Cosmopolitanism and Conflicting Models of World Openness. In: Delanty, G. (ed.) *Handbook of Cosmopolitanism Studies*. London: Routledge.

Strydom, P. 2019b. Critical Theory and Cognitive Sociology. In: Brekhus, W. and Ignatow, G. (eds.) *The Oxford Handbook of Cognitive Sociology*. Oxford: Oxford University Press.

Von Humboldt, A. 2011. *Political Essay on the Island of Cuba*. Chicago, IL: University of Chicago Press.

Walls, D. L. 2009. *The Passage to Cosmos: Alexander von Humboldt and the Shaping of America*. Chicago, IL: University of Chicago Press.

7

COSMOPOLITICS AND THE CHALLENGE OF THE ANTHROPOCENE

The new politics of nature

The idea of the Anthropocene has recently emerged to be not only a major development in the earth sciences, but it has also become influential in the human and social sciences as a critical concept. One of the far-reaching implications of the Anthropocene idea is that it suggests a new way of thinking about nature and the political. In this sense, it is also a more relevant way in which to think through the notion of the risk society, which Ulrich Beck (2006) saw as the basis of a cosmopolitical conception of the political. The Anthropocene is not simply an objective condition of planetary change or an epoch in the geological time scale, but it is also an interpretative category by which contemporary societies reflect upon themselves and upon life itself and reimagine their location and future within space and time.

Major shifts in society occur when human experience and interpretation change, as Koselleck argued in a famous essay (Koselleck 2004). There is much to suggest that today human experience is undergoing a significant shift due to major spacio-temporal transformations. The implications for how such transformations should be interpreted are less clear, but what is evident is that the notion of the Anthropocene has become an important interpretative category for making sense of the world today and of the future of human societies within a trajectory of time that encompasses planetary time.

The Anthropocene is not then a politically neutral concept but contains strong normative and cognitive elements including imaginary significations. As Latour has argued, the normative dimensions are not clear-cut in that the course of political action is, like the scientific account, contested (Latour 2004). It is contested in many ways in terms of who is the political subject, whether it includes nonhumans and future generations, the nature of objective problems, historical and geological periodization, and the potential solutions. The politics of the Anthropocene can be seen in interpretative terms as ways of knowing and containing an imaginary component in that it is about imagining future possibilities and re-defining the present

Cosmopolitics, the Anthropocene challenge **145**

in order to realize such possibilities. This would appear to come close to the idea of cosmopolitanism, which, as discussed in the previous chapter, is also centrally concerned with a vision of the world as the scope of the political. However, it raises new and more challenging questions for cosmopolitan notions of justice (Dryzek and Pickering 2019). The notion of the Anthropocene can be cast in the terms of cosmopolitanism, but it can also offer critical theory a new relevance that allows it to challenge more firmly neoliberalism and its enthusiastic response to globalization.

This chapter seeks to bring together the idea of the Anthropocene, critical theory, and cosmopolitan social and political thought. These bodies of literature are rarely considered together.[1] On the one side, the idea of the Anthropocene can give cosmopolitanism a new significance and political relevance by bringing to the fore new conceptions of nature, and, on the other side, cosmopolitanism can offer the emerging theory of the Anthropocene with a critical social theory around, for example, notions of reflexivity, dialogue, and justice. There would therefore appear to be some value in greater dialogue between these paradigms of thought, which in their very different ways are both concerned with the nature of the encounter, the encounter of one culture with another, and the encounter of the human and the natural world.

The concept of nature has been one of the background ideas in critical theory since Marx, and before him with Rousseau, who saw modern society as destructive of the natural and social worlds. For Marx, capitalism is first and foremost based on the exploitation of nature; human alienation in capitalism is based on human alienation from nature. This theme was developed by Adorno and Horkheimer in the *Dialectic of Enlightenment* for whom societal domination was based on the domination of nature. However, despite their notion of the need for reconciliation with nature, the question of nature remained ambivalent. On the one side, critical theory since Marx was concerned with the problem of the domination of nature with the implicit assumption that emancipation from domination would lead to a different relation to nature; while on the other side, tradition, especially since Lukács to Habermas, saw nature as a domain external to society and thus required social science to accept a non-naturalistic foundation. More problematically, nature is related to through control rather than understanding.[2] Habermas has clearly operated with a problematical anthropocentric framework that sees human emancipation as separate from nature. The ecological implications of his social theory are far from clear or satisfactory. More recent accounts, especially those influenced by Latour, emphasize the social construction of nature with the implication that nature is not a category outside human agency and culture (MacNaghten and Urry 1998).[3] This latter position reduces nature to the human world. It is clearly time to revisit the category of nature in light of the escalation of the politics of nature in late modernity and especially in the context of the Anthropocene.

The idea of the Anthropocene

The notion of the Anthropocene emerged initially as a temporal concept in geologic time but arguably now has a wider sphere of signification as the concept is

146 Capitalism, cosmopolitanism, Anthropocene

taken up in the human and social sciences.[4] Although a temporal condition, as a recent period in the long history of the earth, it is also a spatial concept in that it refers to a process that happened on the planet as a whole. In that sense, it is more than the notion of the globe, which refers to the human-dominated surface of the earth. But the earth is more than the globe and more than the global environment. Indeed, the notion of the earth as famously commented on by Lovejoy (1979) and others, is a misnomer since more than two-thirds consists of oceans, which are integral to the life of the planet. The notion of the Anthropocene invokes a planetary sense of time and space that requires a rethinking of the notion of the globe, which does not fully capture the co-evolution of the natural and social worlds and the deep historical time of human and planetary life.

The notion of the Anthropocene gained currency in 2000 with the proposal that the current geologic Epoch is the Anthropocene and that therefore the Holocene Epoch should be regarded as over (Crutzen 2002).[5] The Holocene, which was officially named and dated in 2008 as the Epoch[6] that followed the Pleistocene, commenced just under 12,000 years ago when an interglacial period of global warming began bringing an end to the last Ice Age. This Epoch was the period in which human civilization began with the emergence of farming and later the creation of cities and the subsequent birth of, what are now referred to, following Eisenstadt's (1986) re-interpretation of Karl Jaspers, as the Axial Age civilizations. In 2018, not without controversy, the Holocene was divided into three Ages, the most recent of which, the Age in which we now live in, the Late Holocene Meghalayan Age, began c 4,250 years ago after a 200-year-long period of cooling that led, following a mega drought, to the collapse of ancient civilizations in Egypt, Greece, and the Middle East, the Indus Valley, and the Yangtze River Valley. However, the notion of the Anthropocene is not currently recognized as an official geologic time scale, despite the efforts of many to have it designated a new Epoch in geological time and thus signal the end of the Holocene. It is arguably the case that the contested concept of the Anthropocene is not only a question of geological time, but it is a cultural and political concept in critical thought. Stratigraphy has now entered public consciousness as well as social and political theory.

The notion of the Anthropocene holds that the earth is now moving out of the Holocene Epoch due to the extent of human activity on the planet. The new planetary time consciousness is the result of humanity having becoming a geologic force that has fundamentally transformed the earth to an extent that it may have created the geo-physical conditions that will postpone if not prevent another Ice Age in the future, thus possibly bringing to an end the periodic inter-glacial nature of geologic time that has characterized the history of the earth for some 2 million years. If the Holocene were to end with a new Epoch beginning, the Quaternary Period, which began some 2.6 million years ago, would need to be reconsidered in terms of three Epochs, with the Anthropocene of a very recent origin. Geological time, biological time, and historical time are now inextricably intertwined in ways that require a rethinking of the relationship of the cosmic order of planetary time with the human order of polis.

Much of the debate on the Anthropocene has been about its origin, whether it began with the Industrial Revolution or earlier in the seventeenth century following the Spanish conquest of Central and South America, as Maslin and Lewis argue;[7] or should be taken back to the origin of civilization, as Ruddiman et al. argue (2015); or even to the late Pleistocene when hunter societies wiped out mega fauna. It is now generally agreed that the commencement of the Anthropocene – even if not an official period on the geologic time scale – is in the middle of the twentieth century, when a major planetary transformation took place. This is the 'Great Acceleration' thesis (Steffen et al 2007, 2015; McNeill and Engelke 2014). The thesis, which is inspired by Polanyi's *Great Transformation*, is based on the claim that planetary change must be demonstrable on the earth system as a whole and must be considerably greater than natural variability. In the footsteps of Karl Polanyi (1944), the notion affirms the need for a holistic view of societal change, but, unlike Polanyi's limited conception of the thesis of a Great Transformation, includes the relationship of society and the earth and moreover has a global scope but with a stratigraphic footprint.

The decade that followed the Second World War offers clear evidence of human-induced changes to the earth system in which a marked increase in the three greenhouse gases of carbon dioxide, methane, and nitrous oxide occur, and when a globally linked societal system based on industrialization and massive demographic explosion coincide. The Second World War marked a general rise since 1950 of the influence of human activity on the earth of which the fallout of nuclear testing is only one. The war itself was a major contributory factor, as was the Cold War that followed in its wake, in that it led to the rapid development of new technologies which all required increased energy on a scale previously unknown (see Steffen 2011; McNeill and Engelke 2014). The key factors are the scale and significance of human activity on the earth system taken as a whole that take such changes beyond the range of variability for the Holocene. The scientific consensus appears to point in this direction of a staged formation of the Anthropocene culminating in the second half of the twentieth century; the notion of modernity needs to be reconsidered as the fundamental threshold in history in so far as this commenced in the eighteenth century. The concerns of western social science around post-industrialization and postmodernity fail to fully capture the take-off of Asia in this period, which is a period of industrialization and of the global expansion of capitalism.

The implications of the advent of the notion of the Anthropocene do not necessarily invalidate the notion of modernity but point to a new contextualization of modernity and of historical time to account for the accepted fact that we live in a human-dominated geological time unit. The Great Acceleration now includes new industrial and extractivistic countries – Brazil, China, India, Russia, South Africa, Indonesia – and has led to an intensification of a process that more or less coincides with the emergence of modernity in western Europe but matures only in the second half of the twentieth century at a time when many other projects of modernity are consolidated through different civilizational routes. Both modernity and the Anthropocene are brought together through the long-lasting consequences of the imprints of the western world, since there is no doubt that despite the global extension of the human imprint on the earth system that the western world, even since the Great Acceleration became a global phenomenon, has played a far greater role. Now it would appear that the entire world is embroiled in societal and technological modes of organization that began in Europe in the nineteenth century. Modernity, too, has been strongly influenced by the European and later the North American variants (Mota and Delanty 2015). It would seem to be the case that the diverse routes of modernity throughout the world, while departing in significant ways from the western world, have nonetheless embarked on much the same project of relentless growth and environmental destruction. This would appear to diminish the significance of major varieties of modernity if in the final analysis all varieties of modernity are embroiled in much the same practices. However, it does not necessarily entirely diminish all dimensions of modernity, other than placing modernity in a much larger timescale. The fact of a certain co-emergence of modernity, at least in western Europe, and the early stages of the Anthropocene does not reduce one to the other. The real confluence is between the Anthropocene and the Great Acceleration (see McNeill and Engelke 2014). There can be little doubt that capitalism has been one of the main drivers of the Anthropocene, as argued by Dipesh Chakrabarty (2009, 2014) and Jason Moore (2015) in that the unrelenting accumulation of capital since the industrial revolution created the social conditions for the domination of humans over the natural world.

A major question for the present day, then, is whether or not the cultural and political currents of modernity can be harnessed to challenge the self-destructive forces that the modern age has unleashed in creating the Anthropocene. In this sense, the challenge of governing the Anthropocene – or transforming it into a positive political project as opposed to a dystopia vision of catastrophe – is also about overcoming the limits of modernity whose presuppositions, it has been much noted, have been based on the separation of human history from natural history (Latour 1993; Rossi 1984). Modernity begins with the presumption of a rupture of human history from nature and is based on a logic of human autonomy and a capacity for the radical transformation of the present in the image of an imaginary future, to take an influential formulation of the nature of modernity associated with the writings of Castoriadis (1987). But if this condition is also the dystopic condition of the Anthropocene, the transformative powers of human agency will need to be considerably rethought. An alternative account, then, would be to see the advent of the Anthropocene moment as not only a product of modernity or a condition coeval with modernity and capitalism but as a condition that can be challenged by the affirmation of modernity and a cosmopolitan cultural model that can be located within the modern as opposed to some post or non-modern condition. Whether or not the social and political institutions of modernity have the capacity to bring about a further transformation is clearly one of the major questions for the present day. From a theoretical perspective, despite the entwinement of modernity and the Anthropocene, and the resulting transformation in the temporal horizons of human and planetary life, the radicalization of the cosmopolitan currents within the modern condition is probably the best way to envisage a livable future.

Cosmopolitics, the Anthropocene challenge **149**

The Anthropocene can be seen as the outcome of the instrumental rationality of modernity, to invoke the Weberian concept of rationality, but modernity always entails more than this condition that has often been equated with capitalism.

The question of agency: reconstitution of subjectivity

At the core of the Anthropocene debate is the question about the nature of agency, of the consequences for history of human action, and the very constitution of human subjectivity and its relation to the nonhuman (see for example Danowski and Viveiros de Castro 2017). Modernity gave rise to the notion of the autonomy of the human being and heralded a view of history as the emancipation of humanity from nature, a condition that was equated with domination. Modern subjectivity is thus constituted through the domination of nature. As noted above, in the critical tradition, from Marx to Adorno and Horkheimer, the domination of nature went with the domination of society and was underpinned by capitalism. Emancipation from domination in this tradition of thought is the emancipation of humanity, not of nature, and does not question the capacity of human agency to recover autonomy. The very foundation of western liberal thought lies in the Anthropo-centric myth of human society arising from the exit from the state of nature. The Anthropocene debate raises some doubts about this western and Enlightenment conception of human agency as the compass of emancipation. There are a number of related dimensions to this.

The first and most important implication is that nature is not an objective and inert entity but holds sway over human life, which is embodied in nature, and, moreover, human agency is operative in nature. Even long before the advent of the Anthropocene – at least in terms of the conventional location of this in the modern world – human beings have been acting upon and transforming nature, beginning with the domestication and extinction of species. In acting upon nature as a biomorphic force and later as a geophysical force, humans are also transforming themselves. In this way, human subjectivity is shaped in a process of co-evolution with nature. However, it does not follow from this, as implied in post-humanist theorizing, that agency is no longer a relevant category.[8]

As most cogently outlined by Strydom, the Anthropocene is not merely a natu-ral condition of the earth but is also a cultural model in so far as it is a category of cultural interpretation or sense making (Strydom 2015, 2017). In terms of the previously mentioned dynamic between human experience and interpretation, the significance of the Anthropocene in one important respect is that it is an interpreta-tion of a new dimension of human experience, namely, the perception that human beings are part of nature and that the quintessence of human life does not reside in the promethean domination of nature. In Strydom's analysis, there is a double logic to this. The Anthropocene is more than a concept; it is also a cultural model in which contemporary society today seeks to interpret itself by recourse to cogni-tively structured referents, such as responsibility, truth, and justice. In other words, the notion of the Anthropocene now captures a wider domain of experience and interpretation about the present and future of the world. It incorporates within it

150 Capitalism, cosmopolitanism, Anthropocene

evolutionary thresholds of learning and thus has acquired a strongly normative and critical character. In the present day, with the effects of climate change increasingly manifest, this is beginning to have an impact on the ways in which human subjectivity is constituted. In terms of agency, it points in the direction of a reflexive conception of agency that is no longer predicated on the destructive separation of society and nature.

The implications of this remodelling of the relationship between nature and society go beyond the present in relation to the future and extend far into the past. An embedded concept of subjectivity, which is implied by the notion of the Anthropocene, suggests an alternative and more cosmopolitan account of the world and its relation to the earth. In this account, human beings are not only embedded in society but are also embedded in nature, the evolution of life, and the earth. As Hannah Arendt (1958: 2) has commented: 'The earth is the very quintessence of the human condition, and earthly nature, for all we know, may be unique in the universe in providing human beings with a habitat in which they can move and breathe without effort and with artifice'.

One of the most promising avenues for further work in understanding the formation of human subjectivity is to explore the developmental or evolutionary logics and their interactions between geological time, biological time, and historical time as well as the history of consciousness. Current theorizing on such interconnections has been mostly confined to the study of environmental influences on human history. The work of Braudel (1990) was the first major attempt to explore a long-term historical formation in the context of environmental influences. Diamond (1998, 2005) has contributed two path-breaking studies on the influences of biological life on human societies and what happens to societies that fail to locate themselves in their natural environment, and, more recently, inspired by the Anthropocene, Costanza et al (2007) have attempted to produce an integrated history of human life in relation to natural history with the general conclusion that societies respond to climatic signals in multiple ways, which can include collapse or failure, migration, and creative mitigation. In their view, future response and feedbacks with the human-environmental system will depend on understanding the global past. This work makes a strong argument that 'examining socioecological systems across multiple timescales can identify the antecedents further back in time of major phenomena that occur in a particular era or time' (2007: 13). Brooke (2014) has written the first global history of human life in the context of the history of the earth showing how human and biological evolution and earth history are interwoven. Dukes (2011), in *Minutes to Midnight*, sought to locate the current Anthropocene era in the context of the history of modern society.

Although most of this literature is confined to the analysis of the environmental limits of human societies, the implications are wider. Some of these have been identified by Clark and Gunaratnam (2017), who highlight, following Brooke (2014) and Davis (2001), that significant social upheaval coincided with major geophysical change. For present purposes, it will suffice to mention here that the direction that this emerging work highlights is that human subjectivity must be seen in deep historical terms as embedded in the natural history of the earth. If the Anthropocene is located in the present, from the mid-twentieth century, it is a moment in a long time scale in which human life and natural history have interacted. The Anthropocene idea draws attention to the need for society today to form a new relation to nature. The history of *Homo sapiens* shows considerable variability and learning potential both in the creation of societal organization, technological mastery, and environmental interaction. Even since the advent of modernity, this is by no means a simple case of the instrumental domination of nature. As Norblad (2017) points out with respect to the governance of forests, throughout European history examples can be found that illustrate a long-term view of the relationship with nature and that the administration of the forest was a model for the management of other things and which does not quite fit into the model of instrumental domination.

Mithen (1998) has shown how the evolution of the modern mind took shape in three main phases, beginning with the formation of general intelligence in primates and early hominids, which was followed by specific or modular intelligences in early *Homo sapiens* and Neanderthals, with the third and most characteristically human intelligence of, what he calls, 'the cognitively fluid mind' appearing 60,000 to 30,000 years ago with the consolidation of a human mind capable of communicating between the different forms of intelligence. The evolution of this cognitively fluid mind, which was marked by the final evolution of *Homo sapiens sapiens*, along with the later invention of farming, which made possible human societies, were in the long historical perspective the most significant developments in shaping human subjectivity.

It may be objected that the Anthropocene is a present or even future condition with only limited historical antecedents. That is indeed the case, but the argument for contextualizing the present in the deep past is that a long-term evolutionary view of human life reveals the learning capacities of the human mind and that the relation of the human and natural world is one of constant change. That relation must also be seen as unfolding through different temporalities, namely the geological, the biological, and the historical (the history of human societies) and the related temporality of consciousness. All of these involve different manifestations of the logic of evolution.

The present time, the past 50 years or so, is a decisive time in the relationship between humans and nature. A relevant consideration in the evolutionary perspective is the fact that the very category of the human being has undergone a major transformation in the past few decades, more or less coinciding with the Great Acceleration of the Anthropocene. As Thomas (2014) argues, it is possible that the chemical acceleration of human life now separates us physiologically from pre-1950 human beings. With the natural world transformed by human beings and synthetic forms of life now possible, the result is that human beings are themselves transformed as a result of their very agency. History and human evolution drove the reflective capacities of the human mind, but it also created the toxic body, which may be an evolutionary new creation challenging the very notion of the human

152 Capitalism, cosmopolitanism, Anthropocene

being.[9] Once life can be synthesized, it ceases to be a natural entity. Bryan S. Turner (2017) concludes that the influence of the Axial Age religions with their theology of suffering and unhappiness may be waning as a result of major neurological, bio-technical, and physiological changes to the human body that offer new possibilities for human agency. In this account, the age of the Anthropocene is also the age of a radical shift in human nature in which the human body itself is undergoing transformation. There are also questions here about the possible end of the evolutionary process, at least as based on chance. According to Darwin, evolution is triggered by the chance occurrence of a mutation. But there may now be forms of life that are no longer determined by chance. However, it is unlikely that chance will altogether disappear in that whatever humans do, it is evident that they do not entirely master the earth and that major pathogenic forms of life may develop as a result of catastrophes to come, and there is always the chance of an impact from the outside, (e.g. cosmic radiation). The human species probably therefore remains permeable and consequently open to chance occurrences.

The second problem concerns Anthropocentrism. In highlighting the centrality of human agency, there is a danger of a certain Anthropocentrism, namely, a view of the planet as shaped by human beings who through science and technology have become its masters. Global warming has preceded the existence of human life, and unless human action does not prevent a future Ice Age, undoubtedly the current interglacial period will come to an end due to circumstances that have nothing to do with humans, who may only succeed in delaying it. Humans may make the planet unlivable, but they are earthbound and, as yet, cannot escape it. As Hannah Arendt (1958: 3) argued in the opening of the *Human Condition* 'we are earth bound creatures and have begun to act as though we were dwellers of the universe'. It is unlikely that whatever they do they will end up destroying it before it ends its existence. This would be to exaggerate the power of human agency, including the non-intentional consequences of human action. What is more realistic is that human agency will destroy conditions for human life or, more likely, create the conditions for the collapse of existing societal systems (Wallace-Wells 2019). The current situation might be characterized as a paradoxical one in which human beings have established themselves as the agents of change over nature while at the same time they are in thrall to nature, which in the final analysis they cannot entirely master since they are part of it (see Chernilo 2017b). It is also the strongest rejoinder to the position of skeptics, who, in contrast to climate change deniers, hold that the climate change is normal and that there have been more intense periods of heat in the deep past of the planet.

The political challenge of the Anthropocene

In discussing the Anthropocene in terms of major temporal and existential shifts there is a distinct danger of neglecting any consideration of power and inequality, which from a social science perspective are essential to any account of societal change. The Anthropocene is generally discussed with a general reference to

Cosmopolitics, the Anthropocene challenge   **153**

humanity as a whole and consequently is in danger of being depoliticized. This is where critical cosmopolitan considerations of justice are relevant. The problem is that humanity as a species being is rather abstract when it comes to human agency. There can be little doubt that the imprint of the Anthropocene can be attributed to the modern western world, which has contributed the vast bulk of the greenhouse gases emitted since the industrial revolution (Bradshaw 2014). This has led to a catching-up situation with the developing world but in a context in which global social inequalities are bound up with climate change (Beck 2010). In addition to global warming the West also led the way toward laying down a new kind of 'rock' stratum though nuclear technology, both industrial and military, and, since it was invented in 1907, through plastic (see Corcoran et al 2014).

These considerations are important because much of the debate on how the Anthropocene should be understood is dominated by a post-humanist perspective whereby agency becomes dissolved. Representatives of this position are Latour (2013, 2014) and Haraway (2015). Critics of the post-humanist position, such as Hornborg (2017) have counterposed a Marxist-influenced position that places capitalism at the core of the problems of the Anthropocene which concern exploitative global power (see Malm and Hornborg 2014; Moore 2015). In this account, the so-called Cartesian legacy is not to be entirely dismissed, even if we have to question the now untenable separation of humans and nature. The post-humanist perspective is indeed problematical if it jettisons human agency, which Hornborg correctly argues must be retained as an analytical and explanatory category, although it leaves open the question of what would happen in a future postcapitalist world. This is a critique that is just as much addressed to de-referentialized mainstream accounts that posit humanity as a whole as the agent or attribute everything to progress or development. In this view, agency is inexorably connected with the human condition and is characterized by purpose. The fact that society and nature have become embroiled in each other does not mean that these categories are not distinct.

The foregoing is relevant to the debate concerning the designation of the Anthropocene as 'Capitalocene', given the coincidence of the Anthropocene and capitalism. Here, too, analytical distinctions must be made between the different concepts. Capitalism, as argued in Chapter 3, is an economic system characterized by accumulation and the private appropriation of profit, while the Anthropocene is a condition of the world and the earth system in which major change has been brought about by human action. Not all human action can be explained by capitalism but a very large measure can be, and this is especially true with the worldwide expansion of capitalism following its adoption in China and Russia since 1991. Moreover, capitalism is part of a complex global system of production, distribution, and consumption, all of which contribute to the Great Acceleration. It makes irrelevant Eurocentric notions such as the post-industrial society. From a critical theory perspective, locating the Anthropocene in social and economic processes as well cultural processes, rather than in an abstract and de-politicized human condition, is essential to an understanding of how major societal and environmental change have come about and how it has diverse effects. It is simply not the case that humanity

154 Capitalism, cosmopolitanism, Anthropocene

as a whole is in the same boat. There are significant global variations in the negative effects of climate change, for example, rising sea levels, as well as in the causes. Invoking humanity as a whole, as in the notion of the Anthropocene as the new age of humans, can be a misleading way to see the current global situation. Such a myopic view is not only Eurocentric but attributes a certain determinism to a condition that is essentially social and political. For these reasons, the notion of agency must be retained and cannot be dismissed as in the post-humanist position. Indeed, this affirmation of human agency and hence human responsibility is essential to the challenge of governing the Anthropocene and needs to be linked to a normative notion of humanity as a species being.

The idea of the Anthropocene, I have suggested, offers a new way in which to interpret not only the earth system, but the human world. It shows how the human-inhabited world is embedded in the physical and biochemical processes of the earth and is inserted in a vastly different scale of time and histories. The social and human sciences have operated with a very different understanding of the world as an entirely human creation and as the dominant force on the planet. Now it would appear that the human world is merely inhabiting the earth for a brief period and will one day vanish for reasons that have nothing to do with what humans will do but with future cosmic changes to the solar system and the orbital cycles of the earth.

The notion of the Anthropocene raises both epistemological and ontological questions for the human and social sciences concerning the very conception of the human world and its relation to the earth. It challenges existing epistemological frameworks of knowledge in a number of ways that all foreground the space of the encounter. The first and most important is in moving beyond the society-versus-nature dualism that has been a fundamental assumption of social science. This does not mean that these analytical categories as such need to be abandoned, but social science can no longer operate with an epistemology of blindness to nature as outside of the domain of the social and the human. The social sciences have long been bifurcated between those that are modelled on the natural sciences and those that are essentially interpretative and based on quite different epistemological assumptions. Both are now in question in their fundamental philosophical assumptions. The naturalistic or neopositivistic conception of social science sees scientific knowledge as based on causal explanation and value-free with society as an object of analysis akin to the model of natural reality. This is a model of knowledge that no longer accords with the self-understanding of the natural sciences. The idea that the earth somehow provides a stable ground on which the social or human world is constructed must be abandoned as incompatible with developments in Earth System Science over the past two decades.

The emerging paradigm of Anthropocene science within Earth System Science challenges some of the epistemological assumptions made by the philosophy of social science about the practice of science and its role in the world. On the other side, the interpretative sciences since Weber have clung onto a model of interpretation that assumes the existence of a social world entirely divorced from the natural world. A tradition of social science became firmly established since the early twentieth century that regarded the natural sciences as the enemy of the emerging social sciences. Here the main controversies concerned the political engagement of the social sciences and their relation with the humanities. For the interpretative sciences shaped by hermeneutics and phenomenology, the interpreting subject was the central category for sciences that operated with an entirely de-naturalized conception of society. Where the neo-positivistic philosophy of social science was heavily naturalistic, the interpretative tradition strove to de-naturalize science, effectively putting culture in place of nature. The result is that, as things stand now, the social sciences are not the best equipped to deal with major reorientations in the natural sciences.

One of the striking developments in recent years is a transformation in the understanding of ontology. The interpretative social sciences have operated with a strongly social ontology, as in the long-established sociological tradition of the social construction of reality. In this tradition, reality is entirely social and is the product of routinized social interaction. The Anthropocene debate, since it first emerged within geology, offers a new view of ontology and in ways that challenge the neo-positivistic philosophy of science. This most naturalistic of all the sciences has produced a major shift in thinking about ontological questions in a new key with the insight that humans are now authoring rocks (Yusoff 2016). The geologic notion of the Anthropocene recasts physical ontology to include the human imprint on nature. Biology was for long the model science of the social sciences, especially sociology and anthropology, which borrowed many of their foundational concepts from biology. It would be an oversimplification to say that the Anthropocene shift has put geology forward as the source of new thinking, not least because the major innovations are within the wider earth science. However, it does require a resituating of biology in relation to geology and to social science. This does not mean that geologic models must replace social scientific ones or diminish biology as the primary relation of humanity to the earth. Until now, the impetus has come from geology, but the social and human sciences have yet to respond. It does not seem likely that the geological conception of the Anthropocene exhausts all possible meanings of the notion. While I agree that this designation of the present age – not necessarily on the geologic time scale – as the Anthropocene is the best of the alternatives – for example the postmodern or the posthuman or global era – and suggest it is not incompatible with all currents in modern thought.

So, we do not need to draw the conclusion that the philosophy of the social sciences has nothing to offer and that Earth System Science has all the answers and that therefore what is required is a geologization of social science. The Anthropocene debate has exaggerated the crisis of science and modern thought. I believe that the critical and interpretative approaches – for there is not just one – in social science, in particular in critical theory, can be radicalized to address the Anthropocene challenge. For example, notwithstanding the problem of the over-sociocentric conception of the social within sociology, in sociological light, the Anthropocene is a political construction because it is first and foremost a means by which contemporary societies interpret their place in the world in light of major shifts in experience. It is certainly the case that place is now part of a deeper history of the earth; however, it is not an exclusively naturalistic category but an interpretative one. It is for this reason that geologists, despite their concern for a rigorous definition of the geologic time scale, cannot extricate themselves from the politicization of the concept. The new division of the Holocene into three ages is itself ironic in that the Meghalayan Age does not take account of human activity and thus does not recognize the present time but is nonetheless defined by a mega-drought that impacted heavily on human societies such that many major civilizations collapsed. Indeed, it is often said that the Holocene is a particularly brief Epoch, having commenced only 12,000 years ago, and is itself an Epoch because of human societies emerged within it.

The fact is that all these processes have different temporalities, scales, and spacialties and, while interacting with each other, are driven by different forces. The forces that can be attributed to human life can be more easily demonstrated to have an impact on the composition of the oceans and atmosphere than on the deep history of rock formation. Since Lovelock's famous book in 1979, *Gaia: A New Look at Life on Earth*, it is now customary to include life as part of the earth, which is a system in which physical, chemical, and biological (including human) processes interact through positive and negative feedback communication.

One of the attractions of the idea of the Anthropocene is that it offers a narrative that links the present to the past and the future in which the human subject is the author. Narratives are essentially interpretative categories by which people – whether individuals or collective actors – make sense of their situation and give continuity to their lives. The Anthropocene fulfils that function even if the dominant narrative portends doom. However, the catastrophic narrative of a dystopic future is not the only one. Other Anthropocene narratives offer a more positive account of human potential to bring about change (Schwägerl 2014). Anthropologists and sociologists have much to contribute in grasping subjectivities, including spatio-temporal orientations and perceptions of epochal transformation. Narratives are important, but in so far as it is a cultural model, the Anthropocene is more than a question of narratives but also entails normative and explanatory components that go beyond the subjective dimension of narratives.

It is undoubtedly the case that in order for the social and human sciences to respond to the challenges of the Anthropocene, greater integration of the sciences will be necessary. This may be the moment for an integrated social science, following the example of earth science, and for greater dialogue between the natural sciences and the human and social sciences. Until now this has mostly been in interdisciplinary areas such as environmental science and the disciplines of geography and archaeology, with global history taking the lead in the human sciences. Such a call is in line with Horkheimer's vision of critical theory as an interdisciplinary engagement with social and political reality with respect to interpretation and the analysis of objective contradictions in social rationality, as well as for political praxis (see Chapter 1).

Cosmopolitics, the Anthropocene challenge **157**

There is also the question of consciousness. Human history is not only a logic of societal formation but of the evolution of consciousness and in particular of meta-representational consciousness. It is ultimately what marks the human from other forms of life and geophysical entities. Human beings at a point in their history – roughly the evolution of *Homo sapiens* sapiens 60,000 to 30,000 years ago – acquired the capacity for consciousness, by which is meant here the ability to reflect upon and self-problematize themselves and devise modes of action that will allow them to act upon the world in light of their vision of how the world should be. While research on other species has revealed similar abilities in some instances, at best non-human forms of consciousness are highly limited in scope. This can be attributed to the larger brain size of *Homo sapiens*, which made possible the cognitively fluid mind, and is possibly not more mysterious than the evolution of the front lobe of the brain (Strydom 2015: 240–1). Whether or not this amounts to a species difference is a matter of some contention; the important point is that the condition of the Anthropocene is one in which consciousness of the condition has entered into the play of forces.

The self-understanding of contemporary societies is now very centrally articulated in the language of the Anthropocene. Although I depart from the post-humanist position, the implication of the critical-interpretative position put forward here is that from a social theoretical perspective the Anthropocene is a discursively constructed reality in which science, including the social and human sciences, are now actively participants. This constructivist position does not dispense with the notion of nature as a domain only of interest to the natural sciences. As argued by Strydom (2015, 2017), there are essentially two models of nature interacting: external nature and human nature. Both act upon each other, and their interaction is mediated through society. Human nature is not entirely determined, and neither is it totally outside external nature, but is formed reflexively in relation to it. The epistemological and ontological implications of this point in the direction of a philosophy of naturalism have nothing to do with the older and now discredited positivistic naturalism. But neither do they support the post-humanist position that seeks to overcome the category of the human and that of nature. As Chernilo (2017a, 2017b) has argued, a feature of the human condition is the capacity for reflexivity which makes possible self-transcendence. Dryzek and Pickering (2019) demonstrate how reflexivity, as a self-critical capacity of a structure or process, can change itself through scrutiny and self-problematization, is a necessary basis for a politics of the Anthropocene. There is today already a limited degree of reflexivity present in the global climate regime, though far from what is required to bring about the necessary changes. Their analysis, which reflects the relevance of cosmopolitan politics and critical thought as discussed in the previous chapter, demonstrates the significance of a movement from recognition of planetary crisis to the reflexive moment of rethinking core values and practices to a practical politics of response to the challenges.

Conclusion: the cosmopolitics of the Anthropocene

One of the most promising directions for critical theory in the age of the Anthropocene might lie in a cosmopolitics of nature, that is, a political conception of cosmopolitanism. This should not entirely be seen as a rupture with the older traditions of cosmopolitanism, for it is itself of ancient origins and has been central to the political thought of the modern age. However, in light of global justice, as discussed in the previous chapter, and the new challenge of the Anthropocene, the cosmopolitan turn in contemporary thought will be a reconsideration.

A distinct tendency in the literature, under the influence of postcolonialism, has been in the direction of a culturally rooted conception of cosmopolitanism and with a strong emphasis on a variety of cosmopolitanisms than a singular and universal one. Such post-universalistic and pluralist conceptions of cosmopolitanism have had a greater resonance in the culturally oriented social sciences than in political philosophy and have been significant in moving beyond Eurocentric conceptions of history and politics. This, perhaps, has led to the result that cosmopolitanism has tended to become a celebration of pluralism and, consequently, loses its political impetus in addressing effectively truly global challenges. Though global justice clearly remains the concern of grassroots cosmopolitan movements, global justice cannot be achieved, by definition, by different groups pursuing different objectives. For this reason, what is required is a stronger political conception of cosmopolitanism, a cosmopolitics, which is one of the most appropriate responses to the political challenges of the Anthropocene.

The notion of cosmopolitanism invokes not only a global response to climate change but one that goes to the core of the problem in linking the human polis with the cosmic order of the planet. It challenges the reduction of solidarity and loyalty to narrow conceptions of human community kept apart in different spaces and times as well as instrumental forms of rationality that are divorced from the more substantive forms of rationality. Moreover, cosmopolitanism is also a normative and critical idea that counter-opposes an alternative to the present while at the same time seeking in the present the sources to make possible a better future. Habermas's deliberative conception of democracy fits very well into the cosmopolitan tradition in that both are underpinned by reasoned communication as the medium by which political issues are handled. Argumentation, as the record of history attests, has a capacity to bring about fundamental shifts in collective self-understanding and cultural recognition (see Crawford 2002). The basis of cosmopolitanism is that in the encounter with the other, the self undergoes change. This can only come about when Self and Other engage in communication, which can be said to be constitutive of subject formation. This cosmopolitan sensibility accords with the deliberative understanding of democracy. Moreover, it affirms the centrality of agency and an ethic of care and responsibility.

The signs of such political formation in *Homo sapiens* are evident in shifts in consciousness since the 1980s. Before the mid-1980s, discussion of ecological issues was mostly confined to the world of science and when there was little if no awareness of a major planetary crisis, as opposed to ecological devastation. The Club of Rome's 1972 report, *Limits to Growth,* was perhaps the first official change in thinking on the need for a new global environmental policy on growth (Meadows et al 1972). Since the Chernobyl explosion in 1986 and the discovery of the Ozone hole in the Antarctic in 1985, that changed with the rise of climate politics and global environmental movements, such that by the 1990s environmental issues entered the agenda of every government and have entered into new orders of governance around sustainability as the leitmotif and the search for renewable sources of energy. There can be little doubt that these developments in governance around green politics have been accompanied by shifts in self-understanding even if they do not, as yet, translate into a new kind of democracy, which is still confined to the increasingly incapacitated politics of the right and left. Relevant, too, are new social movements addressed to planetary politics or political movements challenging neoliberal projects in particular places throughout the world.

For all these reasons, the political challenge of the Anthropocene is very much one that can be cast in terms of cosmopolitics. Some of the central objectives of the Anthropocene as a political condition resonate with cosmopolitical ideas, for example, increasing biological diversity, the need for a global dialogue between the developed and developing world on reducing carbon emissions in ways that respect the desire of the non-western world to have a share in the benefits it has had until now, and the need to strike a balance between short- and long-term thinking. Neoliberalism encourages short-term thinking, while long-term thinking runs the danger of being a justification for doing nothing, but with the resolution that only a deliberative process can offer a way forward. Thus, it would seem that only a cosmopolitical order of governance can offer the only possible political solution to problems that are often objectified as ones that can be resolved by purely technological fixes, as in climate engineering (see Hamilton 2013) or are simply ignored or even denied. Technology and science are certainly the key to the future, since calls for reducing greenhouse gases are empty gestures if they simply put the individual as the culprit and saviour. Alternative technologies will be required to provide carbon-free energy, but such measures will require major re-organization of the governance of societies. It therefore makes no sense to blame science and technology when science and technology are needed to provide the solution to the problem of how contemporary societies can advance human well-being without endangering the very conditions of social possibility. The current discourse of sustainability will undoubtedly prove to be inadequate when it comes to addressing the challenges because it is locked in a hopeless compromise between the instrumental appropriation of nature and inadequate measures of conservation without offering a viable vision for a future that will inexorably increase production to meet the new consumption demands in the developing world. In this scenario, the reduction of poverty comes at a cost that cannot be met within the prevailing system, which was predicated on the assumption that only recently has become evident that western civilization was able to enjoy its privileged ascent only because of poverty elsewhere, much of which was contributed to, if not caused by, the West.

160 Capitalism, cosmopolitanism, Anthropocene

This has now changed and has opened up new political scenarios that require fundamentally new thinking that recognizes that climate change as well as other manifestations of the Anthropocene cannot be contained within national orders of governance. The earth system is not itself constrained by the human–made boundaries of nations. This implies possible geopolitics (Clark 2014). Such politics would require a fundamental rethinking of governance in a cosmopolitan direction, for instance, in re-defining boundaries in terms of what Rockstrom et al (2009) have referred to as 'planetary boundaries'.

As argued above, cosmopolitanism was born with the notion of hospitality, as in Kant's argument in *Perpetual Peace* that the cosmopolitan law requires the recognition of the right of the stranger. In the epochal scale of time of the Anthropocene, it is now humanity as a whole that is the stranger on the earth which it inhabits for what will be a short time in the history of the planet. The 'Cosmopolocene' might be the new name for the descriptively unpolitical Anthropocene and in terms that are more readily translatable into the language of the human and social sciences. While the current preference for the Anthropocene is not likely to give way to any of the alternatives it has provoked, such as 'Capitalocene' or 'Technocene', it is worth reflecting on the value in naming the current age by its oppositional forces. It is possibly something like this that Nietzsche was anticipating when he wrote in a famous section called 'Masters of the Earth' in *The Will to Power*: 'Inexorably, hesitantly, terrible as fate, the great task and question is approaching: how shall the earth as a whole be governed? And to what end shall "man" as a whole – and no longer as a people, a race – be raised and trained?' (1967: 501). The theme of governing the earth and the subsequent discussion of agency in this work was such an attempt to raise the prospect of a new kind of agency, though not in this case with a geophysical crisis in mind.

In sum, the argument leads us in the normative direction of a politicization of the concept of the Anthropocene as a cosmopolitical project. This is both a utopia and a critique of the dystopic narrative of the Anthropocene signalling that it can be transformed into an order of governance.

Notes

1 This chapter is based on a longer article co-authored with Aurea Mota in 2017 and has been extensively re-revised and updated, Governing the Anthropocene: Agency, Governance and Knowledge' *European Journal of Social Theory* 20 (1): 9–38. A shorter version of the paper was given as a keynote lecture at the Brazilian Sociological Association annual conference, Brasilia, 26th–29th July 2017. I am grateful to Aurea Mota for advice in writing the original paper and to Piet Strydom and Frederic Vandenberghe for comments on an earlier version.
2 See the classic account by Alfred Schmidt (2014–1962), which was based on a doctoral thesis supervised by Adorno and Horkheimer. See also Vogel's (1996) reconstruction of the concept of nature in critical theory. For other contributions, see Brulle (2002), Eckersley (1990) and Gunderson (2014).
3 See also from a more critical theory perspective, Eder (1996).
4 For some of the general literature, see Bonneuil and Fressoz (2015), Chakrabarty (2009), Davis (2016), Dukes (2011), Hamilton et al (2015), Steffen et al (2011a, 2011b), Zalasiewicz

et al (2011, 2015a, 2015b). See also the special issues of the *European Journal of Social Theory* edited by Skillington (2015) and Delanty (2017).
5 Initially in a short paper in 2000 (Crutzen and Stoermer 2000). See also Cruzen and Steffen (2003).
6 The geologic time scale (GTS) unlike historical time scales is rigorously defined and periodized into Eons, Era, Period, Epoch, Ages and indicated by capital letters. An Epoch in the GTS refers to a unit within a Period. The current Period is the Quaternary, which has two Epochs, the Pleistocene and Holocene. Epochs may be divided into Ages, as with the current Meghalayan Age.
7 See their article in *Nature*, Lewis and Maslin (2015), Maslin and Lewis (2015). See also Crosby (2003).
8 For other perspectives on this, see Archer (2008) and Chernilo (2017a, 2017b).
9 See Thomas (2014) for an account on the relation between biology and history.

References

Archer, M. 2008. *Being Human: The Problem of Agency*. Cambridge: Cambridge University Press.
Arendt, H. 1958. *The Human Condition*. Chicago, IL: Chicago University Press.
Beck, U. 2006. *The Cosmopolitan Outlook*. Cambridge: Polity Press.
Beck, U. 2010. Climate for Change: How to Create a Green Modernity? *Theory, Culture and Society*, 27: 254–66.
Bonneuil, C. and Fressoz, J-B. 2015. *The Shock of the Anthropocene*. London: Verso.
Bradshaw, M. 2014. *Global Energy Dilemmas*. Cambridge: Polity Press.
Braudel, F. 1990/1987. *The Mediterranean and the Mediterranean World in the Age of Philip 11*. London: Penguin Books.
Brooke, J. 2014. *Climate Change and the Course of Global History*. Cambridge: Cambridge University Press.
Brulle, R. 2002. Habermas and Green Political Thought: Two Roads Converging. *Environmental Politics*, 11 (4): 1–20.
Castoriadis, C. 1987. *The Imaginary Institution of Society*. Cambridge: Polity Press.
Chakrabarty, D. 2009. The Climate of History: Four Theses. *Critical Inquiry*, 35: 197–22.
Chakrabarty, D. 2014. Climate and Capital: On Conjoined Histories. *Critical Inquiry*, 41: 1–23.
Chernilo, D. 2017a. *Debating Humanity: Towards a Philosophical Sociology*. Cambridge: Cambridge University Press.
Chernilo, D. 2017b. The Question of the Human in the Anthropocene. *European Journal of Social Theory*, 20 (1): 44–60.
Clark, N. 2014. Geopolitics and the Disaster of the Anthropocene. *The Sociological Review*, 62 (3): 19–37.
Clark, N. and Gunaratnam, Y. 2017. Earthing the *Anthropos*? From 'Socializing the Anthropocene' to Geologizing the Social. *European Journal of Social Theory*, 20 (1): 146–63.
Corcoran, P., Moore, J. and Jazvac, K. 2014. An Anthropogenic Marker Horizon in the Future Rock Record. *The Geological Society of America*, 24 (6): 4–8.
Costanza, R., Graumlich, L. and Steffen, W. (eds.) 2007/2011. *Sustainability or Collapse? An Integrated History and Future of People on Earth*. Cambridge, MA: MIT Press.
Crawford, N. 2002. *Argument and Change in World Politics: Ethics, Decolonization, and Humanitarian Intervention*. Cambridge: Cambridge University Press.
Crosby, A. 2003. *The Columbia Exchange: Biological and Cultural Consequences of 1492*. Westport, CT: Greenwood Press.

Crutzen, P. J. 2002. Geology of Mankind: The Anthropocene. *Nature*, 415: 23.

Cruzen, P. J. and Steffen, W. 2003. How Long Have We Been Living in the Anthropocene Era? *Climatic Change*, 61 (3): 251–7.

Crutzen, P. J. and Stoermer, E. F. 2000. The 'Anthropocene'. *IGBP Newsletter*, 41: 17–18.

Danowski, D. and Viveiros de Castro, E. 2017. *The Ends of the Earth*. Cambridge: Polity Press.

Davis, J. 2016. *The Birth of the Anthropocene*. Berkeley: University of California Press.

Davis, M. 2001. *Late Victorian Holocausts: El Nino Famines and the Making of the Third World*. London: Verso.

Delanty, G. (ed.) 2017. The Anthropocene and Social Theory. Special Issue of the *European Journal of Social Theory*, 20 (1).

Diamond, J. 1998. *Guns, Germs and Steel: A Short History of Everybody for the Last 13,000 Years*. New York: Vintage.

Diamond, J. 2005/2011. *Collapse: How Societies Chose to Fall or Survive*. London: Penguin Books.

Dryzek, J. and Pickering, J. 2019. *The Politics of the Anthropocene*. Oxford: Oxford University Press.

Dukes, P. 2011. *Minutes to Midnight: History and the Anthropocene Era from 1763*. New York: Anthem Press.

Eckersley, R. 1990. Habermas and Green Political Thought. *Theory and Society*, 19: 739–76.

Eder, K. 1996. *The Social Construction of Nature*. London: Sage.

Eisenstadt, S. N. (ed.) 1986. *On the Origin and Diversity of Axial Age Civilisations*. New York: SUNY Press.

Gunderson, R. 2014. Habermas in Environmental Thought: Anthropocentric Kantian or Forefather of Ecological Democracy. *Sociological Inquiry*, 84 (4): 626–53.

Hamilton, C. 2013. *Earthmasters: The Dawn of the Age of Climate Engineering*. New Haven: Yale University Press.

Hamilton, C., Bonneuil, C. and Gemenne, F. (eds.) 2015. *The Anthropocene and the Global Environmental Crisis: Rethinking Modernity in a New Epoch*. London: Routledge.

Haraway, D. 2015. Anthropocene, Capitalocena, Planationocena, Chthulucene: Making Kin. *Environmental Humanities*, 6: 159–65.

Hornborg, A. 2017. Artefacts Have Consequences, not Agency: Toward a Critical Theory of Global Environmental History. *European Journal of Social Theory*, 20 (1): 95–110.

Koselleck, R. 2004. *Futures Past: On the Semantics of Historical Time*. New York: Columbia University Press.

Latour, B. 1993. *We Have Never Been Modern*. Hempel Hempstead: Harvester Wheatsheaf.

Latour, B. 2004. *Politics of Nature: How to Bring Science Into Democracy*. Cambridge, MA: Harvard University Press.

Latour, B. 2013. *Facing Gaia: Six Lectures on the Political Theology of Nature*. The Gifford Lectures on Natural Religion.

Latour, B. 2014. Agency at the Time of the Anthropocene. *New Literary History*, 45: 1–18.

Lewis, S. and Maslin, M. 2015. Defining the Anthropocene. *Nature*, 519: 171–80.

Lovejoy, A. 1979/2000. *Gaia: A New Look at Life on Earth*. Oxford: Oxford University Press.

Malm, A. and Hornborg, A. 2014. The Geology of Mankind? A Critique of the Anthropocene Narrative. *The Anthropocene Review*, 1: 62–9.

Maslin, M. and Lewis, S. 2015. Anthropocene: Earth System, Geological, Philosophical and Political Paradigm Shifts. *The Anthropocene Review*, 2 (2): 108–16.

McNeill, J. R. and Engelke, P. 2014. *The Great Acceleration: An Environmental History of the Anthropocene*. Cambridge, MA: Harvard University Press.

MacNaghten, P. and Urry, J. 1998. *Contested Natures*. London: Sage.

Meadows, D. et al 1972. *Limits to Growth*. New York: Universe Books.

Mithen, S. 1998. *The Prehistory of the Mind*. London: Phoenix.

Moore, J. W. 2015. *Capitalism and the Web of Life: Ecology and the Accumulation of Capital*. London: Verso.

Mota, M. and Delanty, G. 2015. Eisenstadt, Brazil and the Multiple Modernities Framework: Revisions and Reconsiderations. *Journal of Classical Sociology*, 15 (2): 39–57.

Nietzsche, F. 1967. *The Will to Power*. New York: Vintage.

Norblad, J. 2017. Time for Politics: How a Conceptual History of Forests Can Help Us to Politicize the Long Term. *European Journal of Social Theory*, 20 (1): 164–82.

Polanyi, K. 1944. *The Great Transformation*. New York: Rinehart.

Rockstrom, J. et al 2009. Planetary Boundaries: Exploring the Safe Operating Space for Humanity. *Ecology and Society*, 14 (2). On-line URL.

Rossi, P. 1984. *The Dark Abyss of Time: The History of the Earth and the History of Nations from Hooke to Vico*. Chicago, IL: Chicago University Press.

Ruddiman, W. F. et al 2015. Defining the Epoch We Live in. *Science*, 348: 389.

Schmidt, A. 2014 [1962]. *The Concept of Nature in Marx*. London: Verso.

Schwägerl, C. 2014. *The Anthropocene: The Human Era and How It Shapes Our Planet*. Santa Fe, NM: Synergetic Press.

Skillington, T. 2015. Theorizing the Anthropocene. *European Journal of Social Theory*, 18 (3): 229–35.

Steffen, W., Crutzen, P. and McNeill, J. R. 2007. The Anthropocene: Are Humans Now Overwhelming the Great Forces of Nature? *Ambio*, 36 (8): 614–21.

Steffen, W., Grinevald, J., Crutzen, P. and McNeil, J. 2011. The Anthropocene: Conceptual and Historical Perspectives. *Philosophical Transactions of the Royal Society A*, 369: 842–67.

Steffen, W., Persson, A. and Deutsch, L. 2011. The Anthropocene: From Global Change to Planetary Stewardship. *AMBIO*, 40: 739–61.

Steffen, W. et al 2015. The Trajectory of the Anthropocene: The Great Acceleration. *The Anthropocene Review*, 2 (1): 81–98.

Strydom, P. 2015. Cognitive Fluidity and Climate Change: A Critical Social-Theoretical Approach to the Current Challenge. *European Journal of Social Theory*, 18 (3): 236–56.

Strydom, P. 2017. The Sociocultural Self-creation of a Natural Category: Sociotheoretical Reflections on Human Agency Under the Temporal Conditions of the Anthropocene. *European Journal of Social Theory*, 20 (1): 61–79.

Thomas, J. A. 2014. History and Biology in the Anthropocene: Problems of Scale, Problems of Value. *American Historical Review*, 119 (5): 1587–607.

Turner, B. S. 2017. Ritual, Belief and Habituation: Religion and Religions form the Axial Age to the Anthropocene. *European Journal of Social Theory*, 20 (17): 132–45.

Vogel, S. 1996. *Against Nature: The Concept of Nature in Critical Theory*. New York: State University of New York Press.

Wallace-Wells, D. 2019. *The Uninhabitable Earth: A Story of the Future*. London: Penguin Books.

Yusoff, K. 2016. Anthropogenesis: Origins and Endings in the Anthropocene. *Theory, Culture and Society*, 33 (2): 3–28.

Zalasiewicz, J., Williams, M., Haywood, A. and Ellis, M. 2011. The Anthropocene: A New Epoch of Geological Time? *Philosophical Transactions of the Royal Society A*, 369: 835–41.

Zalasiewicz, J. et al 2015a. When Did the Anthropocene Begin? A Mid-Twentieth Century Boundary Level Is Stratigraphically Optimal. *Quaternary International*, 383: 196–203.

Zalasiewicz, J. et al 2015b. Colonization of the Americas 'Little Ice Age' Climate, and Bomb Produced Carbon: Their Role in Defining the Anthropocene. *The Anthropocene Review*, 2 (2): 117–27.

PART 3

Space, memory and legacies of history

8

THE FUTURE OF PUBLIC SPACE

Crisis and renewal

In this chapter, I am interested in exploring the contemporary transformation of public space. Space has been transformed in fundamental ways today. Cyberspace, more than anything else, has radically transformed how we consider space. The digital world is not only a new kind of space but has transformed non-digital space. The question this chapter is addressed to is whether the traditional understanding of public space is now in decline and exhausted of potential both for public life and for the social life of cities and, if instead, new forms of space are emerging that require a rethinking of the meaning of the public.[1] On the one side, new kinds of digital and post-urban space bring about a transformation in the relation of the citizen to society; on the other side, these new kinds of space present major challenges to traditional understandings of public life in that they can offer cosmopolitan possibilities as well as dangers.

The western urban tradition was based on the centrality of public space: the square, the street, the commons made possible civic life, community, and fostered democracy. This was also the tradition that inspired the related notion of the public sphere, a key concept in critical theory since Habermas, introduced it in his first major work. However, in recent years there has been a major transformation of public space as a result of developments, such as neoliberal commodification, globalization, securitization, and digitalization. There is a greater pluralization of public space − as opposed to a shared space − and a concomitant rise of interstitial and global space. But the spectre of dystopia also haunts our time as our cities lose their connection with community. Against the utopia of Habermas's deliberative model of the public sphere, Foucault's ambivalent notion of the *Heterotopia* − places that are different from the mainstream − captures elements of the contemporary transformation of space. Public space was once based on proximity, the model of dialogue, and commonality between strangers; today it is pluralized but does not foster a culture of pluralism. The central motif of voice in the making of the modern city has been replaced by the motif of the eye.

168 Space, memory and legacies of history

In this chapter, I argue that while the historical forms of public space and the legacy of the Agora have lost much of their relevance, they have not entirely disappeared and can acquire other functions. New kinds of public space have indeed emerged but have not entirely replaced the old forms, even if many of its functions have been rendered redundant.[2] The contemporary crisis has much to do with the decline of the old and the incomplete appearance of the new. Rather than strangers encountering each other in the shared public culture, different groups create their own publics. Yet, public space is still part of the fabric of society and perhaps is best seen in terms of changing social configurations. If space is defined by social relations and the uses that people make of it, it is therefore a matter of changing forms than a question of decline. Public space is ultimately created by the significations that people give to it and, as suggested also by Habermas's notion of the public sphere, it is indeterminate and unbounded. However, it is not disembodied and exists in material and highly mediatized forms. But the role of public space today is less central to the public sphere than it once was, and perhaps its real function today is social rather than political.

Space and the public

The modern understanding of the public has been closely linked to space and in particular to urban space. Cities are spatial zones that are unlike other spatial configurations, such as the nation-state, in that they have always had a stronger connection with the idea of the public. This at least was the basis of the western tradition of the city. The first colonies the Greeks established were all cities and reflected the urban form of the home polis that they sought to replicate in the conquered lands on the shores of the Mediterranean. The Spanish built cities in the New World in much the same way as the ones of the Old World, with the central square and other markers of public life. The Brazilian tradition perhaps signals a break from that European tradition. The foundation of Brasilia in 1960 as the utopian new capital was to be a city without public space as traditionally understood based on an urban centre.[3] But even in this case, forms of public space did take shape, contrary to the programmatic designs of its founders. The very notion of citizenship in modern times was generally seen as pertaining to cities. Public space and public life have been seen as interwoven since the Greek polis. The legacy of the Agora – the free and open space of the city – connects Athens to Rome to Florence in the heritage of the European city of modernity. The modern city inherited the classical understanding of space as the location of public life, but also, as Walter Benjamin (2002) showed in the monumental *Arcades* work, made it the work of memory, since much of the present knows itself only in the memory of that which has been lost. Modernity created a discord between the idea of the city and the reality of modern capitalism.

The quintessential spatial markers of the modern city – above all the square, the street/street life, the park, markets, promenades, public gardens, the commons – are spatial categories. Modern institutions, such as libraries, public parks, town halls, and so on, inherited the spatiality and materiality of the older legacy of public life as expressed in public spaces. The very notion of public space is by definition a contrast to private space and as such captured the escape from the tyranny of the home. The truly free life was to be found in the public domain. The institution of the café since the eighteenth century in European cities cultivated a new kind of public life that also has a political function as a space free of power. Public space makes possible civic autonomy and is the social and material basis of democracy.

In his 1962 work, *The Structural Transformation of the Public Sphere*, Habermas characterized the early public sphere in its formative period in the eighteenth century as a domain of communication that was linked to new public spaces which were reducible neither to the Court Society nor to the private world of domesticity (Habermas 1989). It is, of course, important to note that Habermas's concept of the public sphere was not primarily a spatial one, and the debate on the public sphere in social theory has not been primarily a debate about public space, which has developed into a different body of literature. The German term *Öffentlichkeit* does not correspond to the notion of space as such, and Habermas's concern was not with space as such but with the critical formation of public opinion. The public sphere is a realm of discourse signifying publicness and includes normative elements that are in contradiction to historical reality. Nonetheless, the public sphere is not disembodied; it is based on particular forms of space and the institutions and modes of interaction that they fostered.

While Habermas emphasized communication – in the sense of debate and political contestation based on the emergence of a reading public – as the chief feature of the newly created bourgeois public culture, other more critical perspectives have related it to the space of resistance and social struggles for which the categories of the bourgeois public sphere were less important (see Landes 1988; Calhoun 1992; Negt and Kluge 2011; Tucker 1996; Warner 2002). The age of revolution may have seen the decline of the eighteenth-century bourgeois public sphere associated with Enlightenment culture, as Habermas argued, due to the rise of capitalism and the commodification of the public sphere. However, it also witnessed the creation of new cultural and political movements that were also shaped in the crucible of public space in the modern city. So, on the one side, modern public space becomes the basis of civic life, democracy, recreation, and community and, at the same time, makes possible political radicalness. It is the space of cosmopolitical engagement, where the encounter of the citizen and the stranger opens citizenship to the culture of modernity, which as Benjamin recognized is never contained in fixed structures, such as the glass and steel of the Parisian arcades or the boulevards designed by Haussmann to restrict and control public protests (see Benjamin 1997, 2002).

While Benjamin's reflections on public space capture the ambivalence of modern public space, the dominant story is one of decline. The space of modernity became dominated by the great projects of the modern national state, as in the Haussmann project for the redesign of Paris, great exhibitions, iconic public spaces designed to celebrate the state and often the empire. The example of modernist twentieth-century Brasilia is an extreme case of this drive for the perfectly planned city. Modern space is dominated by the culture of monumentality and capitalist

170 Space, memory and legacies of history

commodification at the same time as it opens itself to something that reaches beyond the new culture of materiality of the nineteenth century. In his account of the phantasmagoria of modernity, Benjamin tried to capture such moments of the modern metropolis, which he saw in the combination of modern technological innovation, bourgeois life, and modernism. As a result, the modern city is also the graveyard of history since it is composed of ruins but also sustained by their memories. Habermas, like Arendt in the *Human Condition*, but following Adorno and Horkheimer, saw the modern public sphere in terminal decline, although this should not be interpreted as nostalgia for a lost reality since the public sphere can be recreated in new forms. In fact, this early work was intended to be an exercise in immanent critique designed to show how the ideas of bourgeois society are not realized in social reality. However, unlike Arendt (1958), in his later work he revised, if not abandoned, what was nonetheless a historical narrative of decline for a theory of collective learning that offered a less historically based model of immanent analysis (see Chapter 1). This sense of modern public space as in decline, eroded by the institutions of modernity and capitalism, was also a theme in Richard Sennett's *The Fall of Public Man*, a work that portrayed the fall of public life with the rise of a privatistic sphere based on narcissism and 'the tyranny of intimacy' (Sennett 1978). In this account, public life has become a place of fear and is depoliticized. However, Sennett's later work on the re-humanization of the city reflected a more forward-looking view of the possibility of the open city as a place where people can have autonomous lives.

In the writings of Georg Simmel and Walter Benjamin, the modern city makes possible a specific kind of intensified experience in which relations of proximity alternate with relations of distance. In his famous essay of 1903, 'The Metropolis and Mental Life', Simmel (1972) referred to this as a nervousness. Metropolitan experience encapsulates the spirit of modernity, especially the sense of things being in flux and fluid (see Gilloch 1997; Frisby 1986, 2001). The city is characterized by the money economy, exchange and circulation, which produce new sensations and cultural representations or images. Modern urban experience is shaped by motion, which tends to lead to a fragmentation of what might once have been a more holistic experience of the world. The urban crowd, street life, and mechanical transportation intensified the inner life of individuals who react in different ways to the stimuli of the city. In the writings of both Simmel and Benjamin, with their respective concerns with Berlin and Paris, the modern metropolis offers the individual possibilities of liberty and creativity that would otherwise not be possible. Influenced by Simmel, Siegfried Kracauer, one of the early Frankfurt School theorists and close to Adorno, wrote in a similar vein about the modern city but gave greater centrality to the critique of capitalism. Common to these interpretations of the modern city was a sense of public space as a domain in which new experiences could be forged. In the writings of Simmel and especially Benjamin, the city is an essentially open space which has a material reality but one that is inseparable from its cultural forms and social relations. For Simmel, the key category was the idea of sociability: the city as the space of social relations. Both authors saw the modern city as marked by the dynamics of the crowd and not primarily as a basis of political community. Their critique of modernity was more of an aesthetic critique than a straightforwardly political one.

The reception of Simmel's work in twentieth-century sociology, above all in the United States, led to a conception of modern society based on the form of the city. Max Weber also saw the city as formative of modern society more generally. In this sociological tradition, space is seen in terms of social relations. The work of Henri Lefebvre developed this perspective on space as a social category with a more elaborate critical theory of the social production of space. For the purposes of this chapter, the important point is that public space should be seen as a social category as a space of relations and is therefore not fixed in a specific form. In the Frankfurt School critical theory tradition, Benjamin came closest to this position in that he saw the spatial categories of the modern metropolis as the basis of new kinds of experience and remembering. Benjamin's reflections on the city offered the additional and important perspective that a city is not based only on people but has a certain materiality in its conditions of existence. The modern metropolis is a product of the interaction of people and technological and material creations that all together give it its vibrancy. This perspective is somewhat lost in later accounts, such as Habermas's purely deliberative vision of the modernity.

The transformation of public space

There is much to suggest that the presuppositions of the conception of public space in critical theory, as discussed in the foregoing, are undermined, if not invalidated, by the transformation of capitalism in the past three or four decades. There is also the further question of the relationship between public space and, as in Habermas's conception, the public sphere as a realm of communication between strangers. It is clear that today the public sphere is no longer rooted in public space; it has found other modalities of existence. While the public sphere has not been entirely disembodied, it has ceased to be a spatial category. Where, then, does public space reside and why should it be cultivated?

To begin, public space is no longer necessarily confined only to urban locations. The modern city inherited the basic structure of the ancient city in having a centre that was the focus of public life. The relation between centre and periphery in cities has now changed the spatiality of the city. There are new sites of space that lie beyond the bounded space of the historical cities of Europe. These sites would include refugee camps, which are not public spaces but spaces of confinement that are also sites of dwelling for many people where they often seek to preserve the life of the spaces they left behind. Many large cities have peripheries that are disconnected with the urban centres and in many cities, especially in North America and in Latin America, the centres have often become empty of civic life. In some cases, the social life of the city is maintained precisely by ensuring that it is disconnected from the periphery. This is illustrated by the way the centre of Brasilia has limited public transport to the satellite towns around it to ensure that the poor people who

172 Space, memory and legacies of history

service the needs of the city on weekdays do not come to the city for recreation on Sundays. The upper-class district of Higienopolis in São Paulo does not have a metro line so that poor people will not spoil the urban tranquillity of its residents. While many cities have reversed the descent into urban decay, they have become beholden to empty or pseudo-public space. Much of this has come about as a result of post-industrialization, which in destroying the modernist city that was the focus of the writing of Simmel and Benjamin created forms of public space that are not designed to foster public life. Thus, one finds in the centre of many cities new kinds of urban spaces created by artists but devoid of lived life. Re-gentrification reverses some trends but brings about others, such as dispossession and fragmentation. A more general trend toward post-urban space can be found with the creation of recreational zones outside the city and, of course, the creation of the post-1945 era, middle-class suburbia.

Public space is defined to a large degree by reference to private space. It follows that changes in the private domain will have consequences for public space. Such transformations have become more important than in the first half of the twentieth century. New kinds of private space have emerged to replace much of what once took place in public. The private realm can no longer be seen in terms of a tyranny from which the only escape was the public domain, which was clearly how Walter Benjamin saw things. There are new kinds of autonomous private space that offer the individual the liberty that once could only be found in public space. While this has led to a decline in communal life, it has clearly shifted the balance in the relation between the private and the public, producing more hybrid forms. However, the changed relationship has also taken more insipient forms with the undermining of the old forms of public space by the private domain.

With the ascent of neoliberalism, the demise of a certain tradition of the public was inevitable. The fundamental rationale of neoliberalism is the onslaught on public life. The valorization of the market and a more expansive and aggressive capitalism has led to the citizen becoming a consumer who is immunized from the experiences of phantasmagoria that Benjamin described as part of the experience of city life. Over the past few decades in almost every part of the world there is clear evidence of growing privatization of public space. Public space is no longer composed of democratic spaces but sites of consumption and control (Low and Smith 2005). Neoliberal commodification is perhaps exemplified in the shopping mall and the golf course.

Much of what is regarded as public space is often not so public. A recent trend in the United States is POPS, or privately-owned public space. A famous example, where the Occupy Wall Street movement began in 2011, is what is now Zuccotti Park, which is owned by a corporation. Other historical examples are a reminder that much of public space has always been private, as is illustrated by Hyde Park, London, which, as with many other public parks, is owned by the crown. Many shopping centres exercise their property rights to impose their rules on what can be 'public', for example, banning people wearing hoods. Permission has to be sought for protests outside the British parliament in Westminster. In many European cities

The future of public space **173**

there is today a concern with Muslim headscarves, and especially the burka, with demands for banning burkas in public space and a more general ban on head-scarves in the public domain. Clearly clothing – which both conceals and reveals the body – has always had a certain signification in public space. In the case of the burka, which requires the total concealment of the body, it has led to demands that the human face cannot be concealed in the public domain. There is an interest-ing tension with this requirement for the visibility of the face and the theme of anonymity that has traditionally characterized the modern city. However, as far as I know, an item of female clothing has not before been connected with security.

Public space nonetheless has always been an area of securitization. This, as men-tioned, was the driving force behind the Haussmann design of Paris, following the Paris Commune uprising in 1871. Recent developments in relation to terror have led to new regimes of securitization and policing that have had a detrimental effect on public space in many cities. Much of this goes along with the expansion in private space. As Sennett argued, in *The Fall of Public Life*, public life has become an area of anxiety rather than a shared space. Notwithstanding these developments, it should be noted that modernity has always been accompanied by such concerns with the con-trol of population and the regulation of space. The ordering of space and the order-ing of societies have been coeval. The extent to which this all is to be seen in terms of domination is questionable. The commodification of public space is ambivalent in that it represents, on the one side, the demise of the older forms of space, while, on the other side, it reverses the urban decay following from de-industrialization and re-introduces conviviality. This ambivalence is perhaps best seen in terms of re-gentrification: large swathes of city life have been saved from stagnation if not decay at the cost of a loss in the older organization of space. The gated community, to take a different but similar example, is also ambivalent. The phenomenon of gating takes many forms, from hard to soft forms (see Bagaeen and Uduku 2015). It is also not entirely a creation of neoliberal times: the medieval cities of Europe have mostly been gated in some form or another, and it was this particular form of the organiza-tion of space that gave them their autonomy.

Clearly one of the most important transformations in public space in recent times is digital space, which often intersects with the older forms of space and may even replace them in certain contexts. It is predicated on private space, even mak-ing possible new kinds of public life, since it is mostly individuals as private persons who connect in virtual space. In the age of YouTube and Facebook, space is no longer local or necessarily based on place. Such kinds of space are both public and private. Much of the digital space is a market place but is accessed from the private sphere, which increasingly enters into cyberspace. The screen replaces the plaza. Digital space creates new kinds of communities but also brings about new kinds of exclusion. Facebook Marketplace, for example, is owned privately and serves simul-taneously to include/exclude people. Those who do not engage with the digital are simply excluded, while those who share the same digital space are included.

The arrival of the smart mobile phone has fundamentally transformed the nature of space. The social theory of modernity emphasized the fleeting and momentary

174 Space, memory and legacies of history

nature of modern urban life, as famously captured in Baudelaire's understanding of modernity as 'the transitory, the fugitive, the contingent'.[4] The mobile phone has made permanent what was once of the moment (see Greenfield 2017). One's location is recorded by the phone's technology; phone networks capture every movement and transaction of the user. The photographs that the user now takes with ease, whether as a tourist or consumer, retain a memory of what was once a fleeting moment. The stroller is more often than not connected to a mobile device rather than to the physical reality of the street, which is traversed with the aid of an online map. The iconic feature of modern urban public space, the phone booth, has now lost is function. Instagram is another example of a significant transformation in how we see space. The dominance of Instagram now has implications for architecture.[5]

These developments are, of course, a feature of the big city. Large cities are now intensively networked spaces which have the effect of bringing about an increased intensification in social relations. According to Paul Mason, the injection of networked technologies into big cities and the resulting intensification in social relations produces a new contrast between the big city and the small town.[6] Arguably this distinction has replaced the older one of urban versus rural. This comes at a time when more than half of the world's population lives in cities. In this context the novelty of the city is no longer marked by a contrast to countryside but by urban transformations that create very different kinds of cities, for example, livable cities as opposed to fortress cities.

According to Castells (1997), flows do not create new kinds of place but replace place. Technology has made private and public space less demarcated and has opened up alternative possibilities for spatial experience that are not contained within the urban form. This radical turn to the post-urban is also reflected in the making of public space as something that is necessarily on the outside: it can also be found indoors, as in new architectural designs that have transformed buildings such as museums where spatial experience facilitates changes in self-understanding. Post-urban public space is by no means regressive or a sign of total reification; it can rise to new kinds of experiences leading to the enhancement of the social life of cities and can make possible new forms of public life. Such transformation in experience is also part of a more general linguistic and cognitive transformation in that the digital world serves a new spatial language: terms that were previously material are now purely digital, for example, 'storage', 'sharing', 'access', 'open access', 'mining', and so on.

Public space is no longer local or even urban but is intermeshed with global flows. The increasing presence of social media through mobile devices has created new transnational spaces that enable greater reflexivity and cultural fluidity. There are numerous modes of mediatized interaction in contemporary public spaces across national borders that express new global flows. New kinds of digital technology make possible transnational space within the context of what was once only local space. Examples range from the instantaneous access to social media that most people have through their mobile phones to the ambient screens that are increasingly a feature of city centres and modes of surveillance (Papastergiadis

2016; De Sousa 2012). In view of these developments, it is difficult to disagree with Ash Amin in an insightful essay that human dynamics in public space are centrally influenced by the entanglement and circulation of human and non-human bodies. He argues that sociality in urban public space is not a sufficient condition for civic and political citizenship' (Amin 2008: 7). His post-humanist perspective stresses the importance of technology and material infrastructure as an intrinsic part of the urban and human condition; that is to say, the social life of the city cannot be seen only in terms of individuals interacting with each other. Such forms of interaction are mediated by technology such that technology is also an active agent in the construction of social realities.

An example of the technologization of social relations can be found in digital cartography, which is having an increasing impact on space. Google Maps requires companies to pay for adverts. One will not know about a café or restaurant unless it has paid to be on Google maps as a priority location. This is not only a new approach to mapping but directly impacts on everyday life. The eventual arrival of the driverless car will be an additional step in the entanglement of technology and cartography in creating ways people navigate urban space.

Digital technology is just one expression of technological change. John Urry has commented on the push for verticality in current futuristic cities, such as Shanghai, Dubai, Qatar, Hong Kong, Rio, São Paulo, Seoul, and Singapore (Urry 2016: 138–40). The space above the surface of cities is becoming more and more important. As a result, helicopters become increasingly common, especially in Sao Paulo. Urry claims micro-light flying will become more a feature of the 'fast mobility city' of the future. Currently Amazon is experimenting with automated drones for the delivery of packages.

The rise of the *Heterotopia*? Towards cosmopolitan space

How then are we to understand the contemporary transformation of urban space? Does it signal the end of the kind of space that was the basis of the European city? Or could such interstitial forms of space be the basis of cosmopolitan space?

The interstitial notion of space is reflected in Foucault's notion of heterotopia. The concept of *Heterotopia*, meaning literally 'other spaces', is one of the more interesting ways to interpret the current transformation of space and the creation of locations that are not spaces as conventionally understood. In his 1967 text, 'Of Other Spaces: Utopias and Heterotopias', Foucault wrote that in contrast to the great obsession of the nineteenth century with history: 'The present epoch will perhaps be above all the epoch of space' and, he wrote, that 'the anxiety of our era has to do fundamentally with space, no doubt a great deal more than with time' (Foucault 1984). The enigmatic and obscure text characterized the present time as a moment 'when our experience of the world is less that of a long life developing through time than that of a network that connects points and intersects with its own skein'. His argument that space takes the 'form of relations among sites' is not too far away from the sociological notion of social reality as relational, as put

176 Space, memory and legacies of history

forward by Simmel, among others. But the heterotopia is not only a domain of social interaction; it is underpinned by materiality.

Heterotopias are a contrast to utopias in that they are real places that exist, often at the margins of societies or the margins of cities. They are counter-sites and are varied (Foucault distinguishes between crisis and deviant heterotopias), and there can be a juxtaposition of several incompatible sites. Foucault drew attention to an aspect of space that did not figure into the earlier accounts, namely, a plural sense of space. Nonetheless, the notion of heterotopias is not entirely foreign to critical theory in that it has some similarities with Benjamin's characterization of the diffuseness of urban life and the possibility of something different (see Dehaene and De Cauter 2001). For Hetherington, they are 'spaces of alternative ordering', where things are done differently than in their surroundings (Hetherington 1992).

Foucault's essay was unclear and suggestive, but it did not have a clear political sense of heterotopias as ways of organizing space. He had in mind examples as diverse as cemeteries, brothels, boarding schools, even colonies. The notion of the heterotopia – at least in terms of its reception – opens up new ways of thinking about spaces for dwelling, living, and encounters. The concept is relevant to the contemporary interest in cosmopolitan space, for example, migrant spaces. One of the major challenges for European societies is the integration of minorities. To achieve this, it has increasingly been recognized that new kinds of interactive space need to be created that facilitate interaction between migrants/refugees and citizens. Many migrant groups cross, inhabit, or complicate the borderlands of Europe: some of these are literal borders; others are those interstitial liminal spaces (such as the securitized zone of Ceuta and the camps in Malta) where international law makes new kinds of citizens, ones not granted full rights. Such spaces are also a part of the making of European public space. In 2015, during a time of unprecedented migration into Europe, public space took on a new significance in several European cities, including schools in Athens used as homes for migrants and tents in public spaces in German cities in the summer of 2015. The physical presence of refugees in cities in Germany, particularly their arrival at the train stations, led to what has been called, *Willkommenskultur*. Clearly, such uses of public space are not a basis for the future in that they are responses to crises. A challenge for Europe is to create spaces of inclusivity for migrants that are more durable and a basis for inclusion and autonomy.

Other examples of cosmopolitan heterotopias would include new and often ephemeral uses of public space, such as festivals, which have become key cultural players in contemporary transformations. It is also possible to speak of radical youth heterotopias. The experience of squatting and the construction of squatter identity in Europe is a manifestation of the transformation in the way that the public, the private, and the collective are reconfigured in contemporary Europe. The phenomenon of squatting in European cities is an example of a radicalized notion of the public and the need to rethink the limits of the private. Other examples would include movement-parties such as *Podemos* in Spain, which emerged out of the transformations in the use of public spaces. Such protest movements can empower their protagonists and reinvigorate democracy through the creation of meaning-ful forms of participation and public engagement. The significant development is the emergence of, what can be called, spaces of engagement whereby public space becomes a location of transformations in self-understanding by making possible new experiences.

The question of public space is not only a question of the transformation of space. The public itself is no longer only the national citizenry but includes oth-ers who are disenfranchised (migrants, refugees, youth). In this sense, the public includes counter-publics. As noted, the large influx of refugees into Europe in the past few years has made its impact on public space.

Many of these developments cannot be understood only in terms of the reifica-tion of public space or the loss of something – the agora – once possessed. They should be seen as expressions of public engagement and the making of embodied cosmopolitan experiences (see Rumford 2011). Space is not something territorially fixed but, following the philosophy of Castoriadis (1987), has an imaginary dimen-sion that gives to it creative – leading to what he called its 'instituting' – possibilities. Public space is ultimately created by the significations that people give to it and is indeterminate. It is evident that today these significations are rapidly changing. Such spaces are cosmopolitan in the sense that they are not only driven by people who themselves have experienced a transnational life, but above all because they enlarge the moral and political horizons of citizens. Cosmopolitan space refers to how majority cultures open themselves up to other forms of space-making (see Rumford 2011). The opening up of such forms of space should be seen as part of growing cosmopolitan trends in contemporary societies. Such trends are of course ambiguous in that they are not entirely new and they produce counter-movements, as is clearly illustrated by the surge of different kinds of populism across Europe.

It is possible to imagine in the not-too-distant future an entirely new and radical transformation of rural space. Under the condition of a new politics of the Anthro-pocene, new uses will have to be found for the large expanses of space devoted to environmentally destructive dairy farming, as well as other kinds of farming. If such a transformation of space were to occur, it would have major implications for public space.

At this point, a general argument can be formulated. Public space was once based on proximity, the model of dialogue, and the promise of commonality; in the classical and modern European city, it had a close connection with public life. Or, put differently, public life was once based on public space and thus had a close connection with the making of cities. Today public space is to a far greater degree pluralized and a site of difference. Rather than similar people encountering each other, diverse people construct their own 'publics'. Increasingly digital algorithms serve people with the content they desire and thus present less difference than sameness. The digitalization of the public creates a new kind of segmented kind of public space. Thus, while society as a whole may be becoming more diverse, digital space, rather than expanding the horizons of cyber communities, tends to strengthen social media silos whereby communities stick to their own 'bubbles'. In

178 Space, memory and legacies of history

the developing world, this is underpinned by a much stronger divide between the various classes and the spaces that they can access.

We can speak of a shift in the category of the public person from a citizen to a stranger. It is only within digital communities that a restricted kind of community of strangers is possible. Public space was once bounded but is now unbounded. However, this unbounded space makes possible new borders and exclusions. It is also reorganized as a result of tremendous material and technological transformations in the organization of cities. This transformation of space presents both dangers and opportunities for cities and for public life.

Mourning and sorrow in public space

Public space has always been a place of collective remembrance, sites where public displays of memory are enacted. The performative function of public space is still relevant today and can be seen in new forms of commemoration. James E. Young, in a classic essay in 1992, referred to the rise of the counter-memorial, or as it is sometimes called the 'counter-monument' (from the German, *Gegendenkmal*). This idea, which recalls Foucault's notion of counter-memories, relates to the ways in which previously excluded peoples – mostly minorities – affirm and insert themselves into national or mainstream narratives by subverting or challenging the official or unexamined taken-for-granted heritage. Such acts of commemoration are reflected in the shift from the monument (to the hero or victor) to the anti-monumental memorial. With this comes a greater recognition of the dark side of history and the need for the present to atone for the crimes of the past, as well as for the victim to have a voice.

Now, while memorials have been erected to the memories of fallen soldiers, especially since 1918, they have now been opened up to a wider sphere of experiences for all kinds of groups and take less the form of the heroic commemoration of, for example, sacrifice for the nation, for king and country. It has led cultural heritage into the difficult waters of contested histories and traumas, since the hero and the victim are often not so easily separated: the victim may be a perpetrator in the eyes of a previously silenced group. Those who made great sacrifices may not have done so for a noble cause (see Chapter 10).

The broadening of the scope of the memorial along with the wider democratization of memory has given to cultural heritage a new and more cosmopolitan task. Instead of being a celebration of a past now in ruins, it is now more likely to be a reflection on atonement, mourning, and grief. It is possible that only such sentiments are all that can unite what are often deeply divided societies today. All that is left of universal values is sorrow, loss, and remorse (this topic will be discussed in relation to memory in the next chapter).

In these very much-changed circumstances, in highly pluralized societies in which everyone is a stranger, cultural heritage can no longer so easily create unity for a nation or community. Instead, its task is to offer ways for the political community to live with the past and find in the figure of the stranger new and more

The future of public space **179**

positive ways of being. To do so will also be a way of reconciling the often difficult work of remembrance with the task of cultural regeneration. Cultural heritage is now being defined in new contexts in which atonement, sorrow, mourning, and grief become the markers by which the present is expressed through a more critical response to the past. The new sites of remembrance are less concerned about representation because often there is nothing left to represent but absence, pain, and suffering. Since the 9/11 memorial in New York, this has set a new trend that goes back to 2001 with Daniel Liebeskind's Jewish Museum in Berlin (see Young 2016; Walkowitz and Knauer (2004).

Such acts of signification are re-shaping public space and have given local communities new ways of expressing their histories. For example, there has been a notable change in abstract designs in spatial memorials, which are also now designed to enhance active participation and dialogue so that the viewer is no longer a passive spectator. The space of experience is enlarged to make possible new and often more personal interpretations. As Quentin Stevens and Karen Franck (2016) show, abstract designs encourage remembrance in ways that encourage the viewer to look inwards, not outwards. Instead of awe and distance, they cultivate a more direct experience that requires interpretation.

Cultural heritage can take a variety of more cosmopolitan forms when it is reclaimed by those previously excluded or marginalized, such as migrant or ethnic communities, national minorities, or those, such as youth groups, who have not been able to articulate their identities around the dominant narratives. Public space can thus be reclaimed and made more relevant for cultural regeneration without presuming a common culture or nostalgia for monumentality. There is also no reason why it should be the space of the nation but the space of forms of community and for the pursuit of the good life.

Conclusion

In this chapter, I have argued that the historical forms of public space have lost much of their relevance. While the spectre of dystopia haunts the very vision of the city today, the historical forms have not entirely disappeared. The contemporary crisis has much to do with the decline of the old and the incomplete appearance of the new. New kinds of public space have emerged but have not replaced the old forms, which lose their function as the container of the public sphere. Political movements, power, and so on no longer depend on public space. As the public moves into other domains, public space is still a key dimension of the social life of the city. Invoking Foucault's notion of the heterotopia, there is today a greater pluralization of public space and interstitial space. The impact of mobility in relation to communal life and sociality has also changed the nature of public space, giving it different material forms. A critical perspective on public space today should not be nostalgic for the past of the European city nor should it see only dystopia in the ruins of the present. There is an urgent need for a new political imagination for the creation of more relevant forms of public space.

180 Space, memory and legacies of history

Notes

1 This chapter is based on a lecture given at the National University of Brasilia in August 2018. I am grateful to Professor Carlos Benito Martins for the invitation and to the audience for comments on the lecture. I am grateful to Aurea Mota and Neal Harris for helpful comments on an earlier version.
2 For some general perspectives, see Innerarity (2006), Madaninipour et al (2013), Low (2000), Low and Smith (2005), Tonkiss 2005).
3 Brasilia was designed in the shape of an airplane. See Holston (1989).
4 Baudelaire (1964: 13).
5 www.theguardian.com/artanddesign/2018/nov/23/snapping-point-how-the-worlds-leading-architects-fell-under-the-instagram-spell
6 www.socialeurope.eu/to-the-postcapitalist-city

References

Amin, A. 2008. Collective Culture and Urban Public Space. *City*, 12 (1): 5–24.

Arendt, A. 1958. *The Human Condition*. Chicago, IL: University of Chicago Press.

Bagaeen, S. and Uduku, O. (eds.) 2015. *Beyond Gated Communities*. London: Routledge.

Baudelaire, C. 1964. The Painter of Modern Life. In: *The Painter of Modern Life and Other Essays*. London: Phaidon Press.

Benjamin, W. 1997. *Charles Baudelaire: A Lyric Poet in the Era of High Capitalism*. London: Verso.

Benjamin, W. 2002. *The Arcades Project*. Cambridge, MA: Harvard University Press.

Castoriadis, C. 1987. *The Imaginary Institution of Society*. London: Polity Press.

Calhoun, C. (ed.) 1992. *Habermas and the Public Sphere*. Cambridge, MA: MIT Press.

Castells, M. 1997. *The Rise of the Network Society*. Oxford: Blackwell.

De Souza E Silva, A. 2012. *Mobile Interfaces in Public Spaces*. London: Routledge.

Dehaene, M. and De Cauter, L. (eds.) 2001. *Heterotopias and the City*. London: Routledge.

Foucault, M. 1984 [1967]. Of Other Spaces: Utopia ad Heterotopias. In: *Architecture /Mouvement/ Continuité*. http://web.mit.edu/allanmc/www/foucault1.pdf.

Frisby, D. 1986. *Fragments of Modernity: Theories of Modernity in the Works of Simmel, Benjamin and Kracauer*. London: Routledge.

Frisby, D. 2001. *Cityscapes of Modernity*. Cambridge: Polity Press.

Gilloch, G. 1997. *Myth and Metropole: Walter Benjamin and the City*. Cambridge: Polity Press.

Greenfield, A. 2017. *Radical Technologies of Everyday Life*. London: Verso.

Habermas, J. 1989 [1962]. *The Structural Transformation of the Public Sphere*. Cambridge: Polity Press.

Hetherington, K. 1992. *The Badlands of Modernity: Heterotopias and Social Ordering*. London: Routledge.

Holston, J. 1989. *The Modernity City: An Anthropological Critique of Brasilia*. Chicago, IL: University of Chicago Press.

Innerarity, D. 2006. *El nuevo espacio público*. Madrid: Espasa.

Landes, J. B. 1988. *Women and the Public Sphere in the Age of the French Revolution*. Ithaca, NY: Cornell University Press.

Low, S. 2000. *On the Plaza: The Politics of Public Space and Culture*. Austin: University of Texas Press.

Low, S. and Smith, N. (eds.) 2005. *The Politics of Public Space*. London: Routledge.

Madaninipour, A., Knierbein, S. and Degros, A. (eds.) 2013. *Public Spaces and the Challenge of Urban Transformation in Europe*. London: Routledge.

Negt, O. and Kluge, O. 2011 [1972]. *Public Sphere and Experience: An Analysis of the Bourgeois and Proletarian Public Sphere*. London: Verso.

Papastergiadis, N. 2016. *Ambient Screens and Transnational Public Spaces*. Hong Kong: Hong Kong University Press.

Rumford, C. 2011. *Cosmopolitan Space*. London: Routledge.

Sennett, R. 1978. *The Fall of Public Man*. New York: Vintage.

Simmell, G. 1972 [1903]. *The Metropolis and Mental Life. In: On Individuality and Social Forms*. Chicago, IL: University of Chicago Press.

Stevens, Q. and Franck, K. (eds.) 2016. *Memorials as Spaces of Engagement: Design, Use and Meaning*. London: Routledge.

Tonkiss, K. 2005. *Space, the City and Social Theory*. Cambridge: Polity Press.

Tucker, K. H. 1996. *French Revolutionary Syndicalism and the Public Sphere*. Cambridge: Cambridge University Press.

Urry, J. 2016. *What Is the Future?* Cambridge: Polity Press.

Walkowitz, D. and Knauer, L. M. (eds.) 2004. *Memory and the Political Transformation in Public Space*. Durham: Duke University Press.

Warner, M. 2002. *Publics and Counter-Publics*. New York: Zone Books.

Young, J. 1992. The Counter-Monument: Memory Against Itself in Germany Today. *Critical Inquiry*, 18 (2): 267–96.

Young, J. 2016. *The Stages of Memory: Reflections on Memorial Art, Loss, and the Spaces Between*. Amherst: Massachusetts University Press.

9

MODERNITY AND MEMORY

Historical self-understanding and the burden of the past

The writings of the Frankfurt school, from Benjamin and Adorno to Habermas, offer important perspectives on critical approaches to historical self-understanding. The legacy of the Holocaust gave critical theory a strong normative and critical orientation in addressing the relation of the present to the past. It led to the view that the orientation to the future requires a rethinking of the present in its relation to the past. Since the incorporation of Freud into critical theory in the 1930s, entirely new approaches to memory were opened that emphasized the subject undergoing a process of interpretation in which the past would be redefined for the emancipation of the present. Understanding the present is inescapably bound up with the critique of the past, but it requires a capacity for critical thought and reflexivity. In their different ways, Benjamin, Adorno, and Habermas developed insights into the analysis of memory as a basis for social transformation. Benjamin's conception of redemptive critique played a major role in the Frankfurt School's approach to memory and history and is also reflected in Habermas's interventions on the public use of history.

These concerns have become highly relevant today with a new interest in memory and cultural heritage as expressed through mourning and remembrance. The past was once seen as something that gave to the present an orientation and identity, but it is increasingly seen as a burden or a trauma.[1] For many people, the relation to the past continues to be one of trauma, loss, and historical injustice. The very category of heritage reflects this problem of which legacy of history is relevant for the present and to what limits should the critique of the past be taken. Critical approaches to memory and heritage today, I argue, need to become more cosmopolitan in that there is now a wider plurality of voices in public culture. The memory of the Holocaust has now opened up a much wider range of memories and has made it possible for many previously silenced peoples to articulate their memories in the public sphere.[2] The position taken in this chapter is that cultural

Modernity and memory **183**

heritage can take cosmopolitan forms when it is reclaimed by those previously excluded from the dominant narratives of public culture. I do not agree with the criticism frequently made that critical theory is based on an historical narrative that sees the future determined by the past and that consequently is tied to a Eurocentric vision of modernity. The key perspective in critical theory on the contrary is that critique entails a capacity to learn from the catastrophes of the past, above all the horrors of the twentieth century. This was central to the thought of Adorno, Benjamin, and Habermas.

The chapter begins with a discussion of the problem of memory more generally in modernity and its relationship with utopia. The argument is that the decline of utopia, which for the left was an expression of the failure of all revolutionary aspiration, led to a preoccupation with memory and a loss of perspective on the future. The second section provides a reconstruction of the idea of memory in critical theory for an alternative account of the trap of memory. The writings of Benjamin, Adorno, and Habermas demonstrate that the engagement with memory is a learning process and a medium of reflexivity and self-transcendence that enables a re-interpretation of the present. Historical experience is not constant and uncontested; it is always subject to new interpretations, making possible shifts in meaning. The final section considers new perspectives on cultural heritage and the relevance of a cosmopolitan perspective.

Modernity: between utopia and memory

Modernity by definition entails an affirmation of the present. It is the new and the time of the now. In signalling a break from that which went before it, it was also tied to the past for its own self-definition in that modernity requires the memory of something anterior to it. Without a past there could be no present. In overcoming the past, the moderns have, paradoxically, almost always appealed to a more ancient past than the recent past, which the present repudiates. The present, even as it seeks to escape the hold of the past, is always tied to history in a deeper sense for its legitimation. Thus, classical antiquity was often seen as the real source of modernity than the more recent medieval age. As has been widely documented, in supposedly overcoming tradition, modernity created tradition as much as destroyed it, for what is generally taken to be traditional is in fact a product of modernity (Hobsbawm and Ranger 1986). Much of the modern world is the product of institutions, culture, and social practices created in the nineteenth century (see Matsuda 1996). Modernity, it would seem, constantly redefines the past, which perhaps explains the excessive preoccupation of modernity with the past, whether it is repudiation or preservation. This is reflected in modern nationalism, which required a collective memory of a particular version of history in order to organize the population into a national state. Modernity is, on the one side, saturated in memory and, on the other, it is also a future-oriented condition in that in its most characteristic forms, it seeks to create the future.

This tendency for the radical movements of modernity to locate themselves in the past was perfectly captured by Marx in 1852 in the *Preface to the Eighteenth*

184 Space, memory and legacies of history

Brumaire of Louis Bonaparte when he mockingly criticized the February Revolution of 1848 in France, which sought to emulate 1789 but led to the dictatorship of Louis Bonaparte in 1851:

> The tradition of all dead generations weighs like a nightmare on the brains of the living. And just as they seem to be occupied with revolutionizing themselves and things, creating something that did not exist before, precisely in such epochs of revolutionary crisis they anxiously conjure up the spirits of the past to their service, borrowing from them names, battle slogans, and costumes in order to present this new scene in world history in time-honored disguise and borrowed language. Thus Luther put on the mask of the Apostle Paul, the Revolution of 1789–1814 draped itself alternately in the guise of the Roman Republic and the Roman Empire, and the Revolution of 1848 knew nothing better to do than to parody, now 1789, now the revolutionary tradition of 1793–95.

This famous passage is a reminder of the how the present remains trapped by the past, and consequently the future is constrained by the memories of earlier struggles. Perhaps it is the fate of all radical utopias that in creating political memories they lose the capacity to realize their vision and retreat into the past. Marx believed that this was not necessarily always the case, and the great revolution of the working class would break the spell of the past: 'The social revolution of the nineteenth century cannot take its poetry from the past but only from the future. It cannot begin with itself before it has stripped away all superstition about the past. The former revolutions required recollections of past world history in order to smother their own content. The revolution of the nineteenth century must let the dead bury their dead in order to arrive at its own content'. The term 'Eighteenth Brumaire' itself refers to a date in the revolutionary calendar (9 November in the modern Gregorian Calendar) that the French revolutionaries created in 1793 and which marked the day in 1799 when Napoleon Bonaparte became head of state. The abolition of the Gregorian calendar was itself a symbolic act to break the power of the past over the present, but the end result was that the past did triumph over the present. Marx's point was that 1848 was a bourgeois revolution and could only be a parody of 1789. However, the real revolution was yet to come. But was Marx right? The twentieth century would suggest that he was wrong and that all revolutions became in the end counter-revolutions.

Most of the most programmatic movements of modernity were based on radical utopias that sought to transform the present according to a particular vision of the future. This list would include the programmatic ideas of the Enlightenment: nationalism, anarchism, socialism and its various off-shoots, and positivism. Modern society was animated by the vision of a future condition that was promised by the present as a radical rupture from the past. For this reason, memory has to be made to work to bind the future to the present. Thus, the French revolutionaries created a new calendar with a different symbolism than the Gregorian calendar. Memory is not just about the recollection of the past; it is also about the active construction of a narrative in which the present becomes its own past. Karl Mannheim in *Ideology and Utopia* noted how utopias are future-oriented ideas, while ideologies are rooted in an historical origin, which gives them a legitimacy (Mannheim 1936). But many modern ideas incorporate elements of both in that utopias take on the character of ideology when they are realized and thus lose their radical future orientation. Nationalism and socialism were driven by utopian impulses but took on an ideological form when they became political programmes that succeeded in implementing a certain vision of the future. It would seem, then, that as the legacy of the French Revolution attests, the radical vision of a new future cannot be sustained only by a utopia that has broken from the past. There are many examples that illustrate this. One has only to consider the early history of Christianity to see how the utopian promise of the kingdom to come had to be not only postponed but subordinated to the commemoration of the saints (see Le Goff 1992).

According to Susan Buck-Morss, in *Dreamworld and Catastrophe*, one of the hallmarks of the twentieth century was the construction of mass utopia. 'The construction of mass utopia was the dream of the twentieth century. It was the driving force of industrial modernization – mass production and mass consumption – in both its capitalist and socialist forms (2000: ix). By the end of the twentieth century, that dream was left behind. Industrial societies discarded the great social project of creating a better world through industrialization and material happiness. That was the founding myth of the Soviet Union, and in different ways it was the basis of the cultural project of the western liberal democracies. The desire for commodities still remains, but it is not connected with a utopian dream. The dream has become a nightmare. The fall of communism in 1989-90 brought about a fundamental shift in historical consciousness and, according to Buck-Morss, 'shattered an entire conception of the world on both sides' (2000: x). What was shattered was, following Walter Benjamin, a 'dreamworld', a concept that captures the ways in which modernity seeks a re-enchantment of the world. This is the forward-looking and utopian spirit of modernity and the promise that a better world is possible. The USSR was founded on this belief as were the post-1945 capitalist democracies. This promise was potentially dangerous in that it could potentially legitimatize violence to achieve the goal of social and political transformation. As Buck-Morss observes, the most inspiring of these mass-utopian projects in both the West and East left a history of disasters in their wake. The dream of mass sovereignty led to wars of nationalism and terror, and the capitalist dream of abundance has led to the exploitation of the human and natural worlds. It was sustained by totalitarianism in the East and by supine acquiescence and conformism in the West, as the Frankfurt School theorists claimed. The end of mass utopia was perhaps most abruptly felt in the communist world due both to the extreme nature of its project of social transformation and the fact of its sudden and complete demise. In the West, modernity did not experience such a radical break from history. Modernity in its various incarnations was always tied to the past by memory, even if the past was reinvented by memory, which in general is a poor guide to history. Since 1990, the former

186 Space, memory and legacies of history

communist states have sought to redefine themselves in time. Inevitably, this has involved a retreat to the past.

Furet (1999), in his history of the idea of communism in the twentieth century, tells the story of how communism lost its connection with utopia. It became at most a technocratic ideology. The demise of communism does not, however, spell the end of utopias, as democracy by its nature keeps alive the spirit of hope for a better world. This at least is how the champions of liberal democracy, including Furet, saw the world after 1990 when capitalism became the future of communism. The 'End of History' scenario is perhaps the more extreme version of this idea that the end of utopia is also the end of ideology. However, another reading of the twentieth century is that the end of utopia portends the arrival of dystopia or the end of any vision of history leading to universal freedom. For many the twentieth century was a century of catastrophe. From a global perspective, such a view would have to be extended to the history of western colonialism.

The notion of dystopia was itself invented in the nineteenth century, coined by J. S. Mill in a parliamentary speech in November 1868 in which he criticized British government land policy in Ireland. In this case, it meant simply the opposite of good. The term has taken on a different reality with the imagination of catastrophe and the collapse of whole societies, even human civilization itself in the face of ecological disaster and the threat of nuclear war still ever present (see Diamond 2019). Major intimations of dystopia were in Max Weber's motif of the 'iron cage' of modern rationalism and the various prognoses of the decline of civilization, perhaps most famously Freud's, *Civilization and its Discontent*, in 1930. Twentieth century thought was fascinated by the prospect of a dystopian future, as in H. G. Wells's 1910 novel, *The Sleeper Awakens*; Fritz Lang's 1927 film of urban dystopia, *Metropolis*; Chaplin's masterpiece of dystopian modern capitalism 'Modern Times' in 1936; Aldous Huxley's *Brave New World* in 1931; Arthur Koestler's *Darkness at Noon* in 1940; and George Orwell's *1984* in 1949.

Modernity was premised on the basis of hope; the postmodern world no longer believes in hope. The simple reality is that the catastrophes of the previous two centuries have undermined if not eliminated hope, which rested on a particular interpretation of history as the unfolding of a plan or at least the possibility that history could be directed by a plan of human design. This was the basic faith of Marxism in all its variants. The history of communism in the twentieth century shattered that belief. Without a future to look forward to, the past was always there. This perhaps explains two tendencies over the past 30 years or so, namely, the retreat into the present and the obsession with the past.

François Hartog has provided a far-reaching analysis of these related currents, which replace the future with an endless present that extends into the deep realms of memory. The past exists only as memory, and the future has disappeared. Whether in the belief in utopia or the idea of progress or Churchill's 'sunlit uplands of democracy', the future does not point to anything that is not available in the present. If the future exists, it is only in the imagination of catastrophe (see Horn 2018). Presentism is a temporality that extends the present into a past but not one that has anything to offer the present. This partly accounts for the obsession with memory as 'an all embracing term, a metaphysical and even at time a theological category' (Hartog 2015: 7).

The disappearance of the future is a particular problem for the left, which unlike the right or conservative thought invests heavily in the future. The past is not there for the present to find refuge; it should serve the needs of the present. Enzo Traverso has diagnosed the condition of 'left-wing melancholy' as a hidden dimension of the left, but one that has come to the surface since the fall of communism as a pervasive condition. Left culture has had a long fascination with both utopia and melancholy. However defined, melancholy concerns the sense of a loss and is expressed in mourning and resignation. 'In Freud's terms, we could define "left melancholy" as the result of an impossible mourning: communism is both a finished experience and an irreplaceable loss, in an age in which the end of utopias obstructs the separation from the lost beloved ideal as well as a libidinal transfer toward a new object of love' (Traverso 2016: 45).

This condition is not confined to the left with its sense of a resignation and loss in face of the failure of revolutionary projects. It is also reflected more generally in the conservative appropriation of memory and with the preoccupation around national memory. On the one side, modernity creates national cultures based on collective memories of the national community; on the other side, modernity erodes the conditions of memory, which is also challenged by history. Memory is thus destined to be nostalgia but without a link with living memories. Pierre Nora, in *Realms of Memory,* sees memory as silenced by history. The result is that memory – the memory of the national community – is now confined to the nostalgic *lieux de mémoire*, or 'sites of memory' as effectively dead remnants of cultural heritage that adorn the present landscape: 'Memory is constantly on our lips because it no longer exists' (Nora 1996: 1). Modernity has accelerated history, making impossible a *mileux de mémoire* in the sense of the living gathering collective memories that are part of everyday life and give life to the nation. The past is irrecoverable and lives on only in ruins that remind the present of a now fragmented collective memory. Nora regretted the passing of collective memory and its dismissal as subjective by the triumph of history, which debunks memory as an objective approach to the past.

Taken further, it is not the case that memory is subjective and history objective: history is now increasingly also seen as subjective. Postmodern thought has undermined the idea of history revealing an objective reality. Postcolonial scholarship and more critical approaches to history, especially since the so-called global turn in historical scholarship of recent years, also requires a rethinking of the presuppositions of much of historical analysis. Recent controversies on history and memory – for instance, colonial legacies – illustrate that it is not just a case of re-establishing lost or hidden memories, but what is required is a questioning of historical self-understanding. Such controversies also require a questioning of the foundations of modernity. It is in this context that a critical theory perspective can offer useful perspectives on memory and history.

188 Space, memory and legacies of history

Critical theory and historical self-understanding

As discussed in Chapter 1, it is not immediately obvious that the writings of the Frankfurt School have much to say that is useful on memory and history. Their work has been limited by a Eurocentric horizon. However, as I argued, notwithstanding the limited scope of critical theory in addressing global issues, the concepts, and in many cases some of the specific examples they were concerned with, are of relevance in the very different circumstances of the present and thus merit re-visiting.

The first and most obvious general theme is the Holocaust, not as an episode in western history but as the defining moment of modernity. The writings of the Frankfurt School provide important resources for contemporary critical theory in addressing current challenges on the historical self-understanding. From a critical theory perspective, neither memory nor history are a reliable guide to the past or the present. History does not offer a refuge from memory, since it is replete with unexamined values and presuppositions which need to be subject to critical examination; memory is also not something that can be invoked as authentic as if it were self-evident. The present is part of the past, but it must also re-define its relation to the past. The writings of Benjamin, Adorno, and Habermas provide important reflections on how the present should relate to the past.

Benjamin's depiction of Paul Klee's 1920 modernist painting, *Angelus Novus*, which he had himself purchased in Munich in 1921, has been a source of inspiration for much of his work and has inspired critical approaches to history ever since. After Benjamin's death at Port Bou in 1940, the painting, which was to become the icon of the Frankfurt School, remained in the personal possession of Adorno until his death in 1969 when Gerholm Sholem acquired it and brought it to Israel. The Angel of History suggested a theological-historical meaning in that in the Talmundic mystical tradition, angels made their appearance in the present as a reminder of the past. Although this could not have been Klee's intention, it lent itself to Benjamin's preoccupation with theology and history and took on a renewed significance in view of the persecution of the Jewish people since 1933. Benjamin's reflection in the *Theses on the Philosophy History* has remained the main interpretation of the painting. Since Benjamin, the Jewish tradition of mourning and remembrance forms the basis for a new and critical approach to history. From this perspective, historical progress does not move from the present to a future but proceeds by the present looking backwards at the catastrophes of the past. This is what Benjamin saw depicted in Klee's painting: the Angelus Novus is moving towards the future, perhaps is hurled towards it by the tumultuous times of the present, but his face is not looking to the future. His face shows an open mouth with an expression of horror; he is looking to the past. The motif gave expression to Benjamin's preoccupation with the theme of historical redemption. The present can redeem the past by confronting it rather than by fleeing from it. In the famous words of the ninth thesis in the 'Theses on the Philosophy of History', 'Where we perceive a chain of events, he sees one single catastrophe which keeps piling wreckage upon

Modernity and memory **189**

wreckage and hurls it in front of his feet. The angel would like to stay to, awaken the dead, and make whole what has been smashed. But a storm is blowing from Paradise; it has caught in his wings with such violence that the angel can no longer close them. This storm irresistibly propels him into the future to which [h]is back is turned, while the pile of debris before him grows skyward. This storm is what we call progress'.

It is clear from this that Benjamin, like Adorno and the critical theory tradition, were deeply critical of the idea of progress, which had to be measured by recognition of the catastrophes of history. Yet, there is also a future to be found, even if it could not be identified. As he wrote in his study of Goethe's *Elective Affinities*: 'It is only for the sake of the hopeless that we are given hope' (cited in Jay 1996/1973: 105). It is also clear that despite the sense of despair in Benjamin's thought, he was not advocating nostalgia since mystical hope was also present in his interpretation of the present. The present may not be able to create a prefect future, and the lesson of history is that progress does not simply unfold. Benjamin's critical theology of history has generally been interpreted to offer a conception of revolution based on the confrontation of the past whereby both history and memory can be subjected to new interpretations. In this critical perspective, the present can face the future only if it liberates itself from the past. The past, with its memories and conflicting histories, is like a theatre for the present to emancipate itself. As he wrote in *A Berlin Chronicle*, 'Memory is not an instrument for exploring the past but its theatre. It is the medium of past experience, just as the earth is the medium in which dead cities lie interred. He who seeks to approach his own buried past must conduct himself like a man digging' (1978: 25–6). Benjamin's critical theory of memory was thus an integral part of his theory of revolution as redemption. As he wrote in the Second Thesis, 'our image of happiness is indissolubly bound up with the image of redemption'. The same applies to our view of the past, which is the concern of history. The past carries with it a temporal index by which it is referred to redemption. There is a secret agreement between past generations and the present one. Our coming was expected on earth. Like every generation that preceded us, we have been endowed with a *weak* Messianic power, a power to which the past has a claim'. Memories are not then to be dismissed by history. To articulate the past, he wrote in the Sixth Thesis, 'means to seize hold of a memory as it flashes up at a moment of danger'. Benjamin's preoccupation with the fragments of the past contained in the present is to be seen as an interpretation of revolution as a mystical redemption for the present 'as the "time of the now", which is shot through with chips of Messianic time' (Benjamin 1970a). The category of experience, so central to Benjamin's thought, is also present in everyday life and is an integral part both of collective and individual memory. Commenting on Bergson and Baudelaire, he wrote that experience 'is less the product of facts firmly anchored in memory than of a convergence in memory of accumulated and frequently unconscious data' (Benjamin 1970b: 159).

Adorno was deeply influenced by Benjamin's writings. The theme of the redemptive, shorn of Benjamin's mysticism, became a theme in his work, as was the immanent approach to many of the ideas of modernity (see Chapter 1). His best-known essay on memory and the present is undoubtedly the 1959 essay and radio broadcast, 'The Meaning of Working Through the Past'. The essay was an intervention into the debate on how the Federal Republic should relate to the Nazi period. His contribution was not only to argue that the past needs to be worked through – since there was agreement on that – but to say that engagement with the legacy of history cannot be lightly done or glossed over without a serious confrontation with objective forces. Against the compliancy in public discussion, he argued that National Socialism lives on in a variety of guises. 'I consider the survival of National Socialism *within* democracy to be potentially more menacing than the survival of fascist tendencies *against* democracy' (1998: 90).

The essay criticizes the language and arguments on the question of German guilt, for example, the tendency to deny or minimize what happened; the search for a balance sheet of guilt as in the claim the destruction of Dresden compensated for Auschwitz; the claim that the Holocaust could only have been caused if the victims had instigated it; or the notion that the burden falls on those who failed to resist Hitler rather than those who cheered him on, and so on. Adorno sees these arguments as attempts to prevent self-reflection and reflect the 'desire to get on with things'. He criticizes the 'loss of history' and the 'effacement of memory' in widespread lack of knowledge and a weak capacity for critical thinking. A key point is his rejection of the popular notion of a 'guilt complex': 'forgetting of National Socialism surely should be understood far more in terms of the general situation of society than in terms of psychopathology' (p. 91). Adorno's critique of the culture of forgetting should be seen in the context of his more general perspectives on the culture industry, which cultivates a culture of conformity. As stated in the *Dialectic of Enlightenment*: 'All objectification is a forgetting' (Adorno and Horkheimer 1979: 230). Against the superficial culture of forgetting, which like the culture industry is a form of reification, he argues for a more critical 'working through the past'.

Negative Dialectics put this historical perspective into a yet broader vision of history: 'Universal history must be construed and denied. After the catastrophes that have happened, and in view of the catastrophes to come, it would be cynical to say that a plan for a better world is manifested in history and unites it. Not to be denied for that reason, however, is the unity that cements the continuous, chaotically splintered moments and phases of history – the unity of the control over nature, progressing to rule over men, and finally to that of men's inner nature. No universal history leads from the savagery to humanitarianism, but there is one leading from the slingshot to the megaton bomb' (Adorno 1990: 320).

Since the incorporation of Freud into critical theory, the Frankfurt School theorists conceived memory as an act of liberation from the past, not its pacification. As Marcuse wrote in *One Dimensional Man*: 'Remembrance of the past may give rise to dangerous insights, and the established society seems to be apprehensive of the subversive contents of memory. Remembrance is a mode of dissociation from the given facts, a mode of "mediation" which breaks, for short moments, the omnipresent power of the given facts' (Marcuse 1964: 98). For Marcuse, memory is what makes possible hope.

The social theory of Habermas gave a firmer foundation to the writings of the early Frankfurt School on memory as a form of critical remembrance. Although his work is not normally discussed in the context of memory, there are important insights. The most direct and well known is the 1986 *Historikerstreit*, 'Historians' controversy'. Habermas's contribution recalls Adorno's seminal essay in his rebuttal of the arguments of influential German historians that the German past can be normalized or the claim that the crimes of the Nazis can be compared to other totalitarian regimes (Stalin or Pol Pot). A number of German historians, most notably Ernst Nolte, attempted to normalize German history by denying the exceptionality of Nazism. Their attempt to redefine the legacy of German history led to a denunciation from Habermas, who invoked the legacy of Benjamin, with the argument that there is an obligation incumbent on the present generation to keep alive the memory of the vanquished: 'It is especially these dead who have a claim to the weak anamnestic power of a solidarity that later generations can continue to practice only in the medium of a remembrance that is repeatedly renewed, often desperate, and continually on one's mind (Habermas 1989: 233). Habermas's position was that the link between memory and history cannot be so easily broken. This is because of the exceptionality of the Holocaust, which means for Germany that the relation to the recent past cannot be a normal one. The present generation, even if they were not directly responsible, bears historical responsibility for the crimes of the past.[3] Habermas's position thus represents a move from Adorno's argument based on guilt to one based on responsibility. The present generation are thus responsible for the crimes of the past even though they are not guilty.

Habermas's intervention into the public debate was also a political attack on what he regarded as a 'neo-conservatism' that was in part a reaction to the cultural politics of 1968. The intervention concerned a specific German issue, but some of the issues it raised are relevant to a broader range of contemporary problems on the burden of the past. Habermas's argument that Germany cannot have a normal relation to the past must now be seen in the wider context of a more complicated situation in which no country has such a 'normal' relation with its past. This perspective can easily be related to similar controversies in other countries, a relevant case being the legacy of the Spanish Civil War and the Francoist dictatorship in Spain.

In the terms of Habermas's social theory, there are two other theoretical contributions that are important: critical hermeneutics and social learning. For reasons of space, only a brief comment will be made on these dimensions of Habermas's social theory (see Apel 1971; Habermas 1977; Thompson 2008). The first concerns the critique of tradition and more generally hermeneutical interpretation. Habermas's position against advocators of interpretative philosophy, most notably Hans-Georg Gadamer, hermeneutical interpretation cannot avoid the difficult challenge of evaluating the past. Tradition is not simply handed down but must be critically interrogated by the present. Against what he felt was a conservative tendency by thinkers such as Gadamer to divorce hermeneutics from normative and critical questions, Habermas, drawing on Freud, advanced critical hermeneutics. From this perspective, historical questions including those of memory require not

192 Space, memory and legacies of history

simply interpretation but also need to address the critical task of emancipation since memory is the key to domination.

Habermas's critical hermeneutics shaped his later theory of communicative action. Relevant in the present context is the notion of social learning. The basis of the theory of communicative action and the foundation of Habermas's entire work is the idea that human beings have the capacity for learning, which is based on the capacity for communication through language. However, not only individuals learn, but so do societies (see Habermas 1979). Collective learning is a core dimension of the evolution of society, which should be noted is not based on a theory of historical progress but on socio-cognitive development and includes pathologies.[4] This insight is important in relation to memory and history in that in light of this theory the past is recalled by the present to broaden the horizons of the present and confront the problems of the present as inherited from the past. The past is engaged with by not emulating it but learning from it.

The critical theory of the Frankfurt School, taken as a whole and taken out of its immediate German context, offers important insights into the nature of memory, heritage, and history. In interpreting the past – with respect to tradition, memory, and heritage – there is a strong emphasis on the need for judgment and evaluation, as opposed to what is increasingly common today, namely, pluralism. It is not enough to recognize the plurality of memories without a critical attitude towards the content and form of memory, since not all memories are equally valid. In this light, historical self-understanding cannot evade a concern with truth and must accept that justice requires to some degree truth. With Benjamin, there is a commitment towards anamnestic solidarity, that is, an identification with the victims of history. Adorno's work in particular stressed the need to dispel illusions and address the dark side of history. It resists not only nostalgia but also the presentism of the culture industry, for example, the 'heritage industry' today can be seen as a form of reification. The use of Freud in critical theory drew attention to mechanisms of repression in memory and the need for a deeper and more critical approach. Finally, a feature of critical theory is to place memory in a broader context of analysis, for, as Adorno remarked, memory cannot be separated from the general structure of society.

The treatment of memory and history in critical theory is distinctive and offers contemporary scholarship with important critical perspectives on historical self-understanding. However, aside from moving on from the German context of the literature, other perspectives need to be brought to bear. As discussed in Chapter 1, postcolonial criticisms need to be considered. While some will see postcolonialism as offering an alternative approach, I believe such a case is unwarranted in that these criticisms are best seen as correctives and, in any case, postcolonial theory does not have an alternative as such. Indeed, most postcolonial theories base their arguments on other western thinkers, such as Foucault. While Foucault's work did place a strong emphasis on rupture, this was even more strongly the case with the theorists of the Frankfurt School who saw the historical experience of the twentieth century as a fundamental rupture from the past. To 'learn from catastrophe' is a key message of critical theory for the present (see also Verovsek 2018).

One problem can be mentioned to conclude the present discussion. In placing at the centre of historical self-understanding the traumas of history, the Frankfurt School has tended to emphasize trauma from the perspective of mainstream society. So post-war Germany is traumatized in having to carry the burden of the past. The problem of German guilt is that it silences the victims' experience of trauma in order to address the guilt of the perpetrators. Perhaps it is not entirely a case of the trauma of the perpetrators if the notion of anamnestic solidarity is given more centrality. However, this is probably also not enough to capture the voice of the oppressed, as in, for example, the perspective offered by Franz Fanon in his 1961 classic work, *Wretched of the Earth* (Fanon 2001). New developments and debates on memory and cultural heritage offer some directions for critical approaches that also reflect greater cosmopolitan engagement than that which characterized the Frankfurt School tradition. It is perhaps the case that their critical perspectives on history and memory were ultimately shaded by their own life histories as upper-middle-class German intellectuals forced into exile rather than members of a persecuted people. While their writings offer great resources for the critique of European and national cultures, their perspectives are limited when it comes to the experience of historical injustice. Although the writings of Benjamin go much further than Adorno's or Habermas's in this regard, the problem remains that the critical theorists were preoccupied with the crisis of European culture, and society and did not look further afield.

The next section offers a reconstruction of new approaches to cultural heritage and memory which give greater place to the voice of the oppressed.

Cultural heritage and the politics of memory revisited

Over the past three decades there has been a tremendous transformation in cultural heritage, both in terms of practices and in the understanding of cultural heritage (see Assmann and Conrad 2000; Harrison 2012). These changes are very much connected to wider changes in the very nature of culture and reflect major social and political transformation. As discussed in the previous chapter, they are also very much evident in the re-shaping of public space in more inclusive ways for diverse histories and experiences.

Heritage is above all a category of memory. It is about how the present defines itself through a relation with the past. It is therefore a dimension of historical self-understanding. All remembrance is selective, since no society or community can recall the entirety of the past. And no social group can exist without a relation to the past. The fundamental problem that heritage presents, then, is what should be retained from the past and how, following Adorno, its legacies should be worked through in a way that does not involve an effacement of memory.

Contrary to the received view of heritage as the handing down of the past to the present, where the past holds sway over the present, heritage should be seen as of the present, how the present time sees itself. This inevitably means that the memories of any one time will be different from earlier times. It means too that

194 Space, memory and legacies of history

the heritage of our time will reflect the concerns of the present. For these reasons, heritage is both a form of historical experience – how we experience ourselves in time – and an interpretation of such experience. It is most often expressed in the form of narratives and in symbolic forms.

The traditional understanding and function of heritage in modern societies was to serve the needs of the national state. It was a form of mass adoration of the national state. It affirmed the grandeur and splendour of the state. In the second half of the twentieth century, especially since the foundation of UNESCO after the Second World War, this view of cultural heritage, which was typically reflected in material forms such as monuments and buildings, was complemented by a more universal notion of cultural heritage as the patrimony of humanity. This shift was accompanied by the idea of intangible culture. Of course, all culture is intangible, but nonetheless the notion of intangible heritage extended – or democratized heritage – to include wider domains of historical experience and had the effect of giving greater prominence to local communities to affirm themselves and generally gave greater weight to the recognition of cultural diversity.

Now, while the two notions of heritage – the national and the universal – became increasingly blurred, further developments took place and have opened up new visions of cultural heritage and the possibility of more critical and cosmopolitan practices. They stand in a relation of tension with the managerial attempt to exploit the economic implications of cultural diversity rather than see opportunities for the good life. Effectively what has happened is that capitalism has stepped in to the void opened up by the decline of the national function of heritage.

The first is what can be called the interactive moment. It has increasingly been recognized across a wide spectrum of perspectives in the human and social sciences that cultures and societies more generally are formed through cross-cultural interactions. These may be between a limited number of locations or they may be global. What was once seen as separated and unique is now seen as a product of global interconnectivity and thus no longer unique or exceptional. Cultures are formed through processes of interaction and exchange out of which come entanglements of various forms, and often new hybrid forms emerge. A basic pattern is that culture undergoes change when it encounters another culture. This may happen as a result of cultural transfers such as borrowings, translation, and theft. Indeed, all culture is a form of theft.

The implication of this is that while there has been much attention given to cultural pluralization, it has been to the neglect of inter-culturalism, that is the encounter of cultures and the fact that all cultures are shaped by such interactions. So, what is needed, then, is greater recognition of the entanglement of cultures. This perspective does not replace the unity in diversity idea of cultural diversity, which has been central to the Council of Europe's cultural policy, but gives to it a stronger emphasis on encounters and entanglements and the possibility of learning as a result. In this way, remembrance can lead to the regeneration of communities by expanding their horizons.

The emphasis on the encounter has become the focus on much scholarly attention in recent years. As Michael Rothberg has shown in his path-breaking book, *Multidirectional Memory* (2009), memories are not self-contained but are shaped by influences drawn from other memories through borrowing, referencing, and negotiation. Thus, the Holocaust memory has been influential in the re-revival of other memories and histories, such as the heritage of slavery. New and silenced memories build on older ones and undergo re-signification (see Delanty 2018).

A second development that must be highlighted is, as discussed in the previous chapter, the rise of the counter-memorial, which instead of being a celebration of a past now in ruins, is now more likely to be a reflection on atonement, mourning, and grief (see Young 1992, 2016; Stevens and Franck 2016).

In these very much changed circumstances, in highly pluralized societies in which everyone is a stranger, cultural heritage can no longer so easily create unity for a nation or community. Instead, its task is to offer ways for the political community to live with the past and find in the figure of the stranger new and more positive ways of being. To do so will also be a way of reconciling the often-difficult work of remembrance with the task of cultural regeneration.

Such shifts in memory and commemoration are also a reflection of the close tie that now exists between cultural heritage and mobility. Memory today is more likely to be a product of the experience of mobility – travel, displacement, migration – than of settled societies. In a world of movement, flux, and fluidity, both of people and artefacts, it is inevitable that culture also shifts along with the new experiences that come with mobility. It presents a challenge for cultural heritage and has been in part reflected in the relatively recent phenomenon of the mobile exhibition and memorial of cultural heritage.

Heritage is thus not constant or durable. Time is the enemy of the past. No longer based on stability or the enduring traditions that have survived the test of time, heritage has moved beyond the traditional understanding of the curatorial tasks of selection, collecting, preserving, and representing. Whether it is issues of ownership, voice or representation, heritage, like all of culture, is now contested.

Another development that can be briefly commented on is the extension of rights to the sphere of culture, as in cultural rights and more recently heritage rights. While this is clearly important, and part of the general democratization of culture, it should not detract from the more fundamental problem of cultural fluidity and entanglement and the conflicts that may result. This can happen when the rights of one group are asserted over the rights of another, since in many cases the privileging of one culture will be at the expense of another.

Such conflicts are a reminder that not all cultural encounters are positive: they can advance adversity as much as enrich the societies or cultures that encounter each other.

In view of these multifarious developments, what I think needs to be more strongly affirmed today is that cultural heritage is very much infused with critical-normative tasks. Heritage is centrally about evaluation or judgement: it is

196 Space, memory and legacies of history

not simply repetition and derivation. Nor is it only about the space of the encounter and diversity. It requires the affirmation of the present in the critical appropriation of the past in order to liberate the present. The practice of cultural heritage by curators, educators, urban planners, and architects of memorials and other sites of heritage thus carries responsibilities. It is a form of engagement and allows for cultural re-interpretation in light of changing experiences and the sense that everyone is a stranger. As Jacques Derrida has written, 'Inheritance is never a given, it is always a task' (1994: 67).

Notes

1 For some perspectives on this, see Alexander et al (2004), Macdonald (2009), Ricoeur (2004), Terdman (1993), Winter and Emmanuel (2000), Wood (1999).
2 See Alexander (2002), Levy and Snaider (2002), Novick (2000), Rothberg (2009).
3 See Baldwin (1990) for further perspectives.
4 See Eder's study on political pathologies in the formation of modernity in Germany (Eder 1985).

References

Adorno, T. W. 1990 [1966]. *Negative Dialectics*. London: Routledge.
Adorno, T. 1998 [1959]. What Does Coming to Terms with the Past Mean? In: *Critical Models: Interventions and Catchwords*. New York: Columbia University Press.
Adorno, T. W. and Horkheimer, M. 1979 [1944]. *Dialectic of Enlightenment*. London: Verso.
Alexander, J. 2002. On the Social Construction of Moral Universals: The 'Holocaust' from War Crime to Trauma Drama. *European Journal of Social Theory*, 5 (1): 5–85.
Alexander, J., Everman, J., Geisen, B., Smelser, N. J. and Sztompka, P. 2004. *Cultural Trauma and Collective Identity*. Berkeley: University of California Press.
Apel, K-O., Bormann, C., Bubner, R., Gadamer, H-G., Giegel, H. and Habermas, J. (eds.) 1971. *Hermeneutik und Ideologiekritik*. Frankfurt: Suhrkamp.
Assmann, A. and Conrad, S. (eds.) 2000. *Memory in a Global Age: Discourses, Practices and Trajectories*. London: Palgrave Macmillan.
Baldwin, P. (ed.) 1990. *Reworking the Past: Hitler, the Holocaust, and the German Historians Dispute*. Boston, MA: Beacon Press.
Benjamin, W. 1970a. Theses on the Philosophy of History. In: *Illuminations*. London: Fontana.
Benjamin, W. 1970b. On Some Motifs in Baudelaire. In: *Illuminations*. London: Fontana.
Benjamin, W. 1978. A Berlin Chronicle. In: *Reflections*. New York: Schocken Books.
Benjamin, W. 2006. *A Berlin Childhood Around 1900*. Cambridge, MA: Harvard University Press.
Buck-Morss, S. 2000. *Dreamworld and Catastrophe: The Passing of Mass Utopia in East and West*. Cambridge, MA: MIT Press.
Delanty, G. 2018. *The European Heritage: A Critical Re-Interpretation*. London: Routledge.
Derrida, J. 1994 [1993]. *Specters of Marx: The State of the Debt, the Work of Mourning and the New History*. London: Routledge.
Diamond, G. 2019. *Upheaval: How Nations Cope with Crisis and Change*. London: Allen Lane.
Eder, K. 1985. *Geschichte als Lernprozess? Zur Pathogenese politischer Modernität in Deutschland*. Frankfurt: Suhrkamp.
Fanon, F. 2001 [1961]. *Wretched of the Earth*. London: Penguin Books.

Furet, F. 1999. *The Passing of an Illusion: The Idea of Communism in the Twentieth Century*. Chicago, IL: University of Chicago Press.

Habermas, J. 1977. A Review of Gadamer's *Truth and Method*. In: Dallmayr, F. and McCarthy, T. (eds.) *Understanding and Social Inquiry*. Notre Dame: University of Notre Dame Press.

Habermas, J. 1979. *Communications and the Evolution of Society*. London: Heinemann.

Habermas, J. 1989. On the Public Use of History. In: *The New Conservatism: Cultural Criticism and the Historians' Debate*. Cambridge, MA: MIT Press.

Harrison, R. 2012. *Heritage: Critical Appraisals*. London: Routledge.

Hartog, F. 2015. *Regimes of Historicity: Presentism and Experiences of Time*. New York: Columbia University Press.

Hobsbawm, E. and Ranger, T. (eds.) 1986. *The Invention of Tradition*. Cambridge: Cambridge University Press.

Horn, E. 2018. *The Future as Catastrophe: Imagining Disaster in the Modern Age*. Cambridge: Cambridge University Press.

Jay, M. 1996/1973. *The Dialectical Imagination: A History of the Frankfurt School and the Institute of Social Research, 1923–1950*. London: Heinemann.

Le Goff, J. 1992. *History and Memory*. New York: Columbia University Press.

Levy, D. and Sznaider, N. 2002. Memory Unbound: The Holocaust and the Formation of Cosmopolitan Memory. *European Journal of Social Theory*, 5 (1): 87–106.

MacDonald, S. 2009. *Difficult Heritage: Negotiating the Nazi Past in Nuremberg and Beyond*. London: Routledge.

Mannheim, K. 1936. *Ideology and Utopia*. London: Routledge & Kegan Paul.

Marcuse, H. 1964. *One-Dimensional Man*. London: Routledge & Kegan Paul.

Matsuda, M. 1996. *The Memory of the Modern*. Oxford: Oxford University Press.

Nora, P. 1996, 1997, 1998. *Realms of Memory: Rethinking the French Past*. 3 Vols. New York: Columbia University Press.

Novick, P. 2000. *The Holocaust and Collective Memory: The American Experience*. London: Bloomsbury.

Ricoeur, P. 2004. *History, Memory and Forgetting*. Chicago, IL: University of Chicago Press.

Rothberg, M. 2009. *Multidirectional Memory: Remembering the Holocaust in the Age of Decolonization*. Stanford: Stanford University Press.

Stevens, Q. and Franck, K. 2016. *Memorials as Spaces of Engagement: Design, Use and Meanings*. London: Routledge.

Terdman, R. 1993. *Present Past: Modernity and the Memory Crisis*. Ithaca, NY: Cornell University Press.

Thompson, J. B. 2008. *Critical Hermeneutics: A Study of the Thought of Paul Ricoeur and Jurgen Habermas*. New edition. Cambridge: Cambridge University Press.

Traverso, E. 2016. *Left-Wing Melancholia: Marxism, History, and Memory*. New York: Columbia University Press.

Verovsek, P. 2018. Historical Criticism Without Progress: Memory as an Emancipatory Resource for Critical Theory. *Constellations*, 26: 132–47.

Winter, J. and Emmanuel, S. 2000. *War and Remembrance in the Twentieth Century*. Cambridge: Cambridge University Press.

Wood, N. 1999. *Vectors of Memory: Legacies of Trauma in Postwar Europe*. Oxford: Berg.

Young, J. 1992. The Counter-Monument: Memory Against Itself in Germany Today. *Critical Inquiry*, 18 (2): 267–96.

Young, J. 2016. *The Stages of Memory: Reflections on Memorial Art, Loss, and the Spaces Between*. Amherst: Massachusetts University Press.

10

LOOKING BACK AT THE TWENTIETH CENTURY

Europe's contested legacies of history

A backward glance at the twentieth century in Europe from the standpoint of the present day reveals not just several legacies of history but also contested interpretations of those legacies. It is no longer credible to see in the past just one dominant legacy. Attempts to reduce history to one logic inevitably run up against a counter-narrative. All legacies are in some way defined by the basic form of a narrative, which is to say there is a starting point and an end point. But these are rarely fixed and move as the sands of the present shift.[1]

As with all narratives, a legacy tells a story that has meaning and significance for the present. Perhaps because of the deep divisions and the diversity of Europe, there will always be different ways of narrating the past. The facts of history in many cases are easy to agree on, but more difficult is what story to tell, since such stories are central to identities, which are unavoidably constructed around adversity. There is also the simple fact that history can rarely be told to reveal a happy story in which all can rejoice. Legacies of history can at most offer the present ways of re-orientation, problematization and the opening of new horizons.

There is perhaps another advantage with the European preoccupation with the past. It is that narratives change as they are told and retold, and these narratives often over-lap, leading not to a common narrative but to mutually influenced ones. That which has been silenced by the dominant narratives can be awakened. In this context, it should also be noted that legacies, as forms of memory, over time change, accordingly as new interpretations of history emerge or when the presuppositions of the older interpretations become invalid.

These considerations are all relevant to the legacies of 1918 and 1968, which roughly cover the era of the Frankfurt School from its beginning to the death of Adorno in 1969 and Horkheimer in 1973. The tumultuous twentieth century was the era that critical theory sought to interpret. What these dates signify is three-fold. They were first events that were of major historical importance in modernity.

Second, they can be seen in terms of a moment of rupture: a break with what went before and thus a re-definition of historical time. In that sense they were epochal in terms of historical time. Third, they are also events that brought about significant re-interpretations of politics and in socio-cultural self-understanding. For these reasons it is possible to say that they provided later times with a legacy, whether good or bad, contested or not. Yet, it is difficult to avoid the conclusion that their legacies were failures in that the hope that they nurtured quickly turned to despair. There is possibly a wider narrative here of how the utopian impulse turns to despair. This was the temptation of the Frankfurt School theorists and to which Herbert Marcuse, despite embodying the revolutionary temperament, finally also succumbed. However, I think something positive for the present can be salvaged from a period brutalized by the memory of war. To have a better understanding of the past is a way in which to have a better understanding of the present. This invariably involves re-visiting political memories. As Walter Benjamin showed, glimpses of future possibility are revealed only through the images that are recovered from the past. To recall a past event is a way to reveal the future. Those in search of the future are sent back into the past. What Benjamin intended by this is that it is possible to imagine the future only through a reflection on the past. As discussed in the previous chapter, the much-cited remark in *A Berlin Chronicle* captures this sense of history embroiled in critical memories: 'Memory is not an instrument for exploring the past but its theatre. It is the medium of past experience, just as the earth is the medium in which dead cities lie interred. He who seeks to approach his own buried past must conduct himself like a man digging' (Benjamin 1978: 25–6).

The lost generation and catastrophe

The end of the First World War in 1918 marked a point at which the legacy of the nineteenth century was finally buried. The First World War — which was the most brutal war the world had known, with between 15 to 19 million killed in what was a pointless and avoidable endeavor, extinguished the values and ideals of the nineteenth century around progress, knowledge, and liberty. The outbreak of war in 1914 marked the end of *La Belle Epoque*, the glorious period since 1871, after the Franco-Prussian War and the Paris Commune, that saw peace, growth, scientific advancement, and cultural flourishment in Europe. The catastrophe of the war was followed in early 1918 by the so-called and misnamed Spanish flu epidemic that left 50 to 100 million dead by 1920. The October Revolution of the previous year marked the rise of a new model of modernity that had terrified the old European elites, both conservatives and liberals. The bourgeois culture of nineteenth-century Europe and much of its worldwide imperial dominance had come to an end in 1918-19. There can be little doubt that this was a moment that defined the beginning of the twentieth century and not the tremendous changes that occurred since the 1890s or during *La Belle Epoque*. At the end of 1918, the *ancien regime* had come to a final end with the fall of the central European empires of the Habsburg, Romanov, Hohenzollern imperial dynasties. The fall of the Ottoman Empire

200 Space, memory and legacies of history

between 1918 and 1920 changed much of the external landscape around the core European world. Nations emerged out of the debris of empires. The old European bourgeois culture and society entered into new and unsettling times with the 'rise of the masses' and what was everywhere felt to be a rebellion against the elites, as in the famous book in 1930 by the Spanish philosopher Ortega Y Gasset, *The Revolt of the Masses* (Ortega Y Gasset 1994).

The year 1918 was a turning point in European consciousness in many ways, above all it signalled a deep and far-reaching pessimism of the received values of European culture, which appeared to be meaningless in the fundamentally changed circumstances that the war produced as well as the wider external context of the rise of the United States of America, the collapse of the vast Ottoman Empire, and the spectre of communism after October 1917. In place of the older belief in the idea of Europe, modernity, and the Enlightenment's celebration of progress was a new pessimism of spirit and a profound sense of the crisis of European civilization, which was reflected in a pronounced anti-modernism in European thought, as testified by the writings of Freud, as in *Civilization and its Discontents*, Nietzsche, Heidegger, and above all epitomized in the popular book of Oswald Spengler, *The Decline of the West* in 1926 (Spengler 1991).

Beyond that common starting point of catastrophe, crisis, and epochal change, it is difficult to point to a single legacy that might have emerged from the debris of the war. Certainly we can speak of the beginning of the twentieth century, but whether it is a short one that ended with the revolutions of 1989-90 when a new European order emerged, as Hobsbawm claimed, is perhaps a question of whose century it is (Hobsbawm 1994). The notion of a short twentieth century does not quite work as a global periodization. The significance of 1945, on the other hand, is clearly more compelling in global terms, as it was an epochal change more or less everywhere. However, as has often been noted, for much of central and eastern Europe, the surrender of the Third Reich marked only the transition from one totalitarian state to another. For others, for example, Czechoslovakia, created in October 1918, it was the moment when, to follow Milan Kundera's words in his seminal 1984 essay, 'The Tragedy of Central Europe', it disappeared from history, and when it reemerged in 1989 it lasted hardly three years until its dissolution in 1993. Nonetheless, all things considered, the period 1918 to 1989 is probably the most meaningful time frame for Europe's twentieth century. As regards 1918 itself, one should probably place it in a wider time frame, at least from 1917 (if not 1914) to 1920, since the armistice in November 1918 was just one moment in a series of events that marked a major turning point in modern European history that saw, amongst other developments, the German Reich transformed into the Weimar Republic. The war itself was not formally over until the Paris Peace Conference in January 1919. It was a period in which a fragile and doomed balance existed between peace and democracy in that the conditions for establishing democracy were peace, but this was highly tenuous.

It is clear that one concrete outcome of 1918 and the events that followed was the worldwide belief in the nation-state and the vision of history it cultivated. Until 1918 republican nationalism was on the whole relatively constrained, and many nations coexisted within wider imperial forms. But with the advance of democracy, the notion of self-determination gained increased influence, and liberal bourgeois nationalism reconciled itself to the rise of separatist nationalist movements. The circumstances of 1918 provided a new context for nationalism, and self-determination was embraced as part of the Versailles Order. I do not need to recount here the catastrophic long-term outcomes that were engendered when nation-states were created more or less overnight out of territories that did not have long traditions of statehood or nationhood. This appeared at the time to be the price for peace in Europe and the territories that fell under European (mostly French and British) mandates. The peace afforded the rise of new democracies, but democracy alone did not prevent the descent in war and civil war, as the examples of Weimar, Italy, and Spain illustrate.

Perhaps one of the enduring outcomes of 1918 was a new culture of commemoration that became part of cultural heritage in a new age of mass politics. The past becomes a resource for the present to invent for an era that had no future. As marked, most notably, at least within the UK and the British Commonwealth, Remembrance Day – held annually on 11 November to mark the armistice signed on that day in 1918 – set a new trend in how the past is commemorated since it was instituted in 1919. It was widely adopted in many countries (the production of nostalgia is a good British export) and became part of their national identities. The older forms of remembrance were based on commemoration of heroes or the exploits of dynastic leaders. For example, the Arc of Triumph built by Napoleon to honour the French army bore only the names of the generals. But the Tomb of the Unknown Soldier after 1918 at the Arc de Triumph marked a shift in the commemoration of the fallen, who came to symbolize the nation. A similar event occurred in London, with the creation of the Tomb of the Unknown Soldier (originally called Warrior) in Westminster Abbey. As George Mosse pointed out, there was also the political context of the rise of Bolshevism, which the British government feared might gain a foothold in Britain, indeed as it briefly did in Germany after the war (see Mosse 1990: 94–5). In place of the cry for revolution was the two-minute silence and the solemn ceremony to remember the dead.

Since 1918, as symbolically marked by the Tomb of the Unknown Soldier, the past is commemorated through the remembrance of the individual rather than the ruler. The creation of the Cenotaph (meaning in Greek 'an empty tomb') in Whitehall, London, in 1919 provided a symbolic reference for the enactment of collective national bereavement in the UK. Rather than triumph and heroic sacrifice, the tone shifts to suffering and the experience of loss. It is possible to speak of a fundamental shift in the relation of the present to the past with the creation of a new public culture of mourning for what became known as the 'Lost Generation' (see Winter 2014). This all had a lot to do with the simple fact of the enormous volume of death created by the war and the problem of how to bring the dead home and bury them (see also Fussell 2000; Gregory 2008; Winter and Immanuel 2000). *La Belle Epoque* had celebrated life, but after 1918 the Zeitgeist turned to death and the preoccupation with victimhood and the decline of civilization.

202 Space, memory and legacies of history

The notion of the 'Lost Generation' has a both a wider and a narrower reference. Apparently coined by Gertrude Stein but famously associated with Hemmingway's 1926 novel, *The Sun Also Rises*, it referred to the post-war expatriate generation of American writers who settled in Europe, mostly France, where they led somewhat decadent and rootless lives. However, the term has a wider meaning than this literary trope in that it captured the epochal sense of loss and has been used to refer to those born during the war as well as those who perished in it (see for example Wohl 1979). The Lost Generation were those who lost hope for a better future. In many ways the notion expresses the profound sense of loss that 1918 produced in the encounter with mass death and the absence of the possibility of redemption. It is in this wider sense of the term that I use it here.

For these reasons I suggest that the legacy of 1918 was the trauma of war and the problem of how to commemorate its memory for a generation for whom the promises of modernity had turned into a living nightmare. This was quite literally the case since many of those who returned from the front were permanently traumatized. While in Russia the October Revolution opened up the vision of a new future, for most of Europe the experience was the end of utopia (though, to follow Furet (1999), the same lesson was eventually learnt by the 1950s when communism also lost its utopian impulse). While 1918 marked the moment of rupture with the recent past, it did not, nonetheless, translate mourning into opposition to war, and it also did not signal opposition to the empire, which, if anything, was strengthened after 1918 in both Britain and France. The cessation of hostilities on 11 November 1918 did not bring about an end to war. On the contrary, and I do not think this is an insight reached by hindsight, it led to a new appetite for war in Germany, while in Britain it resulted in what was widely regarded to be a temporary peace. The seeds of the Second World War were set in the peace negotiations, as anticipated by John Maynard Keynes in his 1919 book *The Economic Consequences of the Peace*. The period 1914 to 1945 can thus be seen, as has often been claimed, as a long European war. Despite the armistice – which is all it was, a cessation of hostilities; it was not a peace in any significant sense – the foundation of what was to become the ill-fated League of Nations; widespread progress in science and in public health, 1918 did not mark the transition to a new European order based on the older ideas of the nineteenth century, such as peace and progress, which seemed to be cast aside in the new times of political turbulence that saw civil wars in Ireland and Spain and the rise of fascism. The liberal establishment, unable to halt the rise of political violence, preferred to turn inwards or, in the case of Britain, to stem the stirring of nationalism in the empire. It was a time when the left, internally divided, was unable to offer a new vision. In contrast, the radical political right was ascendant. So, in saying that the legacy of 1918 was the trauma of war it was not the case that this experience translated into hope for a better world. Undoubtedly many tried, but they failed. They failed either because their efforts were not adequate to the task or because of a lack of political imagination and fortitude. The Great War, so avoidable, did not lead to reconciliation but to the return to the path of war.

The memory of 1918 is today somewhat ambivalent. It has lost much of its direct relevance to the present. That is hardly surprising since it is the case with all events that with the passage of time they cease to be a collective memory and become – if the memory survives at all – what can be called a cultural memory, whereby the memory ceases to be tied to those who experienced the event – the Lost Generation – and becomes instead sustained by other cultural means that make it possible to be a memory for a wider spectrum of people. But in saying that 1918 has lost its memorial significance, I am suggesting that it is also losing this wider cultural memory and has become a kind of amnesia.

Why is this? It is because the memory of the Great War is a memory that has few if any lessons for the present, at least as institutionalized in the national days of commemoration. The Great War was not a just war and nor was it a successful war that can be celebrated for its achievement. Remembrance Day became a symbol of the British nation and was more or less interwoven with reverence for the monarchy. Its creation had an anti-Bolshevist role in binding the nation in a public culture of mourning. The declining power of Remembrance Day today to define the British nation – with the obligatory wearing of the traditional red poppy – is not only a question of the loss of symbolic power of the event and its hollow annual performance. The public culture of mourning instituted since 1918 around monumental shrines was, despite the shift it brought about in the nature of commemoration, an expression of the national community as part of a wider empire.

The myth of the fallen soldier and the creation of war memorials everywhere was ambivalent and could also be deployed to serve the fascist cause, as illustrated by the controversial Valley of the Fallen erected outside Madrid during the Franco dictatorship. While the figure of the fallen soldier is also to a large degree a reflection of the weakening of the integrative power of national culture to bind the nation, I think the significance of its decline goes beyond this dimension, and it has a lot to do with a shift in the public mood around war and its commemoration in a post-imperial age. Until recently the dominant narrative around 1918 – at least in the UK – was the motif of sacrifice as reflected in the abstract figure of the fallen soldier. I suggest that this figure is no longer compelling and no longer makes possible collective bereavement and that collective mourning ceases to define national identity. It was certainly a departure from the older forms of representation and commemoration and served an age that still paid service to sacrifice as a noble deed. This was also an era in which the relationship of the masses and elites was characterized by deference and, crucially, when to die for the homeland or king and country was a worthy cause. Such forms of symbolic representation of glorification were underpinned by the ideal of the nation, which stood above the heads of the individual whose glory was tied to the glory of the nation. But today, for many, nations are inglorious.

The figure of the fallen soldier belongs to a former age. It no longer resonates with the times in which we live in. The symbolic culture of the fallen soldier – with its themes of manliness, camaraderie, heroism, sacrifice, and those of the Christian liturgy – has lost its relevance for today. Moreover, the commemoration of the fallen

204 Space, memory and legacies of history

solder hides other histories that are no longer silenced. For example, recent years have seen the widespread re-commemoration of those who were condemned for cowardice. There were some 16,000 conscientious war objectors in Britain between 1914 and 1918. The official commemoration of 1918 thus runs into many problems when new symbolic orders offer counter-narratives. For example, the exclusion in the official narratives of around one million Indian soldiers who fought in the British army has been criticized as an attempt to construct a false image of a predominantly white British army. But including those marginalized or silenced is not enough if the narrative is itself in question, as I think it must be if we question war and sacrifice for the nation and empire as a good cause. There is, for example, the question of Gallipoli in this narrative, which is a story of the recklessness of elites who regarded the common solider as disposable (58,000 soldiers died on 25 April 1915 on a pointless landing on the Dardanelles ordered by Churchill, then the First Lord of the Admiralty). In this case, sacrifice was a testimony to the folly of elites. The questioning of the official narrative is not just a recent event. Since the late 1920s there was a counter-narrative of anti-war and pacifism that has mostly been silenced. In recent years it has enjoyed a revival[2] and has taken the white poppy as the symbol of peace and anti-war. In contrast to the red poppy, which commemorates British soldiers, the white poppy is the symbol of all casualties of war. The black poppy has been another counter-memory that highlights the memory of black soldiers who fought in the war, and the purple poppy commemorates more than 8 million horses, mules, and donkeys killed in the Great War.

There is also a wider philosophical question, namely, why an event should be commemorated in the first instance. The dominant assumption, since 1918, was to remember those who died. Now, while as I said memory had become a national narrative absorbed into an annual state pageantry, it maintained a link to the dead only by exclusion, since not all were remembered, and it silenced public debate on why they died. I will not pursue further the philosophical ramifications of this and issues of the just war, but it can be suggested that commemoration today has shifted in a more critical direction to incorporate reflection on war. This also includes reflection on the legacy of colonialism. While 1918 saw the crash of several empires (Ottoman, Russian, Habsburg), the western sea-based empires, especially the British and French, survived and reached their zenith in the period until 1945, when the descent into de-colonization began (see Kumar 2017). This is the moment to consider the legacy of 1968 and the arrival of a postcolonial Europe.

One final reflection on 1918 is in order: it was also the year in the UK that women got the right to vote and to stand for election (though restricted to women over 30 who met certain property requirements); 8.5 million got the right to vote, and in the general election of December 1918 the franchise was three times larger than the previous election. Although equality with men did not come until 1928, it was nonetheless a breakthrough and a testimony to the suffragette movement and a positive outcome of the war years. However, it did not lead to a new political utopia, and the overwhelming political memory of 1918 remained the trauma of war and a culture of amnesia and nostalgia for an irrecoverable past.

The Disobedient Generation and the recovery of utopia

Like 1918, 1968 was also a European-wide memory, though with greater global dimensions.[3] It was also the year that defined a generation, but unlike the memory of the Lost Generation, many of whom perished in the Great War, its memory is still one that is a living memory. But the contrasts are greater. The year 1918 saw the rise of a new generation of male youth who were dissatisfied with the old order that appeared to have come to an end, and, for the greater part, there was a turn to radical right-wing politics. The radical youth movement, especially in Germany, was in many ways a rebellion against modernity. The year 1968 in contrast is the year that is most characteristically associated with the rise of the cultural left; it was the event that defined a new generation of European youth who had become dissatisfied with the post-1945 world. Unlike the Lost Generation, this now included the voices of women, though feminism was to have an ambivalent relation with 1968. The post-1945 world was first shaken not in Europe but in the United States of America. It was a tumultuous year that saw the assassinations of Martin Luther King, Jr. and Robert F. Kennedy and widespread opposition to the war in Vietnam, which was a global impetus for the movement. It showed that war was not in fact a thing of the past. But 1968 was more than a year, it was a period that is marked, at least for France, at its outer limits by the end of the Algerian War in 1962 and the election of Mitterrand to the French presidency in 1981. In that sense one should speak of the '68 years, what Richard Vinen has referred to as the 'long '68 (see Vinen 2018: 14–15). A short framing would be from 1968 to 1973.

The generation of '68 – the 'Disobedient Generation' to use the title of a collection by Sica and Turner (Sica and Turner 2005) – brought about a seismic shift in the moral and political horizons of modern society. It was as much a cultural revolution as a political one, at least for Europe as a whole (May 1968 in Paris clearly was a political movement, as Ross (2003) has argued). If 1918 signalled the end of nineteenth-century European bourgeois civilization, 1968 signified the crisis of the post-1945 status quo everywhere, in both the Western and Eastern Bloc countries. In a famous book written in 1968 on the counter-culture, Theodor Roszak described it as a revolt against technocratic society (Roszak 1969). The post-1918 world was still one in which elites commanded the allegiance of the masses; 1968 marked the point in which that relation broke down with the rise of a new kind of radical politics that questioned the authority of elites. It was thus part of a turn towards anti-authoritarianism and a new spirit of emancipation in which collective self-determination had to include personal self-determination. Instead of self-sacrifice for king and country, self-determination and freedom were the new motifs.

The '68 generation shaped Europe in the West and in the East in ways that were far-reaching in terms of new values around personal autonomy, quality of life, justice, and peace. The consensus that was worked out in both East and West since 1945 ended in 1968. Both Soviet socialism and western democratic capitalism by 1968 had ossified into rigid frameworks that reduced politics to a highly regulated and institutionalized modes of operation that had effectively obliterated the

206 Space, memory and legacies of history

possibility of real emancipation. The two decades or so of prosperity in the West had created the conditions for opposition that could not be contained within the status quo. It was above all the university-educated middle class that provided the initial impetus for change and a rejection of many of the values of the post-war years.

The 1968 movement was a genuinely European-wide movement in that it arose spontaneously in the Warsaw Pact countries and in West Europe. May 1968 in Paris and Spring 1968 in Prague were two of its iconic moments. Arnason has suggested that the crisis of 1968 in Prague was experienced as a more general crisis of modernity. Previously marginalized currents of Marxist thought formed a bridge between East and West in 1968 in articulating a new critique of domination (Arnason 2002). But 1968 had wider European reverberations, especially in the Federal Republic of Germany and a more docile one in Britain despite the lead there in the aesthetic and intellectual side of the counter-culture. It was the case that the context everywhere was different, and, as a result, generalizations are difficult: in France it was the background of the Algerian War; in West Germany anti-fascism; in Prague the search for a mid-way between western democracy and Soviet socialism. The American origins of the movement in opposition to the Vietnam War gave to the European movement a strong opposition to war and the consciousness that peace needed a fundamental change in self-understanding. The confluence of the anti-imperialist and anti-fascist background was perhaps the real legacy of 1968 and what marked it off from 1918 when the desire for peace did not lead to a rejection of war. There is perhaps more research needed on this connection. It was a time in Europe when there were dictatorships in the east and in the south, with dictatorships in Portugal (until 1979), Spain (until 1980) and Greece (from 1967 to 1974) and the liberal democracies were actively pursuing wars in the colonial territories. The university-educated youth of 1968 were radicalized in a different way than the new cadres that were formed in 1918. 1968 may not have been as epochal as 1918, but it did lead to a shift in historical self-understanding and the formation of a new cultural model for Europe. Much of it was forged in radical campuses (in France at Nanterre; in the UK at Essex, Birmingham, Sussex; in Germany at the Free University in Berlin and Frankfurt; in Italy in Turin and Milan, and in the US at Berkeley and Columbia) and driven by student radicals, as in the iconic figures of Daniel Cohn-Bendit in France and Rudi Dutschke in Germany. New radical ideas, based on new interpretations of Marx and Freud, as in the writings of Herbert Marcuse and Michel Foucault, changed the intellectual context and gave to the political imaginary a way to challenge power and conceive of alternative political orders (see Brown 2013; Horn 2008; Bhambra and Demir 2009; Marwick 1999; Sica and Turner 2005). In this sense it can be said that 1968 revived the utopian dimension of a politics of hope for a better world. This utopia, as Marcuse (1979) recognized in his final work, *The Aesthetic Dimension*, did not last for long.

It might also be argued that 1968 saw the birth of European identity with the emergence of a generation of young people whose identities were formed in the consciousness of being part of a larger world than the national community. The larger sense of Europe was also becoming increasingly a reality, despite the limitations of European integration in the 1960s. The consolidation of a new generation of young people was in many ways a product of travel. Increased numbers of young people through travel and activism came to see themselves belonging to a European-wide transnational community (see Jobs 2009). Many were activists. Gildea et al (2017) in their survey of 1968 argue that activists across Europe often had a sense of being part of a wider revolt that went beyond their own national context and which also had a European dimension that included the experiences of Central and Eastern Europe (see also Passerini 1996). They thus speak of a 'European 1968' that was wider than Paris, Berlin, and Milan. This European-wide movement, which was underpinned by cultural developments in music, the arts, and popular culture, represented a different kind of cultural engagement to the intergovernmental and technocratic project of European integration. It was marked by a strong 'cultural effervescence', to use Durkheim's term, which was manifest in outbursts of politico-cultural creativity that led to the formation of a new consciousness of changing times. Unlike the Lost Generation of the post-1918 world, the generation of 1968 had hopes for a better world.

A wider perspective on 1968 would need to take into account the years that followed, which saw a growing crisis develop in the western world, culminating in the economic and political crisis of 1973. The oil crisis of October 1973, the final end of the Vietnam War that year and the end of the Bretton Woods System, which had been the basis of economic stability over the previous two decades but had been crumbling since 1968, all marked the end of the era of post-Second World War stability. The year 1973 saw Pinochet's coup in Chile. This wider international context is important in assessing the legacy of 1968. It requires a more critical perspective.

A backward look at the period shows that the cultural left of '68 failed to make a political impact of much significance. The revolutionary power attributed by the French Press to May 1968 was not matched by what in fact happened in Paris (Seidman 2004). Though this is a view that is disputed by Ross (2003), who argues that the dominant narrative and political memory of May 1968 in Paris as a cultural protest erased the radical politics of the events. The political and economic crisis that had been brewing since 1968 and culminated in 1973 was not primarily driven by radical politics, which had little immediate impact. The societal crisis was primarily a crisis in capitalism, and the generation of '68 had no real solutions and failed to stop the tide of repression, which was more pronounced in the socialist East. We should not forget that the Prague Spring – the experiment that began in January with so-called socialist humanism in Czechoslovakia by the government of Alexander Dubcek – came to an abrupt end on 20 August that year when Soviet tanks invaded. It is the spectre of the tanks rolling into Prague, not the Spring days that has shaped the political memory of the year. So, one reading of August 1968 was the end of the short-lived experiment with an alternative kind of socialism. In Warsaw, 1968 was dominated by the anti-Semitic purge of Jewish intellectuals. In March of that year, the Polish Communist Party forced thousands of Jewish people to leave Poland on the dubious grounds of being anti-Polish. And what did May 1968 lead to in Paris? The return of a hardline centre right rule of Charles de

208 Space, memory and legacies of history

Gaulle and the reaffirmation of the status quo amidst the fragmentation of the left. The period more generally saw the election of centre-right governments and the beginning of the crisis of social democracy and the obsolescence of the old left. In November 1968 Richard Nixon was elected president of the USA. It marked the end of progressive politics.

The new cultural left that was born in 1968 lacked political potency and failed to stop the rising ride of neoliberalism, which (at least in the English-speaking world) was the solution that was eventually found for the problems of what have been referred to as a crisis of governability that surfaced between 1968 and 1973. The year 1968 was a year of European-wide revolt, but it was not a revolution. It did not bring about a transformation in the political system. It had the ingredients of revolution, but they did not come together. The 1969 Woodstock Festival in the US was an expression of the normalization of the counter-culture, as perhaps marked by Matthews Southern Comfort. The cry for revolution easily slipped into reform and accommodation (as illustrated by the careers of Bill Clinton and the former British foreign secretary Jack Straw). Boltanski and Chiapello (2005: 167) have noted how many of the left-wing and extreme militants in 1968 went into official government positions in the 1980s. In positions close to political power they underwent a conversion to power and assimilated employers' demands into their own culture that proved to be highly flexible. This trend is also reflected in the political career of Joska Fisher in Germany, a figure who encapsulated the '68 generation in the journey from street demonstrations to liberal democracy. Revolution and counter-revolutionary currents flowed easily together, and one should not forget that it was the latter that triumphed. For Central and Eastern Europe, the real revolution was in 1989, but that did not follow in the footsteps of 1968 (when the Prague Spring sought to find a mid-way between socialism and liberal democracy) in that it was a movement that was in the name of liberal democracy.

Perhaps there is a more general point to be made here about the fate of European revolutions. In contrast to revolutions in other parts of the world – the American (1775) and Mexican (1910) Revolutions come to mind – European revolutions have been, in their own terms, failures, even if they laid the foundations for long-term political transformation. The revolutions of 1789 and 1848 resulted in the reestablishment of the *ancien regime*, as did England's Glorious Revolution of 1688. The year 1968 did not itself lead to political counter-revolution – as in the example of the Arab Spring – but it did not succeed in its political aims and, as argued, the aftermath was the consolidation of the political right. The political hope it nurtured did not translate into effective political programmes. The alliance between workers and students was a short one, and the ultimate legacy of 1968 was the end of a common political struggle. The counter-culture could easily provide fuel for the new spirit of capitalism. Indeed, much of it was not particularly political but more about self-discovery and personal freedom. The writings of Michel Foucault contained a message about the end of collective political struggles. Where Marx announced the end of interpretation, postmodern thought declared that all is now a matter of interpretation. This is not to neglect the fact that many of the

'68 generation were the children of anti-fascist fighters, and, while they were not feminists, their ideas fostered the feminist revolution.

Some qualifications are needed. The year 1968 did bring about a shift in self-understanding more generally in Europe, even if it failed to offer a political alternative. In West Germany the '68 generation brought about political change of some significance, as reflected in particular by the rise of the Green Party and the politicization of the German university system (see Kundnani 2009). One of the enduring legacies of the '68 years was antifascism, which can be seen as part of the wider legacy of anti-war that was also more generally part of European self-understanding in the post-war decades, but did not reach the level of significant cultural transformation until 1968. It was predominantly confined to the universities. However, political reform took longer. There can be no doubt that this was a considerable achievement, since until then what Adorno (1998) in 1959 referred to as 'working through the past' in the Federal Republic was more or less nonexistent. In this respect, the '68 years were very much defined by a generational conflict between right-wing parents of the Nazi period and their left-wing children. The myth of revolution may not have been matched by reality, but it did lead to a shift in self-understanding.

But the generation of 1968 was not a common one and included what Habermas in 1968 has called 'left-wing fascism', as reflected in the extreme left in Germany in 1970s in the figure of Andreas Baader, whose favourite film, Richard Vinen points out (2018: 287), was Sergio Leone's 1968 spaghetti western, *Once Upon a Time in the West*. Nonetheless, despite the escalation in violence since 1968, it should be noted that May 1968 in Paris, the epicentre of the European movement, was not in fact violent: no one was killed. In Germany, aside from the non-fatal shooting of Dutschke, no one was killed in 1968. This is a stark contrast to the Paris Commune uprising in 1871, when some 25,000 people were massacred. It is true that the memory of the murder of Benno Ohnesorg by a policeman the previous year cast its shadow over radical politics in West Germany for several years to come. Certainly, in Northern Ireland, with the rise of the civil rights movements, it was the beginning of a period of long-lasting political violence. However, it is worth reflecting on the very different experience Algerian activists had when they organized a peaceful protest in Paris in October 1961: some 200 were murdered by the security forces and their bodies thrown into the Seine, and thousands were imprisoned (House and Macmaster 2006)

Any consideration of the legacy of 1968 will also need to address what might be described as a certain Eurocentrism. Although it can be seen as an expression of a new cultural and political cosmopolitanism, this was very much a western one that was not always necessarily political. Indeed, much was about hedonistic travel and hippie culture. More than this, it was a movement that did not have much to say on racism and the inclusion of minorities. I do not think it is a case of applying the perspective of the present day to an earlier time to say that a striking failure of 1968 was its silence about empire and coloniality. The language and political horizons of the era did not extend beyond a preoccupation with issues that were confined to

210 Space, memory and legacies of history

a limited conception of Europe. It must be recalled that this was a time when the European powers had only recently relinquished their colonies: the post-imperial age had begun, but a postcolonial Europe had not yet emerged. Portugal still held on to its African territories until the collapse of the dictatorship in 1979, but most other countries lost their colonies by 1968. In France the memory of the Algerian War of Independence (1954-62) was still strong and was a background context for 1968, but it did not lead to much reflection on colonialism and legacies of empire. In fact, only just over ten years earlier (in 1956-7) Britain and France went to war against Egypt over the closure of the Suez Canal in order to preserve the passage to their overseas territories.

The May '68 movement, which was a predominantly white and middle-class movement, did not significantly involve black activists. This issue may be less relevant to Germany and Central Europe where anti-fascism was a more pressing and dominating issue, but the question of empire cannot be separated from domestic politics for much of the western European colonial powers. It took another generation to broaden the European compass to include those previously excluded. It is significant that 1968 did not have much to contribute to the advancement of cultural pluralism, even if it widened the moral and political horizons of European societies. That is not to say that European activists were unconcerned about struggles in other parts of the world. Anti-imperialism, as I mentioned earlier, certainly complemented anti-fascism in shaping the political consciousness of activists throughout Europe. As epitomized by the figure of the Argentinian revolutionary who died in 1967, Che Guevara, who was the cult hero of the wider revolutionary movement, European activists were inspired by anti-imperial struggles in Europe's colonies and ex-colonies and Vietnamese resistance to US imperialism was an important catalyst. This could lead to extraordinary naivety as the widespread endorsement of the Chinese Cultural Revolution (from 1966) by Maoist radicals in western countries as somehow a signal of a radical cultural transformation, despite claiming almost 2 million victims. However, it would appear that the preoccupations of the 1968 generation were with an imagined revolution in Europe that never happened, at least not in terms comparable to anti-imperial struggles in other parts of the world. They were keen to condemn imperialism abroad but did not pay much attention to their own country's legacies of colonialism. As with everything, there are some exceptions and it is true, as Enzo Traverso (2016: 13) argues, that the legacy of the Holocaust played a role for French activists in May 1968 in drawing parallels with French and American colonialism, as also reflected in Aimé Césaire's, *Discourse on Colonialism* in 1950 (Césaire [1950] 2000). It is certainly the case that anti-imperialism was more strongly present in 1968 than in 1918 when the myth of empire remained strong and mostly unquestioned.

I am also mindful of the fact that in Britain, 1968 was probably the year that marked the rise of racist xenophobia: in April of that year Enoch Powell gave his famous 'Rivers of Blood' speech in Birmingham. The notorious speech was targeted at the progressive Race Relations Act in the UK of that year, which made it illegal to discriminate on housing, public services, or employment on the grounds of race.

Conclusion

To conclude, while it can be shown that 1918 and 1968 reflect two different narratives of Europe and modernity deriving from very different legacies – one of the political right and one of the cultural and political left – and two generational legacies (the Lost Generation and the Disobedient Generation) – I believe it is possible to see in both a legacy that has real significance for our time, namely, opposition to war. The year 1918 marked the beginning of the brutalization of war and its commemoration to an extent, as Mosse (1990) argued, led to its trivialization and thus its greater acceptance. The Second World War and the wars that followed in so-called peace-time – the Algerian War and the Vietnam War – shaped a new consciousness that cultivated a more critical attitude to war. The ultimate legacy of the 1968 years was the end of the era defined by the two world wars and the beginning of a new era in which different values would shape the future.

Notes

1 This chapter is based on a keynote lecture given to the conference *Contested Europes: Legacies, Legitimacies, and (Dis)Integration*, Södertörn University, Sweden, 29–30 November 2018. The lecture and theme of the conference concerned the centenary of 1918 and the 50th anniversary of 1968. My thanks to Neal Harris, Jo Moran-Ellis, William Outhwaite, Monica Sassatelli, and Heinz Sünker for comments on an earlier draft and to participants at the conference for their comments.
2 For example, the Veterans for Peace movement, founded in 2011.
3 See Gassert and Klimke 2018; Ingo and Waters 2010; Klimke and Scarloth 2008; Kurlansky 2005.

References

Adorno, T. 1998 [1959]. What Does Coming to Terms with the Past Mean? In: *Critical Models: Interventions and Catchwords*. New York: Columbia University Press.
Arnason, J. 2002. The Forgotten 1968 and the False End of History. *Thesis Eleven*, 68: 89–94.
Benjamin, W. 1978. A Berlin Chronicle. In: *Reflections*. New York: Schocken Books.
Bhambra, G. and Demir, I. (eds.) 2009. *1968 in Retrospect: History, Theory and Alterity*. London: Palgrave Macmillan.
Boltanski, L. and Chiapello, E. 2005. *The New Spirit of Capitalism*. London: Verso.
Brown, T. 2013. *West Germany and the Global Sixties: The Anti-Authoritarian Revolt, 1962–1978*. Cambridge: Cambridge University Press.
Césaire, A. 2000 [1950]. *Discourse on Colonialism*. New York: Monthly Review.
Furet, F. 1999. *The Passing of an Illusion: The Idea of Communism in the Twentieth Century*. Chicago, IL: The University of Chicago Press.
Fussell, P. 2000. *The Great War and Modern Memory*. Oxford: Oxford University Press.
Gassert, P. and Klimke, H. 2018. *1968 On the Edge of Revolution*. Portland, OR: Black Rose Books.
Gildea, R., Mark, J. and Warring, A. 2017. *Europe's 1968: Voices of Revolt*. Oxford: Oxford University Press.
Gregory, A. 2008. *The Last Great War: British Society and the First World War*. Cambridge: Cambridge University Press.

Hobsbawm, E. 1994. *Age of Extremes: The Short Twentieth Century, 1914–1991*. London: Michael Joseph.

Horn, G. H. 2008. *The Spirit of '68: Rebellion in Western Europe and North America, 1956–1976*. Oxford: Oxford University Press.

House, J. and MacMaster, N. 2006. *Paris 1961: Algerians, State Terror, and Memory*. Oxford: Oxford University Press.

Ingo, C. and Waters, S. (eds.) 2010. *Memories of 1968: International Perspectives*. Bern: Peter Lang.

Jobs, R. I. 2009. Youth Movements: Travel, Protest, and Europe in 1968. *American Historical Review*, 114 (2): 376–404.

Klimke, M. and Scarloth, J. (eds.) 2008. *1968 in Europe: A History of Protest and Activism*. London: Palgrave Macmillan.

Kumar, K. 2017. *Visions of Empire: How Five Imperial Regimes Shaped the World*. Princeton, NJ: Princeton University Press.

Kundnani, H. 2009. *Utopia or Auschwitz: Germany's 1968 Generation and the Holocaust*. London: Hurst.

Kurlansky, M. 2005. *1968: The Year that Rocked the World*. London: Vintage.

Marcuse, H. 1979. *The Aesthetic Dimension: Critique of Marxist Aesthetics*. Boston: Beacon Press.

Marwick, A. 1999. *The Sixties: Social and Cultural Transformation in Britain, France, Italy and the United States 1958–1974*. Oxford: Oxford University Press.

Mosse, G. 1990. *Fallen Soldiers: Reshaping the Memory of the World War*. Oxford: Oxford University Press.

Ortega Y Gasset, J. 1994. *The Revolt of the Masses*. New York: Norton.

Passerini, L. 1996. *Autobiography of a Generation: Italy in 1968*. Middletown, CT: Wesleyan University Press.

Ross, K. 2003. *May '68 and Its Afterlives*. Chicago, IL: University of Chicago Press.

Roszak, T. 1969. *The Making of a Counter-Culture: Reflections of the Technocratic Society and Its Youthful Opposition*. New York: Doubleday.

Seidman, M. 2004. *The Imaginary Revolutionary: Parisian Students and Workers in 1968*. Oxford: Berghahn.

Sica, A. and Turner, S. (eds.) 2005. *The Disobedient Generation: Social Theory in the Sixties*. Chicago, IL: University of Chicago Press.

Spengler, O. 1991 [1926]. *The Decline of the West*. Oxford: Oxford University Press.

Traverso, E. 2016. *Left-Wing Melancholia: Marxism, History and Memory*. New York: Columbia University Press.

Vinen, R. 2018. *The Long '68: Radical Politics and Its Enemies*. London: Allen Lane.

Winter, J. 2014. *Sites of Memory, Sites of Mourning*. Cambridge: Cambridge University Press.

Winter, J. and Emmanuel, S. 2000. *War and Remembrance in the Twentieth Century*. Cambridge: Cambridge University Press.

Wohl, L. 1979. *The Lost Generation of 1914*. Cambridge, MA: Harvard University Press.

11

THE CRISIS OF THE PRESENT
Authoritarianism and social pathologies

This chapter offers an analysis and exploration from a critical theory perspective of major societal crises of the present. It has been widely recognized that contemporary societies are undergoing a crisis that is deeper than a periodic political or economic crisis and could be described as civilizational. Democracy has not only failed to prevent an increase in inequality but has also failed to stop the rising tide of authoritarianism. There is now a deep and pervasive sense of the futility of progressive collective action. In Chapters 4 and 5 I looked at some aspects of the current situation with respect to developments related to capitalism and, in particular, to the post-2008 financial crisis and the general malaise of neoliberalism. In this chapter, I am concerned with the on-set of a range of crises in contemporary society that can be related to the more general societal context of contemporary capitalism and the unravelling of what has been referred to as a democratic capitalism. One of the most obvious manifestations of the sense of a world in crisis has been the prevalence of a new wave of what is generally termed populism and which takes a predominantly right-wing form, while in many cases incorporating left-wing elements. The Trump presidency is the most significant expression of radical right-wing populism. However, populism is not unique, something aberrant from the norm, and, it is important to consider, populism is also not historically novel. Other expressions of current trends would include Brexit in the UK and the growth of anti-migration movements across Europe and more generally in the world, and the rise of varieties of political authoritarianism. I return to these movements and events later in this chapter.

Since 2016, social and political scientists have struggled to understand these developments as social and political phenomena and the extent to which they can be historically understood and explained. Not surprisingly, the spectre of fascism is often invoked, and comparisons are made with Germany in the 1930s. In this chapter, I argue that a feature of the crisis in many countries – whether with Trump in

214 Space, memory and legacies of history

the USA, Johnson in the UK, Bolsonaro in Brazil, Erdogan in Turkey – is authoritarianism and that it takes both political forms as well as socio-cultural. It cannot all be explained by capitalism; authoritarianism is a phenomenon in its own right and is fully compatible with democracy even as it exhibits anti-democratic characteristics. Fascism emerged in the context of failing democracies; the current situation is different even if the sense of a crisis in civilization is also present: liberal democracy is well established and has provided the fertile ground for a very different kind of authoritarianism, which I call authoritarian democracy. However, I argue that one major additional factor also needs to be incorporated into the picture, namely, the background of failing neoliberalism. The catastrophic effects of several decades of neoliberalism have generated the conditions for the emergence of a new wave of authoritarianism.

The contribution this chapter makes to the current discussion is to apply the social theory of the Frankfurt School to the present crisis of democracy and the on-set of social pathologies in social integration. There is much value in doing this since the early Frankfurt School sought to understand the nature of fascism and, more importantly, the continuation of fascism in liberal democracies. As I shall demonstrate, their work on authoritarianism offers important insights into social pathologies and societal regression. However, I am not proposing that their social theory can be unproblematically applied without some modifications; other and more recent developments in critical social theory will also need to be brought to bear on the current situation, which I argue is different from both the pre-1945 context as well as the post-war years in which the authoritarian personality project began. Above all, the current situation is shaped by the societal consequences of neoliberalism, which sowed the seeds for virulent forms of nationalism to emerge today.

The first section of the chapter looks at the Studies in Prejudice research programme of the Frankfurt School, and especially the influential *Authoritarian Personality* published in 1950. In light of the theoretical framework developed in these studies and in particular with reference to Adorno's own contributions, the second section will examine current trends in light of these theories. Here I argue that a pervasive trend in liberal democracy is authoritarian democracy, whereby democracy produces anti-democratic currents. Trump, Bolsonaro in Brazil and Johnson in the UK are key examples of this trend and reflect wider authoritarian currents and regressions in society. The third section offers an excursus on Brexit as an example of societal regressions and pathologies within democracy.

The Frankfurt School and *The Authoritarian Personality*

As noted in Chapter 3, the Frankfurt School in exile in New York developed a highly successful programme of empirical social research that sought to understand the nature and significance of anti-Semitism from a largely psychoanalytical perspective. The driving force in this re-orientation of critical theory was Max Horkheimer, who brought together an interdisciplinary group of German-Jewish émigré scholars at Columbia University, including Marcuse, Adorno, Fromm, Lowenthal, Neumann, Kirchheimer, and Pollock. The early studies in the 1940s were widely recognized to be important in understanding the nature of anti-Semitism and attracted significant funding beyond what the Institute of Social Research itself funded.[1] The critical theorists, and those who funded their research, believed that in order to combat anti-Semitism it was first of all necessary to understand it. The social research was also an important demonstration of the interdisciplinary task of critical theory to combine philosophical inquiry with empirical social research in order to educate society. In bringing together social psychology, sociology, philosophy, and political science, it was an innovative programme that sought to advance critical thought in both social science and in the wider society. The series, edited and directed by Horkheimer, published five major works, including *The Authoritarian Personality*, which were strongly influenced by psychoanalysis and the idea that weak personality structures were conducive to being receptive to political propaganda. The research noted similarities in the manipulation of public opinion on the USA and in Nazi Germany by fascist movements and proposed that similar psychological traits and social conditions were present in the different social contexts. Other topics included the historical emergence of anti-Semitism in imperial Germany.

Underlying the studies was the Freudian notion that an autonomous ego is better placed to resist prejudice, fascist propaganda, and anti-Semitism than egos insufficiently differentiated from their social environment. A fully autonomous person does not internalize social stimuli in the way a weaker ego does. This idea was accompanied by a more general sociological and social psychological argument that in the twentieth century there was a change in the relationship between personality and prejudice due to the weakening of the bourgeois ego. Moreover, a weakened ego is more likely to degenerate into narcissism, which leads to identification with fascist leaders. This thesis of ego weakness, which was suggested by Freud (1974) himself in *Group Psychology and the Analysis of the Ego* in 1922, was developed in the writings of Erich Fromm in *The Working Class in Weimar Germany* and later by Herbert Marcuse in, for example, 'The Obsolescence of the Freudian Concept of Man' (Fromm 1984; Marcuse 1970). Research also conducted by Horkheimer et al (1936), *Studies on Authority and Family*, provided a further elaboration of this argument with the thesis that changes in the nature of family life – in particular increased financial security and the related insecurity in paternal authority – increased people's vulnerability to anti-democratic influences. Fromm, however, believed ego weakening was only one element in a more complicated picture of psycho-social forces, which included sado-masochism, which he regarded as the core of the authoritarian personality (Jay 1996/1973: 128). The Frankfurt School theorists placed a strong emphasis on the family as a major institution in society in which authority is founded. It follows, then, that changes in the nature of family life will have wider implications for the nature of authority. Nazism, for example, led to an attack on the family with the result that individuals sought authority outside the family. More generally, changes in capitalism led to a weakening of the

216 Space, memory and legacies of history

bourgeois family and its model of authority. In essence, the weakening of the ego and the resulting loss in personal autonomy cultivates a type of personality that sees in the fascist leader a mirror of one's self. The basic thesis is that there is a difference between the truly autonomous individual and the individual who submits to standardization and is thus de-individualized. This theory, and the seminal work of Freud, made possible the explanatory framework for the empirical research. It showed for the first time how political ideologies are rooted in psychological forces that in turn are related to socio-economic structures.

Adorno and Horkheimer (1979) themselves, independently of the wider circle, developed a larger philosophical framework for understanding anti-Semitism in the *Dialectic of Enlightenment*. The philosophical arguments in the section, 'Elements of Antisemitism', were a contrast to the more social scientific approach adopted in the various publications of the Studies in Prejudice programme. The most famous work in the Studies of Prejudice was *The Authoritarian Personality*, which should be seen in the context of the earlier philosophical work (Müller-Doohm 2005: 292). Before looking at this work in more detail, a few points of a more general nature can be said about the theoretical framework. The first is that anti-Semitism is not simply one specific kind of prejudice but reflects a more general and pervasive culture of prejudice. While Horkheimer was particularly interested in anti-Semitism, which was hardly surprising in view of the Holocaust, its characteristics have a wider relevance for understanding prejudice in general. In the post-1945 period, this wider context became more relevant, but at the time when the studies were developed, it was by no means evident what the outcome of the war might be. A second aspect of anti-Semitism is that it is a false projection onto a victim of repressed impulses. In 'Elements of Anti-Semitism' Adorno and Horkheimer wrote: 'Impulses which the subject will not admit as his own even though they are most assuredly so, are attributed to the object – the prospective victim' (Adorno and Horkheimer 1979: 187). A third point is that anti-Semitism is a condition that is characteristic of the social subject rather than the Jews. This has methodological implications, as noted in the Introduction to *The Authoritarian Personality*, namely, that 'one place to look for determinants of anti-Semitic opinions and attitudes is with the persons who express them'. The fourth point is that anti-Semitism is a medium of domination. In seeking out victims, whether Jews or others, it enables the creation of a more general culture of authoritarianism. So, in sum, anti-Semitism is to be seen as an expression of societal domination, and therefore it needs to be seen as a product of a particular kind of society. It is for this reason that the Studies in Prejudice publications were considered to be significant in that they went to the core of deep pathologies within modern society in uncovering correlations between psychological dispositions, political ideologies, and social context. Although a departure from the study of capitalism, the rationale of the programme was not a rejection of the earlier concern with capitalism. However, the re-orientation was an acknowledgement of other forms of domination beyond those that can be accounted for by reference to class domination or instrumental reason.

The Freudian background to the studies and the social psychological methodological approach adopted in the empirical research should not then be seen in isolation from the wider sociological and philosophical work of Horkheimer's circle of critical theorists at Columbia in the 1940s. The attempt to understand the susceptibility of the individual to anti-democratic influence inevitably required the application of social psychology methods of research. However, one should also not lose sight of the fact that as far as the most influential critical theorists were concerned, this work was part of a wider social theory and included the 'culture industry' and the arrival of the 'totally administered society'. In addition to these themes, also relevant is Benjamin's argument about the fascist uses of aesthetics in mass politics in order to create forms of popular expression that do not challenge capitalism: 'Fascism sees its salvation in giving these masses not their right, but instead a chance to express themselves' (Benjamin 1973: 243).

Against this background, *The Authoritarian Personality* can be discussed. Of the institute's publications of the period, it was the enduring one, and, despite its methodological deficits, it has exerted a considerable influence in critical social research. The research for *The Authoritarian Personality* – authored by T. W. Adorno, Else Frankel-Brunswick, Daniel Levinson, and R. Nevitt Sanford – was conducted in co-operation with the Berkeley Public Opinion Study in California (Adorno et al [1950] 2019). The immediate political context was not fascism but the existence within democracy of anti-democratic tendencies, including deeply rooted social conservatism. It was devised in 1944 but began the following year and thus bore the imprint of a world that had only just seen the defeat of fascism. But this gave it a new relevance. As Adorno later said in 1959, 'I consider the survival of National Socialism *within* democracy to be potentially more menacing than the survival of fascist tendencies *against* democracy' (1998: 90). With this work, the focus shifts from anti-Semitism to authoritarianism. Indeed, it seems that anti-Semitism is a dimension of authoritarianism. The project was concerned with the formation of a specific kind of personality who is anti-democratic and potentially fascist. As boldly stated by Max Horkheimer in in the Preface: 'The central theme of the work is a relatively new concept – the rise of an "anthropological" species we can call the authoritarian type of man' (P. lxxi).

The guiding hypothesis was 'that the political, economic, and social convictions of an individual often form a broad and coherent pattern, as if bound together by a "mentality" or "spirit", and that this pattern is an expression of deep lying trends in his personality' (p. 1). The authors emphasize that they are seeking to examine 'the potentially fascistic individual'. Since fascism was just defeated, it was unlikely that there would be many people avowedly fascistic or belonging to fascist organizations. They emphasize 'potential' because they did not set out to study avowedly fascist individuals but personality structures that are susceptible to fascist tendencies. The important point was that fascist tendencies still exist as certain kinds of prejudice and other character traits and could in different circumstances support fascism, which is always a latent force in society and under certain circumstances can become manifest. The political context of the McCarthy era of the late 1940s

218 Space, memory and legacies of history

and early 1950s provided ample evidence of fascist tendencies within democracy. One of the authors, R. Nevitt Sanford, a professor of psychology, was dismissed from the University of California, Berkeley in 1950 for not signing an oath of loyalty (Gordon 2019: xxiv). The study sought to identify a set of characteristics that when combined constitute a specific 'syndrome'. It is this syndrome that constitutes the 'authoritarian personality'. Although this is referred to as a 'personality', it is not reducible to an individual as such, but is manifest in a syndrome: 'The answer must be sought not in any single personality nor in personality factors found in the mass of people, but in processes at work in society. It seems well understood today that whether or not antidemocratic propaganda is to become a dominant force in this country depends primarily upon the situation of the most powerful economic interests, upon whether they, by conscious design or not, make use of this device for maintaining their dominant status' (p. 7).

This statement makes clear that the social psychological dimension must be located in a wider sociological context. The research, which used both quantitative and qualitative methods of data collection and analysis, sought to correlate ideologies – the organization of opinions, attitudes, and values – and social factors, such as class and economic circumstances. But such correlations do not explain personality formations, such as the authoritarian personality. While being influenced by certain preconditions, this syndrome appears to be a product of psychological dispositions – both personality traits and attitudes – that somehow already exist. Now, while the authoritarian personality has itself been a product of social circumstances, once it has come into existence it is capable of action on the social environment. The authors argue that '[T]his conception is necessary to explain consistency of behaviours in varying situations, to explain the persistence of ideological trends in the face of contradictory facts and radically altered social conditions, to explain why people in the same sociological situation have different or even conflicting views on the social issues, and why it is that people whose behaviour has been changed through psychological manipulation lapse into their old ways as soon as the agencies of manipulation are removed' (p. 6). The study asserts the existence of dispositions that are not explained by economic forces or economic self-interest and may be detrimental to economic self-interest. However, under certain social and economic circumstances, such disposition rise to the surface and can take on a political significance.

The methodological device used in the study was the famous F–Scale – whereby the F refers to fascism – which was designed to measure the authoritarian tendencies within the personality structure of around 2000 people interviewed and which would be indicative of the authoritarian personality. This syndrome is made up of nine variables which can be briefly summed up: conventionalism (rigid adherence to middle-class conventions); authoritarian submission (uncritical attitudes towards moral authorities); authoritarian aggression (tendencies to condemn and to punish people who violate conventional values); anti-intraception (opposition to the subjective, imaginative, the tender-minded); superstition and stereotypy (rigid thinking in categories); power and 'toughness' (preoccupation with strength, dominance); destructiveness and cynicism (generalized hostility, vilification of the

The crisis of the present **219**

human); projectivity (disposition to believe that wild and dangerous things go on in the world); and sex (exaggerated concern with sexual 'goings-on').

These variables exist within the wider population, but they cohere within specific groups to varying degrees. The methodological objective was to demonstrate a close correlation between a number of deeply rooted personality traits – the previously stated nine characteristics – and overt expressions of prejudice. The social contextualization – exposure to external stimuli, such as fascist ideology – was a secondary objective. The authors sum up one of their major findings: 'individuals who show extreme susceptibility to fascist propaganda have a great deal in common. (They exhibit numerous characteristics that go together to form a 'syndrome'.) The study did not clarify the degree to which the results can be generalized, but the authors clearly thought the study uncovered a deep-lying trend in the modern personality structure and which was pervasive within the lower-middle class. The 'authoritarian personality' is thus a syndrome that is composed of a high degree of certain characteristics that tend to coalesce within certain groups, but is independent of any specific groups, such as a class. It is thus not a group-specific phenomenon, such as reducible to a socio-economic group or to an identity, but can be found across the class spectrum. Nonetheless, there is a certain correlation between a certain kind of personality and political orientations.

The Authoritarian Personality has been heavily criticized on methodological grounds, in terms of the sample, the conceptualization of the objectives, and design.[2] Despite its theoretical sophistication, it was methodologically flawed in that the outcomes were more or less anticipated in the research design, which did not take the form of a hypothesis to be tested but a theory that sought confirmation. There results from the various scales used in many instances were contradictory in that high scorers on one scale were low scorers on another. This led to the F- Scale being taken as the indicative measure of both latent and manifest fascist tendencies. There was also political bias – according to neoconservative critics such as the sociologist Edward Shils – in that only right-wing authoritarianism was considered as relevant. From a different and more sympathetic perspective to the core aims of the project, it has often been criticized for its over-reliance on social psychology rather than sociology; this coupled with the Freudian influence tended to see authoritarianism as residing with the structure of the psyche rather than being a social creation. However, as noted above, some of these criticisms are unjustified in that the project should be seen in the context of the overall aims of critical theory. As a multi-authored and interdisciplinary project, it was not primarily sociological (the two senior authors, Frenkel-Brunswik and Levinson, were psychologists, and Sanford was an expert in research methodology). It is also fair to say that the project reflected a social psychological approach and to the extent that it was part of a wider programme, the general reader would not know of the connection with the wider concerns. Adorno's main contribution, aside from Chapters 16 and 19, was with sociological contextualization and the analysis of political ideologies. However, all authors, including Adorno shared the basic psychoanalytical theoretical background to the study.[3] Adorno, for his part, did not see the study as an exercise

220 Space, memory and legacies of history

in inductive hypothesis verification research, even if it employed quantitative and statistical research methods.

Peter Gordon (2018) in a discussion of Adorno's previously unpublished 'remarks' on *The Authoritarian Personality* confirms that Adorno dissented somewhat from the social psychological approach, which tended to see personality formation as the primary reality and not the social reality that produced the personality traits.[4] Adorno was 'convinced that the ultimate source of prejudice has to be sought in social factors which are comparably stronger than the "psyche" of any one individual involved' (Adorno [1948] 2019: xl11). It seems, then, that in the study these traits were not explained but presupposed.[5] Adorno, in contrast, wished to see anti-Semitism, fascism, and authoritarianism as 'due to the total structure of our society' (Adorno [1948] 2019: l). Perhaps this is why in the Conclusion, the authors write: 'It seems obvious therefore that that the modification of the potentially fascist structure cannot be achieved by psychological means alone. The task is comparable to that of eliminating neurosis, or delinquency, or nationalism from the world. These are products of the total organization of society and are to be changed only as that society is changed' (p. 974). The approach adopted otherwise could lead to the mistaken view that authoritarianism is simply the aggregation of subjective traits. It would appear then that Adorno had made a crucial observation in seeing authoritarianism not in the final analysis as a personality system that could be accounted for by individual psychology or even as attitudes but as an expression of a social trend and the emergence of new norms. While the notion of an authoritarian personality might then be the wrong concept, its typifying characteristics nonetheless must correspond, if not to a socio-cultural milieu, then to particular individuals. However, the important point is that authoritarianism is a social phenomenon and is present to varying degrees in different groups. Individuals who exhibit authoritarian traits are more likely to share common opinions, have similar practices (as in child-rearing), and political views. The wider implication of Adorno's argument is that a social pathology is not to be explained by individual psychology because the pathology of authoritarianism is an expression of society in that it leads to regression and oppression. Thus, Adorno's wider concern as reflected also in his interventions in public debate in Germany on his return in 1952 was that democracy itself is not a protection from authoritarianism and can nurture pathologies.

In conclusion, *The Authoritarian Personality* was very unclear as to whether the authoritarian personality was a psychological disposition that could be exploited by political manipulators or was a social phenomenon of its own with its own dynamics. Either way, it is clear that authoritarianism is a powerful trend in modern western societies and is not only a product of totalitarianism. In this respect, the distinction between totalitarianism and authoritarianism is crucial. Liberal democracy prevailed over totalitarianism (at least by 1990) but not over authoritarianism, which found a new life in post-totalitarian democracies (see Tucker 2015). Perhaps the struggle against totalitarianism required authoritarianism. But authoritarianism is also present in liberal democracy, as Adorno recognized and analysed in a lecture in 1967 on the rise of the extreme right in Germany just twenty years after its defeat in 1945

(Adorno 2019b). Authoritarianism is a more general phenomenon that is also, and possibly even more so, amenable to democracy and is sustained by the culture industry which provides it with content that is devoid of critical substance (Trump after all was a TV reality presenter). Although the authors of *The Authoritarian Personality* saw the danger of fascism lurking in liberal democracy of authoritarianism, they did acknowledge in the last words of the work 'that the majority of our subjects do not exhibit the extreme ethnocentric pattern and the fact that there are various ways it may be avoided altogether'. Their conclusion is: 'If fear and destructiveness are the major emotional sources of fascism, *eros* belongs mainly to democracy' (p. 976).

Considerations on neo-authoritarianism today

The critical theory of fascism and authoritarianism has much relevance for our time. Although the circumstances are different, a reading of especially *The Authoritarian Personality* reveals some important perspectives on the figure of Donald Trump, other such demagogues, and right-wing populist movements as well as the social and political phenomenon of Brexit. What was a weakness of the study is perhaps now a strength: the work was regarded as failing to really identify fascists and fascism but could only identify authoritarians and a pervasive culture of authoritarianism. The one enduring and relevant element that is highlighted by the work of the critical theorists in the 1940s is the phenomenon of authoritarianism. This concept and the analysis especially of Adorno and the studies directed by Horkheimer, despite their methodological flaws, suggest that authoritarianism is a phenomenon in its own right and that while certain types of individuals are attracted to authoritarian ideologies, it is a pathological product of society. Rather than see authoritarianism as a feature of specific groups of people, it should rather be seen as residing in what Adorno referred to as 'the general structure of society'. This is an important insight in that it corrects a tendency to see regressive and pathological tendencies as residing within the psyche of individuals or properties of groups. While individuals and groups are the primary agents of social processes, the influences on them come from external sources. More significantly is that the elements constitutive of many social phenomena are a plethora of characteristics that coalesce to varying degrees across a range of social groups. What constitutes a phenomenon such as authoritarianism is often the combination rather than the specific characteristics, many of which alone are insufficient to bring about a shift in social and political organization (thus, for example, Euroscepticism was rife in the British Conservative Party since the mid-1980s but it did not have a capacity to bring about societal transformation). More generally, an orientation towards, for instance, conventionalism or social conservatism alone does not lead to authoritarianism. Other orientations would also need to be present and, additionally, there would also need to be external forces, such as political manipulation, or a golden opportunity, such as the Brexit referendum, which presented an unexpected opportunity for the radical right as well as for the far left of British politics, who paradoxically found in the same entity the means to achieve their different aims.

222 Space, memory and legacies of history

On the basis of this critical perspective informed by the Studies in Prejudice, it can be concluded, then, that certain people exhibit authoritarian characteristics and related cultural orientations, which, when combined with specific circumstances, which include social conservatism and exposure to political ideologies, become increasingly authoritarian. When large numbers of people develop such tendencies, authoritarianism becomes less a marginal pathology than a normalized one. Erich Fromm referred to this as 'pathological normalcy' (Fromm 1991; see also Fromm 1963). This concept draws attention to how pathologies emanate from the mainstream of society, and, while they are often associated with specific groups, it is society itself that is sick. The psychoanalytical slant in the critical theory studies opened up new avenues of critical inquiry, but it also put such investigations on the wrong track in that it tended to lead to a view of pathologies as inherent in the psyche of individuals. It also relied on the questionable model of the crisis of the patriarchal bourgeois family, which furnishes Freudian psychoanalysis with its social content. A sociological correction, as indicated by Adorno's proposals, draws attention to the social construction of cultural orientations, which are not simply given but are created by often contradictory societal processes and cultural dynamics.

This approach is particularly helpful in making sense of one of the most puzzling aspects of the large and diverse social support basis of Trump and Brexit in 2016. Despite the differences between the two phenomena, they share a complex social basis. By all accounts, it is not possible to pin the support basis for Brexit and Trump to a specific social class. Initial responses that it was a rebellion of the white working class – the so called 'losers of globalization' – who see themselves disenfranchised by the liberal and progressive-oriented middle class are unfounded. While there is some truth in this claim, it is only part of a more complicated mosaic of voting behaviour. The USA and the UK, to take these two examples, are certainly deeply divided societies. Trump and Brexit, on one level, can be seen as a clash of two cultures: one pluralist, liberal, and broadly cosmopolitan, and the other closed and nationalistic. On a different level, the colliding cultures are not underpinned by clear-cut groups. White working-class Labour voters did not overwhelmingly vote 'Leave' in the referendum of 26 June 2016. It is now evident that some 70% of Labour voters voted 'Remain'. While the majority of Labour Remain voters were middle class, the majority of conservative voters, who are middle or lower-middle class, voted Leave. Low-income households did vote in large numbers to leave the EU, even if they were voting against their own economic interests.[6] Similarly in the USA, Trump supporters are not all poor or working-class white voters. Education is certainly more of a marker of pro-Brexit and pro-Trump in that, on the whole, people without university education voted for Brexit and Trump in greater numbers. However, education – along with age – alone is only part of the picture, and, while important, it does not account for the wider societal divide. Many not so well-off white working people are vehemently opposed to Trump, and this is also the case with Brexit.

According to MacWilliams, in a study on Trump supporters, one statistical variable tops all others, including education, gender, age, ideology, religiosity even fear

The crisis of the present **223**

of terrorism, namely, authoritarianism (cited in Gordon 2018: 46; see MacWilliams 2016). MacWilliams's study, which recalls *The Authoritarian Personality*, was based on key questions that were designed to elicit authoritarian tendencies pertaining to child-rearing. Respondents who reflected authoritarian approaches were predominantly Trump supporters. Now, while this might invite some skepticism if the conclusion is that views on child-rearing led to specific political outcomes, it has the merit of highlighting a key societal phenomenon, namely, authoritarianism. Rather than conclude that there is a specific psychological personality, a more interesting conclusion, as Gordon argues, is that 'the authoritarian personality signifies not merely a type but an emergent and generalized feature of modern society as such' (Gordon 2018: 47). As Adorno also argued, authoritarism cannot be explained by recourse to ideology as such, but takes on a political form as result of social conditions, including the disappointment with modernity (Adorno 2019b).

Much of the current discussion on Brexit, Trump, and related events and movements in other countries – Bolsonaro, a Brazilian version of Trump – focuses on populism (see for example Müller 2016). Some of this literature offers important perspectives on what are undoubtedly right-wing populist movements, which, while differing greatly have much in common (for example, anti-elite/anti-establishment, anti-migration, nationalistic and xenophobic, and so on). Clearly, Trumpism and Brexit are highly complicated and can be adequately explained by recourse to several causes coming together. However, the thesis suggested in this chapter is that more attention should be placed on authoritarianism as a key feature not only of these political figures and movements but of their underlying societal reality. A consideration of the movements/leaders, ideologies, and voting behaviour alone does not provide sufficient insight into the social preconditions nor the societal trends that make possible such events.

The notion of populism suggests a misleading contrast between democracy and anti-democracy. The spectre of a new era of populist politics is often seen as a reflection of a crisis in democracy for which the antidote is more democracy. There is some truth to this in that liberal democracy appears to be in crisis so far as the mainstream centre left and centre right are no longer as stable as they once were. However, it is highly misleading and a failure to understand the nature of populist politics to see populism as contrary to democracy. The simple reality is that the current wave of right-wing populism is precisely a product of democracy.[7] In this respect, the Frankfurt School perspective needs some re-adjustment. Although Adorno and other critical theorists recognized that the post-1945 western world had defeated fascism and democracy was ascendant, they were writing at a time when democracy was relatively newly established and the ghost of totalitarianism was still present. In southern Europe dictatorships still prevailed, and Central and Eastern Europe was, of course, under the heel of a totalitarian power. The circumstances today are different: right-wing populism is a product of democracy and, at least in Europe, has been nurtured by European integration. Two of the most virulent authoritarian movements of recent times, Trump and Brexit, occurred in long-standing stable liberal democracies. For this reason, right-wing populism is

224 Space, memory and legacies of history

best seen as a form of authoritarian democracy and a contrast to dictatorial forms of political authoritarianism, which can be termed democratic authoritarianism.[8] The later refers to political orders that are primarily authoritarian in the sense of being close to dictatorship with only minimal democratic principles or where democracy is reduced to cosmetic roles (as in Russia under Putin or Egypt under Sisi). These countries cannot seriously be considered functioning democracies, even if they claim to be or are nominally democracies. In contrast, a pervasive trend in the western world, where liberal democracy is well established, as in the UK and USA, is the emergence of authoritarianism.

Authoritarian democracy – as represented by Trump and Bolsonaro – may be regressive but is a product of democracy even if its supporters and its policies display anti-democratic tendencies. Brexit is also a reflection of such regressive tendencies within democracy. It is a mistake to see these phenomena as contrary to democracy, which does not exist in a pure form. There is nothing in the essential nature of democracy to prevent people from being authoritarian or having anti-democratic values. Democracy can nurture such syndromes, especially when it is bereft of critical public debate. It is evident that in the age of post-truth politics, fake news, and 'alternative facts', reality-TV and social media as sources of news for the majority of people that the quality of democracy will suffer. Both Trumpism and Brexit are vivid examples of such regression. Nonetheless, such forms of regression do not simply come from themselves but from the erosion of the social foundations of democracy, which to function properly requires, to follow Habermas, a functioning public sphere, which in turn requires a relatively intact life-world. Several decades of corrosive neoliberalism and global capitalism have undermined these societal presuppositions.

Societal regression: excursus on Brexit as a pathology of democracy

There are so many facets to Brexit that any single account will be problematical and possibly overtaken by events. It is evident that Brexit is not a stable phenomenon but is protean and highly volatile. Trump may be voted out of office; Brexit may collapse under the weight of its contradictions. It is as much in the future as in the past, since it is unlikely to end when, or if at all, the UK leaves the EU. Brexit is constituted not just by the discourses that produced it – Euroscepticism and social discontent – but also by the ones that have come about since June 2016, which include Europhilia and a realization of the diminished significance of the UK. But it also includes an intensification of pro-Brexit positions and a radicalization of Euroscepticism. Looking at Brexit from the perspective of the present time, mid-2019, rather than the circumstances prior to June 2016, suggests one major question that needs further critical reflection, namely, how did it come about that a virulent authoritarian right-wing political ideology within the Conservative Party succeeded in convulsing not only the Westminster political system but brought about a fundamental transformation in the wider society, such that British society

The crisis of the present **225**

is now not only polarized around Brexit, but defined by it. The politics of Brexit penetrate deep into the fabric of everyday life. Few ideologies have this capacity. How is this possible? One possible answer is that it is not due to the rational appeal of an ideology as such but can be accounted for by the rise of authoritarian currents that are exacerbated by the politics of Brexit.

But what is Brexit? There can be no doubt that Brexit is primarily a right-wing political project in which neoliberals and authoritarian English nationalists join forces. Despite the attraction Brexit has for some far left-leaning Labour MPs, it is a product of English (not British) nationalism and has its primary support with older Conservative Party voters. It is this English nationalism, which has been relatively dormant despite occasional moments of activity, that has now surfaced as a triumphant force and has gained, to a large degree by default, considerable support. Justifications and counter-discourses abound such that almost everything has to be positioned in terms of the ever-shifting codes of Brexit. These trends are not entirely new or recent; it is simply that they come to the fore so prominently as a result of the referendum and, since the Trump presidency, the global rise of the radical right.

There can be no example of a self-inflicted catastrophe of such monumental proportions as the exit from the single market, quite aside from all the complex ramifications of the dysfunctional process of withdrawal. There was no reason why Euroscepticism could not have been contained within the Conservative Party. It is arguably plausible that the referendum outcome, if managed differently, might have led to a less polarized society. A variation of the Norway model (membership of the single market without full EU membership) might have been an acceptable compromise in the aftermath of the referendum, but the stakes have been raised to a point that whatever post-Brexit form the UK morphs into the radical conservative right will be dissatisfied.

Brexit, in its current convulsed condition, was by no means inevitable, and one should not forget that the outcome of the referendum was a marginal victory which could easily have been the other way around. It is almost certainly the case that the impact of social media, harnessed by the better-funded campaign of Leave, produced 3 million additional votes that would not otherwise have been the case. This is important in that it was a highly contingent phenomenon and not a tidal wave of the masses rebelling against the elites. But, then, it can be said that many major revolutions or transformative events were also contingent on a number of elements coming together at a specific time. A striking feature of Brexit is the particular combination of contingent events, political-economic realities, and discursive constructions that led to the unfolding of Brexit in its particular trajectory.

A facet of Brexit that has not been sufficiently addressed, if at all, and which is certainly of major sociological interest, is the problem of how societies – or larger entities, such as the EU, or smaller ones, such as cities and regions – make collective decisions about their future. Parliamentary democracy is not designed for this task since it is designed for majority decision-making where small majorities are the norm. It is more or less impossible for referendums to produce majorities

226 Space, memory and legacies of history

of the size, so-called super-majorities, that would be needed to make compelling decisions, which is what they are supposed to achieve. The UK, like most countries, is a representative democracy whereby elected representatives make decisions in complex arrangements between the executive and the legislature. The instrument of a nation-wide consultative referendum (there were only two prior such national referendums, and both produced results that confirmed the status quo) in producing an outcome that was contrary to the status quo but without a sufficiently large majority led to a crisis without end since there was no effective means to translate the outcome into the decision-making structures of parliamentary democracy. Referendums on major open-ended questions easily result in increasing uncertainty rather than certainty and thus contribute to the very forces that give rise to the need for the referendum in the first place. This is quite obviously because there are no mechanisms in place to decide on the multiple possible interpretations of what, in this case, 'leave' means. The question posed did not contain an answer but an invitation to ask more questions. The result of the unspecified alternative that the nation was asked to vote on was a plethora of Brexits. There is the additional paradox that Brexit ceases to be a means to an end, which it was originally supposed to be, but becomes the end in itself.

There are two sociological points here. One is the problem, possibly the impossibility, of establishing legitimate collective decisions in the context of complex and pluralist contemporary societies, especially one that is internally fractured such as is the UK. For such collective decisions to be possible, equally complex constitutional and democratic structures need to be in place. But these exist only for the purpose of electing governments. The attempt to create a collective decision only results in regression. The second problem is how to reverse a mistake to prevent a regression. A bad government can be thrown out at the next election. The results of a referendum cannot be reversed, unless a system is designed for run-off referendums or more robust arrangements for representative and plebiscitarian forms of democracy to connect as opposed to clash. Brexit has been a colossal error, but it appears that it cannot be reversed. Leaving the EU entails the reversal of systemic structures – legal, economic, social, and political – created over the past four decades. The British society that existed before the early 1970s does not exist anymore. It has been systemically transformed by Europeanization. Reversion to a pre-1970s Britain is not possible, and attempts to turn the clock back will result in regressive outcomes.

It is clear to anyone looking at the debacle from the outside that Brexit needs to be corrected, though the point at which correction might be possible without irreparable damage has probably been passed. Most pro-Brexit politicians have not claimed Brexit is a good cause. The sole defence of the indefensible is that the outcome of the referendum must be implemented regardless of the consequences, since it is supposedly a 'decision' of a 'people'. Brexit has thus become a trap: it is taken to be a decision, and in any of its possible forms it leads to undesirable outcomes for which there are no measures to rescind. It is also obvious that the arcane parliamentary motions and meaningful and non-meaningful votes (some of which are in the domain of the absurd) that the mechanisms do not exist to deal with the problem. What is the problem?

The problem, in essence, is embarking on major societal restructuring without a plan and without an assessment of the risks and outcomes. The Iraq war was one such monumental error that the British parliament made. It remains an extraordinary fact that it made another grave error with major consequences in 2015 in legislating for the referendum and passing the Withdrawal Bill. Nothing was learnt from Iraq about the folly of politicians. While the former PM, David Cameron, has been vilified for the high risk of holding the referendum, it must not be forgotten that it was parliament that voted for the Referendum Act, and the two major parties also endorsed the triggering of Article 50 without an inkling of a plan.

Brexit, of course, for many is supposed to be a moment of emancipation akin to a declaration of independence from a foreign power. It is thus supposed to be a constitutive moment in which the nation re-affirms itself. But as has now become evident that there is no British nation, only post-imperial fantasies of an imagined and irrecoverable past. Whatever divisions existed in the disunited kingdom are now such that there is probably no return to the status quo. The cause of Scottish independence will be increased, and the unification of Ireland is only a matter of demographic time. England will discover the costs of a nationalism that has already enhanced the socio-economic and socio-cultural divisions and engendered new pathologies. Brexit has opened a Pandora's box of toxic elements that go beyond the societal divisions that pre-existed Brexit. For this reason, Brexit is not entirely explained by societal divisions even if these constituted the societal conditions of its possibility. This would not explain how the phenomenon has morphed into new, pathological, and regressive forms. In any case, the societal divisions have increased as a result of Brexit, which is perhaps best seen as an expression of authoritarian currents in society. In that respect, it has much in common with Trumpism.

At this point another and wider claim can be ventured. What sustains democratic authoritarianism is a negative logic by which it is defined against the rest of society, namely, the liberal, pluralist mainstream. This is perfectly illustrated by Brexit. While Brexit is ideologically defined by opposition to the European Union, it is quite clearly more than a simple condition of Euroscepticism that will vanish when and if the UK leaves the EU. As evidenced by the rise in hate crimes, anti-migration legislation, the positive embracing of economic harm, and so on, it is clear that it is also a political project that has a wider aim, namely, to reverse several decades of progressive politics, pluralism, and cosmopolitan orientations. Such currents have been intermeshed with neoliberal policies so that they are often difficult to disentangle. This is why Brexit offers for some a revolt against neoliberal austerity politics, while for others it is a strategy to advance aggressive nationalism. For others it is a ploy to erode democracy and the rule of law and order to advance a new neoliberal project. The contradictory logics of the previous decades – neoliberalism and cultural pluralism – have become de-coupled with Brexit: the cosmopolitan and pluralist currents have become the target. This paradoxically allows, except possibly

228 Space, memory and legacies of history

for the Eurosceptic left, neoliberalism off the hook. Thus, the Conservative Party continues to pursue Brexit, which for many of its champions is a way in which to pursue a new era of British neoliberalism models on imperial nostalgia.

Similar dynamics are present with Trump and Bolsonaro, who are also products of democracy; however illiberal it may be, it is nonetheless democracy. Both pursue neoliberal policies while invoking authoritarian values and have widespread appeal to voters who hold authoritarian values. The Brazilian case is a reminder that opposition to minorities is a necessary feature of authoritarianism. In this case, since migrants do not exist in significant numbers, the functional equivalent is fulfilled by the gay community. Hence Bolsonaro's obsession with homosexuality, a characteristic, too, of Putin's Russia, as noted by Snyder (2018). While the targeting of minorities is a major dimension of authoritarian democracy – even in the case of Brexit Britain where it is contrary to the interests of the economy – the true 'other' are not marginalized minorities – but the 'other half' of the population, (i.e. those who are anti-authoritarian). This logic is an illustration of what Horkheimer and Adorno understood by anti-Semitism as an instrument of domination in that it was always more than opposition to Jews. It facilitated the mobilization of an apparatus of domination over society as a whole.

So, in every possible sense, current trends towards right-wing populism are symptomatic of a regression within democratic orders whereby democracy nurtures anti-democratic orientations and cultivates pathologies in social behaviour as well as in social policies.

Conclusion

In this chapter, I have stressed the usefulness of the critical theory notion of authoritarianism as a way to make sense of the rise of right-wing populism. The original conception in *The Authoritarian Personality* offers important insights but needs to be modified in light of some of the difficulties with the psychological and psychoanalytical approach adopted. The wider theoretical framework of the Frankfurt School alone is also insufficient to account for the genesis of authoritarianism. The conundrum is that authoritarianism as a societal syndrome that has considerable appeal to certain individuals and social groups can account for regressive trends in society and politics – Trumpism, Brexit, right-wing populism, hate crimes, post-truth, and so on – but the phenomenon cannot explain itself. *The Authoritarian Personality* study solved this problem by attributing causal power to the psychological dispositions within the mindset of individuals but does not account for large numbers of people having such dispositions in the first instance. This goes a long way in showing how fascist movements or fascist leaders or demagogues alone do not cause fascism but are part of a spectrum of elements, which include psycho-social forces. So, what might be a cause of authoritarianism? In order to account for authoritarianism in terms of widespread dispositions or attitudes latent in the population, recourse to other explanations is necessary.

The crisis of the present **229**

A key factor, I suggest, is breakdowns in social integration. To take up Habermas's theory of social versus system integration, as discussed in Chapter 3, the integration of societies rests on a balance between social forms of integration functioning according to their internal life-world logics, but, when these break down, regression can result when crises are not overcome. Habermas saw such regression caused by the 'colonization of the life-world' by systemic forces or in situations where the systemic integration becomes the dominant form of societal integration. This perspective undoubtedly accounts for many social pathologies – for example, the destruction of communities, excessive consumption, burn-out from over-work, the impact of austerity policies – but it does not account for pathologies generated from within the life-world. To account for regressive forms of social integration that are internal to the life-world one can distinguish between negative and positive forms of integration. The latter are forms of integration that are inclusive and designed to enhance well-being and social worth; the former are forms of integration that seek to exclude and marginalize people. Viewed in such terms, negative forms of integration generate social pathologies and require reactionary values such as those associated with authoritarianism. Such forms of integration are not derived directly from what Habermas referred to as the colonization of the life-world, since they derive from the life-world, but can be provoked by it, as in, for example, the ways in which deprivation nurtures violence and hatred. Authoritarianism is likely to be deeply rooted in social milieus or a life-world that has not developed autonomous forms of life and which rely to a considerable extent on negative integration. In this perspective, the wider societal context is essential to understand authoritarianism, which cannot be reduced neither to the psychology of specific groups nor to capitalism as such. There is also the example of information overload. Today, with information technologies of all kinds, there is more and more information available and with this comes more and more options. But the abundance of information does not lead to people making more enlightened choices. It leads to regressive desires for new kinds of authority, which are easily satisfied by demagogues and a politics of closure nurtured by fantasy and revenge.

The notion of a breakdown in social integration and societal crisis also requires explanation. While the societal preconditions for the rise of neo-authoritarian politics in many parts of the world vary considerably, a major part of an explanation must reside in the pervasive impact of the negative consequences of four decades of neoliberalism, which had the effect of eroding the social foundations of many societies due to the growth of social inequality, the declining prospects not only for the working class but also for the middle class, the erosion of social solidarity as a result of the spread of markets into all spheres of social life, and increased social polarization. This situation, coupled with increased migration, nurtured a culture and consequently a politics of envy and resentment against migrants and against those who appeared to prosper from the new times. Social polarization is reflected in political polarization. Neoliberalism, as noted by Nancy Fraser, has two faces, a culturally progressive one (as reflected in the policies and figures of Bill Clinton

230 Space, memory and legacies of history

and Barack Obama) and a reactionary one as reflected in Trump. The latter's success is due to a considerable extent on the confluence of reactionary neo-conservatism and neoliberalism, for neoliberalism no longer sustains itself on its own, as Wendy Brown has persuasively shown with respect to Trumpism (Brown 2019). As argued in Chapters 4 and 5, neoliberalism is alive and, if not particularly well, is sustaining itself with the help of a radicalized and reactionary social conservatism that has jettisoned partnership with progressive cultural politics. What we have here, to follow Brown, then, is a cultural divide within the right (Brown 2019: 90–3). This divide has played out on a number of fronts and also takes global forms. Some of the major currents would include working class and middle-class reaction to the negative effects of globalization; radicalization among migrants fuelling the Islamist movement; the radicalization of white supremacist movements; the radicalization of nationalism. While such currents are varieties of right-wing ideology, they can easily coalesce with left-wing dissatisfaction with the *status quo* (as the example of Brexit and recent developments in Italian politics). Paradoxically there is a certain convergence with neoliberalism, which, while not causing such currents of rage, created the conditions for their emergence.

I would like to conclude the present discussion with a few remarks on whether the current wave of authoritarian politics, which is what I think it should be called, can be understood by analogy with the 1930s. I disagree with the temptation to see in the present a revival of fascism. While on one level, it is clear that Trump exemplifies the traits of the fascist figure – narcissistic, aggressive, racist, and authoritarian – a sociological perspective requires a wider view of the social and political situation beyond the cult of leaders and their styles of political communication. The rise of neo-fascist movements and the ascendency of the global extreme right suggest some parallels with the 1930s. However, in my view this is the wrong interpretation. Neo-authoritarianism today is different in that it is not primarily a product of fascism and does not necessarily lead towards totalitarianism. Europe in the 1930s witnessed the rise of totalitarianism of the right and the left. The present situation is fundamentally different. Totalitarianism has more or less vanished from the world as a whole. What has survived are varieties of authoritarian political orders. Democracy as such is not in question in the way that it was in the 1930s. In this period, the democracies that did exist were few and fragile, many only products of the post-1918 period. It is true that fascists such as Hitler and Mussolini acquired power through the democratic process, but this was not comparable to today when democracy is on a stronger footing, however much it may have been de-stabilized by Trumpism and Brexit. In any case, once elected, Hitler immediately abolished the shambles of Weimar democracy. Trump has not been able to do this and probably does not wish to become a dictator. Moreover, the 1930s was a period of major re-armament and the creation of militias that gave fascism powers that it otherwise lacked. Additionally, Hitler and Mussolini benefited from what were initially successful economic policies that solved the major economic issue of the day, namely, unemployment and spiraling inflation. The global context is also fundamentally different. Fascism succeeded to a large degree because of the spectre of communism.

The western liberal democracies were petrified by the rise of the USSR and the potential for communism to spread. Fascism was a more attractive option, which led to the liberal democracy standing by rather than aiding the republican government in Spain following Franco's defeat of the new democracy.

Perhaps there is one other significant factor. The post-1945 period witnessed the worldwide spread of democracy and the advancement of considerable social progress in health, education, egalitarianism, and science (see Chapter 6). Despite set-backs, the societal learning processes that have occurred are not easily reversed. The emergence of neo-authoritarianism as a significant reality today has to contend with the reality also of anti-authoritarianism (Witoszek 2018). The conflict between these two syndromes closely corresponds with one of the major cleavages in contemporary society, namely, a closed nationalistic conception of political community and an open one based on pluralism and cosmopolitanism. The latter was weak in the 1930s, though by no means absent (Harrington 2016). Today progressive politics and anti-authoritarianism is arguably in a stronger position than the forces of neo-authoritarianism, which arguably have a limited capacity to lead to world wars. Ultimately, this is what makes the current situation different from the 1930s. The disaster of the Iraq War has quenched the thirst for war in the UK and USA and in many other countries that supported the 2003 war. The left is in crisis today, as it was in the 1930s, but the circumstances are radically different. In the 1930s social democracy was in its infancy and contested by communism, while today social democracy may be in decline but most countries have been shaped by more than a half century of social protectionism. Nonetheless, both neo-authoritarianism today and fascism in the 1930s do have one thing in common, namely, the crisis of authority. Both are solutions to the crisis of authority, and, while the causes are different, they are products of the changed relations between economic conditions, cultural practices, socio-psychological traits, and political actors.

Notes

1 For accounts, see Jay (1973), Wheatland (2009).
2 Brewster Smith (1997), Hyman and Sheatsley (1954), Stone et al (1993), Roiser and Willig (2002).
3 For a clear account of the Freudian background to *The Authoritarian Personality*, see Adorno's reflections in an essay in 1951 (Adorno 1982).
4 The '*Remarks on The Authoritarian Personality*', written in English in 1948 as the project drew to a close, have now been published in a foreword to the new edition of *The Authoritarian Personality* (Adorno 2019a).
5 In addition to Peter Gordon's invaluable essay on the contemporary relevance of *The Authoritarian Personality*, see also the special issue of the *South Atlantic Quarterly* (Marasco 2018).
6 See the Joseph Rowntree Report (1916). www.jrf.org.uk/report/brexit-vote-explained-poverty-low-skills-and-lack-opportunities. On Brexit, see also Evans and Menon (2017) and Outhwaite (2017).
7 See Heitmeyer (2019), who sees right-wing populism as a form of authoritarian radical nationalism.
8 On democratic authoritarianism, see Brancati (2014) and Zakaria (1997). I have also discussed this in Chapter 15 of *Formations of European Modernity*, 2nd edition, 2018, London: Palgrave.

232 Space, memory and legacies of history

References

Adorno, T. 1982 [1951]. Freudian Theory and the Pattern of Fascist Propaganda. In: Arato, A. and Gephardt, E. (eds.) *The Essential Frankfurt School Reader*. London: Bloomsbury.

Adorno, T. 1998 [1959]. What Does Coming to Terms with the Past Mean? In: *Critical Models: Interventions and Catchwords*. New York: Columbia University Press.

Adorno, T. W. 2019a [1948]. Remarks on the Authoritarian Personality. In: Adorno, T. W., Frenkel-Brunswik, E., Levinson, E. and Sanford, R. N. (eds.) *The Authoritarian Personality*. London: Verso.

Adorno, T. W. 2019b. *Aspekte des Neuen Rechts-radicalismus*. Berlin: Suhrkamp.

Adorno, T. W., Frenkel-Brunswik, E., Levinson, E. and Sanford, R. N. 2019 [1950]. *The Authoritarian Personality*. London: Verso.

Adorno, T. W. and Horkheimer, M. 1979 [1944]. *Dialectic of Enlightenment*. London: Verso.

Benjamin, W. 1973. The Work of Art in the Age of Mechanical Reproduction. In: *Illuminations*. London: Fontana.

Brancati, D. 2014. Democratic Authoritarianism: Origins and Effects. *Annual Review of Political Science*, 17 (3): 313–26.

Brewster Smith, M. 1997. *The Authoritarian Personality*: Re-Review 46 Years on. *Political Psychology*, 18 (1): 159–63.

Brown, W. 2019. *In the Ruins of Neoliberalism: The Rise of Antidemocratic Politics in the West*. New York: Columbia University Press.

Evans, G. and Menon, A. 2017. *Brexit and British Politics*. Cambridge: Polity Press.

Freud, S. 1974 [1921]. *Group Psychology and the Analysis of the Ego*. London: Hogarth Press.

Fromm, E. 1963 [1955]. *The Sane Society*. New York: Rinehart and Winston.

Fromm, E. 1984. *The Working Class in Weimar Germany: A Psychological and Sociological Study*. Oxford: Berg.

Fromm, E. 2010 [1991]. *The Pathology of Normalcy*. Riverdale, NY: AMHF.

Gordon, P. 2018. The Authoritarian Personality Revisited. In: Brown, W., Gordon, P. and Pensky, M. (eds.) *Authoritarianism: Three Inquiries in Critical Social Theory*. Chicago, IL: Chicago University Press.

Gordon, P. 2019 [1950]. Introduction. In: Adorno, T. W., Frenkel-Brunswik, E., Levinson, E. and Sanford, R. N. (eds.) *The Authoritarian Personality*. London: Verso.

Harrington, A. 2016. *German Cosmopolitan Social Thought and the Idea of the West*. Cambridge: Cambridge: Cambridge University Press.

Heitmeyer, W. 2019. *Autoritäre Versuchungen: Signaturen der Bedrohung 1*. Berlin: Frankfurt.

Horkheimer, M., Fromm, E. and Marcuse, H. 1936. *Studien über Autorität und Familie*. Paris: Alcan.

Hyman, H. and Sheatsley, B. 1954. The Authoritarian Personality: A Methodological Critique. In: Christie, R. and Jahoda, M. (eds.) *Studies in the Scope and Method of the Authoritarian Personality*. Glencoe, IL: Free Press.

Jay, M. 1973. *The Dialectical Imagination: A History of the Frankfurt School and the Institute of Social Research, 1923–1950*. London: Heinemann.

MacWilliams, M. 2016. *The Rise of Trump: America's Authoritarian Spring*. Amherst: Amherst College Press.

Marasco, R. (ed.) 2018. The Authoritarian Personality. Special Issue of *The South Atlantic Quarterly*. Durham: Duke University Press.

Marcuse, H. 1970. The Obsolescence of the Freudian Concept of Man. In: *Five Lectures: Psychoanalysis, Politics, and Utopia*. Boston: Beacon Press.

Müller, J-W. 2016. *What Is Populism?* Philadelphia: University of Pennsylvania University Press.

Müller-Doohm, D. 2005. *Adorno: A Biography*. Cambridge: Polity Press.

Outhwaite, W. (ed.) 2017. *Brexit Sociological Responses*. London: Anthem Press.

Roiser, M. and Willig, C. 2002. The Strange Death of the Authoritarian Personality: 50 Years of Psychological and Political Debate. *History of the Human Sciences*, 15 (4): 71–96.

Snyder, T. 2018. *The Road to Unfreedom: Russia, Europe, America*. London: Bodley Head.

Stone, W., Lederer, G. and Christie, R. (eds.) 1993. *Strength and Weakness: The Authoritarian Personality Today*. New York: Springer.

Tucker, A. 2015. *The Legacies of Totalitarianism: A Theoretical Framework*. Cambridge: Cambridge University Press.

Wheatland, T. 2009. *The Frankfurt School in Exile*. Minneapolis: University of Minnesota Press.

Witoszek, N. 2018. *The Origins of Anti-Authoritarianism*. London: Routledge.

Zakaria, F. 1997. The Rise of Illiberal Democracy. *Foreign Affairs*, 76 (6): 22–43.

12

CONCLUSION

On the future

Implicit in the critical theory tradition is a strong orientation to the future. Hope for a better future exerts a critical stance towards the present. As a 'diagnosis of the times', critical theory seeks to illuminate the hold of the past over the present in order for future possibilities to be realized. It seeks to break the spell of the past and overcome pathologies and regressions in societal organization and in thinking. Yet, it is clear that critical theory has had relatively little to say on the future. It has been mostly concerned with the grip of the past on the present.[1] Nonetheless, the future played a role in beckoning beyond the present and the immediate past.

In the works of Adorno, Horkheimer, Marcuse, and Benjamin, the idea of a better future was a major part of their conception of critique. The future is also something that we have a responsibility for, rather than being predetermined or residing in an unrealizable utopia. However, it remained at most a hope. As is perhaps most clear in the writings of Benjamin, the future is revealed only in revisiting the past where 'traces of what was to become' can be found in those fleeting moments of consciousness and often only expressed in allegories. The utopian impulse was of course most strongly present in the writings of Ernst Bloch as it was in the work of Herbert Marcuse, who wrote of the promise of happiness as the source of what was left of the revolutionary temperament. Habermas's notion of learning processes suggests an opening to the future that does not simply rest on utopia. Apel also concretized the appeal to the future when he wrote about the need for a macro ethics of responsibility for the future (Apel 1987). Honneth's theory of struggles for recognition would see social struggles as a key dynamic for the making of new societies, though in this rendition the future is more strongly seen as a continuation of the present. To make a general claim, the history of critical theory reveals a notion of the future as a potentiality within the present but can be realized only through forms of critical thought and action that are able to conceive of alternatives to the present.

Conclusion **235**

In this concluding reflection, I argue that critical theory will need to develop a clearer sense of how it sees the future. What kind of society will emerge in the future? What are likely social transformations to come that will shape the future? How should the future be conceived? Much of the current debate in critical theory is focussed on the problem of progress (Allen 2016). Now, while this is clearly one of the principal ways the future has been conceptualized in modern social and political thought, it is the not the only one. As noted in Chapter 1, Adorno in a late essay appeared to go beyond the critique of progress in the *Dialectic of Enlightenment* when he wrote that the 'concept of progress requires critical confrontation with real society' (Adorno 1998: 148). If he was critical of the idea of progress, it was because of its lack of conceptual clarity: 'Even more than other concepts, the concept of progress dissolves upon attempts to specify its exact meaning, for instance what progresses and what does not' (p. 143). Benjamin also rejected the idea of progress (Benjamin 1999: 473–80). In the Arcades Project, he affirmed the centrality of catastrophe in thinking about the present and future: 'The concept of progress must be grounded in the idea of catastrophe. That things are "status quo" is the catastrophe. It is not an ever-present possibility but what in each case is given' (Benjamin 1999: 473). For this reason, it seems to me to be a pointless endeavor either to rescue or reject the notion of progress, which was never central to the intellectual framework of critical theory, which operates with a different conception of the future as latency and potentiality. The concept of progress is too undifferentiated, quite aside from the received perception of western supremacy.[2] Moreover, as I have argued, critical theory has always subordinated the notion of progress to societal learning from historical catastrophe.

The concept of the future has been given insufficient attention more generally in social and political theory. Bertrand de Jouvenel's, *The Art of Conjecture,* is a classic text on a particular understanding of the future as social forecasting (2017 [1964/1967]. The French philosopher de Jouvenel was concerned with the importance of understanding future events as determined by present circumstances and the need to go beyond unreasoned exercises of the imagination. His defence of forecasting was an antidote to the dangers of utopianism as well as deluded claims that are unfounded by reasoned inquiry. This approach to the future naturally lent itself to the predictive rationality that critical theory generally criticized, even though it was not envisioned as a form of instrumental rationality. However, it should be noted, as discussed earlier in this book, that Habermas in his 1968 book, *Knowledge and Human Interests*, argued that prediction and control is precisely the role of the natural sciences (Habermas 1987). He disagreed only with the predictive model as one appropriate for the social sciences.

The Art of Conjecture gave a central place to human agency in determining the future. The future as such is unknown, and a wide range of future possibilities exist. These can be controlled through knowledge. So, in one sense the future is that which comes after the present, but in another less temporal sense the future can be controlled by human beings acting in the present. The future thus serves as a way through which the present is prolonged.

236 Space, memory and legacies of history

A striking contrast to de Jouvenel's view of the future, which gave little place to utopia or the imagination, is Cornelius Castoriadis's notion of the 'imaginary', which is a future-oriented projection that all institutions, and more generally all societies, have to varying degrees. Modern societies, in particular, have a strong vision of their future. They are founded on social imaginaries, and underlying them is a more fundamental radical imaginary that made possible their initial creation. His major work, *The Imaginary Institution of Society,* made a seminal contribution to the idea of the future (1987 [1975]). Castoriadis offered a very different vision to that of de Jouvenel's somewhat conservative concern with the need to master future events. For Castoriadis, the task for critical thought is to articulate a new radical imaginary that could be the basis of a new social imaginary and thus make possible new kinds of social organization, or what he called new kinds of social instituting (see also Adams et al. 2017).

Another classic text on the idea of the future is Reinhart Koselleck's 1976 essay, 'Space of Experience and Horizon of Expectation'. For Koselleck these are categories that make possible history. Expectations are of the present about the future, which is made concrete. Modern societies have expanded the horizon of expectations beyond what has been previously experienced. This conception of the future introduces a stronger sense of rupture in historical continuity in that the future must be not only different from the past, but it must be better and it must be realized in the present. With modernity, the actual space of experience is also changing such that new expectations emerge. Koselleck thus provides a conception of the future as one of expectation. This is different from Castoriadis's social imaginary in that he sees the first manifestation of the redefinition of experience and expectation in the Enlightenment's idea of progress. The dimension of radical transformation is thus domesticated. Koselleck's concerns with the emergence of modernity were confined to a politically conservative conceptual history, as is also apparent from his other well-known book, *Critique and Crisis* (Koselleck 1988). However, his essay has been highly influential in social theory and offers a way to envisage current transformations in consciousness, but which cannot be understood by reference to the older idea of progress.

Since 1986 with the publication of Ulrich Beck's, *The Risk Society,* the idea of the future underwent a major revision (Beck 1992). It is now to be conceived less as a narrative of progress or of utopia. Expectations of a better future were shattered by a sense of the future as already realized in the present. Modern societies have become risk societies in that human agents have created the dangers facing them, as opposed to pre-modern societies where dangers mostly derived from natural occurrences. In risk societies, the future is ever present as potential hazards or catastrophes emanating from modern society. The future is therefore only a matter of calculating and mitigating the risks, the most significant of which are environmental ones. This idea of the future as a shock, which locates the future in the present, was famously first expressed in the book, *Future Shock,* in 1970 by Alvin Toffler. Published in the same year as the Chernobyl explosion, *Risk Society* captures a new sense of existential anxiety over the future and a strong contrast to the idea of the

Conclusion **237**

future as one of expectation. Beck's book also placed at the core of any account of the future the problem of knowledge because it is also a cognitive issue in how risks can be known, since many dangers are invisible and incorporate the phenomenological dimension of experience. Risks therefore require interpretation as they are not objective and real in ways that can be reduced to the art of forecasting, as in, for example, de Jouvenel's work. John Urry's final work, *What is the Future?*, is a significant work on how social science can reclaim the study of the future. In this work, he set out a broader vision of the study of the future that drew heavily on the implications of complex systems for the analysis of social futures, which are contested, varied, and uncertain. Such systems are also fragile and often characterized by innovation, unpredictability, and possible reversal (Urry 2016: 188).[3] Complexity-driven futures is an alternative future thinking based on the individualistic model of human action, but it is also an alternative to conventional approaches based on the relatively fixed and enduring economic and social structures that characterize the present. His position, influenced by Beck, differs in that it implies that the future is radically unknowable and irreducible to risks.

This is also present in Niklas Luhmann's theory of the future but in a much less political direction. According to Luhmann in a work on risk, 'modern society represents the future as risk' (Luhmann 2002: 37). The future for Luhmann loses normative significance since it cannot be known: 'The future can now be perceived only through its characteristics as more or less probable or more or less improbable. For the present this means that no one is in a position to claim knowledge of the future nor a capacity to change it' (Luhmann 2002: 48). This is also the problem that to know the future one would need more time than is realistically possible to acquire all relevant knowledge. The result is that the future is depoliticized (p. 44). In an earlier and seminal essay, 'The Future Cannot Begin', Luhmann emphasized the future as a rupture from the present. The modern concept of the future entails a rupture from the past and becomes an 'open future'. The future is experienced as a horizon of possibilities that disappear as we approach them. 'Future itself, and this means past futures as well as the present future, must now be conceived as possibly quite different from the past. It can no longer be characterized as approaching a turning point where it returns into the past or where the order of this world or even time itself is changed' (Luhmann 1976: 131).

On the basis of these disparate theoretical contributions to the idea of the future, the following is a proposal for a conceptual definition. The concept of the future, I suggest, has four main dimensions: it is a temporal, existential, normative, and epistemic condition. Different visions of the future play out through these dimensions.

The first and most important is that, like the past and present, it is primarily a temporal condition that like all temporal categories relates to the present (Luhmann 1976: 137). Whether the future is seen as something that has yet to occur or has already commenced, it is a form of time consciousness. The idea of the future is defined by its relation to the past and by its relation to the present. It may be seen as a radical rupture with the past and thus something fundamentally new and possibly unknowable. It may be seen as in continuity with the past, as suggested by the idea

238 Space, memory and legacies of history

of progress, namely, an accumulative view of the progress achieved in history. In this case, it is more easily knowable in that it is not seen as determined by events that have not yet occurred (see also Augé 2014). The future also stretches into infinity, since as a temporal condition it does not come to an end.

Clearly, the relation of the future to the past has a bearing on its relation to the present. If it entails a radical rupture, it will invariably involve a break from the present, but if there is a basic continuity in the relation to the past, there will be continuity with the present. The relation to the present will depend on how the present is understood; for example, if the present is seen in continuity with the past or if the present itself has broken from the past, as in the sense of a generational rupture. Or, an endless present may obliterate the very idea of the future as it has of the past. Some of these considerations relate to the time-scale that is bound up with the self-understanding of the present. For example, the common notion that the present began in 1945 suggests a not-to-distant future, but a long-scale present – say, beginning in 1789 – projects the future into a more distant time. However, if the future comes after the present, it may never be realized because the present will always redefine itself, thus re-setting the historical clock forever anew. In this case, there would be only a perpetual present with only the fiction of a future. It is obviously the case in the context of the Anthropocene that these timescales are considerably complicated since they involve the intersection of very different historical temporalities, from the history of human society, to earth or planetary history and biological history (see Chapter 7).

The second dimension is what I would call the existential dimension. The future is not only a temporal condition but has a deep existential and cognitive dimension to it. The existential perspective was put forward by Heidegger in *Being and Time* when he wrote in the section on 'The Temporality of Understanding' that 'if we are to provide a formally undifferentiated term for the future, we may use one which has designated the first structural item of care – the *"ahead of itself"*. Factically Dasein is constantly ahead of itself, but inconstantly anticipating with regard to its existentiell [sic] possibility' (Heidegger [1927] 1980: 386). It is arguably the case that the future is a concept that only makes sense with respect to humans. Only humans have a future. By this, I mean that the idea of the future is literally an idea, and as such it is manifest as a form of consciousness and cognition. Inanimate objects and most forms of non-human life do not have consciousness of a future as a reflective condition. Many of the more advanced non-humans do have consciousness and possess memory, however limited it is, but they do not have a sense of an individual, collective, or even planetary future. The scientific basis of this is the evolution of the prefrontal lobe cortex within the frontal lobe in the human brain, which is the part of the human brain that involves thinking about the future as well as abstract thought and is unique to humans.[4] For this reason, the idea of future is perhaps best seen as integral to the human condition. As such, it is a subjective condition and does not reside in objective facts but in experiences and interpretations of the human, social, and natural worlds.

Conclusion **239**

The third dimension follows from the previous in that in pertaining to existential experiences and cognitive capacities, the future is also normative and ethical. The belief that a better world is possible and that we have a duty to future generations is an ethical idea that is inseparable from the idea of the future. For this reason, the idea of the future is not only an inductive question of prediction or forecasting but is bound up with memory. The critical theory of Benjamin is particularly instructive in this respect. Benjamin shows how the future is discernible only in memory that have now receded into the past but which have meaning for the present. Although it is not what Benjamin had in mind, there is a physiological basis to the tie between memory and the orientation to the future. Humans have a developed memory in order for them to live for the future. (There is a physiological relation in the brain between memory and anticipating the future.) Planning, making, and imagining the future is the basis of human societies, which are all future oriented. Utopian thought is also an expression of this orientation to the future as are all modern movements. In sum, the future is an expectation that entails strong normative – ethical and by extension political – forces. It is ultimately underpinned by human agency.

The fourth dimension to be highlighted is the epistemic. Especially in light of Beck's and Luhmann's notion of the future reduced to the apprehension and managing of risks, whether real or imagined, the future is clearly a cognitive category in that it must be known. Forms of knowledge are designed to make the future knowable to the present. With this goes the notion of imagined futures. The imaginary component is central to all conceptions of the future, whether in the domain of space exploration[5] or in the very nature of capitalism (Beckert 2016; Beckert and Bronk 2018).

In addition to these four dimensions, a few other points should be mentioned. The future is also a cultural category in that it concretely exists in various cultural models. These will vary as do all cultural models in terms of different contexts. As John Urry has also argued, there is no single future as such but different trajectories. 'There is no empty future waiting to be filled' (Urry 2016: 190). However, the future is not reducible to cultural context in that today all forms of life are entangled in different ways and there are in addition irreducible universalistic principles and learning processes that are common to most, if not all, societies. So, while there are varieties of future consciousness and it is possible to speak of multiple futures, the underlying structures are often similar in that common logics are present, even if they are filtered in different ways. The implication, then, is that too much weight should not be given to cultural context; neither should the future be reduced to the imaginary dimension. The imaginary is one important dimension that shapes the future, but it is not the only one. Following Kant, Reason contains ideals and ideas but not imaginaries, which are forms of sensibility that are not based on rules and principles. Ideas, for instance, are not reducible to imaginaries in that they allow the present to understand itself and its future. Imaginaries embody creative visions of social possibility.[6] Visions of the future must therefore include reference

240 Space, memory and legacies of history

to expressions of Reason, such as the development of cultural models that contain learning levels and modes of cognition. There are many very different futures and many ways it is structured. The future is not singular but unfolds in different societal fields according to different modalities and trajectories. In terms of the formal aspects of a critical social theory of the future, there is the evolutionary nature of the future, which, however seen, is related to the evolution both of consciousness and learning mechanisms.

On the basis of the foregoing considerations for a critical theory of the future, a look at current debates and wider societal discourses reveals the following six ways in which the future has been framed in recent literature. The following sketch might be seen as a reconstruction of the idea of the future in contemporary consciousness.

First, a still dominant concept of the future undoubtedly retains the idea of progress. Even if the notion of progress is not always invoked, it is present and influential in liberal thought from the 'end of history' thesis to evolutionary psychology. One of the most compelling arguments for faith in the progressive capacity of modern society is the work of Steven Pinker, whose book, *The Better Angels of our Nature*, is perhaps the best statement and also one of the most compelling arguments from evolutionary psychology (Pinker 2011). Pinker in fact makes the case for evolutionary progress primarily on cultural rather than genetic grounds (see Chapter 9). This is not the place to enter into a discussion of the book and the merits of evolutionary psychology. It will suffice to comment that the book presents a powerful counter-argument to the received view, accepted by the Frankfurt School, that modernity brought an increase in violence and that western civilization tends towards barbarism. Pinker establishes the strongest argument for this position and then systematically demolishes it by referring to four areas of life in which modern society has evolved new dispositions that point to the inescapable conclusion of progress as measured by the decline of violence and barbarism. The four 'better angels of our nature' – a phrase used by Thomas Jefferson – that have prevailed over the darker forces that made violence normal in premodern societies are: the increase in empathy, self-control, the moral sense, and reason. Evolutionary dynamics lead to the development of psychological faculties that steer us from violence and lead people to coexist peacefully. Despite the obvious instances of violence over the past more than one hundred years, the earlier history of humanity displayed far greater levels of violence. Empathy has been significant in cultivating altruism and changes in the normative order of society; one of the greatest reductions of violence in history has been attributed to self-control; the moral sense has come to be increasingly important in regulating social interaction; the capacity for reason tends towards nonviolence solutions.

Pinker's book makes a strong argument for progress in history as an evolutionary and 'civilizing' process. However, a weakness is that it does not tell us much about the future other than it is likely to be a continuation of the forces that have made the present possible. The present and the near future in any case from this perspective acquire their positive character only in comparison to the earlier dark history of human civilization. The worst aspects of the present are only bad in contrast to

Conclusion **241**

an even worse history. The result is that the troubles of the present cannot be given prominence except in relation to the past and are therefore always going to be better since there is no golden age to which we can look back. This approach is clearly inadequate for a perspective on the future as anything other than a continuation of the present. It is possible to envisage a society that has eliminated violence but is otherwise unlivable, as in, for example, a fortress city or a dystopian futuristic city in which humans are the slaves of robots.

Second, related to the previous position, there is the dominant forecasting relation to the future. The conventional view of the future, as expressed also in de Jouvenel's book, is that it can be mastered through knowledge. Science and the capacity for calculation and prediction are the keys to understanding the future. This is the dominant modernization conception of societies as embarked on very similar journeys. It reflects the positivistic legacy of Enlightenment thought and the belief in a more or less singular and linear future. This is a view that the future is somehow discernible in observable data that depicts trends and leads to an emphasis on prediction and thus a basis for planning. It rests on an inductive conception of knowledge. Even in more complex forms, such as scenario-thinking and modelling, the future can be made to reveal itself. Such conceptions of the future are the basis of 'futurology' or 'future studies'.[7]

Third, as a reaction to the shortcoming of the previous, one of the most influential ways of relating to the future is the notion of a sustainable future. Since the Brundtland Report in 1987, *Our Common Future*, this has become an increasingly influential normative view of the future as something that needs to be created by collective political action. Unlike the first liberal view of the future, as in evolutionary psychology or the conventional notion of progress, the emphasis is placed not on the evolution of human nature and psychological dispositions and motivations but on the societal context and the need for macro-economic solutions to the problems that can be largely attributed to modernization and turbo-growth. The notion of sustainable development has come to be one of the main ways of relating to the future that questions the previous model, which more or less accepts current social and economic arrangements. Although, of course, not incompatible per se with forecasting, which is rather a means to an end, the idea of sustainable development is based on the affirmation of new ends, as for example, the notion of a 'green economy' or low-carbon futures. The assertion of new goals for contemporary societies requires rethinking of much of the taken-for-granted means. Thus, sustainable development has become one of the main policies for most states and international organizations (see Blewitt 2017; Sachs 2015). One can locate this in the wider context of the notion of risk as a way of relating to the future. However, the notion of 'a risk society' has been mostly absorbed into the pursuit of policies of sustainability, which has become a more all-embracing term. It can also be noted that there are more radical critics of sustainability, such as the view that a deeper transformation of contemporary societies is required rather than what is often a means to achieve an equilibrium between growth and ecological sustainability (see for example, Caradonna 2014; Foster 2015; Adloff and Neckel 2019). One such

242 Space, memory and legacies of history

position would be the rejection of growth itself and with it the notion of sustainability. (The Andean movement of *buen vivir* is just one example of a rejection of the national and global in favour of a model of harmony between local communities and nature.)

Four, the previously discussed modes of relating to the future see a strong continuity with the past and present. The future will not be fundamentally different from a certain view of the present. Despite the tendency for sustainability to call into question the received wisdom of the benefits of modernization, on the whole – aside from some radical positions – it does not fundamentally question growth. While setting new goals, it is more concerned with finding new means to realize the widely accepted goals – for example, finding non- or low-carbon forms of energy. A fourth and very different view of the future is the penchant for imagining disaster, as in Zizek's *Living in the End Times* (Zizek 2011). The future as catastrophe, to cite the title of Eva Horn's book, is clearly now a popular way of imagining the future. As Horn (2018) shows in her book, the fascination with doom is not a novel feature of the present but has been central to modernity. The idea of a planned future has often been associated with dystopia and, as discussed in Chapter 5, modern capitalism has often been seen as portending the end of society. It is also reflected in Schumpeter's theory of creative destruction, namely, the view that the future is realized through systems of innovation that require the sweeping away of the old (Schumpeter 2010). While creative destruction was in fact a positive view of the future, the vision of catastrophe reflects a sense of doom. The spectre of the apocalypse goes back to the roots of civilization. It has received a new impetus today with the idea of the Anthropocene. As discussed in Chapter 7, the Anthropocene may spell catastrophe for human societies in a not-too-distant future, but there is also a 'good Anthropocene' that can lead people to a new planetary ethic. Catastrophe thinking can be a way to awaken the present, as in Al Gore's book, *The Future* (Gore 2013; see also Smil 2008). In this context, there are also more historical perspectives on past catastrophes, such as the collapse of societies, including complex societies (see Diamond 2011; Tainter 1988). Recent expressions of catastrophe include Brexit and the 2008 financial crash.

Five, an alternative route to looking at the future avoids the temptations of catastrophism and can be termed techno-utopianism. If it has anything in common with received views about the future, it is an unbridled confidence of the capacity of science-driven technology to find solutions for current problems, in particular those relating to the question of new forms of energy and ecological challenges. It is also directly related to post-humanist conceptions of the human being as shaped by technology. Examples of techno-utopianism would include new initiatives by private enterprises to extract valuable minerals from asteroids and bring them back to earth. So far, twelve have been identified as suitable for mining and can be induced to approach the lunar or earth orbit. Space travel has also become the focus for a new generation of super-rich capitalists and embellished with visions of a post-human future beyond the earth. The melting of the icecaps on Mars by detonating hydrogen bombs has been proposed by Elon Musk as a technical feasibility that could release water for a future human settlement. By the end of this century, advances in self-replicating robots and in developments in nanotechnology will probably make possible the production of large quantities of graphene and carbon tubes that could be used for the construction of human settlements on Mars (see Kaku 2018). Less far-fetched examples of techno–utopianism would include climate engineering (Hamilton 2013).

Six, the alternative to the previous five positions is not easily specified, but in light of the foregoing, elements of a critical theory of the future can be outlined. I suggest that a critical theory of the future resides in part in a critique of existing perspectives and incorporates elements of them. I see this as having a stronger critical edge and a greater emphasis on a radical transformation of the present. Against the post-humanist position in much of techno-humanism, a critical theory of the future would place a stronger emphasis on the centrality of human agency and the future as determined by the present. In contrast to the temptations of catastrophism, the future can be shaped by human will and collective action. In view of the centrality of technology to any conception of the future, a more positive view of technology will also be required that goes beyond the notion of instrumental rationality, which, as we have seen in this book, was the dominant conception in the critical theory tradition of technology. Technology cannot be consigned to the domain of technique – that is the instrumental means to achieve goals – nor can it alone be the end itself (see Schatzberg 2018). Technology should rather be embraced as a creative, cultural, and social force that is integral to social organization and future possibility. From a critical theory perspective, the pertinent features of the future are those of conceivability and realizability. It is not something entirely imaginary nor is it inductively determined as in the social forecasting model. In Kantian terms, the future is shaped by certain preconditions, such as epistemic, cognitive, and normative structures and ideas, and so on; in left Hegelianism terms, the future is shaped by transformative processes including the action of human agents in the present.

I have not included this as a distinct current utopianism since it is present to varying degrees earlier (see Kumar 1987). Nor have I considered postmodernism, since this movement in western thought in the late twentieth century has not been primarily addressed to the future, other than to announce its irrelevance as a category of modernist thought.

The present discussion will conclude with a reflection on what kind of societies will be created in the future. Assuming the present refers to the post-1945 period and extends to c 2050, a practical sociological application of the future would see it as the world from the second half of this century. I would suggest that one of the main challenges for a critical theory today is to move beyond the historical experience of modernity as it has become consolidated in the nineteenth and twentieth centuries. In my view, there are at least six reasons why the future will be radically different from the present and the past.

The first is population growth and the related factor of the decline in mortality rates. For most of the c 10,000 years of human societies, the population of the world was less than 500 million (which was reached by 1500). Even by 1900 the

244 Space, memory and legacies of history

world population was 1.6 billion. Today, it is more than 7 billion and will rise by the middle of this century to 9 billion. Demography is something that social theory generally ignores but the sheer force of numbers makes a significant difference to the nature and dynamics of human societies. Second, when combined with changes in mobility, the demographic factor is even more significant. For much of the twentieth century, which saw the greatest explosion in the numbers of people living on the planet, a very large number were severely curtailed in their movement either by poverty or by the barriers erected by totalitarian states. Since the fall of communism in 1989-90 and the opening up of China for travel and markets, this has fundamentally changed. Populations are now on the move, whether for reasons of tourism or migration. Third, closely connected to the demographic change is the related problem of climate change and environmental destruction. As discussed in Chapter 7, the transformation in the relation of human societies to the planet is one of the most important changes today. One of the many implications is the challenge of new sources of energy, alternatives to silicon and plastic, and the disposal of waste. Contemporary societies are more than ever highly intensified zones of energy concentration, and their future development is likely to be very much shaped by new forms of energy and the related politics. Fourth, partly in relation to the ecological modernization but with a much wider salience, technology and especially digital technologies have become more and more part of the fabric of not only societies but of human nature. Future developments in technology are likely to be on a far greater scale than anything that has previously been the case. Fifth, finally since 1968 and with a major impetus again in the 1990s, there has been a worldwide expansion of demands for democratization, which are not likely to be easily silenced, especially as a shift in the scales of economic and political power occurs, tipping the balance away from the western world. It is possible to envisage the continued spread of democratization but also its frustration and transformation into all kinds of movements, including neo-authoritarian ones. Moreover, democracy does not exist in a pure form and becomes entangled in other forces, such as capitalism.

Against these potential scenarios, the future is thus likely to be very different from the kind of society that was the background and basis of much of critical theory. New kinds of power and domination will come into existence, intimations of which we are seeing today with the intrusion of digital technologies into the traditional practices of liberal democracy and the unprecedented destruction of the planet. Critical theory was shaped in its formative period by the experience of totalizing systems of domination and the dissolution of the western industrial working class as the major agent of change. Habermas and Honneth in their different ways offered more up-to-date visions of the nature of domination in post-totalitarian times (the colonization of the life-world, and with Honneth, forms of misrecognition), but these conceptualizations are not enough to comprehend new kinds of domination, which are neither totalizing nor easily corrected by reason or recognition, nor new kinds of progressive politics.

Understanding these challenges offers fertile ground for critical theory today. I have tried to show in this book that the conceptual framework of critical theory, despite its limitations, is well placed to shape critical discussion on the future of society. Critical theory makes possible a mode of interpretation and explanation that shows how alternative forms of social, economic, and political organization can be realized and how societies can learn from the catastrophes of the past and how current pathologies can be identified and overcome. Critical theory shows how transformative ideas enter into social practice and how social structures and institutions evolve in light of the learning accumulated but not realized.

Notes

1 My thanks to Piet Strydom for valuable feedback on an earlier draft.
2 See Wagner's analysis and reconstruction of the idea of progress (Wagner 2016).
3 In Chapter 6, Urry outlined six methods of future research that follow from his perspective on complexity: learning from the past, studying 'failed' futures, developing dystopias, envisaging utopias, extrapolation, and scenario-building. See also Urry (2003).
4 See Matthew Rushworth and Franz-Xaver Neubert research, https:www.livescience.com. html, reported in early 2014
5 See Kaku (2018) and Rees (2018).
6 See Adams et al (2017) for an account of the debate around social imaginaries.
7 See Gidley (2017) for a review from the perspective of critical future studies. See also Slaughter (2003).

References

Adams, S., Blokker, P., Doyle, N., Krummel, J. and Smith, J. 2017. Social Imaginaries in Debate. *Social Imaginaries*, 1 (1): 15–52.
Adloff, F. and Neckel, S. 2019. Futures of Sustainability as Modernization, Transformation, and Control: A Conceptual Framework. *Sustainability Science*, 14: 1015–25.
Adorno, T. W. 1998 [1969]. Progress. In: *Critical Models: Interventions and Catchwords*. New York: Columbia University Press.
Allen, A. 2016. *The End of Progress: Decolonizing the Normative Foundations of Critical Theory*. New York: Columbia University Press.
Apel, K-O. 1987. The Problem of a MacroEthic of Responsibility to the Future in the Crisis of Technological Civilization: An Attempt to Come to Terms with Hans Jonas's 'Principle of Responsibility'. *Man and World*, 20 (1): 3–40.
Augé, M. 2014. *The Future*. London: Verso.
Beck, U. 1992 [1986]. *The Risk Society*. London: Sage.
Beckert, J. 2016. *Imagined Futures: Fictional Expectations and Capitalist Dynamics*. Cambridge, MA: Harvard University Press.
Beckert, J. and Bronk, R. (eds.) 2018. *Uncertain Futures: Imaginaries, Narratives, and Calculation in the Economy*. Oxford: Oxford University Press.
Benjamin, W. 1999. *The Arcades Project*. Cambridge, MA: Harvard University Press.
Blewitt, J. 2017. *Understanding Sustainable Development*. London: Routledge.
Brundtland Report. 1987. *Our Common Future*. New York: World Commission on Environment and Development.
Caradonna, J. 2014. *Sustainability: A History*. Oxford: Oxford University Press.

Castoriadis, C. 1987 [1975]. *The Imaginary Institution of Society*. Cambridge: Polity Press.

de Jouvenel, B. 2017 [1964/1967]. *The Art of Conjecture*. London: Routledge.

Diamond, J. 2011. *Collapse: How Societies Choose to Fail or Succeed*. 2nd edition. London: Penguin Books.

Foster, J. 2015. *After Sustainability*. London: Routledge.

Gidley, J. 2017. *The Future*. Oxford: Oxford University Press.

Gore, A. 2013. *The Future*. London: Allen Lane.

Habermas, J. 1972 [1968]. *Knowledge and Human Interests*. London: Heinemann.

Hamilton, C. 2013. *Earthmasters: The Dawn of the Age of Climate Engineering*. New Haven: Yale University Press.

Heidegger, M. 1980. *Time and Being*. Oxford: Blackwell.

Horn, E. 2018. *The Future as Catastrophe: Imagining Disaster in the Modern Age*. Cambridge: Cambridge University Press.

Kaku, M. 2018. *The Future of Humanity*. London: Penguin Books.

Koselleck, R. 1988. *Critique and Crisis: Enlightenment and the Pathogenesis of Modern Society*. Cambridge, MA: MIT Press.

Koselleck, R. 2004 [1976/1979]. 'Space of Experience' and 'Horizon of Expectation': Two Historical Categories. In: *Futures Past: On the Semantics of Historical Time*. New York: Columbia University Press.

Kumar, K. 1987. *Utopia and Anti-Utopia in Modern Times*. Oxford: Blackwell.

Luhmann, N. 1976. The Future Cannot Begin. *Social Research*, 43 (1): 130–52.

Luhmann, N. 2002. *Risk: A Sociological Analysis*. New Brunswick, NJ: Transaction Publishers.

Pinker, S. 2011. *The Better Angels of Our Nature: A History of Violence and Humanity*. London: Penguin Books.

Rees, M. 2018. *On the Future: Prospects for Humanity*. Princeton, NJ: Princeton University Press.

Sachs, J. 2015. *The Age of Sustainable Development*. New York: Columbia University Press.

Schatzberg, E. 2018. *Technology: Critical History of a Concept*. Chicago, IL: University of Chicago Press.

Schumpeter, J. 2010 [1942]. *Capitalism, Socialism and Democracy*. London: Routledge.

Slaughter, R. 2003. *Futures Beyond Dystopia: Creating Social Foresight*. London: Routledge.

Smil, V. 2008. *Global Catastrophes and Trends: The Next Fifty Years*. Cambridge, MA: MIT Press.

Tainter, J. 1988. *The Collapse of Complex Societies*. Cambridge: Cambridge University Press.

Toffler, A. 1970. *Future Shock*. New York: Random House.

Urry, J. 2003. *Global Complexity*. Cambridge: Polity Press.

Urry, J. 2016. *What Is the Future?* Cambridge: Polity Press.

Wagner, P. 2016. *Progress: A Reconstruction*. Cambridge: Polity Press.

Zizek, S. 2011. *Living in the End Times*. London: Verso.

INDEX

activism 139
Adorno, T. 7, 11, 14, 16–19, 20, 25, 63, 145, 182–4, 190, 213–31; *Authoritarian Personality, The* 16, 64, 213–31; and Foucault, M. 7, 31; and Horkheimer, M. 15, 17, 64, 73, 75, 145; *Minima Moralia* 18–19; *Negative Dialectics* 11, 17–18, 190
agency 149–51
Albert, M. 111
Alexander, J. 48; *see also* digital, algorithmic governance
Allen, A. 28–30, 32–3, 235; *see also* decoloniality; postcoloniality
Amable, B. 111
Amin, A. 175
Anthropocene 144–60; Capitalocene debate 153; and cosmopolitanism (Cosmopolocene) 158, 160; defining 145–6; 'Great Acceleration' thesis 147–8, 153; origins 147; politics 152–7; and post-humanism 153; and reflexivity 157
Anthropocentrism 152
anti-Semitism 17, 38, 64, 214–16; *see also* Holocaust
Apel, K. 20, 22, 234; *see also* hermeneutics
Archer, M. 44, 45
Arendt, H. 150, 152, 170
Arnason, J. 63, 71, 268
Aron, R. 67
austerity 100
authoritarianism 213–31; authoritarian democracy 222–4; *see also* Adorno, T.,

Authoritarian Personality, The; technology, automation
Avicenna 32

Baudelaire, C. 174
Bauer, B. 11
Bayle, P. 40
Beck, U. 131, 144, 236
Beckert, J. 121
Benhabib, S. 43, 139
Benjamin, W. 31, 74–8, 108, 168–73, 182–4, 188–90, 199, 217, 234–6, 239; *Arcades Project* 31, 108, 168–71; and memory 182–4, 188–90; and progress 234–6; and technology 74–8
Berry, D. 80; *see also* technology
Bhaskar, R. 42, 44–5
Bildung 41, 99, 134; *see also* technology, biotechnology
Bloch, E. 31, 108, 234
Boltanski, L. 7, 55; and Chiapello, E. 70, 98, 208; and Thévenot, J. 55; *see also* debt
Bourdieu, P. 42, 47–50, 90
Braudel, F. 150
Braverman, H. 74
Brexit 221–2, 224–8
Bridle, J. 81, 82
Brock, G. 129
Brooke, J. 150
Brown, W. 91, 102, 230
Buck-Morss, S. 11, 185
Burawoy, M. 42

248 Index

Calhoun, C. 109

capitalism: accumulation of capital 114; collapse of 115–16; crises of 112–15; definitions of 67–9; low growth 116–18; and modernity 67–70; surveillance 81–2; varieties of capitalism (VoC) 101, 110–12; *see also* Anthropocene, Capitalocene debate; neoliberalism

Castells, E. 139, 174

Castoriadis, C. 56, 71, 177, 236

Chakrabarty, D. 148

Chernilo, D. 157

climate change 110, 116, 120, 149–52

Collins, R. 113; *see also* Habermas, J., communicative action

Comte, A. 40

consciousness: critical 63, 66; and domination 65; false 14; Hegelian 10, 40; self-consciousness 11

corporate social responsibility 104

cosmopolitanism 31, 124–41; and Anthropocene 145; cosmopolitanization 131; critical 125–7; and domestic politics 140; preconditions for 135–8; prospects for 138–40; and space 175–8; *see also* Anthropocene

Coulthard, G. 28

'counter-monument' 178, 195

crisis/crises 22, 112–15, 116–17

critical realism 44–7; *see also* Bhaskar, R.

critical practice 53–5; for critical sociology (*see* Bourdieu, P.)

critique 17, 38–59, 44; definition of 13; diagnostic 43–4; disclosing 16, 44; Foucauldian 42; genealogical 50–3; from Hegel to Marx 10–11; of ideology 20; immanent 11, 13–14, 17, 18, 20, 44; methodology 22, 44; normative 14, 20, 43–4; of political economy 40; reconstructive 14; reflective 40, 49; varieties of 38–59

Crouch, C. 89, 92, 95, 103

cultural left 208

cultural logic of capitalism 70

culture 48–50

culture industry 190, 191

Dahrendorf, R. 67

Dean, J. 89, 91

debt 101–2

decoloniality 7–8, 27–32, 33, 125, 178

Dejours, C. 66

De Jouvenel, B. 235

Delanty, G. 31, 134–5

Della Porta, D. and Marchetti, R. 139

democracy and capitalism 72–3

Deranty, J.-P. 66; *see also* Adorno and Horkheimer

De Souza Santos, B. 140

dialectics 11, 23, 44; and consciousness 65; dialectical materialism 11, 18; negative dialectics 11, 17, 18

Diamond, J. 115

digital 79–83, 167, 173–8; algorithmic governance 81–2, 177–8; and space 173

discourse 50–3

Disobedient Generation, The 205–10

double movement 71

Douzinas, C. 130

Drucker, P. 119

ecological catastrophe 116, 130, 152–3, 158–60

Eder, K. 43

Eisenstadt, S. 146

empiricism 38–40

Enlightenment 39, 41, 149; *see also* ecological catastrophe

Eurocentricism 27–9, 124, 188; *see also* decoloniality; postcoloniality

Europe 20, 95–6, 198–211

European Union 100; *see also* Brexit

Fanon, F. 193

Favell, A. 100

Feenberg, A. 78; *see also* digital

feminism 89, 99

Feuerbach, L. 11

Forst, R. 25

Foucault, M. 7, 31, 41, 50–3, 91, 167, 175–8; and Adorno, T. 7, 31; and Bourdieu, P. 50; and governmentality 52, 91; and heterotopia 175–8; methodology 50–3; and neoliberalism 91, 92, 98; and technology 80

Fraser, N. 11, 25, 43, 70, 72, 89, 99, 229; and Jaeggi, R. 43, 70

freedom 9–17

French philosophy 40; *see also* revolution, French Revolution

Freud, S. 14, 41, 182, 186, 215

Freyenhagen, F. 19

Fromm, E. 14, 40, 215; pathological normalcy 222

F Scale 218–19

Fuchs, C. 119

Fukuyma, F. 73

Furet, F. 186–9

future 234–45; of capitalism 108–22

Gadamer, H.-G. 43, 191–2; *see also* hermeneutics
Gane, N. 91
Gasset, O.Y. 200
generative mechanisms 46
German idealism 39
Giddens, A. 45
global civil society 139–40
global justice 127–30; *see also* ecological catastrophe
Gouldner, A. 42; *see also* Anthropocene, 'Great Acceleration' thesis; Foucault, M., and governmentality
Great Transformation 68

Habermas, J. 7, 10, 19–22, 23, 27, 28–9, 49, 65–6, 72–3, 115, 145, 167–70, 182, 190, 235; and Anthropocentrism 145; and Bourdieu, P. 49; communicative action 20–1, 27–9, 192; and Foucault, M. 52; and modernity 28–9; and public space 167–70; and technology 77–9; *see also* Bourdieu, P.
Hall, D. and Soskice, P. 101, 110–12; *see also* capitalism
Harris, N. 14, 27
Hartog, F. 186–7
Harvey, D. 73, 90, 117
Hayek, F. 92–3
Hegel, G. 9, 24, 40; and Haitian Revolution 11; Hegelian dialectics 12, 14; Hegelian ontology 9, 11; and Kant, I. 9, 44; and Marxism 11, 13, 20, 40, 51; and needs 71; and recognition 24, 27
Heidegger, M. 74, 238
heritage 182–3, 193–6
hermeneutics 20, 42, 43; critical 191–2
Hetherington K. 176; *see also* Foucault, M., and heterotopia
Hobsbawm, E. 200
Holocaust 16–17, 29, 127, 182, 188, 190; *see also* anti-Semitism
Honneth, A. 7, 10, 22, 23–8; *see also* recognition/recognition theory
Horkheimer, M. 13–17, 20, 64, 73, 75, 145; *see also* Adorno, T.; Horkheimer, M.
Horn, E. 115
Hornborg, A. 153; *see also* Avicenna

ideas of Reason 11
identity thinking 22
immanent critique 11
immanent-transcendence 14, 43–4, 124–5
individualisation and neoliberalism 98–100

injustice 14; *see also* reason
integration (systemic/social) 65
intersubjectivity 25–7; *see also* recognition/recognition theory

Jaeggi, R. 8, 11, 43; *see also* Fraser, N., and Jaeggi, R.
Jameson, F. 7
justice 14; *see also* global justice

Kant, I. 9, 11, 20, 44, 127, 133, 160; and cosmopolitanism 127, 133; and ideas of reason 9; and Hegel, G. 9, 44
Kerner, I. 32
Keynesianism/neo-Keynesianism 120
Klee, P. 188–9
Kondratieff cycles 114
Koselleck, R. 40, 144, 236
Kotz, D. 117
Kracauer, S. 18, 170
Krugman, P. 120
Kundera, M. 200

labour 63, 66; *see also* Marx, K./Marxism, Labour Theory of Value
latency 43–4
Latour, B. 144
Lazarsfeld, P. 38
Lazzarato, M. 90
Left-Hegelianism 7–10, 12, 20, 32–3
'left-wing fascism' 209
'left-wing melancholia' 187
Levi-Strauss, C. 50–1
'Lost Generation, the' 199–204
Lovelock, J. 156
Lowenthal, L. 38
Luhmann, N. 237
Lukács, G. 63–4, 74
Lyotard, J.-F. 7

Malthus, T. 115
managerialism 96–8
Mann, M. 118
Mannheim, K. 91, 185
Marcuse, H. 10, 12, 13, 14, 16, 25, 63–4, 70–1, 190, 215; and memory 190; and technology 76–9
marketisation and privatisation 103
Marx, K./Marxism 11, 13, 18, 41–2, 63, 67–9, 72–3, 112, 113, 121, 133, 183–4; and capitalism 67–74, 109–10, 112–13; and cosmopolitanism 133; and crises 112–13; and Hegel 41–2; Labour Theory of Value 69; and nature 145; primitive accumulation 69, 109

250 Index

Mason, P. 119, 174
McClanahan, A. 102
McNay, L. 26
Mead, G.H. 126
memory 182–97
Meyer, J. 97, 99
Mignolo, W. 125
Miller, M. 43; *see also* Adorno, T., *Minima Moralia*
Mithen, S. 151
modernity 20, 40, 62–83, 148; and Anthropocene 148; and capitalism 67–70; and memory 182–96
Moore, J. 148
'moralisation of the market' 104
mourning 178–9
Mumford, L. 74; *see also* Adorno, T., *Negative Dialectics*

negativism 18
neo-conservatism 92; *see also* Thompson, M. J.
neoliberalism 89–105; and austerity 100, 114; defining 90–105; as economic policy 94–6; 'neoliberal governmentality' 98; totalisation of neoliberalism 102–5; *see also* capitalism
Neumann, F. 38
New Public Management 97
Nietzsche, F. 50
Nora, P. 187
Norblad, J. 151
normative internationalism 138–9
normative justification 39
Nussbaum, M. 129

Object Relation theory 25
ordo-liberalism 97
Outhwaite, W. 47

Parsons, T. 68; *see also* Fromm, E., pathological normalcy
Pedersen, O. and Campbell, J. 92
Peirce, C.S. 20, 22
Pierson, P. 95
Piketty, T. 117
Pinker, S. 240
Polanyi, K. 68, 71
Popper, K. 42
positionality 51
post-capitalism 118–20
post-coloniality 7–8, 27–32, 178, 187, 204
post-humanism 51–2
post-metaphysical theory 10

post-modernism 65
post-structuralism 50–3, 65
post-universalism 126
Powell, W. and DiMaggio, P. 92; *see also* Marx, K. / Marxism, primitive accumulation
progress 30–1, 109
psychoanalysis 14
public space 167–80; cosmopolitanism 175–8; mourning 178–9; technology 173–5

race 8; *see also* reason, technical rationality
rationalisation 65–7, 113
Rawls, J. 23, 127, 131
reason: communicative 20, 23, 29, 72–3; critique of 9; instrumental 13, 16, 17, 64, 67, 72–3, 76–8, 216; and left-Hegelianism 7–11; regulative ideas of 9, 14, 28–32, 33, 44, 63; technical rationality 78–81
recognition/recognition theory 23–8, 28–9, 66
reconstructive critical theory 22
reflexive sociology 49
reification 25, 27, 63
remembrance 199–204; fallen soldier 203; pacifism 204; Remembrance Day 203–4
revolution 184, 199, 208; French Revolution 40, 184
Ricoeur, P. 43
Reich, R. 120
Rosa, H. 8
Rose, N. 98
Roszak, T. 205
Rothberg, M. 195
Rousseau, J.-J. 145
Rouvroy, A. and Burns, K. 80–1

Said, E. 28
Sassen, S. 139
Sayer, A. 44, 47
Scheffler, S. 132
Schumpeter, J. 69, 112–13, 119; *see also* consciousness, self-consciousness
Self, Other, and World relations 126
Sennett, R. 170, 173
Seymour, R. 80; *see also* Holocaust
Simmel, G. 170–3
Singer, P. 128
Sittlichkeit 24
slavery 11, 28
social learning processes 43, 132
social psychology 216–31

Index **251**

social research and philosophy 38–40, 41
societal regression 224–8
socio-cognitive 137; *see also* Strydom, P.
sociological dimension of critical theory 39–42
sociology, critical 47–50
solidarity 128
sorrow 178–9
Soysal, Y. 99
space and public 168–71
Spengler, O. 200
Standing, G. 120
state 89–94
Stehr, N. and Adolf, M. 104
Stiglitz, J. 120
Stirner, M. 11
Streeck, W. 90, 115
Strydom, P. 14, 22, 137, 149, 157
suffering 25; *see also* capitalism, surveillance

Taylor, C. 43
Taylor-Gooby, P. 97
technologies of the self 52
technology 74–83, 229, 244; automation 119; biotechnology 78–9; technological determinism 83; *see also* digital

Thatcherism 94–6; *see also* neoliberalism
Thomas, J. 151
Thompson, M. J. 25
Toffler, A. 236
totalitarianism 30, 64
Touraine, A. 56, 72
Traverso, E. 187
Trumpism/Trump, D. 221–3
Turner, B. 42, 152

Urry, J. 103, 175, 237; *see also* capitalism, varieties of capitalism (VoC)

Von Humboldt, A. 133
Von Mies, L. 93; *see also* neoliberalism

Wagner, P. 72
Wallerstein, I. 69, 113–14
Walzer, M. 43, 130
Weber, M. 13, 20, 63–4, 68, 70, 99, 112, 113, 186
Winnicott, D. 25
Wright Mills, C. 42

Young, J. E. 178; *see also* Left-Hegelianism

Zuboff, S. 81–2